Patchwork States

Patchwork States argues that the subnational politics of conflict and competition in South Asian countries have roots in the history of uneven state formation under colonial rule. Colonial India contained a complex landscape of different governance arrangements and state-society relations. After independence, postcolonial governments revised colonial governance institutions, but only with partial success. The book argues that contemporary India and Pakistan can be usefully understood as patchwork states, with enduring differences in state capacity and state-society relations within their national territories. The complex nature of territorial governance in these countries shapes patterns of political violence, including riots and rebellions, as well as variations in electoral competition and development across the political geography of the Indian subcontinent. By bridging past and present, this book can transform our understanding of both the legacies of colonial rule and the historical roots of violent politics, in South Asia and beyond.

Adnan Naseemullah is Senior Lecturer in International Relations at King's College London. He is the author of *Development after Statism* (2017).

Patchwork States

The Historical Roots of Subnational Conflict and Competition in South Asia

ADNAN NASEEMULLAH
King's College London

CAMBRIDGE
UNIVERSITY PRESS

CAMBRIDGE
UNIVERSITY PRESS

University Printing House, Cambridge CB2 8BS, United Kingdom

One Liberty Plaza, 20th Floor, New York, NY 10006, USA

477 Williamstown Road, Port Melbourne, VIC 3207, Australia

314–321, 3rd Floor, Plot 3, Splendor Forum, Jasola District Centre,
New Delhi – 110025, India

103 Penang Road, #05–06/07, Visioncrest Commercial, Singapore 238467

Cambridge University Press is part of the University of Cambridge.

It furthers the University's mission by disseminating knowledge in the pursuit of
education, learning, and research at the highest international levels of excellence.

www.cambridge.org
Information on this title: www.cambridge.org/9781009158428
DOI: 10.1017/9781009158404

© Adnan Naseemullah 2022

First published 2022

A catalogue record for this publication is available from the British Library.

ISBN 978-1-009-15842-8 Hardback
ISBN 978-1-009-15841-1 Paperback

Cambridge University Press has no responsibility for the persistence or accuracy of
URLs for external or third-party internet websites referred to in this publication
and does not guarantee that any content on such websites is, or will remain,
accurate or appropriate.

Contents

Figures

Tables

Preface

This book has its roots, rather incongruously, in a statement by then-President George W. Bush, in 2007, explaining why the American War in Afghanistan was still raging six years after the attacks of September 11, 2001, and the subsequent US invasion. Bush said, "Taliban and al Qaeda fighters do hide in remote regions of Pakistan. This is wild country; this is wilder than the Wild West."[1]

At the time I heard Bush's statement, I was conducting dissertation fieldwork in the Pakistani metropolis of Lahore, interviewing manufacturers and visiting their textile mills and factories in the plains of central Punjab. This bustling, industrial landscape was just 360 miles – and yet a world – away from the tribal agencies Bush was discussing. Those regions were quickly becoming the epicenter of Pakistan's deadliest insurgency, which lasted over a decade. Bush's statement piqued my interest as a fledgling student of comparative politics. By drawing parallels between the "wildness" of Pakistan's remote regions and America's Wild West, he was highlighting territories within a sovereign state that may not be governed in a sovereign manner. And as with the early American state, the Pakistani state is strong in some regions like central Punjab, yet its presence or strength varies from place to place.

An important difference between America and Pakistan implicit in Bush's comparison is that the American West had been "won": indigenous communities were subjugated, ghettoized, and eliminated; bandits and outlaws no longer operated with impunity; and territories were formed into states under the writ of democratically elected federal, regional, and municipal governments. In the case of Pakistan's Northwest, British colonizers had gained control over the "frontier" territories between the upper Indus Valley and the borders of Afghanistan around the same time as the United States' victory in the Mexican War. Yet until a constitutional amendment in 2018, they were

---

[1] Address to the American Enterprise Institute, February 15, 2007.

governed exceptionally as a set of tribal agencies, in which the footprint of the Pakistani state was light and tribal leadership held significant independent authority. The variation in states' monopoly of violence across their territories, as these two cases show, is not a universal outcome. Instead, processes of state formation are historically specific, and central authority is established in some geographic cases more successfully than others.

Any actual comparison between the two cases would not be particularly welcome in a discipline that sees both the United States and Pakistan as exceptional, though for different reasons. Yet I could not shake the idea that embedded within that comparison was a deeper lesson of how states were built, for what purposes, and with what outcomes. The inquiries that arose from these questions have taken me in lots of different directions over the last decade: to interviews with Pakistani bureaucrats who worked at the very edges of the state's authority; to archival research as a way of uncovering, systematizing, and analyzing the variations in colonial rule; and to data on contemporary subnational variation in areas as distinct as riots and rebellions in India and the effective number of parties in Pakistan. This book represents a culmination of these disparate investigations into how the South Asian state was constructed in the past and with what consequences for the politics of conflict and competition in the present.

Through the course of this research and its eventual integration into the present volume, I have come to appreciate both the benefits and the drawbacks to social science's evolving approaches to history and its legacies. At seminars in college and graduate school, I had gained a deep respect for the comparative-historical tradition that had brought political scientists, sociologists, and historians together in conversation over the deep relationships between violence and the state. Through collaboration and argumentation, they formulated many of the key theories, concepts, and approaches at the core of state-building and discussions of political order. The implicit Euro-centrism of elements of the tradition and its intellectual debts to modernization theory limited its applicability, however, for those of us who wished to study developing countries on their own terms. This limitation is particularly acute when studying variations in the strength of the state not across countries but within them.

In the last couple of decades, a new approach to historical legacies has gained traction, one inspired by institutional analysis and causal inference. A key advantage of this approach is greater attention to comparability among cases and the strategic use of fine-grained data to demonstrate long-term impacts of historical phenomena. But its focus on precisely identifying the effects of historical institutions, especially through the search for natural experiments, also has disadvantages. By choosing exactly comparable cases and finely curating data to increase analytical leverage, we miss out on the complex but legible – and analytically important – *diversities* of institutional form. Such a focus also occludes institutional origins and the (many) cases in which institutional cases are "assigned" in quite deliberate fashion rather than randomly or exogenously. Finally, the application of as-if randomization logics and subsequent path dependence has weaker purchase for understanding the landscapes of political violence than other, more constant social processes, like development.

This book represents an attempt to deploy comparative-historical insights as well as archival research and contemporary data in a more encompassing manner to tell the story of state formation and its variably violent consequences in South Asia. In this effort, an investigation of the origins of different institutions of colonial governance is a key starting point. In common with others writing on the territorially uneven nature of state-building within national boundaries, I explore the political motivations and anxieties that led British colonizers to establish distinctly different forms of governance across the directly ruled provinces, princely states, and political agencies across the subcontinent between the mid-1700s and mid-1800s. I then explore how independent governments after 1947 attempted to revise the fragmented array of governance forms through postcolonial state-building. These efforts were not entirely successful, yielding persistent variations in governance, but decolonization represented a key critical juncture that is often elided by scholars of colonial legacies. Legacies of these differences in state capacity and state–society relations shape patterns of political violence, especially in relation to the sovereignty of the state, in India, Pakistan, and Bangladesh.

Patchwork States contributes to two important, though very different, sets of intellectual debates. The first involves how we analyze the politics of South Asian countries. Much of the scholarship on India has been conducted in the very long shadows of the decline of Congress and the attendant fragmentation of political authority. The purported singularity of purpose among the leaders of the independence struggle has been replaced by increased demands among different communities and heightened competition among politicians for resources and political authority, understood through the idiom of clientelism, and implicated in Hindu–Muslim riots. South Asian comparative analysis has, meanwhile, highlighted stark differences between democratic India and autocratic/hybrid Pakistan (and Bangladesh).

What much of this scholarship has ignored is the complex character of the state itself, as structures different from and indeed prior to the formation of regimes and the character of political competition. State structures vary within national boundaries, but as importantly, they are common in their variation to all three countries. As a result, political competition and violence in all three countries occur across uneven landscapes of state authority, of which India, Pakistan, and Bangladesh are all a part. This book argues that these uneven landscapes can shape patterns of violence, as well as the character of political competition and development trajectories, in all three countries.

The second set of debates involves the relationship among state-building, colonial rule, and political order. Try as we might to escape them, we find ourselves trapped by the intellectual structures of modernization, which privilege questions of national success and failure and invites us to find sources for these differences. Colonialism looms large as a potential explanation for the relative poverty and instability of many developing countries; this is, of course, not an inaccurate assessment! But in the search for systematic cross-national explanations, we tend to treat colonialism – especially in its nonsettler forms – as a perverse but singular institutional treatment.

In South Asia and beyond, however, colonialism represented an *internally complex* system of domination and subjugation, one which needs to be studied on its own terms if we are to understand its true impact. This book represents such an investigation in the subcontinent to understand subnational variation in political violence and other outcomes. But it suggests other factors that are relevant to understanding impacts of colonialism far beyond South Asia: the different motivations of imperial powers in different territories under their domination, and the extent to which postcolonial state-builders were able to revise or erase the concrete institutional legacies of colonial or imperial rule. Applying these questions in comparative perspective can help us understand a broad array of phenomena, from East Asian developmental states to Southeast Asian protection pacts to "ethnic management" and spheres of influence in the Soviet Union and the People's Republic of China to the internally divided American empire in the western hemisphere.

* * *

As with any project that has come together slowly over the course of a decade, there is an immense number of people that deserve enormous thanks, without whom this book would not have been written. Part of the length of time over which it has been written means that I will, inevitably, leave out people whose thoughts and assistance in shaping the book should be recognized. I apologize for any such oversight at the outset.

In the conduct of this research, staff at the Asian and African Studies Reading Room at the British Library as well as those at the National Archives and the Central Secretariat Library in New Delhi have been invaluable. I have benefited greatly from presenting various aspects through various stages to audiences, including at the University of Pennsylvania's Center for the Advanced Study of India, Brown University's Watson Institute, the Institute for Defence and Security Analysis in New Delhi, Ashoka University, the Institute of Commonwealth Studies at the University of London, the Institute for Development Studies at the University of Sussex, and meetings of the American Political Science Association, and the Society for the Advancement of Socio-Economics.

For expertly shepherding this book from a draft manuscript to publication, I am immensely grateful to my editor, Sara Doskow. Two excellent reviews from anonymous reviewers provided key feedback and comments. Other key individuals at Cambridge University Press whose efforts have been essential include Jadyn Fauconier-Herry, John Haslam, Rachel Blaifeder and Claire Sissen. For expert copyediting, typesetting and other aspects of production,

I thank Mathivathini Mareesan and Rashmi Motiwale Ladheriwale. John Beauregard provided me with an excellent index.

Colleagues and collaborators, with whom I worked on some of the ideas that generated the book, warrant particular recognition. Paul Staniland and I wrote an article on the concept of indirect rule that served as the starting point for the typology of colonial and postcolonial governance detailed in Chapters 2 and 5; Paul has since provided excellent feedback on integrating the project into conversations in conflict and security studies and I have benefited tremendously from his perspectives on political violence in print, including his recent book. Pradeep Chhibber and I coauthored a piece on subcontracted governance and the effective number of parties that has served as the basis for analysis in Chapter 7; Pradeep has subsequently made critical interventions in the drafting of the manuscript that sharpened it significantly. Clionadh Raleigh has helped me tremendously in exploring key concepts in the study of political violence in Chapter 6, and ACLED's fine-grained cross-national data have enabled me to demonstrate their utility in practice.

Ashutosh Varshney incisively situated distinctions at the heart of my research on contemporary violence in South Asia in broader comparative context, in a lengthy and enormously helpful exchange. Catherine Boone provided much-needed advice in framing the project and executing the analysis. Amit Ahuja, Christopher Chambers-Ju, Jody LaPorte, Susan Ostermann, and Jessica Rich provided excellent feedback on draft introductory and framework chapters. A fantastic group of historians and historically minded scholars of colonial and early postcolonial India have deeply informed the book: Neilesh Bose, Elizabeth Chatterjee, Mark Condos, Berenice Guyot-Réchard, Barton Scott, Jon Wilson, and especially Taylor Sherman. James Kurth provided invaluable insights across many conversations on the nature of empire, colonial rule, and political order in comparative perspective that have powerfully informed its conceptual and historical apparatus.

I have benefited from conversations, suggestions, critiques, and assistance over the years from Katherine Adeney, Caroline Arnold, Khalid Aziz, Bilal Baloch, Jennifer Brass, James Chiriyankandath, Jennifer Dixon, Caitriona Dowd, Kathy Gannon, Sam Handlin, Kathy Hochstetler, Bill Hurst, Lakshmi Iyer, Christophe Jaffrelot, Francesca Jensenius, Devesh Kapur, Mimi Keck, Peter Kingstone, Bill Kissane, Tomila Lankina, Adrienne LeBas, Mashail Malik, Colin Moore, Pratap Bhanu Mehta, Brian Min, Shuja Nawaz, Paula Newberg, Prerna Singh, Ekaterina Tertychnaya, Anshuman Tiwari, Steven Wilkinson, Andrew Wyatt, Emily Zackin, and Adam Ziegfeld. Conversations with postgraduate students in South Asian politics and international relations at King's and participants in Foreign Office workshops on South Asia have helped me to sharpen the presentation of my ideas. And through the last two years of writing and revising the manuscript during the coronavirus pandemic, I can only express my deepest gratitude for the (socially distanced) love, companionship, and emotional support of friends, family and community.

I dedicate this book to the memory of my grandmother, Freda Mollie Barger, and my grandfather, Muhammad Ziaullah. My grandfather passed away when I was a small child, but his career as a government servant involved an intimate experience with colonial rule and its ongoing legacies. I knew my grandmother very well, however. She graduated from university and was conscripted into work in the India Office in London during the Blitz, experiencing three of the last years of colonial rule as a minor, unwilling functionary of the imperial project at the metropole. Her subsequent life and career were nothing short of astonishing. She has always been a source of inspiration, and this book would not have been possible without her encouragement and support.

Abbreviations

ACLED	Armed Conflict Location and Event Database
AIML	All-India Muslim League
ANP	Awami National Party
BJP	Bharatiya Janata Party
BNP	Bangladesh National Party
CAA	Citizenship Amendment Act
CIA	Central Intelligence Agency
CPI	Communist Party of India
CPI-M	Communist Party of India-Marxist
CRPF	Central Reserve Police Force (India)
EIC	East India Company
ENP	effective number of parties
FATA	Federally Administered Tribal Area (Pakistan)
INC	Indian National Congress
IOR	India Office Records
KMT	Kuomintang (Chinese nationalists)
KP	Kyber Pakhtunkhwa
MQM	Muttahida (Mohajir) Quami Movement
NDA	National Democratic Alliance
NWFP	North-West Frontier Province
OBC	Other Backward Classes
PML-N	Pakistan Muslim League-Nawaz
PML-Q	Pakistan Muslim League-Quaid
PPP	Pakistan People's Party
PTI	Pakistan Tehreek-e-Insaaf

PTL	Pakistan Tehreek-e-Labbaik
SCV	Sovereignty-challenging violence
SNV	Sovereignty-neutral violence
UP	United Provinces (of Agra and Awadh) or Uttar Pradesh
UPA	United Progressive Alliance

PART I

FRAMEWORK

1

Introduction

1.1 SNAPSHOTS FROM A HARD WINTER

On December 11, 2019, the Modi government in India promulgated the Citizenship Amendment Act (CAA), which allowed non-Muslims from surrounding countries to become Indian citizens. Many saw this legislation as a fundamental challenge to principles of secularism enshrined in the Indian Constitution. As a result, citizens staged mass protests throughout India throughout the winter. A group of Muslim women established an activist encampment in Shaheen Bagh, gathering together thousands in the cold, smoggy Delhi winter for four months between mid-December and mid-March. Many similar protests took place throughout the country, from Assam to Punjab and from Kerala to Bihar.[1] Student protests against the actions of the government met with violence from right-wing activists and from the police, including at Jawaharlal Nehru University and Jamia Milla Islamia in New Delhi and Aligarh Muslim University in Uttar Pradesh. Violent altercations between protestors and the police on December 20 led to several deaths in the northern cities of Meerut and Kanpur.

In the context of both these protests and then-President Donald Trump's visit to India in February, Hindu nationalist activists conducted a pogrom among lower middle-class neighborhoods in northeastern Delhi, in which fifty-three people were killed over the course of four days. Most of the fatalities were Muslim, and the police kept hundreds of the wounded from receiving medical attention while subjecting them to physical abuse. The riots began when a local leader of the ruling Bharatiya Janata Party (BJP) called for the removal of a sit-in against the CAA. But the ensuing social violence fanned out through neighborhoods and targeted Muslim communities and businesses, following well-established patterns of Hindu–Muslim riots implicated in organized crime,

---

[1] Ahuja and Singh 2020.

police complicity, electoral politics, and the absence of social integration across religious communities.

Yet other forms of political violence continued at far remove from the CAA agitations and the Delhi pogrom. In the erstwhile state of Jammu and Kashmir, whose constitutional provisions for autonomy were abrogated by the central government in November, incidents of insurgent violence continued despite the presence of a million Army and paramilitary personnel; security forces and militants engaged in armed clashes in the districts of Rajouri, Poonch, Pulwama, Jammu, Srinagar, and Shopian. And elsewhere, Maoist cadres engaged in battles with government forces and violence against civilians in Bihar, Chhattisgarh, and even eastern Maharashtra.

More widespread, though less noticed, lethal political violence also occurred, taking the form of riot-based conflict between activists of political parties, such as in Telangana and West Bengal, and clashes among caste and communal militias and vigilante groups, such as in Punjab and Gujarat. One of the deadliest attacks on civilians occurred in a village in West Singhbhum district in the Maoist-impacted state of Jharkhand, where members of the Pathalgarhi movement for tribal autonomy kidnapped and killed seven villagers opposed to the movement. The Armed Conflict Location and Event Database (ACLED) reported 857 violent incidents, including 516 riots, during December 2019, and January and February 2020 – an average of just under ten incidents of political violence a day.

Insurgent violence is more salient in Pakistan, India's neighbor to the west, particularly since Pakistan's ambiguous involvement in the civil war in Afghanistan and the ensuing terrorism and territorial insurgency. During the winter of 2019–2020, several battles between government forces and militants represented the continuing fallout from the decade-long Taliban insurgency in the northwest of the country. However, separatists in the western province of Balochistan perpetrated even more significant and deadly attacks, including a Baloch Liberation Tigers assault on army personnel in Dera Bugti that left sixteen fatalities. Terrorist attacks associated with both conflicts have continued to occur in Pakistani cities.

For all this emphasis on insurgency, social conflict was also prevalent; riots accounted for more than a quarter of violent incidents between December 2019 and February 2020. These included clashes among rival factions in a tribal jirga in Balochistan, rival party workers in Peshawar, rival student groups in Sindh, and groups representing different Muslim sects in southern Punjab. All told, ACLED reported 121 incidents of conflict in Pakistan over that winter. It also recorded 1,314 mass-organized protests in Pakistan, with civil society organizations, business groups, and unions speaking out against price hikes, the unavailability of electricity and gas, and the murder of journalists, parties staging rallies to protest government policies, and ethnic and religious groups demanding greater recognition.

In Bangladesh, multiple forms of political violence during the winter included acts of terrorism, with unidentified assailants planting improvised explosive devices at police stations in Khulna and Chittagong. But by far the most prevalent among the 171 violent incidents recorded by ACLED during this period was a wide array of riots and armed clashes within Bangladeshi society: among sectarian factions, rival parties, factions within one party, between the police and student groups, party workers or civil society activists. Property and political control, as well as social grievances, were often at the heart of political violence, with many protests turning into riots and armed clashes.

This brief survey of just three months in the political life of three countries in the Indian subcontinent suggests that Naipaul's characterization of the Indian polity in 1990 – as consisting of "a million mutinies" – is just as relevant today and applies equally to India's neighbors as to India itself.[2] In other words, countries in South Asia face multidimensional challenges to civic peace and stability from politically motivated actors. The sheer diversity of different forms of conflict and competition across these South Asian countries suggests that an enduring question of the politics of developing countries – what explains organized political violence? – is very much alive in the Indian subcontinent and important for understanding the politics of countries in the region.

Characterizing the array of South Asia's multiple, complex instances of political violence, in order to uncover their causes, is a difficult task, however. Like many countries in the developing world, India, Pakistan, and Bangladesh lie in the middle of a spectrum between the stable political order enjoyed by prosperous and peaceful countries like Canada and Denmark and the systemic civil conflict associated with the collapse of the state in war-torn countries like South Sudan and Syria. Much of the scholarship on civil conflict has sought systemic explanations for the incidence, duration and intensity of civil wars at the cross-national level, but have little to say about serious, multidimensional – but not regime-threatening – violent conflict within countries. On the other end of the scale, sophisticated studies of the micro-dynamics of violence are conducted within sites of systemic conflict, contexts which are usually seen as exceptional and thus beyond the remit of quotidian politics. Scholars of the contentious and violent politics of South Asia, meanwhile, have investigated the causes of specific conflicts, such as the Taliban insurgency or terrorist violence in Pakistan, Hindu-Muslim riots, the insurgency in Kashmir, or Maoist rebellion in India, but rarely from a systematic comparative perspective either across or within national boundaries.[3]

The variegated nature of political violence in South Asian countries has two specific features that defy extant approaches. First, different species of political violence are present in different areas of the same country. For instance, some

---

[2] Naipaul 1990.
[3] For notable exceptions, see Staniland 2012, 2014, 2021. In other national contexts, see Varshney 2008.

parts of India experience insurgencies, others ethnic riots, even though they are ruled under the same government and policed by the same official organizations tasked with upholding the coercive monopoly of the state. This varying national geography of violence has not been well-accounted for in the literature on political conflict. Second, there are common geographical patterns of violence in South Asian countries – especially India and Pakistan, but even in Bangladesh – despite significant differences in social structure and regime type. These parallels stand awkwardly in relation to scholarship in South Asian politics, which emphasizes national differences rather than similarities.

These geographically diverse threats to political order invite us to investigate their causes within and across India, Pakistan, and Bangladesh, an investigation which can integrate forms of violence like riots, terrorist attacks, and rebellions into a single explanatory framework. Why do different forms of violence occur, in different places, within the same national boundaries? What characteristics of politics and relationships between state and society at the local level might lead to these different patterns of conflict? How might we characterize the linkages among the state's political authority, citizens' engagement with that authority, and different species of conflict? How might these interact with less violent forms of political competition, and over what? To begin such an investigation, I suggest that patterns of political violence in South Asia might be usefully characterized as the concrete consequences of a longstanding geographic unevenness in the authority of the state within and across national territories.

1.2 THE PATCHWORK STATE

This book argues that these varieties of violence are embedded within a more expansive spatial politics of conflict and competition within and across South Asian countries. This spatial politics is the concrete consequence of how the state was built, which was without national coherence at all in mind. The fragmented and diverse character of public institutions at the local level – what I call the patchwork state – shapes the deep and long-lasting character of state capacity and relationships between state and society, prefiguring how citizens and social groups, including violent actors, engage the state's authority and resources. Patchwork governance institutions can thus configure the relative incidence and patterns of political violence in different places within India, Pakistan, and Bangladesh.[4] They can also inform other expressions of conflict and competition, such as local electoral contests and trajectories of

---

[4] This notion of patchwork governance has some family resemblances to the variations in bureaucratic concentration and effectiveness in African countries reflected in McDonnell's (2020) *Patchwork Leviathans*. This book adds to the ongoing conversation on the uneven nature of the state in developing countries by focusing on *spatial* variation and seeking to explain other outcomes, like patterns of political violence.

development, which are similarly embedded in the same variations in state capacity and state–society relations.

It further argues that territorially distinct governance institutions that constitute the modern South Asian state have concrete roots in the process of state-building under colonial rule. In contrast to much of the research on political order in South Asia, which focused on political institutions after independence, and analyses of colonial legacies that identify the long-run effects of specific institutions, I examine the construction and persistence of a *diverse set* of governance arrangements before independence. Over most of the subcontinent for nearly two centuries, British colonial authorities quite deliberately formulated and maintained differentiated forms of rule over subject peoples and suzerain polities. They did so to pursue specific objectives associated with imperial conquest and domination. This had the effect of prefiguring differences in the local capacities of the state and the relationship between state and society in different places, which have had long-lasting influences.

Postcolonial governments certainly attempted to revise and homogenize this diversity of governance through projects of state-building after independence. These efforts were only partially successful, however, due to the constrained capacities of the state for conducting administrative reform and the political divisions that foreclosed the wholesale transformation of the state. The patchwork nature of the postcolonial state and its consequences for geographical patterns of political violence thus have concrete, complex – but explicable – historical roots.

As a result, the state in contemporary India and Pakistan encompasses significant differences in its capacity, authority and relationships with social actors across its territories. The state is powerful and autonomous in some places, weak and captured in others. In some places, state and society penetrate one another, but in others, society and the state are distant from one another, and at the extreme, the latter violently occupies the former.[5] In what follows, I will introduce the ways in which British colonizers shaped variations in governance for their own purposes, and how postcolonial state-builders sought to revise these arrangements. I will then explore how patchwork governance shapes contemporary outcomes in patterns of political violence, as well as electoral competition and development trajectories, through mechanisms of state capacity and state–society relations.

1.3 GREED, FEAR, AND FRUGALITY IN COLONIAL STATE-BUILDING

An investigation into the provenance and explanatory power of the patchwork state concept in South Asia must begin with the motivations and impulses behind state-building efforts during the colonial period, which ultimately led

---

[5] Bangladesh is a more territorially homogenous state that represents an exception to this characterization, but one that is explicable through the same historically informed analytic framework.

to deliberate differentiation in colonial governance. This exercise involves examining the concrete ends and the means of British rule in India. I argue that organizational motivations of *greed*, *fear*, and *frugality* drove the politics of colonial conquest and consolidation.[6]

Scholars and commentators have contended that British rule in India, and colonialism more generally, had a singular purpose, in the extraction of valuable resources, and that the institutions of colonial rule existed to solely enable this purpose.[7] This assumption is not without solid foundations. Yet a framing of colonialism as a straightforwardly extractive enterprise elides some of the complexities of exactly how it extracted, and with what consequences, in different locations.

Colonizers' extractive impulses generally stand in for a broader notion of naked material greed at the very core of the colonial project, but this was expressed in two very different ways: taxation and trade. These accord to extraction and protection, two forms of resource mobilization in Charles Tilly's famous comparison between European state formation and organized crime.[8] Extraction represents the straightforward expropriation of resources by authorities who wield coercive monopolies, just as (nominally less legitimate) gangsters might rob banks. State-building projects, in order to accomplish such extraction, require the building up of significant bureaucratic capacity to calculate and administer taxation, with record-keepers, tax-collectors, and bailiffs. Tilly referred to "protection," by contrast, as the efforts by state-builders to simultaneously encourage and support commercial activity and to threaten its operation unless protection rents are paid, following the logic of racketeers rather than larcenists. Olson located the logic of protection in the successes of capitalist development; "stationary bandits" have incentives to invest in production in the areas of their jurisdiction, and the certainties required for private investment then necessitated investment in state institutions.[9]

British colonial rule in India enabled raw acquisitiveness both through protection and extraction because its activities in the subcontinent constituted at once a mercantile empire and a territorial one. Yet unlike Tilly's framework, either set of activities yielded a strong, coherent state. This was primarily because colonizers also intended their proceeds to flow back to the metropole, while maintaining a weak polity under colonial subjugation; as I will argue later in the text, colonial state-building was governed by objectives of frugality rather than effectiveness. Nevertheless, these two forms of acquisitiveness had quite

---

[6] Here and throughout this book, I use greed, fear, and frugality as shorthand idioms for the organizational goals of and risks to the imperial project writ large, manifested in different places and different times, rather than the emotive responses of individuals. I thank Taylor Sherman for pushing me to clarify this point.

[7] See Acemoglu, Johnson and Robinson 2001 for an influential theoretical treatment. See Tharoor 2018; Dalrymple 2019 for recent popular applications to India.

[8] Tilly 1985.   [9] Olson 1993.

concrete but differentiated consequences for the establishment of different governance arrangements across the subcontinent.

1.3.1 Greed through Trade

At the turn of the seventeenth century, the material wealth of Mughal India – from silk and cotton garments to spices, opium, and indigo – drew the Portuguese, Dutch, British, and French into competition over control of overseas markets for these goods. Early empire-building efforts were purely maritime in nature, concerned with the control of seaborne trade and the domination over commercial relationships at entrepôts – treaty ports or "factories" – rather than affairs further inland. Trade was the primary means by which the English (from 1707, British) state could benefit from colonial enterprises, through collecting duties on imported goods. The East India Company (EIC) was singularly focused on securing and maintaining the wealth associated with unfettered access to overseas markets until the middle of the eighteenth century.[10]

By the middle of the nineteenth century, however, the ways that Britain benefited from trade inverted. Despite continuing demand for Indian products, the British came to see India primarily as a market that could be kept open for their industrial goods following domestic market saturation, while allowing Britain to run trade surpluses that could finance growing deficits with Germany and the United States. The emphasis of the commercial foundations of colonial rule had thus shifted; structurally uneven terms of trade destroyed indigenous industries, while transferring the incomes of Indians to the imperial metropole.[11]

For trade and commerce, certain sites – particularly centers of banking and trade that had long been integrated with overseas markets – were more valuable than others. Ports like Madras, Bombay, and Calcutta and wealthy inland cities like Hyderabad and Bangalore represented capitalist loci in which the authority of the state was relatively extensive and there was an active, though racialized, civil society. This greater administrative capacity and intertwining of state and commercial society enabled the enforcement of contracts and the protection of property rights necessary for complex transactions of debt and finance, which in turn integrated India into global and imperial markets.

Beyond these metropolitan nodes, however, colonial institutions devoted to commerce were less interventionist. Colonial authorities used a variety of formal and informal measures – from plantation agriculture to debt bondage – to maintain the production of key tradable commodities.[12] They

---

[10] For an overview of the activities of the EIC, see Kohli 2020, 21–68.

[11] Digby 1901; Naoroji 1901; Dutt 1902. On how the imperial drain thesis informed Indian nationalism, see Goswami 2004.

[12] Richards 1981.

also made geographically specific investments in communications and transportation, creating webs of infrastructure that linked sites of commodity production and markets for manufactured goods to those of overseas commerce. For much of the agrarian hinterland and far peripheries, however, the powerful institutions of the British mercantile imperial project were simply not evident.

1.3.2   Greed through Taxation

The colonial extraction of agricultural surplus was established through a distinctly different set of historical processes. From the 1760s to the 1840s, the EIC consolidated its territorial dominance, through the conquest of Bengal and subsequent annexations, over most of the territory in the Indian subcontinent. They initially did so to protect their commercial monopolies against indigenous threats to commercial privileges. Yet in so doing, the Company became a continental empire as well as a maritime one. Entrepreneurial colonizers like Robert Clive argued to their superiors that sovereign control of territory could yield significant resources in the extraction of land revenue. As a result, colonial officials conducted surveys over conquered territories and levied revenues regardless of local conditions, periodically causing immense hardship for the peasantry, including several deadly famines.

Over time, however, this form of extraction excited feelings of ambivalence among colonial administrators; revenue administration was costly and the revenues collected were both underwhelming and uncertain. Colonial governments used land revenue and other taxes to defray the costs of empire, including its protection by maintaining the army. Yet the salaries of colonial officials, establishments and supplies, and local expenditures regularly exceeded revenue generation throughout the period of colonial rule, leading to significant, if normatively dubious, structural debts of the Indian government to Britain.

Further, colonial authorities never actually intended the *maximization* of extraction. Evidence for this forbearance can be found in the preservation of India's princely states, together covering a third of the Indian subcontinent, including prosperous states such as Hyderabad, Mysore, and Baroda. These were formally beyond the tax base of the colonial government, even though many yielded much more significant revenue to their rulers than many of the areas under direct colonial administration. While some "native" states engaged in conflict or conspiracy against the EIC had much of their territory annexed, this practice had largely ended by the middle of the nineteenth century. After 1858, the government formally protected princely states from accession and they were key allies of the project of colonial governance.

More significantly for understanding governance variation, colonial revenue authorities, as well as those of princely states, extracted revenues in different ways, to different extents, in different parts of the subcontinent. In much of northern and eastern India, proprietary landlords would collect agricultural surplus from peasants and pay revenues to the government, whereas in much of southern, western, and northwestern India, government officials would collect taxes directly from individual cultivators or from village communities. These different forms of land tenure and taxation were associated with different levels of state capacity and intervention in society, with significant long-term effects, as scholars have recognized.[13] The origins of these institutions were in turn bound up in the particular politics of colonial conquests across the subcontinent. The straightforward perspective of empire as simply an extractive enterprise is thus muddied by these complexities, which become clearer if one takes a more territorially informed perspective to how India was ruled and why.

1.3.3   Fear

Beyond material greed, existential insecurity was ever-present as a powerful motivation for governance arrangements in colonial India, as historians of the British Empire have persuasively argued but social scientists have largely ignored.[14] This accords, following Tilly, to the ways that the existential nature of geopolitical competition drove the construction of states and necessitated extraction for defense and expansion. Colonial state-building and the practice of governance was thus at least as much a reaction to challenges from its opponents as an extractive enterprise.

These threats to colonial rule were the result of colonial activities. The increasingly successful efforts of British colonial agents in dominating commerce and controlling trade provoked armed backlash from indigenous elites as well as other colonial powers. This led the British to engage in a series of armed conflicts with powerful indigenous states, from the Anglo-Mysore Wars and the Anglo-Maratha Wars spanning the turn of the nineteenth century to the Anglo-Sikh Wars in the 1840s. These conflicts massively increased the size of the Indian Army, placing military mobilization and deployment at the very center of the colonial project.[15]

Through eventual victory in these conflicts, the colonial government controlled more territory in the hinterland – increasing its territorial power but also multiplying its vulnerabilities – until by the mid-nineteenth century, the entire subcontinent was under the EIC's influence or outright control. For all the blustering triumphalism of imperial historiography, however, the first century of territorial rule under the EIC was marked by constant threats, which persisted even after it achieved territorial paramountcy over India. The

---

[13] See Banerjee and Iyer 2005 for an influential articulation of these distinctions.
[14] Guha 1997; Wilson 2008; Condos 2017. For an alternative view, see Ehrlich 2020a.
[15] Bayly 1994; Condos 2017.

Rebellion of 1857–8 represented the most visceral manifestation of British anxieties, when "native armies" with the support of former princely rulers revolted against the agents and officers of the EIC. While it was brutally crushed over the course of a year, the Rebellion cast long shadows. The perceived necessity of avoiding such an uprising drove colonial policy over the next nine decades.

Myriad other real or imagined threats to their continued domination continued to arise, from the infiltration of foreign agents to cause social unrest to nationalist uprisings and tribal insurgencies. The Russian Empire, spreading its influence over Central Asia throughout the nineteenth century, was a particular object of focused alarm and the cause of disastrous conflicts in Afghanistan. This concentrated the imperial defense and security apparatus toward India's northwest, with significant consequences in state–society relations saturated by military mobilization in the territories that would become Pakistan. As importantly, however, the legacies of the 1857 Rebellion led the government to perceive more diffuse threats from within Indian society, from princely rulers and rebellious tribes to the nationalist movement.

In response, British agents formulated and deployed a diverse array of coercive tools, as well as relationships of collaboration with indigenous elites, in different forms in different places, for interdicting both concrete and inchoate threats. Throughout British India, colonial administrators and agents established a complex, overlapping set of security arrangements against both internal and external threats. The British Indian army represented the core of this interdiction; in combination with the Royal Navy, it served to defend the interests of the broader British Empire as well as a coercer of last resort in India.[16] In addition, paramilitaries, police forces, intelligence agents, spies, and local informants, backed up by a repressive judicial apparatus of magistracies and higher courts, worked together to manage this endemic insecurity, both in the heartland and in far peripheries, and in both directly ruled provinces and princely states. The British Indian state also managed complex networks of patronage, support, and legitimation to key local elites as a means to divide opposition and undermine resistance.

There were, to be sure, some attempts at homogenizing the coercive state apparatus across the subcontinent, through all-India legal codes that were adopted even by princely states, as well as fixed templates for the organization of police forces and the military. However, the specific nature of different threats varied from place to place, with the result that formally similar law and order and coercive apparatuses were mobilized and deployed in different ways and to different extents across territory. In areas of exceptional governance along the frontier, special tools of security were formulated, from "political agents" to paramilitaries to tribal militias, and the state would even subcontract coercive monopoly to local elites to limit long and costly military

---

[16] Darwin 2009.

engagements aimed at complete subjection.[17] Thus, British India's security apparatus was very real, but it was also heterogeneous across space, yielding different governance arrangements in different places in the same ways that extractive mandates also differentiated governance arrangements.

1.3.4   Frugality

Finally, governance followed the strict accounting of administrative cost as a particular feature of colonial state formation in India. Frugality had deep roots in the earliest structures of British colonialism. The early organizing structure of colonial enterprise, the EIC, chartered in 1600, was an overseas joint-stock company, or in more modern parlance, a multinational corporation.[18] Analysis of multinationals in the twentieth century has highlighted structural conflicts of interest – essentially principal-agent problems – between corporations operating abroad and those of their home governments as well as between the agents of multinationals operating in foreign countries and principals – directors representing stockholders – at home.[19]

With the EIC, these principal-agent problems were very much in evidence. From the seventeenth century, there were regular disagreements between the agents of the Company in India, who executed trade and extended territorial control while privately enriching themselves, and directors at the Company's headquarters, who were alarmed that the rising expenditures from military expeditions and civil investments were eating away at their returns on investment. The Company and the British government also clashed frequently; the latter initially chartered and then affirmed its monopolies to receive customs revenue from its trade, while simultaneously being obliged to defend its expansion through expensive military force. Parliament passed a series of legislative measures to increase control, culminating in the formal transfer of power from the EIC to the British government in 1858. Even after this point, however, principals at home remained suspicious of wasteful and wanton expenditure in state-building activities by the agents of empire. As a concrete consequence of these principal-agent difficulties, cost-benefit calculations pervaded the very viscera of the colonial project. Government officials continuously bemoaned the public cost of empire even while private shareholders, agents, and associates reaped its rewards and while Britain established global hegemony due, in part, to ruthless exploitation of India's resources and overseas deployment of its military power.

Thus, the machinery of colonial government operated on structurally and deliberately straitened circumstances as less of a bug than a feature of colonial domination. It continued to accrue debt to City of London bondholders, which further justified British control and policies of openness to trade. Agents of the

---

[17] Naseemullah 2014.   [18] Dalrymple 2019; Kohli 2020.   [19] Gilpin 1975.

colonial government – whether civil or military officers, residents at princely courts, or political agents – maintained significant freedom of movement, as long as they did not incur significant or ongoing demands on this truncated fisc. The different forms of colonial governance thus operated not on a logic of monopolization of coercive power or the maximization of extracted resources but rather the minimization of expenditure.

The frugality mandate had two consequences. First, it acted as a balancing mechanism between greed and fear in the construction of the state in different places. Colonial agents continuously weighed extraction against the potential for insecurity, just as they weighed the economic benefits of greater security through the application of coercion against its ongoing costs. Second, it meant that the variations in governance arrangements tended to persist over the many decades of colonial rule, because transformations of governance were costly. Policymakers, officers, and agents at every level of the colonial government, as well as residents influencing princely rulers, generally upheld the principle of maintaining extant structures. Authorities directed expenditure that followed patterns of investment in earlier state-building, embedding mechanisms of path-dependence deeply into colonial governing practices. The spatial diversity of extractive and coercive mandates – greed and fear – associated with conquest and consolidation under the Company thus continued to shape governance arrangements during the last century of British influence.

***

Indians were, of course, far from passive observers in the ways that India was conquered and governed during colonial rule. Their actions and strategies, in terms of both resistance and collaboration, critically shaped British strategies of governance. Yet until the rise of the mass nationalist movement and even afterward, there was no coherent Indian response to the many ways that the British exercised their influence over the subcontinent, adding to the fragmented nature of rule.

Indians in different geographical and social locations formulated strategies and practices for benefiting from, coping with, or resisting British domination: from wealthy merchant and banking communities to princely rulers whose authority was affirmed and supported by the Empire, from landlords dependent on state power for protection to indigenous government officials charged with enforcing it, and finally from nationalist leaders challenging the spirit of colonial rule in the public sphere to rebels working to undermine colonial power and tribal insurgents that violently challenged British authority at the limits of its power. Thus, British colonizers did not shape diverse governance arrangements in isolation, but rather in response to and sometimes in cooperation with the actions and strategies of many different Indian actors.

The various combinations of the imperatives of greed and fear, along with the mandates of frugality, led to the establishment of different sets of governance arrangements in different spaces across the Indian subcontinent, from metropolitan capitals through the agrarian hinterland to far peripheries, across directly administered provinces, princely states, and political agencies. These can be categorized into legibly different forms of colonial governance. Integrating and building upon insights from previous studies on colonial institutions, I formulate a typology of governance arrangements in colonial India: *metropolitan, modernizing, intermediate, conservative, chieftaincy*, and *exceptional*.[20] These categories incorporate administrative districts, princely states, and political agencies in what is now India, Pakistan, and Bangladesh into a common conceptual landscape of variation in colonial governance.

1.4 POSTCOLONIAL STATE-BUILDING

The Indian subcontinent on the eve of independence and partition contained a patchwork array of different forms of governance and authority. When independence was finally achieved for India and the new country of Pakistan, postcolonial governments sought to unite their countries and provide subject populations with common identities as citizens through the construction of new state institutions. In so doing, they sought to address and indeed counteract the patchwork nature of governance, and their efforts represent a key critical juncture in the governance of South Asia. Their limited successes in this effort, and thus the hard limits to the erasure of the legacies of colonial rule, were a consequence of the nature of postcolonial politics.

The leaders of postcolonial India tried to address the legacies of colonial rule by engaging in nationalist mobilization and postcolonial state-building, largely under the idiom of development. As many nationalist thinkers had argued, the British actively underdeveloped the subcontinent, creating the poverty and economic backwardness that represented a dramatic reversal of fortunes from the wealth of precolonial India.[21] As a result, the provision of basic goods and services and the expansion of economic opportunities, to counteract colonial inequities, emerged as the basis for the postcolonial state's legitimacy. This was, after all, the primary appeal of the Congress party, which served as the key mobilizing force against colonial policies, the mass movement that strove for and achieved freedom from British rule and ultimately, the governing party for decades after Independence.

Prime Minister Jawaharlal Nehru, as well as many socialists in Congress, sought to effect a fundamental transformation of the Indian political economy through statist planning, to address these mandates of development. However, these efforts were challenged from within. This is because the Congress party in the states and districts of India did not represent an ideologically unitary

[20] The particular categorization of colonial governance is described in detail in Chapter 2.
[21] For more on reversal of fortunes, see Acemoglu, Johnson and Robinson 2002.

organization, singularly committed to this incorporative program of statist development. Rather, it was an arena of conflicting interests among political actors, many of whom were agrarian conservatives who actively resisted pressures to homogenize social and political structures and free up resources for industrialization.[22] As a result, pressures for economic transformation and political incorporation were strong in some locations, but weak in the many others, particularly where proprietary elites dominated the Congress organization in rural areas.[23] Further, threats to national security from without and within led to the persistence and augmentation of exceptional governance. Cleavages within early postcolonial politics reinforced rather than unraveled the patchwork state.

Meanwhile in Pakistan, post-partition governments, and particularly Ayub Khan's bureaucratic–authoritarian regime from 1958 to 1969, were primarily concerned with security rather than development. Yet, they nonetheless understood development and the strengthening of state capacity as a vital component part of a national project of self-preservation in the face of systemic vulnerability, as well as a powerful source of the state's legitimacy.[24] Industrial development in Pakistan, just as in India, transformed some institutional landscapes but not others. The strategic orientation of the Pakistani state also supported the continuation of a more formally differentiated set of governance practices, aimed at managing populations at the periphery rather than transforming their circumstances. This yielded an even more extreme patchwork.

There were other sources of patchwork persistence. In both Pakistan and India, the key instruments for reform were themselves institutions inherited from colonial India. The civil service – especially the district officials responsible for policing, taxation, and judicial affairs – represented at once a source of stability and a mechanism for the continuity of colonial structures into postcolonial societies. Bureaucracies did extend their authority, particularly by integrating princely states, but in variable fashion across national territory (and in India more vigorously than Pakistan), recapitulating more narrowly the diversity of governance arrangements that was present under colonial rule. Just as greed, fear, and frugality fashioned diverse forms of governance in colonial India, the persistent effects of this spatial diversity in how the state was equipped and how it engaged with social actors has fashioned how postcolonial governments could provide development and achieve security across their territories.

The politics of Bangladesh, after independence from Pakistan in 1971, stand in stark contrast to those of India and Pakistan, because they are not particularly territorial in nature. Rather, they involve contention over the meaning of statehood, rooted in either secular nationalism around Bengali ethnic identity or religious nationalism based in Islam. Yet the underlying

[22] Kothari 1964; Frankel 2005.   [23] Weiner 1967; Kochanek 1968.
[24] Jalal 1990; Naseemullah and Arnold 2015.

consensus over the nature of territorial governance and political competition at the local level in the Bangladeshi hinterland is in itself a product of the relative lack of variation in colonial governance arrangements in the eastern half of Bengal, which have carried forward to shape the character of Bangladesh today.[25] The lack of patchwork variation in Bangladesh, leading to startlingly different consequences, thus suggests the utility and validity of the concept.

***

This book thus argues that patterns of violence, national political systems, and struggles over development in the three countries are endogenous to relatively unreconstructed diversities in state institutions that have persisted from colonial rule. In South Asia, in contrast to several countries in East and Southeast Asia, revolutionary upheaval or systemic conflict did not transform the state.[26] No matter how (partially) revised by postcolonial politics, Pakistan and India remained patchwork states, while the territory that would become Bangladesh did not constitute a patchwork to begin with.

The deliberate if limited efforts of postcolonial governments to construct new state institutions and transform governance for the national goals of development and security did lead to the limited convergence of the diverse range of colonial governance arrangements. This has yielded a narrower set of postcolonial governance categories: *metropolitan, modernizing, conservative,* and *exceptional.*[27] This spatial framework of governance diversity, with roots in colonial rule and postcolonial politics, represents the key to understanding the politics of conflict and competition across India, Pakistan, and Bangladesh.

1.5 PATCHWORK STATES AND CONTEMPORARY SUBNATIONAL OUTCOMES

Through the historical investigations mentioned earlier, this book ultimately seeks to explain spatial diversities in forms of violence within and across contemporary South Asian countries. It argues that the patchwork state concept, and its varying governance categories from colonial rule and postcolonial state-building, can help us to understand the variations in the authority of the state and its relationships with society. These have consequences in the nature and patterns of political violence as well as other important outcomes implicated in political competition. In what follows, I explore the mechanisms that translate patchwork governance to contemporary outcomes at the subnational level as well as the implications of these outcomes in national politics. Figure 1.1 represents a schematic representation of the book's full argument.

---

[25] Khan 1999.   [26] Skocpol 1979; Slater 2010; Vu 2010.
[27] Processes of revision and the categorization of postcolonial variation will be discussed in Chapter 5.

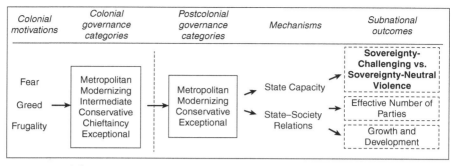

FIGURE 1.1 The argument

1.5.1 Mechanisms

Before explicating how the patchwork state informs particular outcomes, it is important to lay out the ways that legacies of colonial governance (and postcolonial revision to that governance) persist and impact the present. Scholars of colonial legacies, explaining contemporary variations in development but also violence, tend to treat these legacies as a matter of state capacity: the internal strength, coercive power, and normative authority of state organizations, from the bureaucracy to the police to the military, to successfully subject their will on social actors. This is indeed an important formulation of the impacts of colonial rule; there are many places in India, Pakistan, and even Bangladesh in which agencies of the state are understaffed and under-resourced, with deficiencies that go back before the establishment of independent statehood. These deficiencies have serious consequences for political order.

But if state capacity is a necessary tool for understanding the contemporary outcomes, it is hardly sufficient; it presents the state's side of the picture, analytically privileging its capacities to bend society to its will. Further, it begs the answer to a vexing question: capacity for and in relation to what? What is missing from accounts of the strength of the state is this relationality – a sense of what society expects of state actors, as well as what the state expects of social actors.

These relationships – which are often institutionalized, though subject to change either from external shocks or internal processes – vary quite significantly within and across South Asian countries. The terms of engagement between the regular police or municipal agencies and the residents of elite housing communities in Mumbai, Dhaka, or Karachi are dramatically different from those between paramilitary officials and tribal communities in Jharkhand, the Chittagong Hill Tracts, or the erstwhile Federally Administered Tribal Area (FATA) of Pakistan's Northwest; these differences are not straightforwardly reducible to measures of state strength, such as personnel, budgets, or training.

As a result, we need to understand variations in the relationships between state and society as well as those in state capacity. Research into these relationships has tended to view state strength and the strength of social actors resisting the state's monopolizing imperatives as zero-sum.[28] In this book, I take a more ambivalent view by introducing two distinct dimensions of state–society relations.

The first is relatively well-known: that of *state capture*, which is usually understood as the capacity of dominant social actors to dominate the state at the local level and deploy its resources for their own purposes, against their rivals or subordinates. Social science often employs state capture as a diagnosis for corruption. Here, I use state capture to assess the extent to which social actors, particularly powerful ones, might be able to use the resources and authority of the state to accomplish their own objectives. This in turn suggests the cohesiveness of social dominance, as opposed to the fragmentation of elites in competition with one another, and a local state apparatus that serves as their enforcer rather than an adjudicator of rival claims to public resources and coercive power.

A second dimension of state–society relations is the extent to which state and social actors are intertwined. South Asia is replete with "embedded particularism,"[29] or the ways that informal social ties can exist within formal structures of the state; a bureaucrat might do a regulatory favor for an entrepreneur with whom she went to college, for example. Common ethnic ties between politicians and community leaders might influence distributional outcomes. At the same time, the state also embeds itself in society and influences its structure and composition, from regulation and its forbearance to establishing caste and ethnic categories around which groups mobilize. On the other end of the scale, such as in national peripheries and tribal hinterlands, agents of the state and social actors are distant from and wary of one another, such that the state is an alien institution or even an occupying force. Thus, the extent of *state–society penetration* is an important indicator that reflects the two-way nature of influence.

Together, state capacity and the terms of state–society engagement, as they vary across the districts of India, Pakistan, and Bangladesh, have shaped various spatial politics of conflict and competition. The capacities of the state, but also mutual expectations and relations between state and social actors, can powerfully transmit the legacies of colonial governance, and postcolonial revision, in ways that shape contemporary politics. They have a profound influence on the patterns and varieties of violence across the three countries, complementing but integrating extant examinations of insurgencies and riot-based conflict. These spatial politics help us understand other associated

---

[28] For influential treatments, see Migdal 1988, 2001; Scott 1999, 2009. For an overview of the literature, see Migdal, Kohli and Shue 1994.

[29] Herring 1999.

outcomes as well, from electoral competition to economic and social development.

1.5.2   Patterns of Violence and Sovereignty

Patchwork governance arrangements across South Asia have profound consequences for the patterns of violent conflict in Bangladesh, India, and Pakistan, because they shape how social actors contentiously and violently engage with the state's authority and why. As a result, differing theoretical relationships between sovereignty and violence lie at the very heart of explaining political violence and how it varies. To explicate these linkages, I propose the following framework for understanding the causal relationship between the nature of the state and state–society relationships and the incidence of riot- and insurgency-based violence at the local level.

In geographical contexts where the state has significant capacity and there is significant state–society interpenetration – in modernizing and especially metropolitan districts – social groups and political actors actively compete over control of the state's authority and access to associated rents and resources, often using violence to polarize communities or demonstrate their strength to gain or maintain control. In so doing, this political violence affirms the legitimacy and sovereign authority of the state by competing (often contentiously, sometimes violently) over its spoils, in terms of the distribution of resources and the direction of policies. The violent aspect of this competition is what I term *sovereignty-neutral violence*.

It suggests systemic violence and contention can be consistent with settled, institutionalized, interpenetrative relationships between state and society, or in other words, our everyday notions of political order. Ethnic riots, electoral clashes, and even targeted killings are characteristic of sovereignty-neutral violence; they represent the darker but no less real side of political competition – the struggle of who gets what, when, and how. They represent those who are fighting over control of the state, not fighting to overthrow it.[30]

In geographical contexts where there is much less capacity and negligible interpenetration between the state and social groups – especially in exceptional districts – actors have a greater propensity for engaging in conflict over the very terms of state's authority. This is what I term *sovereignty-contesting violence*. Such conflicts arise and persist when there are fewer institutionalized resources that might draw different groups into competition over them, and the relative absence of interpenetration between society and the state that would

---

[30] Metropolitan districts are also sites of significant terrorist attacks, which are not normally characterized as sovereignty-neutral. However, terrorists target major cities, when they are able, to demonstrate their power to national governments, rather than arising from local governance relationships, except in the very particular circumstances of urban insurgency.

institutionalize this competition. Instead, groups violently reject the legitimacy of the state and its ability to organize social relations.

This rejection often follows more recent attempts of the state to intervene more forcefully in areas where it had maintained traditions of "standoffishness."[31] Rebellions in northwestern Pakistan, Bangladesh's uplands, northeastern India, the "red belt" of Maoist rebellion in the jungles of central and eastern India, and the erstwhile state of Jammu and Kashmir represent particular political geographies where agents of the colonial state established a variety of heterodox practices of governance and traditions of self-restraint. Postcolonial states inherited these practices with only limited modification. The state's subsequent, often-unilateral abrogation of these traditions of self-restraint in areas of governance heterodoxy, based on geopolitical imperatives or incentives for resource mobilization and extraction, has led to systemic political disorder and rebellion. Insurgent violence, terrorism, and the building of alternative sources of authority are thus the products of qualitatively different engagements with a very different avatar of the state than riot-based social conflict.

Hinterland areas that at lower points on a scale of state–society interpenetration – many of which I categorize as conservative districts – represent long-term under-investments in the state's capacity. The capture of the state by dominant social groups and the reproduction of social hierarchies are common in these contexts. As such, these districts see a more mixed picture of various forms of violence, as some groups seek to capture the state and others to challenge it, in ways that are at once explicable through this framework and understudied by extant approaches.

1.5.3 Electoral Competition and Development

The patchwork nature of state institutions influence not just the different forms of violence but also the peaceful, institutionalized, and quotidian acts of individual citizens, namely voting in elections. Classic studies of political order have tended to concentrate on the presence or absence – or rise and fall – of incorporative political parties with high degrees of internal institutionalization and programmatic direction in shaping party systems.[32] In India, these included the Congress during the height of its power but also the Communist Party of India-Marxist (CPI-M) in certain states. These parties are thought capable of channeling the passions of citizens toward progressive ends, and away from violent means of achieving those ends; party competition, in this view, involves choosing the "right" options for peace, progress, and prosperity.

But how social actors engage with the state's capacity and authority can have important consequences for how voters view the meaning and consequence of electoral choices. The fragmented, intense nature of electoral competition

[31] Slater and Kim 2015. [32] Huntington 1968, 397–462.

today – in India, but also in Pakistan[33] – suggests that differences in the character of that competition may be a consequence of the nature of the state and its relationship with citizens in different places. When the state is capacious and interpenetrates with active groups in civil society – particularly in metropolitan and modernizing districts – we see a tendency toward competition among two or three parties, consistent with our expectations in systems with single-member plurality electoral rules.[34] In these cases, competition is conducted over control of the state by democratic governments and thus the direction of policy and patterns of public distribution. In cases where there are more distant and fraught relationships between society and the state, however, we might see either one-party capture or extreme fragmentation of the vote among parties and candidates in constituencies. In many of these cases, the more limited aim among competitors is gaining the particular office and the rents associated with it. In others, elections represent vehicles for the perpetuation of subnational authoritarianism, either driven by the state or challenging its authority.

These differences in electoral competition at the constituency level – measured by the effective number of parties (ENP) – may not be as dramatic as political violence. However, they indicate another crucial way in which the patchwork nature of state institutions influences the operation of South Asian political competition, in democratic India as well as hybrid Pakistan and Bangladesh. They suggest that different dimensions of political competition and conflict have a common cause in the way the state was built.

The patchwork state in India, Pakistan, and Bangladesh has significant implications for the political economy of development, which is inextricably intertwined with competition and indeed conflict. I suggest that subnational variation in growth and development are implicated in patchwork state institutions and differentiated state–society relationships. Forms of investment by the state in both security and development, and the ways that social actors engage with these investments, are not straightforwardly separable from the patchwork nature of the state itself. Violent conflict, electoral competition, and economic development can thus be seen as outcomes of a common causal framework: that of the differentiated construction of governance arrangement during the period of colonial rule and the limited revision of governance arrangements by postcolonial states.

1.6   RESEARCH DESIGN AND ANALYTIC APPROACH

This book takes the historical roots of contemporary political geographies as a starting point for its empirical investigations into the influence of the

---

[33] Bangladesh's elections are increasingly uncompetitive, with the single-party dominance of the Awami League.

[34] Duverger 1954; Cox 1997.

patchwork state on forms of contemporary competition and conflict. In contrast to much of the work on subnational politics in South Asia, my analytical focus is at the district (second administrative or ADMIN2) level, a unit roughly equivalent to counties in the United States. Emphasis on Indian states in the study of subnational politics is predicated on the idea that the constitution, policies, strategic decisions, and capabilities of state governments drive outcomes. This book does not deny the powerful influence of regional governments, for good or ill. Yet in focusing on the district level, it suggests that there are historically rooted variations in state capacity and state–society relations that operate within states (and Pakistani provinces), and thus constitute a distinct but complementary explanation for subnational politics, particularly in relation to patterns of political violence.

Further, districts or *zillas* – around 650 in India, 120 in Pakistan, and 70 in Bangladesh – represent the lowest level of administration at which bureaucrats and police officers have independent, everyday decision-making autonomy in a tradition that goes back to colonial rule, and so represent meaningful variations in the bureaucratic apparatus and how it engages with society. They also reflect greater continuity from the colonial past than Indian state boundaries, which were substantially reorganized in the early 1960s. District boundaries have not changed significantly over the past 250 years; colonial districts have been subdivided, but very few contemporary districts do not fit wholly within districts or princely states in the colonial period.

To investigate patchwork governance arrangements in the Indian subcontinent before independence, I classify 344 administrative districts, princely states, and political agencies in 1911 – any unit that is associated with at least one contemporary district in India, Pakistan, or Bangladesh – into six governance categories using information on juridical status and land tenure arrangements from the Imperial Gazetteer, an encyclopedia of governance that provides a minimum level of comparability across units. I then match these colonial districts, princely states, and political agencies to contemporary districts in the three countries. I use extant colonial classifications, as well as data from national censuses for the three countries in the early 1970s that reflect discrete dynamics of postcolonial politics, to reclassify these contemporary districts into metropolitan, modernizing, conservative, and exceptional governance categories.

I deploy these categories to explore the key subnational politics of conflict and competition in the three countries. For the analysis of conflict, I examine the dispersion of two types of violence – sovereignty-contesting and sovereignty-neutral – across the governance categories of India, Pakistan, and Bangladesh, based on two of the leading cross-national datasets of geocoded conflict events and a third Pakistan-specific dataset.[35] For analysis of electoral competition at the constituency level, I analyze the ENP across recent elections in the three

---

[35] Naseemullah 2018.

countries, based on an argument that relates governance, structures of patronage, and the goals of political competition.[36] To assess the implications of the patchwork state concept on the political economy of development, I analyze key development indicators and explanatory mechanisms in relation to governance categories.

1.7 PATCHWORK STATES IN COMPARATIVE PERSPECTIVE

This subnational enquiry also has implications for understanding South Asian politics at the national level. By coding contemporary districts by governance categories across the three countries, we can see the relative incidence of these categories in the three countries, which has influenced how each has been governed. The vastness and political complexity of India, for instance, inevitably produces significant variation in governance and associated violence. This has not been unraveled by processes of development and bureaucratic reform, which themselves have been spatially uneven in nature. Characterizations of political violence in India, such as Hindu-Muslim riots, are a product of popular attention to forms of competition and conflict in the most salient and successful components of the country's national political geography. Meanwhile, the hinterlands and far peripheries that host rebellions against the state itself have received much less attention in the majoritarian politics of Modi's India and trajectories of growth and investment located in cities. Yet rebellions and riots are both a consequence of how the Indian state was built and how India is governed, variably, across its sovereign territory.

Pakistan and Bangladesh represent a study in contrasts, though before 1971, both were ruled under the same government. Pakistan, relative to India, is even more diverse in terms of governance. Its western and northwestern provinces represented the long and fractious frontier of British colonial authority. In the past two decades, these have been sites of endemic insurgencies, the impacts of which have been felt throughout the country, framing Pakistan in the popular imagination as a failed state. Just as India's insurgencies are often overlooked, there is serious and significant violence in Pakistan over the distribution of the state's resources in cities and the prosperous countryside, which is just as much a product of the patchwork state as in India. Further, patchwork governance may also reflect an overlooked territorial manifestation of Pakistan's chronically hybrid regime, with large swaths of the country's frontier, particularly Balochistan, under de facto military control, while vigorous competition among political parties and social groups, over the goods of the state, continues in populous provinces to the east.

Bangladesh, by contrast, is an instance of a much less uneven political geography, and thus greater governance homogeneity, than either India or Pakistan. This is due to the fact that the country was once the eastern half of

[36] Naseemullah and Chhibber 2018.

one province of British India, at the very fount of colonial rule. The pre-independence politics of Bangladesh has meant an intense modernizing political transformation, first because of the separation of western Bengal in 1947 and then a bloody and successful struggle for independence in 1971. As a result, Bangladesh's violent politics are nationally convergent and, with some exceptions, not particularly territorial in nature. This has resulted in endemic political violence that is national in nature. Competition and conflict thus have occurred over the very meaning of the state as a whole, rather than variations in capacity and authority at the local level.

This book more generally provides a new approach to investigating the processes by which the national authority of modern states spreads across territories under its jurisdiction placing South Asia in greater comparative perspective. In Europe and Latin America, state-building processes are located in the more distant past, while for most of Africa, they were essentially postcolonial in nature. In important cases in East and Southeast Asia, the dramatic events of the mid-twentieth century and their consequences yielded revolutionary and developmental states that in effect transformed territorial authority. South Asian countries provide an illustration of patchwork state-building in the era of high colonialism and its consequences in enduring governance differentiation, thus helping understand the patchwork state as a meaningful way of understanding colonial legacies and their concrete impacts on political competition and conflict.

1.8 THE STRUCTURE OF THE BOOK

This book proceeds as follows. Chapter 2 builds the foundations of the rest of the analysis, in two directions. First, it places the patchwork states framework in greater theoretical perspective, through a discussion of work on conflict and political order and then an introduction to the book's approach, grounded in uneven state-building, state capacity, and state–society relations. It then constructs a typology of colonial governance by integrating discussions of direct and indirect rule and land tenure institutions, across what is now India, Pakistan, and Bangladesh, which have been treated separately by researchers focused on colonial legacies.

Part II investigates the historical roots of the patchwork state in South Asia. Chapter 3 explores the spatial dimensions of colonial conquest from the mid-eighteenth century. I lay out how different forms of governance arose based on greed – the acquisitive nature of the colonial enterprise both in mercantile and extractive forms – on fear, or the insecurity of colonial possessions from indigenous projects of sovereignty, and the overall mandates of frugality. Chapter 4 focuses its analysis on the second century of colonial rule over the Indian subcontinent. I classify districts, princely states, and political agencies into six colonial governance categories at the apotheosis of British rule in India, and then use data gleaned from colonial archives to explore how these different categories reflected differences in the way that districts and states were governed, taxed, policed, and how the army was recruited and where it was deployed in the early twentieth century. I then look at how these governance practices might have changed in the 1940s, with the rise of the nationalist movement, greater participation of Indians in colonial governance and investments in state capacity for wartime mobilization. Chapter 5 examines the state-building efforts and governance practices of postcolonial regimes in India and Pakistan after independence. As the subcontinent was partitioned, princely states were integrated, and the sovereign states of India and Pakistan embarked on separate trajectories of postcolonial nation-building, I investigate the nature and limits of the revision to governance arrangements inherited from colonial rule. I also detail how Bangladesh represents a significant exception to the patchwork states of India and Pakistan, due to the contingent and tragic consequences for independence for the eastern half of a single province in British India.

Part III explores the consequences of the patchwork state on subnational politics of conflict and competition. Chapter 6 examines the key outcomes that motivated the book: the nature of patterns of political violence and conflict in South Asia using the patchwork state concept. Building on earlier work on political violence in India, I use conflict events datasets to integrate insurgency- and riot-based violence into a common conceptual framework, in order to analyze their relative incidence across the political geography of India, Pakistan, and Bangladesh. While these analyses constitute snapshots with varying exposures rather than the dynamics of violence over time, they do allow us to see how different categories of governance might be associated with the preponderance of one kind of violence or the other. This data also reveal significant national variations across the three countries, arising from both the circumstances of conflict but also the patchwork nature of the state – from Pakistan through India to Bangladesh – that can shape the patterns of conflict. Chapter 7 relates patchwork governance to electoral competition. I locate in different governance categories of the patchwork state in India and Pakistan different ways in which citizens engage with the state, which have an impact on variation in constituency-level indicators. Chapter 8 explores the implications of the patchwork state concept on the politics of development and the ways that security and development are intertwined.

Part IV concludes the book with some broader reflections on the impact of the patchwork state concept on the study of comparative politics. Chapter 9 examines the state of research into colonial legacies, and highlights critical shortcomings from undue attention to causal identification, which might be remedied by an analytical focus on processes of state-building. Chapter 10 then discusses more generally how the patchwork state concept might make us think differently about the politics of developing countries, the role of colonial legacies in driving these politics, and neglected factors in the impact of colonialism on understanding political order.

2

Political Order, State Formation, and Typologizing Colonial Rule

Political violence has long been a central preoccupation of political science, international relations, and cognate fields. But it is also a virtual Tower of Babel, in which scholars from different disciplinary and methodological traditions speak in mutually unintelligible conceptual languages. This book seeks to provide a common lexicon to understand the patterns of violence in South Asia, through the lens of uneven state-building and the patchwork state. In exploring the roots of different kinds of violence, embedded within the broader politics of conflict and competition in South Asia, I take an approach that situates this violence in the disparate construction of governance arrangements across territory, informing the incentives and interests of violent actors. This conceptual and empirical approach will be laid out in the next several chapters, focusing on the spatially specific histories of colonial state formation and postcolonial governance revisions, providing us with stable and causally prior predictions of the interests and strategies of political actors within and across national territories.

But before undertaking such an investigation, this chapter will survey extant theoretical approaches on the relationship among conflict, society, and the state to highlight what is novel about this book. There are several venerable intellectual traditions of understanding political order and disorder. This book draws on these traditions for insights while filling in certain key lacunae vital for explaining the dynamics of different forms of political violence in developing countries like those in South Asia. It begins with approaches to political violence that are drawn largely from studies of conflict. It then presents a dominant, if implicit, tradition in comparative politics, especially for understanding contention and violence: that of political order, its attendant institutions, and its variation across countries and over time. *Patchwork States* departs from some of the assumptions embedded in this institutional tradition by focusing on the comparative-historical study of state-building. I outline this approach and more recent advances that recognize the unevenness in state formation within national borders. I then place this unevenness in the context of state capacity and state–society relations in order to arrive at a workable architecture that can link historical processes to contemporary outcomes.

The second half of this chapter lays out the analytic foundations of the book's framework by explaining the rationale behind the characterization and categorization of complex but legible diversity in colonial governance arrangements. To do so, I construct a typology by intersecting two extant categories of differentiation – between direct and indirect rule on one hand and forms of land tenure institutions on the other – each of which represent differences in colonial investments in state capacity and the formation of state–society relations. The resulting typology can encompass administrative districts, princely states, and political agencies in what is now India, Pakistan, and Bangladesh; it represents the first such effort in the examination of colonial legacies across all of South Asia. The typology forms the basis of the historical analysis in subsequent chapters and – following revisions to the typology following postcolonial state-building – serves as the explanatory framework for patterns of varieties of violence and other key outcomes.

This chapter proceeds as follows. First, it surveys approaches to explaining political conflict. Second, it lays out the political order framework that serves as the basis of most examinations of political violence in comparative politics. Third, it introduces state-building in an uneven fashion in postcolonial countries and relates it to variations in state capacity and state–society relations that serve as key mechanisms for reproduction. Lastly, the chapter presents the typology of colonial governance categories that serves as the starting point for analytical investigations for the rest of the book.

2.1 STUDYING POLITICAL CONFLICT

The direction of scholarship on widespread political violence in developing countries has always followed the interests and anxieties of academics, analysts, and commentators of the period. During the Cold War, civil conflict was understood through the destabilizing pressures of modernization, as the gap between the rising expectations of society and the relative inability of state institutions to manage those expectations.[1] By the 1990s, however, the breakup of multiethnic states and the rise of civil conflict among identity groups focused attention on the causes and dynamics of ethnic conflict.[2] Much of this research has aimed at formulating policies of conflict management and resolution and favored instrumental and incentive-based explanations for such conflict.[3] Following the attacks of September 11, such theories of civil conflict were

---

[1] Gurr 1970.
[2] On ethnic conflict and intrastate wars, see Posen 1993; Chua 2002; Eck 2009; Kaldor 2012.
[3] Lake and Rothschild 1997; McGarry and O'Leary 2013.

incorporated into a larger policy apparatus associated with the Global War on Terror, when both Afghanistan and Iraq descended into civil war.[4] State failure, and the strategies of identity groups to maximize their power in response to that failure, became a critical part of the conceptual lexicon.

Debates about the determinants of the failure of the state and systemic civil conflict have consolidated into a debate about "greed versus grievance," or more accurately, grievance versus feasibility, on the part of violent actors. Long-standing accounts hold that the ethnic dimensions of intrastate conflict arise from group-based inequalities and associated grievances, especially when states have limited capacities or motivations for redressal.[5] Scholars have more recently explored these causal associations through rigorous cross-national research into ethnolinguistic fractionalization and the provision of public goods.[6] Other researchers, more skeptical of the association between inequality-based grievances and the incidence of conflict, have argued that structural factors enable the guerrilla insurgencies that characterize many of the civil wars in developing countries, including weak state capacity, insurgent-friendly geography, and *rentier* resources.[7] These debates seek accurate predictors for the preponderance of civil war cross-nationally, though they cannot easily explore its internal character or the actors that drive it.[8]

If explaining patterns of violence within countries, rather than predicting the eruption of civil conflict among them, is our aim, these macro-approaches have limited utility. A different tradition of research has investigated the micro-dynamics of social interaction among violent actors within contexts of civil conflict by exploring their moral and ideological motivations or the maximization of their opportunities for survival or benefit in information-poor conflict environments.[9] Work by a range of scholars has further suggested the importance of organizational logics, group cohesion, motivating ideologies, and strategic interactions among armed actors in diverse contexts of intrastate conflict.[10] Yet, by and large, these studies are still conducted in the particular context of sustained, widespread violence, in which quotidian politics are often suspended. In developing countries such as India, Pakistan, and Bangladesh, in which insurgencies might occur in peripheries and hinterlands alongside a durable state, presiding over "normal" (though often

---

[4] The choice-theoretic foundations of the study of conflict during this era obscures a less-policy tractable intellectual tradition of relating civil war to existential crises in the legitimacy of the state. See Holsti 1996; Kissane 2016.

[5] Horowitz 1985; Stewart 2008.

[6] Cederman, Wimmer, and Min 2010; Cederman, Gleditsch, and Buhaug 2013.

[7] Fearon and Laitin 2003; Collier, Hoeffler, and Rohner 2009.

[8] Some scholars have used "big data" approaches to explore the internal dynamics of insurgent violence, but they do so across radically different contexts that defy systematically comparative analysis. See Berman et al. 2018.

[9] Wood 2003; Kalyvas 2006; Balcells 2017.

[10] Weinstein 2007; Cunningham 2011; Staniland 2014; Arjona 2016.

quite violent) politics in most of the rest of the country. If we want to understand patterns of conflict across the full extent of these countries, we must take a broader approach that incorporates both quotidian and exceptional contexts of violence.

This, in turn, suggests novel approaches to understanding conflict that are more closely associated with violent actors in *domestic* politics, yet still acknowledges and investigates violence as an integral component of these politics.[11] In the South Asian context, Staniland has developed an excellent theoretical framework that interacts the ideologies of state actors with those of violent groups, both within everyday society as well as in rebellion against the state.[12] Yet such a focus on the discrete strategies and tactics of state actors and such groups still occludes the constant, everyday practices of the state and its relationships with society, as they vary across national geographies, which are a vital part of the story of political violence in South Asia. Further, state-armed group interaction is rooted in ideological motivations developed in the postcolonial period, where aspirants to national power achieved the sovereignty necessary to translate their ideologies into policy backed up by force.[13]

More broadly, actor-centric perspectives clash with broader questions on the nature of political authority that stand at the heart of analysis of national and subnational patterns of violence most salient to comparative politics. These are, in turn, capable of integrating political violence with other important arenas of inquiry, from democratic transition and regime dynamics to electoral competition to growth and development. For this, we turn to objects of analysis – institutions – and an intellectual tradition that deployed variation in their presence and power to understand political violence in comparative perspective: that of political order.

2.2   POLITICAL ORDER AND INSTITUTIONS IN THE DEVELOPING WORLD

Inquiries into national authority and political order in developing countries initially responded to specific concerns of American imperial power in the postwar international system.[14] To counter Soviet influence, the United States

---

[11] Auyero 2007; Arias and Goldstein 2010; Skarbek 2014; Barnes 2017; Lessing 2017; Matanock and Staniland 2018; Birch, Daxecker, and Höglund 2020.
[12] Staniland 2020.
[13] There have been attempts to explain civil conflict through colonial legacies, but these do not directly engage with theoretical debates. See Blanton, Mason, and Athow 2001; Lange and Dawson 2009; Mukherjee 2021.
[14] The idea of political order in international relations, by contrast, arose as a liberal critique of anarchy, with political orders in "international society" characterized by the density of interaction between nations even in the absence of a hegemon. Subsequent discussions of "world order" have largely remained within the field of international relations. See Bull 1977; Slaughter 2004; Hurrell 2007; Kissinger 2014.

undertook development assistance through bilateral agencies and multilateral organizations. The intellectual scaffolding supporting such policies was that of modernization theory: that developing countries could uncomplicatedly follow the economic and political trajectories of more "advanced" countries, as long as foreign powers could help to facilitate and finance this modernization.[15] But by the mid-1960s, these pollyannish expectations were faltering. Many countries across the developing world were suffering from coups and revolts against (weak, unstable) governments as well as guerrilla insurgencies, riots, and other forms of endemic political violence.

This perceived crisis of governance led political scientists to seek explanations for modernization's discontents. Samuel Huntington's *Political Order in Changing Societies* represented a powerful and wide-ranging analysis that specifically addressed this problem. Huntington argued that the key distinction among developing countries is "not their form of government but their degree of government."[16] For him, violence and instability were the inevitable product of the underdevelopment of institutions capable of disciplining popular energies toward productive, common ends. Developing countries thus required powerful institutions to manage the disruptive and conflict-ridden transition from tradition to modernity.[17]

Huntington's rather conservative diagnosis of the problem was coupled with an ecumenical approach to potential solutions; as long as political institutions were capable of managing the complex disruptions of social change, they represented viable options for constructing and maintaining political order.[18] Broad, encompassing political parties, in particular, represented modal political institutions for "organizing the expansion of political participation" without attendant destabilization.[19] The Congress party in India represented such a durable, organized, electorally hegemonic party, capable of structuring political participation and social mobilization, even while incorporating traditional agrarian perspectives that might otherwise revolt against modernizing measures.[20]

But he also viewed the praetorian regime of Ayub Khan in Pakistan as a viable alternative means of addressing instability and political violence. It explicitly and self-consciously built innovative political institutions – particularly, the system of "Basic Democracy" – which could provide for greater participation, but in a tutelary and controlled fashion, and cultivated

---

[15] Rostow 1960; Lerner 1964.   [16] Huntington 1968.
[17] Huntington's understanding of political institutions as "arrangements for maintaining order, resolving disputes and selective leaders" (Huntington 1968, 8) is at once narrower and more explicitly political than modern social science's definition of institutions as "the humanly devised constraints that structure political, economic and social interaction" (North 1991). I use institutions and arrangements interchangeably here and throughout the book.
[18] Remarkably for the high Cold War era, Huntington praised Leninist party-regimes for providing durable institutions for containing disorder. Huntington 1968, 334–343.
[19] North 1991, 398.   [20] North 1991, 409–410, 439, 446–448. See also Weiner 1967.

political parties as necessary evils in order to manage increased participation within this system.[21] Thus, for Huntington, South Asia contained two important cases of effective political institutionalization that represented solutions to the problems of instability and violence that seemed endemic to developing countries during this period.

The year of *Political Order in Changing Society*'s publication, 1968, proved to be inauspicious for making predictions. The following year saw the 84-year-old Indian National Congress split apart along ideological cleavages, with the populist Indira Gandhi ultimately capturing the party. At about the same time, waves of mass popular protests in East and West Pakistan forced Ayub Khan from power. Neither the hegemonic party nor the bureaucratic-authoritarian regime represented durable long-term solutions to the problem of political order.

Political order as an explicit concept has since faded from prominence in the conceptual lexicon of comparative politics, as comparativists have been drawn less to explaining the general problem of political instability and more toward discrete outcomes, like economic performance, democratic transition, and authoritarian persistence.[22] Yet a more implicit emphasis on powerful institutions has remained central to the comparative politics of developing countries. The causal import of disciplinary institutions, particularly when embedded within powerful regimes, continues to loom large for explaining national stability and success.

In particular, the "developmental state" framework posited that postwar Japanese economic success arose from puissant institutions that embedded the strategic orientations of the bureaucratic elite in key economic locations, from banks to industrial conglomerates.[23] Scholars have used developmental state institutions to explain the astounding growth of East Asian countries like Taiwan and South Korea from inauspicious origins.[24] Subsequent comparative research has explored the social prerequisites of such institutions, the social coalitions that might support them, and their capacity to discipline the national bourgeoisie in the service of stability and economic success.[25] And in a broader sense, the relative and varying autonomy of the state and its institutional capacities has had a powerful, permanent impact across the subfield of comparative politics.[26]

2.2.1   Political Order in South Asia?

Beyond his particular assessments of institutions and regimes, Huntington's animating concerns have not disappeared from the subcontinent. From the

[21] Huntington 1968, 250–255.
[22] Studies by Fukuyama 2011, 2015 represent a notable exception.   [23] Johnson 1982.
[24] Amsden 1989; Wade 1990; Woo-Cumings 1991. For an excellent overview, see Haggard 2018.
[25] Waldner 1999; Chibber 2003; Kohli 2004; Slater 2010; Vu 2010.
[26] E.g., Skocpol 1979; Collier and Collier 1991; Evans 1995.

1980s, scholars of Indian politics faced a particular set of pressing questions that related to political order. Relative to the 1950s and 1960s, India was experiencing party system fragmentation, rising contention and violence, and declines in public investment. Echoing Huntington's analysis of political order, Kohli attributed India's "crisis of governability" at the time – signified by increases in riots and everyday violence as well as uprisings such as those in Kashmir, Assam, and Punjab – to the decline of the Congress party.[27] For him, the early post-independence Congress party represented a party-regime with high degrees of legitimacy through popular mobilization, providing stability while accommodating new forces and incorporating business, landed, and class elites into a ruling coalition committed to nationalism, development, and social progress.[28]

By the 1980s, however, Congress is thought to have suffered a serious institutional decline, ending both its organizational cohesion and hegemonic legitimacy over the polity. Huntington's theme of increasing violence arising from economic and social change was powerfully represented in the analysis; "developmental successes" had led to the erosion of hierarchical ties within society and rising political assertion among "demand" groups, with a dominant party no longer capable of accommodating these demands, due to faltering institutions.[29] This incapacity, in turn, arose from leaders' decisions to undermine party institutions for short-term, populist goals. Thus, according to this framework, instability and violence in India were rising as a consequence of the erosion of an incorporating party-regime with strong disciplinary institutions, resulting in pessimistic assessments of India's prospects for civic peace and stability.

For all the narratives of decline, however, there has been substantial subnational variation in political authority and developmental success across India's states. Those ruled by the CPI-M, for instance, seemed to have arrested institutional decline and rising disorder and established regional regimes with astonishing records of human development.[30] Scholars have subsequently deployed case-specific and comparative subnational analysis that assesses the causes and strength of state-level subnational regimes based on social coalitions, political institutions, and party competition, which in turn have been deployed to explain differences in growth and development as well as bureaucratic effectiveness and stability.[31] While the specific anxieties of violence and instability of the 1980s have declined, the notion of institutions driving outcomes has remained at the core of comparative questions within Indian politics.

---

[27] Kohli 1990.   [28] Kohli 1990, 4–5. See also Tudor 2013.
[29] Kohli 1990, 6–7. See also Rudolph and Rudolph 1987.
[30] See Kohli 1990, 267–296; Heller 1999.
[31] Sinha 2005; Bussell 2012; Kohli 2012; Singh 2016; Murali 2017. For an early survey of state-level regimes, see Frankel and Rao 1989.

2.2.2   The Limitations of Institutional Frameworks

Powerful as these institutional approaches are for understanding the politics of Indian states and their economic and social consequences, including political violence, there are some drawbacks as well. First and most obviously, it is not easy to translate approaches that were formulated to explain Indian politics to Pakistan and Bangladesh. Until recently, much of the cross-national research within the region has emphasized and sought to explain the regime differences between India and Pakistan, usually leaving out Bangladesh entirely.[32] Recent convergence in the politics of the two countries suggests the greater feasibility of "cross-national subnational" analysis. However, many of the key variables that are used to analyze Indian politics at the subnational level do not fare well on the journey across international borders.

Second, institutional analysis has tended to locate the origins of national political institutions under the powerful Congress organization after independence, with subsequent but regionally uneven decline in the following decades.[33] But alternative political assessments dispute this narrative. For prominent historians and analysts of Indian politics and political economy, the Congress regime, even at its height under Jawaharlal Nehru, did not constitute a cohesive set of institutions with a common purpose but rather a complex arena of diverse and conflicting interests.[34] This was especially true beyond New Delhi; the everyday operation of political and bureaucratic institutions at the local level was deeply implicated in differentiated patterns of social domination, challenges to that domination, and competition among groups, over which the party and government at the center had limited control. Another way of looking at institutional decline and crises of governance, then, is that it represented the steadily more visible and explicit manifestation of conflicts among these interests, which were present in more muted form in 1947, and existed as much in Pakistan and what became Bangladesh as in India.[35]

This institutional diversity has its roots before the assumption of independent statehood, from the construction of state institutions and social relationships under colonial rule. Unlike those of revolutionary or developmental postcolonial regimes in East and Southeast Asia, these

---

[32] See Oldenburg 2010; Tudor 2013; Wilkinson 2015. For an argument that highlights similarity, see Jalal 1995.

[33] Singh 2016; Lee 2019a represent exceptions, with explanations reaching back before independence. This book does not wholly dispute the very real tensions that accompanied the development of a more fragmented and contentious polity over India's postindependence history, but it does question its applicability to the variation in the subnational politics of South Asia.

[34] Kothari 1964; Frankel 2005; Sherman 2022.

[35] Indeed, challenges to political order were obvious in the first decade after independence in India, from the Naga rebellion to continuing insurgency in Telangana to the cancellation of Communist electoral victory in Kerala to subnational authoritarian rule as a means of ensuring stability in Kashmir.

institutions, particularly those of the quotidian bureaucracy, were impacted but not wholly transformed by decolonization.[36] Post-independence political institutions were built upon the already-existing uneven ground laid during colonial rule. As a result, an investigation into the institutions that shape contemporary politics of competition and conflict in South Asia might fruitfully begin before independence. This in turn entails an examination of the way that the state was initially built across the subcontinent under colonial rule. It also solves the problem of translation across national boundaries; despite regime differences, Pakistan (and Bangladesh) also absorbed, with little revision, the institutions that represented structurally similar legacies of colonial rule. This book's central concept of the patchwork state in South Asia brings together uneven state formation under colonial rule, postcolonial efforts to revise state structures, and the resulting territorial politics of conflict and competition in South Asia today.

***

What would such an inquiry into state-building and its consequences in the subnational politics of conflict and competition in South Asia look like? To introduce its components, I proceed in three parts. First, I discuss state formation as an intellectual tradition in social science and recent advances that highlight subnational unevenness in its processes under colonial rule in developing countries. Second, I lay out some of the key mechanisms that enable the transmission of colonial (and postcolonial) state-building to shape contemporary outcomes. Third, I lay out the logics behind key institutional distinctions embedded in colonial state-building that serve as a foundation for subsequent analysis.

2.3 UNEVEN STATE FORMATION UNDER COLONIAL RULE

To begin understanding state-building in a patchwork fashion under colonial domination, we must explore the historical processes involved in the building of the state. There is a long and distinguished tradition of studying state formation at the very core of the broader comparative-historical approach in the social sciences.[37] This research has largely focused on the European experience, which resulted in the consolidation of several hundred states and statelets into a handful of powerful, cohesive ones.

From the fifteenth century, strong states in Europe were consolidated through interlinked processes of agricultural commercialization, mercantile revolution, imperial expansion, and increased military competition. The

---

[36] For comparisons with these cases, see the concluding chapter.
[37] For an overview, see Mahoney and Rueschemeyer 2003; Mahoney and Thelen 2015. Neither state formation nor comparative-historical analysis has been well integrated into recent analysis of colonial legacies. This will be discussed further in Chapter 9.

emergence of interstate conflict led to the building up of the capacities of surviving contenders and ultimately to successful states through establishing methods of taxation and associated administrative apparatus, formulating internal security apparatuses, and instantiating mechanisms of "protection" over commercial activity.[38] These processes connected trade and commerce to taxation, internal coercion, and war-making. In turn, different trajectories of state formation have resulted in divergent economic, political, and social outcomes at the national level.[39]

Most countries in the developing world have not emulated the processes that led to the powerful states of Europe. Dependency theorists proposed a straightforward and compelling explanation of these failures: that colonialism and imperialism extracted and expatriated the resources that could be used for the construction of states and the development of economies.[40] Yet the experiences of East Asian states succeeding in state formation despite infelicitous starting points and intimate connections with the West complicated this explanation.[41] African states, by virtue of fixed borders and the relative lack of interstate conflict, saw state structures focused around cities and national frontiers, with the absence of state capacity in the hinterland, reflecting the mismatch between "juridical" and "empirical" statehood.[42] Limited interstate conflict in nineteenth century Latin America, funded by external debt or rentier resources, meanwhile, led to the relative incapacity of state institutions.[43] In East relative to most of Southeast Asia, "systemic vulnerability" drove serious investments in postwar state-building.[44] Such comparative analysis usefully highlights different values on common variables that explain different outcomes in terms of state strength between Europe and East Asia on one hand and Latin America and Africa on the other.

These narratives tend to follow methodological nationalism, however, resulting in assessments of the relative success or failure of states as a whole. State formation itself is often a locally uneven process, however. Some researchers have sought to go beyond such cross-national comparisons by examining developing countries as arenas of political contention and competition in their own right, explaining subnational outcomes in comparative perspective by investigating the making of uneven institutional terrain through the particular politics of colonial and postcolonial state-building.[45] This research points to a way of understanding variations within developing countries that arise from the past and can explain the present, and providing a nuanced and more tractable subnational perspective to ambivalent national outcomes in developing countries.

---

[38] Tilly 1985, 1991.   [39] Moore 1966; Luebbert 1991; Downing 1993; Ertman 1997.
[40] For a classical synthesis, see Cardoso and Faletto 1979 [1971].   [41] Amsden 1989.
[42] Jackson and Rosberg 1982; Herbst 2000.   [43] Centeno 2000.
[44] Doner, Ritchie and Slater 2005.
[45] O'Donnell 1993; Mamdani 1996; Boone 2003; Scott 2009; Soifer 2015.

In particular, the causal roots of institutional distinctions in the ways that territories are governed – disciplined, policed, judged, taxed, organized in terms of ownership – can have enormous implications in conflict and competition. In exploring the institutional roots of conflict over land in Africa, Boone has powerfully deployed distinctions in land tenure arrangements under colonial rule (and postcolonial governance) to explain patterns of violence within and across countries.[46] Rural property regimes at the subnational level across Africa's colonies and independent states, which had constituted political order across agrarian hinterlands in the past, are now shaping diverse patterns of land-related political conflict in the present.

This book follows a similar approach for understanding geographic variations in the politics of competition and conflict in South Asian countries, but takes a state-institutionalist perspective beyond agrarian relations, reflecting the multifaceted nature of the colonial enterprise in India. The sources of conflict and related forms of violence in South Asia are over divisions within society and the nature of state authority, within which conflicts over land represent a part. Further, some of the most extreme variations in the patterns of conflict and competition in South Asian states occurs in locations distant from agrarian society: in cities, or in tribal peripheries with limited agricultural production. Yet both Boone's analysis and mine are grounded in the relational dimension of institutions, which necessitates exploring how the state and society engage with one another differently across territory and how this generates conflict. In the following section, I will delineate such relational mechanisms, which are underemphasized in the study of the legacies of colonial institutions.

2.4 STATE, SOCIETY, AND PATCHWORK INSTITUTIONS

The patchwork state, the central explanatory concept of this book, constitutes variegated sets of state institutions, operating differently across territory, that together constitute public authority within national boundaries. What are the key dimensions of variation along which these institutions might vary, producing different outcomes? I highlight two dimensions in this regard: state capacity and state–society relations. This book argues that these attributes differ significantly at the district level based on historically informed governance arrangements in contemporary South Asian states, shaping spatial variations in the general politics of conflict and competition.

For students of politics and sociology, the modern state, famously defined by Weber as "a human community that (successfully) claims the monopoly of the legitimate use of physical force within a given territory," represents the modal actor in political and social life.[47] Its effectiveness, cross-nationally and within national territories, is thus hugely consequential for civic peace as well as for

[46] Boone 2014.   [47] Weber 1991 [1919], 82.

prosperity. Even economists have turned to the presence and absence of capacious state institutions as a key explanation for differences in stability and economic success, through a variety of different mechanisms.[48] The World Bank has increasingly emphasized the importance of state institutions to create and implement development policies and programs and has developed governance indicators – drawn largely from assessments by experts – to measure their effectiveness.[49]

Scholars of comparative politics have often used state capacity as a key intervening variable for explaining economic and social outcomes. A primary reason for this is our engagement with public policy. Policy-driven scholarship is often drawn to analyzing state institutions in relative isolation because they wish to understand how key demands of citizens might be achieved through policy interventions by the state, as well as why policies might not be successfully executed because of the lack of state capacity to implement them.[50] As a result, scholars have tended to "see like the state."[51] In the study of Indian politics, the worldviews, incentives, and capacities of bureaucratic actors to implement policies have been treated as keys to effective social enquiry.[52] Recent analysis of the impact of colonial legacies has relied on differences in state capacity as causal mechanisms translating colonial institutions to contemporary outcomes.[53]

Powerful as it is, however, the concept of state capacity runs the danger of ambiguity and endogeneity. The state is most often identified as incapable in cases of violence and underdevelopment, suggesting blurry boundaries between the concept and the outcomes associated with it. Indirect proxies of state capacity are regularly far too blunt and can confuse explanations with outcomes.[54] Further, state capacity is understood in relation to implicit but contested objectives of the state, thus suggesting essential disagreement on the nature and purposes of the concept.[55]

As difficult as it is to measure, state presence and capacity at the local level are certainly relevant for understanding the politics of conflict and competition in South Asia. Differences in the legitimacy and effectiveness of the bureaucracy in Tamil Nadu relative to Bihar are significant, and the everyday Pakistani state is self-evidently more present and powerful in Lahore than it is in Dera Ghazi Khan, let alone the former tribal agencies of the frontier. Assessments of state strength, as they vary across territory, are thus important ingredients for this analysis.

---

[48] See North, Wallis and Weingast 2008; Besley and Persson 2011; Acemoglu and Robinson 2012.
[49] World Bank 1997, 2002, 2007.   [50] See Evans 1995 for a key example.   [51] Scott 1999.
[52] Gupta (2012) and Singh (2016) represent important exceptions of bureaucrats being embedded in wider social fields. Recent work on the micro-politics of public goods provision also highlights the ways that poor citizens engage the state. See Kruks-Wisner 2018; Auerbach 2020.
[53] Banerjee and Iyer 2005; Iyer 2010; Lee 2017, 2019b; Mukherjee 2021.
[54] See, for example, Fearon and Laitin 2003.
[55] For a theoretical discussion, see Naseemullah 2016.

But to understand the politics of competition and conflict in a context like South Asia, attention to the relationship between state and society is unavoidable. The colonial "state" was explicitly delimited in terms of its resources and dependent on various forms of social collaboration to accomplish goals that differ across territory. In this, it was self-consciously the polar opposite of the consolidated, rational-legal Prussian state that most closely approximated Weber's ideal type. The postcolonial states in South Asia have also been porous and weak relative to social forces.[56] Patterns of political violence – and broader political dynamics of competition and conflict – are not the product of the state in isolation but rather the interaction between state and society.

A more nuanced perspective assesses the state in relation to its requirements for engaging society. For Migdal, state capacity is best understood as the ability of its agents to "*penetrate* society, *regulate* social relationships, *extract* resources and *appropriate* or use resources in determined ways" in order to achieve its stated objectives.[57] For Mann, state power can be divided into two forms: despotic, where the state exercises coercive authority without reference to civil society, and infrastructural, referring to the state's ability to penetrate society in order to achieve its objectives.[58] This leads to a different approach toward understanding the state, as a field of power characterized by coercion and constituting the actual practices of agents of public authority, but symbolized by a coherent, controlling organization.[59] This "state-in-society" approach usefully understands the state as an ambivalent and porous entity with blurred boundaries with society, such that state capacity is incomplete without reference to its engagement with social forces. Governance is, thus, rarely authored by the state alone but accomplished by state and non-state actors working in collaboration, competition, and contestation.[60]

Two aspects of state–society relations require particular examination. The first is whether the state at the local level can be neutral and independent in pursuit of its interests, in the presence of powerful social actors. This question recapitulates an old debate in Marxism regarding the state's "relative autonomy," or the extent to which the state may act independently of the immediate interests of dominant (bourgeois) class, to preserve the overall capitalist system.[61]

In South Asia, bourgeois interests are not cohesively articulated, but the question still stands in relation to the state and dominant proprietary actors at the local level; do police officers, magistrates, and local administrators act as their agents, or can they stand up to local notables in the service of the principles

---

[56] Migdal 1988.   [57] Migdal 1988, 4. Emphasis original.   [58] Mann 1984, 2008.
[59] Migdal 2001; see also Migdal, Kohli and Shue 1994.
[60] See, for instance, Brass 2016 on the role of non-state actors in public service delivery in Africa.
[61] See Poulantzas 1969; Miliband 1970 for the debate's contours. For a powerful application, see Skocpol 1979.

and objectives of the state? This accords to a commonsensical notion of the extent of state capture, reproduced at the local level and varying across national territories. In some instances, notables represent a coherent body capable of bending the local state as instruments of their will, whereas in others, a "relatively autonomous" state engages with a more fragmented set of elites, who have to compete for its attention.

A second, related aspect of state–society relations in the South Asian context is the levels of *interpenetration* between society and the state. Herring has described India's political economy as that of "embedded particularism," where the state is subject to social influences even as it attempts to influence society.[62] There is, however, significant variation in the extent of distance between state and society, based on different governance institutions. Consider, for example, governance in the city of Calcutta. Chatterjee has argued that even as the state – in the avatar of the municipal corporation, state-level agencies and even the Union government – might intervene to shape, disrupt, or coerce society, contentious forms of social organization shape the scope of state action in turn.[63] In cities all over India, Pakistan, and Bangladesh, the local state is powerful and coercive in its attempts to intervene in and regulate society, but social actors intervene in the state, controlling it through elections, limiting its power through contention and wielding all kinds of particularistic influences in public life. The relationship between state and society is constant, intimate, violent but ultimately mutually constitutive through repeated interaction.

At the other extreme, as in the state of Kashmir in India or the province of Balochistan in Pakistan, the state is alien and aloof, following directions from central ministries, security agencies and army headquarters hundreds of miles away, rather than responding to local conditions and social demands. At the extreme, this can mean the state acting as an occupying force, impervious to the interests and grievances of the society under occupation. A significant distance between state and society – thus, competition over the very nature of public authority – is as characteristic of these deep hinterlands and far peripheries as proximity is characteristic of metropolises.

In other words, one might think of the various spatially differentiated public institutions in South Asia as varying institutionalized arrangements of positions, roles, and practices among state actors (the police, revenue collectors, judges, paramilitaries) and various social groups. The capacity of the state is an important attribute to local governance, but so is its level of capture and interpenetration. Together, these dimensions, I argue, have a defining impact on the nature of conflict, contestation, and competition.

***

Exploring the mechanisms that translate differentiated arrangements of governance in the past to outcomes in the present is important for any work

---

[62] Herring 1999.   [63] Chatterjee 2004.

on the contemporary impacts of historical institutions. What of the origins of these institutions, and their differentiation, in the first instance? Why did colonizers deliberately fashion such differentiation in their practices of governance? In what follows, I will begin laying out institutional origins by surveying key distinctions between indirect and direct rule, which have been highlighted by extant literature on colonial legacies in India, to arrive at an integrated typology of governance arrangements that will serve as the foundation for subsequent analysis. Chapter 3 will explore the historical roots of these variations, but the rest of the chapter will build a typology of these differences using a key distinction in any discussion of colonialism and its legacies: that of direct and indirect rule.

2.5 A CONCEPTUAL TYPOLOGY OF COLONIAL GOVERNANCE

If institutional differentiation characterized colonial state formation and its consequences, we need a framework for understanding these distinctions. I provide this through a typology of colonial governance. Typologies are organized systems of conceptual types or categories that help us structure our explanations. They order our analysis by delineating discrete and meaningful distinctions in our explanatory variables, thus providing hypotheses and predictions on how they might shape outcomes. Conceptual typologies – typologies highlight the different dimensions of an explanatory concept – constitute powerful tools for social science research.[64] In particular, typologies can elucidate and make tractable the multidimensionality of a particular concept by providing substance, and thus explanatory power, to cells or types in relation to one another. Conceptual typologies are especially important tools for historical investigations into critical junctures and resulting, impactful path-dependent institutions – including that of state formation – especially when those institutions are internally differentiated.[65]

2.5.1 The Elements of the Typology

As discussed in the last chapter, British colonial agents sought the extraction of resources through taxation and trade and effective defense against challenges to their authority, but also to limit costs. It follows that they would strategically deploy investments in state-building to achieve these objectives rather than uniformly monopolize coercion. This means that in some places, we might have seen substantial deployments of state capacity, and close, interpenetrative relations with society. In others, state-builders would delimit their presence by allowing elites in society to govern in their name, thereby pursuing their objectives without incurring costs. The variegated nature of

---

[64] Collier, LaPorte and Seawright 2012.
[65] See Collier and Collier 1991; Luebbert 1991; Kohli 2004; Slater 2010; Vu 2010.

colonial governance is thus implicated in a debate within history, law, and social science about whether colonial powers would seek to destroy and then replace existing governance arrangements, or to preserve these arrangements, at least formally, for the sake of stability, and for what reasons.[66]

These represent, in turn, a well-known distinction in the study of colonial governance and its legacies: that of indirect versus direct rule. "Indirect rule" is traditionally described as a form of political arrangement in which state authorities delegate day-to-day governance to local powerholders, often endowed with traditional or customary authority.[67] Indirect rule was therefore associated with limited state capacity and distance from society. Under direct rule, by contrast, a capacious and putatively autonomous state apparatus governs citizens without any such intermediation, or in other words, a form of public authority that approximates the Weberian state. Studies of colonial governance have used the conceptual dyad as a signifier of different forms of state presence and capacity, with significant long-term outcomes across territory, highlighting the distinction between citizens in the modernizing state and subjects in "native authorities."[68] Social scientists have profitably used aspects of these conceptual distinctions and their legacies to explain subnational variations in development and violence in contemporary India.[69]

While they serve as useful starting points for a discussion of the distinctions among colonial governance forms, indirect and direct rule are not unproblematic categories. Most seriously, the dichotomy is imbalanced. Direct rule implies a putatively isomorphic ideal-type of a monopolizing state, whereas indirect rule refers to a heterogeneous category of structures with discretely different governance institutions in it. In addressing this problem, Staniland and I distinguished different forms of indirect rule with reference to colonial India and its postcolonial consequences.[70]

In so doing, we highlighted two governance hierarchies that arise from direct and indirect rule. The first relates to what we normally understand as direct and indirect rule: the distinction between directly administered districts on one hand and notionally independent princely states on the other. The second relates to the extent to which government authorities – whether princely or British – subcontract key state functions, like policing and the collecting of taxes, to social elites, or implement these functions more directly. Both are critical to

---

[66] See Benton 1999; Gerring et al. 2011; Mamdani 2012.

[67] See Furnivall 1957 for a classic treatment.

[68] See Mamdani 1996, 2012. Some research into the impact of direct versus indirect rule is cross-national in nature, reflecting distinctions between settler colonization and indigenous societies under imperial domination. See Acemoglu, Johnson and Robinson 2001; Lange 2009; Mahoney 2010.

[69] Banerjee and Iyer 2005; Iyer 2010; Verghese 2016; Lee 2017, 2019b; Verghese and Teitelbaum 2019; Mukherjee 2021.

[70] Naseemullah and Staniland 2016.

understanding how colonial India was governed, differently, across space, and together they form the basis for a typology of colonial governance institutions.

2.5.2 Direct and Indirect Rule: Formal-Legal Distinctions

Perhaps the most significant feature of India under British rule was that the colonial government directly ruled only two-thirds of the total territory of the subcontinent; the remainder comprised 565 so-called native or princely states. These were nominally independent entities that were nevertheless under the influence – "paramount authority" – of the British imperial apparatus; in other words, they constituted classical indirect rule.[71] While paramountcy arrangements were present informally from the early eighteenth century, the formal treaties – "subsidiary alliances" – were established in the late eighteenth and early nineteenth centuries.

Princely rulers primarily sought to preserve their nominal independence and authority, even at the cost of furthering British interests. Treaties and alliances allowed imperial control over defense, foreign policy, communications, and coinage and the quartering and maintenance of troops in princely territory. However, these relationships also entailed flexibility and imprecision, represented by significant freedom of action for colonial residents in princely courts within overall policy guidelines and the limited autonomy of princely rulers.[72] This treaty system developed into a template for the relationship between princely rule and British authority in territories that persisted until independence.

In territories under formally direct rule, by contrast, British (or British-employed Indian) administrators, judges, policemen, and revenue collectors ruled populations under the supervision of governors in provincial capitals and ultimately the Governor-General or Viceroy-in-Council. The colonial government collected taxes and enforced laws. This government, either under the East India Company or after 1858, the Government of India, was formally separate from but under the supervision and control of authorities in the British government in London.

Some institutional aspects did transcend the divide between directly ruled and princely territories. Most princely states adopted colonial legal codes and some established convergent technocratic practices, such as revenue settlements, forest management, and smallpox vaccination. Yet there remained important formal-juridical distinctions. It mattered significantly for decision-making whether the ultimate seat of authority was a princely court embedded within structures of aristocracy, albeit under the influence of a resident, or the bureaucratic offices of collectors, governors, and Government House in Calcutta and then the Secretariat in New Delhi.

---

[71] Ramusack 2004.   [72] Fisher 1984, 1991.

The immense heterogeneity of indirect rule represents an underlying difficulty with the category that precludes its simple application. Princely states varied significantly both in terms of size – many princely states involved tiny parcels of land, others like Hyderabad and Kashmir were the size of European countries – and the degree of "statedness." This heterogeneity makes generalizations of colonial policy toward all princely states difficult, and as such, variations must be recognized in any typology of governance. There were also more exotic forms of governance that fall under the overall category of indirect rule. Governance arrangements in the frontiers of the empire, particularly to the extreme west, northwest, and northeast, saw colonial authorities deliberately delimit the footprint of the coercive state and negotiate with tribal actors to establish and maintain stability, thus juridically subcontracting governance, but in a manner qualitatively different from princely states.

2.5.3   Distinctions in Administrative Practice

Even in the regions that the colonial government ruled directly, however, there was substantial variation in how colonial agents implemented governance, and particularly the taxation of land, in practice. From 1765, land revenue and the social structures associated with its collection constituted the modal pillar of district governance. The title of "collector" for the most senior official in the bureaucracy at the district level, still in use today, reflected the centrality of the alienation of agricultural surpluses through taxation as the most basic form of extraction and governance.

Three broad arrangements for revenue collection emerged within the districts of colonial India in the late eighteenth and early nineteenth century.[73] The first, landlord-based or *zamindari*, represented a system in which a class of hereditary and feudal proprietors – *zamindars*, *taluqdars*, *jagirdars*, or holders of *inam* grants – met the government's revenue demands by extracting surpluses from tenants and cultivators, and passing along a portion of this surplus to the government – in other words, tax-farming. The second, cultivator-based or *ryotwari*, represented a system whereby land revenues were assessed to and paid by cultivators (*ryots*) directly to the government, without intermediaries. The third, village-based or *mahalwari* – represented an intermediate arrangement where land revenue was assessed to village communities in common and paid by village headmen or the heads of clan lineages.[74] The long-term implications of

---

[73] Banerjee and Iyer (2005) popularized these distinctions among social scientists, but they were not the first to indicate their importance. The British consistently highlighted these categories in reports on provincial administration and they were at the heart of debates on land reform among scholars of South Asian politics and history since at least the 1950s.

[74] In Punjab and Uttar Pradesh, these arrangements were called pattidari or bhaicharya; in the Central Provinces, these were referred to as malguzari tenures.

landlord-based arrangements involved the subcontracting of significant tax-gathering and other governance powers to social elites, thus delimiting the presence of state institutions on the ground. Cultivator-based arrangements, by contrast, required a more developed administrative apparatus and engagements between individual cultivators and agencies of the state, operated by indigenous elites incorporated into the bureaucracy.[75]

But in addition, there was significant, if underrecognized, variation in land revenue administration in princely states. For example, the Kingdom of Mysore had a sophisticated land taxation apparatus, with the state government extracting revenue directly from cultivators, through the *ryotwari* system that was established under direct British administration between 1831 and 1881, after which the monarchy was restored. In Jammu and Kashmir, by contrast, land revenue was collected indirectly from villages by an intermediary class of landlord-brokers, "robbing cultivators and the State."[76] In still other states, particularly in central India and Rajputana, the ruler directly administered only the *khalsa* or crown lands, which often constituted a fraction of the total, with the rest being controlled by hereditary proprietors (*jagirdars*) with alienated estates, who farmed revenue in return for maintaining order and providing military service in a feudal arrangement. In the smallest and most feeble princely states, the land was essentially untaxed and ungoverned, and princely families were no more than chieftains with paltry private treasuries. Thus, a spectrum of administrative practice that was evident in directly administered districts was also replicated in princely rule.

2.5.4 Assembling the Typology

If we combine these two hierarchies without any subsequent modification, we would get six categories (Table 2.1). In practice, however, this way of categorizing governance is at once too limited and too detailed.

First, governance distinctions based on agrarian relations leaves out locations where agriculture is not the dominant activity. Two of these represent the extremes of state presence and absence: metropolitan cities and political agencies in tribal-majority regions along the northwestern and northeastern frontier. In the former, constituting only a few significant cases, both taxation and administrative activities were more dense and diverse than in agrarian society and thus represent a polar case of direct rule. In the latter,

[75] Naseemullah and Staniland 2016; Lee 2019b. Contrary to Banerjee and Iyer's (2005, 1190) characterization of land tenure forms as "the result of certain historical accidents," and Lee's (2017) deployment of European wars as a quasi-experimental instrument for the deployment of zamindari arrangements, I argue in the next chapter that the establishment of different forms of land tenure was the concrete and deliberate consequence of the specific politics of colonial conquest.
[76] Imperial Gazetter of India, vol 15, p. 138.

TABLE 2.1 *Indirect and direct rule along two dimensions*

	Indirect versus Direct rule	
Land Tenure Arrangements	Princely state; Cultivator-based tenure (Mysore; Cochin)	District; Cultivator-based tenure (Malabar; Satara)
	Princely state; Intermediate or mixed tenure (Baroda)	District; Intermediate or mixed tenure (Julundar, Saharanpur)
	Princely state; Landlord-based tenure (Kashmir, Jaipur)	District; Landlord-based tenure (24 Parganas, Buxar)

exceptional governance arrangements preclude any significant taxation; colonial agents would provide allowances – conceptually the reverse of extraction – to tribal *jirgas* in return for alliance with the colonial state's objectives.

Second, directly administered districts and provinces and princely states exhibited a significant degree of convergence of governance practice for cultivator-based or intermediate/mixed forms of land tenure, suggesting that districts and princely states with these forms of land tenure institutions might in practice belong in common categories.[77] Figure 2.1 uses data from the Imperial Gazetteer to separate princely states and districts by land tenure institutions and measures per capita income in 2004[78] and a composite of public goods indicators from Iyer's data.

We see that land tenure institutions have potentially greater impact than the juridical distinctions between direct and indirect rule, except in terms of formerly landlord-based districts in terms of per capita income. This constitutes at least circumstantial evidence that princely states and administrative districts are convergent in the first two categories, but not in the third.

The resulting typology includes six colonial governance arrangements: metropolitan, modernizing, intermediate, conservative, chieftaincy, and exceptional. The first and the last refer to metropolitan cities and tribal

---

[77] Desai 2005; Boehme 2015.

[78] District GDP measures in the mid-2000s are available from state-level development data in an archived website of the Planning Commission, now under the Niti Udyog website. https://niti .gov.in/planningcommission.gov.in/docs/plans/stateplan/ssphd.php?state=ssphdbody.htm

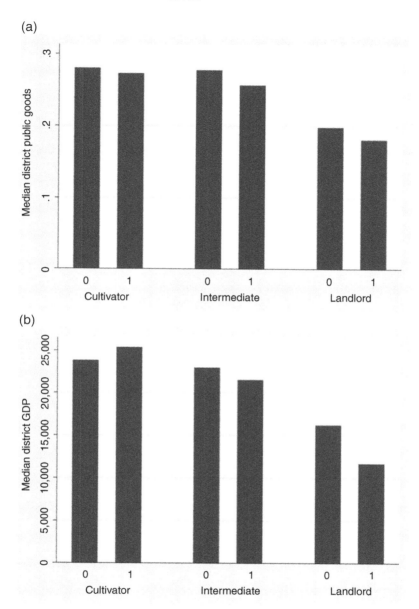

FIGURE 2.1 Public goods and per capita income by indirect rule and land tenure

regions or frontier political agencies, respectively, the middle four reflect formal-juridical distinctions interacting with the practices of land tenure in the countryside. For cultivator-based and intermediate/mixed forms of land tenure, I include princely states and directly administered districts together in modernizing and intermediate political orders, respectively. For landlord-based tenures, however, I separate districts and princely states into conservative and chieftaincy tribal orders, because the subcontracting of revenue collection had dramatically different consequences for administrative districts and princely states. The coding for these categories will be explained in Appendix A. The final typology for colonial governance is presented in Table 2.2.

Figure 2.2 represents a map of what is now Pakistan, India, and Bangladesh around 1911, by governance category, based on present-day district boundaries:

TABLE 2.2 *Typology of colonial governance institutions*

	Direct rule	Indirect rule
State capacity State–Society Interpenetration →	**Metropolitan** (n: 5) Examples: Bombay, Calcutta.	
	Modernizing (n: 75) Examples: Belgaum, Karachi, Nasik, Guntur, Malabar, North and South Kanara, Lyallpur; Mysore State, Tehri Garwal State, Hill Tippera State, Cochin State.	
	Intermediate (n: 97) Examples: Amritsar, Jullundur, Agra, Saharanpur, Rawalpindi, Multan, Bannu, Nimar, Jubbulpur; Chittagong, Goalpara, Ahmedabad, Madurai; Tonk State, Pudukottai State, Baroda State.	
	Conservative (n: 80) Examples: Noakhali, Mymensingh, Nadia, Larkana, Champaran, Gaya, Palamau, Etah, Raipur.	**Chieftaincy** (n: 67) Examples: States of Jaipur, Jammu and Kashmir, Bastar, Saraikela, Bahawalpur, Kalat, Swat.
		Exceptional (n: 19) Examples: Khyber Agency, Waziristan Agency, Chittagong Hill Tracts, Khasi and Jainta Hills.

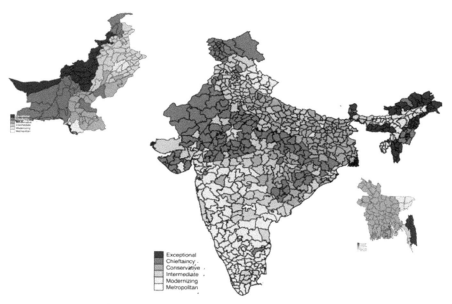

FIGURE 2.2 Map of colonial India by governance category

2.6 CONCLUSION

In a search for the appropriate theoretical lens through which we might understand the politics of conflict and competition in South Asia, the approaches of security studies clarify dynamics among violent actors but occlude questions of political authority. Investigations of political order, preoccupied with the rise and fall of political institutions, can explore such political violence alongside other important outcomes, but they often locate causal factors in postcolonial contexts and are most powerful at the national level. I argue that the examination of political competition and conflict, as it varies across territory, entails an investigation of the initial construction (and subsequent revision) of local governance institutions, under colonial rule and postcolonial regimes. State capacity and different aspects of state–society relations are key dimensions of those governance institutions, representing important causal mechanisms that can relate patchwork state institutions to political outcomes such as varieties of violence, forms of electoral competition, and development trajectories at the local level. Typologizing these differences through the key institutional distinction in studies of colonial governance – direct and indirect rule – provide the foundation for the rest of the book's empirical investigations.

In Chapter 3, I pursue the historical roots of differing colonial governance, implicated in the East India Company's conquest of the subcontinent from the 1760s to the 1840s. As discussed in Chapter 1, the colonial mandates of fear, greed, and frugality are key explanations of why different forms of governance were deployed in different places. Differences in strength of these mandates across newly conquered territory are in turn a product of the complex but legible politics of early colonial domination; the chapter surveys these politics.

PART II

HISTORICAL ROOTS

3

The Making of Patchwork Authority

The Indian subcontinent in the late summer of 1947, stretching from the Himalayas to Kanyakumari and from the borders of Afghanistan to the borders of Burma, contained a diverse patchwork of different forms of governance. How did this diversity come about? I argue that the organizational motivations of greed, fear, and frugality at the core of the colonial state-building enterprise represent an essential starting point for this inquiry. Yet these motivations need to be tethered to the actual politics of the making of colonial India. The British *raj* was not a unitary, coherent precursor to weak South Asian states but rather as a complex object of political enquiry itself, one that generated the institutions internal to patchwork states. We need an account of the roots of this complexity, and the incentives, interests, and strategies that drove it.

Part of the challenge in understanding the establishment of these institutions is that we have tended to heed one set of objectives of the imperial project to the exclusion of others. Many students of colonialism, particularly in the social sciences, have emphasized the fundamentally extractive nature of the colonial enterprise. Colonial rule in India was certainly an archetype of an extractive project, starting its life as a multinational corporation, the East India Company (EIC, or Company).[1] This framing, however, elides the fact that the extractive mandate itself was spatially uneven, with some sites far more valuable than others, and was divided between classical extraction, represented by taxation, and the extraction of value through uneven trade in commodities and later, the import of manufactured goods. In other words, greed did indeed drive colonial rule, but greed by itself cannot easily explain the complex nature of colonial governance, nor indeed discrete variations within it.

Another perspective sees colonialism as part of geopolitical conflicts among European powers, which included competition over colonial conquest. In South

[1] Dalrymple 2019; Kohli 2020.

Asia, there were significant strategic challenges to European colonial projects from the powerful indigenous polities that succeeded or displaced the Mughal Empire. Competitive and violent processes of the assertion of authority among indigenous state-making enterprises in the eighteenth century intersected with competition and conflict among European overseas mercantile projects. To defend themselves against these overseas and indigenous threats, political agents and Company armies embarked on a long process of undermining, subverting and eventually defeating indigenous states, which led to the establishment of territorial control or indirect influence over most of the subcontinent from the mid-eighteenth to early nineteenth centuries. Both the extractive perspective and the geostrategic perspective, each in their own way, drove the complex motives and more proximate interests of colonial actors and indigenous interlocutors, who formed relationships and invested institutional resources that congealed into forms of governance. Following Tilly, they represented important foundations of state-building under colonial rule.

There was also significant disagreement internal to the colonial enterprise among the strategies of its agents and far-off principals, and between individual and corporate interests. Colonial agents had to obey a strict mandate of governance frugality, deeply embedding a logic of the limitation of costs into state-building investments and subsequent governance practices. Frugality would have significant consequences in the ways that India would be governed, producing weak impulses toward homogenization and path dependence from initial investments and subsequent governance arrangements.

Colonial agents formed governance practices based on the relative strength of the organizational motivations of greed, fear, and frugality, but they also reacted to spatially specific events and processes over which they did not have direct control, thus creating webs of causation that defy any simple narrative of institutional sorting. In other words, colonial state-building became implicated in the variously distributive, contentious, and violent politics of early colonial India, contingent and disjointed but no less real and consequential. To understand the legacies of colonial rule and its contemporary consequences, then, we need to understand these generative politics.

Fortunately, the intentions and objectives of the colonial enterprise followed some useful regularities during the critical periods in the establishment of colonial rule. Specifically, the importance of extraction relative to other objectives, as well as different kinds of threats to security and the means to interdict these threats without bankrupting the government, can explain many of the differences in state-building across political geography. The primacy of the extractive mandate and inchoate threats from peasant rebellion rather than from strategic rivals led to the early absorption of the Mughal heartlands of northern and eastern India, then the subsequent hollowing out of precolonial governance and the empowerment of new elites in order to achieve stability. In central, southern, and western India, by contrast, early and imminent threats to colonial rule from powerful indigenous polities meant sustained conflict, and thus necessitated military mobilization. Bifurcated responses followed the violent suppression of these challenges to British hegemony. In some areas, the destruction and wholesale replacement of governance arrangements led to more explicit state-building efforts and ongoing government intervention in economy and society. In others, colonial rulers affirmed the suzerainty and autonomy of various kinds of princely states, with governance associated more with indirect domination than formal subordination.

The extremes of state presence and absence beyond agrarian society were also explicable through the mandates of greed and fear. In the metropolitan cities, key nodes of engagement between India and the world economy, the importance of liberal norms around the operation of commerce and finance yielded the formation of a dense, interpenetrating network of state and social institutions. Frontier regions in the northwest and northeast, by (extreme) contrast, represented the virtual absence of extractive or commercial potential and heightened security threats from external powers, which, combined with frugality, produced particular forms of heterodox coercive and pact-making practices that yielded extreme restraint in state-building. This chapter will introduce these varied landscapes, to provide the reader a better sense of the historical origins of institutional difference.

3.1 BEFORE TERRITORIAL EMPIRE

Between 1601 and 1765, the EIC's ambitions and activities were not territorial in nature. Its agents relied entirely upon indirect influence to achieve their commercial objectives. In the seventeenth century, when the EIC started trading operations to India, the Mughal Empire was a powerful and cohesive, if also heterogeneous, imperial polity.[2] The Company established "factories" or treaty ports – in Surat in 1612, in Madras in 1640, in Bombay in 1668, and finally in Calcutta in 1690 – to facilitate the trade of valuable commodities to Britain and further East, through relationships with rulers of adjacent kingdoms and artisan or agrarian communities producing such commodities.

For its first 164 years, the EIC was itself a strictly mercantile, if often bellicose and always obstreperous, enterprise. The Company initially operated at the sufferance of regional Mughal authorities and was often subject to challenge from other increasingly powerful indigenous forces, such as the Maratha navy. Formed as a joint-stock company with a royal charter guaranteeing monopolies over eastern trade, it stood at the center of multiple, overlapping forms of contention – between its shareholders and directors in London and the agents of the Company in India, between the Company and the government in London, between the Company and unlicensed traders – while of course being subject to the vicissitudes of Mughal politics and competition with other European powers over Indian trade, like the Dutch, the Portuguese, and the

---

[2] Alam and Subrahmanyam 1998.

French.[3] From unspectacular seventeenth-century foundations through the middle of the eighteenth century, the Company establishments had a strictly delimited territorial presence, limited to enclaves surrounding fortified ports, with small military detachments and scant administrative capacities.

It was relatively successful in expanding markets, in part due to the ultimately long-term alignment of interests between agents and principals, along with that of both British and Mughal governments in maximizing the customs duties from overseas trade. The institutional flexibility of the Company was also important. Exploration of market opportunities throughout Asia required decentralization and the interconnection of Company goals with the interests and objectives of their own employees and private traders.[4] The EIC's operations during this period was less a tightly coordinated, extractive imperial project and more a loose association of official traders and freebooters operating out of armed trading posts at the outer edge of a vast, powerful Mughal polity.

The Mughal Empire itself began to stagnate and fragment following the death of Emperor Aurangzeb in 1707. Its decline provided opportunities for the Company to capture and control Indian commerce. Alone among European companies, it received an imperial *firman* from the cash-strapped Moghul crown in 1717, which entitled the EIC to duty-free commerce in return for generous payments.

The fragmentation of the Moghul Empire also presented serious hazards. Regional governors, vassal kingdoms, and enemies of the Mughals attempted to consolidate the mantle of territorial authority for their purposes, posing serious strategic threats to the activities of the EIC by the middle of the century. Threats to the Company interests were especially acute in southern India, which Aurangzeb had brought under Mughal rule only a half century before and which became a site of intense conflict among European and indigenous regional powers. Between 1746 and 1763, the armed mercenaries of the Company – along with British naval vessels and army units – engaged the French in the Carnatic Wars, a series of armed conflicts over control of the Carnatic coast in present-day Tamil Nadu and Andhra Pradesh. These lay at the intersection of military competition in the War of Austrian Succession and the Seven Years' War in Europe and over the state formation project of the Nizam of Hyderabad, a powerful Mughal successor state initially allied with the French.[5]

Though ultimately resulting in British victory, the Carnatic Wars represented an existential challenge to the Company's position in southern India. Early in this conflict, a French military expedition from Pondicherry captured Madras. By the conclusion of both the Carnatic Wars and the Seven Years' War in 1763, however, British power had frustrated France's political ambitions in India, and

---

[3] For overviews of the EIC, see Chaudhuri 1978; Bowen 2005; Dalrymple 2019; Kohli 2020, ch. 1.
[4] Erikson 2014.   [5] Bryant 2013, 35–106.

Hyderabad became a British ally. Victory over France and its allies in the South paved the way for territorial hegemony over India. Yet the nature of that domination lay in a complex transition in the Company rule from a belligerent mercantile enterprise to an expansionary territorial empire. This transition occurred first and most prominently in Bengal, a thousand miles to the northeast.

3.2 GREED, THEN FEAR: NORTHERN AND EASTERN INDIA

In the mid-1700s, Bengal and its hinterlands became the center of colonial power in India. Calcutta served as the capital of British India until it was replaced by New Delhi in 1911. Its hinterland in the north and east of the subcontinent, including Bangladesh and the present-day Indian states of West Bengal, Bihar, Jharkhand, and parts of Orissa and Uttar Pradesh, was absorbed first and most decisively into British territorial rule from 1765. For much of the early colonial period, colonial rule in these regions formed the standard of governance. Yet such governance traditions, including substantial variations around the norm, were the particular outcome of political dynamics in the establishment of territorial empire in India. These were in turn implicated in the complex nature of extraction and profiteering inherent in early colonial rule.

The events that culminated in territorial conquest occurred in the late 1750s, when the modernizing Nawab of Bengal, Siraj ud-Daula, challenged the Company's trading abuses, leading to armed conflict between the Company and the Nawab's armies.[6] The Company's victory at the Battle of Plassey in 1757 and the subsequent Battle of Buxar in 1764 yielded territorial control over much of northeastern India. To affirm this control, the Mughal emperor granted the *diwani*, or paramount tax-collecting authority, in Bengal to the Company in 1865.[7]

3.2.1 The Ambivalence of Revenue

Robert Clive, the Governor of Bengal and commander of forces against the Nawab, persuaded his risk-averse superiors in the Company that the acquisition of land revenue through territorial conquest would yield a fortune for its shareholders. Following Bengal's conquest, the Company's government increasingly relied on land revenue as a major source of income, particularly when the British government restricted its trading privileges, culminating in the loss of its monopoly in 1833. By 1841, land revenue accounted for 60 percent of total revenue for the company.[8] In practice, however, the taxation of land yielded rather disappointing outcomes, at least directly. Spiraling costs of administration and military mobilization, in Bengal and beyond, met and exceeded the uncertain income from land revenue; between 1793 and 1810,

---

[6] Bryant 2013, 153–185. [7] Stern 2011. [8] Richards 2011.

the Company's debt in India rose from £9 m to £39 m, or $3.8 bn today.[9] But territorial conquest also meant fortunes for private actors, including Clive, who received personal land grants from Mughal officials.

The extractive mandates of the colonial enterprise in northern India manifested in greater control over the production of key commodities at the heart of the Company's overseas commerce. British imports of tea from China became a focus of the Company's mercantile efforts, producing huge profits for its directors, while creating a trade deficit for Britain. The infamous reverse trade in trafficked opium from India to China by private trading firms created a triangular trade pattern and enabled Britain to sustain these negative trade balances. The cultivation of opium was thus a strategic priority; it came under a Company monopsony, concentrated in districts in Bihar under direct British rule and princely states in western India under increasing British influence.[10] Territorial control meant control over the production of other valuable commodities such as indigo and jute, the export of which constituted a key source of profits for the Company. The import of these commodities meant significant revenue for the British government through customs duties. Territorial control thus enabled the extractive tendencies of a variety of different actors, even though the realization of the revenue itself was far less profitable than the commerce it enabled.

3.2.2   Governing Bengal

At the same time, there were serious anxieties embedded in the nature of territorial conquest. The EIC's assumption of direct rule in Bengal came with a deep sense of unease, as British administrators lacked any real understanding of how Bengali agrarian society could be governed and taxed. For this reason, historians have argued that the origins of colonial rule in India, especially in its first decades in Calcutta, were characterized not by confidence but by existential uncertainty.[11] While Company officials sought to rationalize land revenue through restructuring agrarian institutions, such rationalization was difficult because of the fundamental non-legibility of indigenous society. To govern, administer, and ultimately to tax, British colonial agents sought fixed rules, even though these activities under the Mughals were embedded within flexible and fluid social relationships.[12] Moreover, eighteenth-century Bengal itself represented a fragmenting Mughal society, in which social norms and relationships were subject to significant flux.

Individual Company officers attempted to formulate fixed and timeless forms of meaning in law, statute, and policy. They did so to maximize predictability in land revenue without being implicated in the complexity and turbulence of the

---

[9] Wilson 2008, 115; Richards 2011.   [10] Richards 2002; Markovits 2009.
[11] Guha 1963, 1997; Wilson 2008. See Ehrlich 2020a for a dissenting perspective.
[12] Wilson 2008.

everyday politics of receiving petitions and adjudicating disputes. However, the consequences of these quests for fixed rules were destructive; they led to a collapse of revenue soon after 1765 and a devastating famine in 1770, stoking fears of an agrarian revolt. Subsequent colonial administrators sought to manage agrarian relations based on their own models and frameworks from English agrarian society, which led to a deep, implicit transformation in colonial governance. This transformation occurred in two stages.

The first stage involved British intentions to bolster the local "aristocracy," or rulers under Mughals. After 1765, Governor-General Warren Hastings established a form of indirect rule, replacing Siraj ud-Daula with a more pliant Nawab, Mir Jafar, but otherwise keeping the Nawab's government in place. Colonial officials collected revenue under the authority of the Nawab. Hastings sought to preserve the Mughal Empire in Bengal to protect its legitimacy as a tool for colonial rule. As a longstanding Company official in India and thus a man devoted to overseas commerce, he allowed only limited intervention in extant structures of territorial governance.

Under his tenure, however, agents of the Company (the "Nabobs") made flagrant use of their authority to amass great fortunes through graft and venality in Bengal, and then transferred their fortunes home, wielding huge influence in the debased politics of Georgian Britain. Whig reformers in Westminster accused Hastings of enabling this corruption by refraining from greater intervention and allowing corruption, while vilifying him for continuing Mughal-era practices of tax-farming. They argued that such practices disrupted the customary rights of the "gentry" and contributed to the collapse of revenue administration. Hastings was recalled to London and impeached for high crimes and misdemeanors before Parliament in 1788 – Edmund Burke was a principal prosecutor – in a trial that lasted seven years but ultimately resulted in acquittal.

Charles Cornwallis, an appointee of the British government, replaced Hastings as Governor-General in 1786. Under Cornwallis' tenure, Philip Francis and other liberal reformers in the Council in Calcutta instituted a wide-ranging set of governance reforms that constituted the second stage in agrarian transformation. The most prominent among these was the Permanent Settlement in 1793, in which the colonial government fixed revenue demands on the estates of the "landowning gentry" (zamindars, taluqdars, jagirdars) in perpetuity.

Some social scientists have suggested that Company rule in Bengal and the surrounding regions simply represented the continuity of rule by Mughal-era landlords, but historians disagree, and with good reason. Permanent Settlement entailed the radical empowerment of a set of new agrarian elites and produced a massive transfer of landed wealth and authority away from the traditional Persianate aristocracy. It enabled, as Ranajit Guha has powerfully argued, a revolution in the ideational, material, and institutional structures of property associated with colonial rule in this region.[13]

---

[13] Guha 1963.

This represented a radical departure from Mughal governance. Inalienable land ownership among "proprietors" was foreign to a Mughal world of fluid relationships of trusteeship, mutual obligation, and courtly practices. The Permanent Settlement was rooted in principles of eighteenth-century European moral and political philosophy, which held that rights to landed property was the only basis for a stable and prosperous polity, in a wholly inappropriate context.[14] Colonial administrators had imagined that the protection of property rights might serve as a source of stability and legitimacy for the persistence of colonial rule. This meant, in effect, disestablishing the system of governance under Hastings that preserved the power of Nawabs and reestablishing authority at the level of a new "gentry," thus a different form of de facto indirect rule under *de jure* direct rule.

A decade after its establishment, Permanent Settlement and associated regulations had not really succeeded in providing a new basis for stability in governing the agrarian hinterland. They led in practice to a spasm of the commodification of land. Many Mughal notables faced bankruptcy because they could not pay revenue demands and were thus forced to sell their estates, often to portfolio capitalists and the rising class of upper-caste Hindus who served as "native" clerks and officials in the Company administration. The new proprietors of the land found agrarian production and taxation challenging due to the continuing social power of the old zamindari families, which further destabilized agrarian relations and threatened grain shortages and unrest across Bengal and Bihar.[15] By the early 1800s, philosophies of governance gave way to more pragmatic actions that endowed the surviving landed gentry with almost complete autonomy, as well as the active support of the coercive state, to strengthen their power over cultivators and enable the payment of revenue.[16] Landlords in colonial Bengal, thus empowered, provided a comforting, if misleading, cognitive consonance in the relationship between the gentry and peasants in eighteenth-century England.[17]

Yet an underlying reason why the Company empowered the proprietary class in northern India was that peasant insurrection was imagined as a greater threat to political order than elite revolt.[18] Landlords were the first, as well as essentially the last, line of defense against such insurrection.[19] Thus, inchoate insecurity from a restive subaltern peasantry, with the potential power to disrupt the imperial project at its core, led colonial rulers of Bengal and its hinterlands to, in effect, subcontract governance. The power of zamindars in agrarian society and the relative weakness and anxiety of the colonial state, at least as an independent entity on the ground, persisted long after the initial establishment of these institutions. These elites dominated the social order in the many decades following the Permanent Settlement, while managing to subvert

[14] Guha 1963; Sartori 2014.   [15] Kolff 2010.   [16] Wilson 2008, 122–123.
[17] Cannadine 2001; Wilson 2008, 111.   [18] Bose 1993.
[19] Stokes 1978; Guha 1983; Wilson 2008, 124–126.

potential modernizing reforms and collaborating with commodity producers to limit government intrusion into the affairs of the countryside.[20]

The Permanent Settlement thus ultimately succeeded in solidifying the colonial landed order in northern India, but not in the ways that colonial officials had imagined. Landlords were able to create and maintain a barrier that limited directed state involvement, thus necessitating the colonial state's continued relations with social elites. Zamindars were themselves constrained in shaping agrarian relations by village-level power brokers (*jotedars*) who controlled local patronage relationships, building and maintaining structures that resisted the control of either "modernizing" landlords or colonial reformers.[21] Thus the empowerment of landowners in northern India had long-term consequences, in state capacity and the nature of local politics. These accounts suggest a complex network of social relationships in agrarian northern India, governed at the top by a British colonial state whose actual authority did not extend deeply, as a result of early mandates of stabilizing extraction and subsequently countering insecurity from peasant rebellion.

3.2.3 Variations in North India

While the establishment of landlord-based tenures under the direct rule of the colonial government represented the norm in northern and eastern India under the *raj* in Bengal, there were important exceptions. First, instances of princely or classical indirect rule were rare but not completely absent. Colonial rulers subsumed most minor princely states in the region as feudatory estates under British administration. However, a few – mostly at the Himalayan periphery in the north, where agrarian production was marginal and buffers were needed against Tibet and China – persisted as formally independent entities under British influence. The Nepalese Kingdom itself represented a particularly independent form of princely rule, with the Rana rulers after the Anglo-Nepalese War of 1814–1816 adopting policies of close alignment with the colonial government on external and military affairs, while consolidating their power domestically. The British would formally recognize Nepal as an independent, sovereign state in 1923.

Second, while the Company replaced the Nawabs of Bengal with direct British administration, it preserved the nominal independence of the Nawabs of Awadh, the Mughal-era province directly to the west (now central and eastern Uttar Pradesh), and augmented their territories. British influence over Awadh was significant, however. There was a powerful residency and large military establishment headquartered in Lucknow. This arrangement of notionally indirect rule continued until 1856, when the Company annexed Awadh outright, due to the putative corruption and ineptitude of the Nawabi establishment.

[20] Palit 1975.   [21] Ray 1979.

Third, colonial administrators used a starkly different approach to administer the territories in the hinterland of Delhi to the northwest, including Agra and the Doab (now western Uttar Pradesh). These territories were notionally under the direct control of the Mughal emperor, but were conquered by Afghan Rohilla and Maratha armies in the early 1700s. Subsequent British conflict against the Rohillas and the Marathas brought these territories under British administration, first in the name of the emperor and then directly under the Company. However, these prior conquests had demolished the Mughal-era aristocratic order. Moreover, Jat and Rajput communities in these regions had long established practices of cultivating the land based on clan and lineage structures at the village level. These "martial" communities were part of a wider precolonial soldier–peasant society.[22] Colonial administrators in northwestern India affirmed these clan-based community structures, yielding the *mahalwari* or village-based land revenue settlements. They also recruited many of these armed peasants into the Bengal Army, a military force crucial for the defense and expansion of imperial interests both in the subcontinent and beyond.[23]

The establishment of the mahalwari system was not without adverse consequences. The high land taxation levied on Rajput communities, especially relative to the permanently settled estates under zamindars in Bengal and Bihar, was a crucial background factor for the 1857 Rebellion.[24] Yet the governance over what is now western Uttar Pradesh also created a qualitatively different agrarian society from that of Bengal. It also influenced the ways the colonial apparatus ruled over other "martial" Sikh, Punjabi, and Pashtun communities further to the northwest several decades later, as we shall see later in the text.

***

The British conquest of northern India, from Bengal, Bihar, and Orissa to the hinterlands of Delhi, was primarily a product of extractive opportunism. However, the transformation of the Company's colonial enterprise from a mercantile to a territorial empire was destabilizing, leading to a series of profound transformations in governance in northern and eastern India. Agents of the colonial enterprise sought first to rule "indirectly" under existing structures of the Nawabs and the Persianate aristocracy while deriving the benefits of land tenure. When that failed to achieve the requisite stability and were faced by the threats of peasant insurrection, they attempted to stabilize agrarian relations by consolidating and then empowering a "gentry" of feudal landowners, in line with a set of philosophical priors from eighteenth-century thought, in the invention of rights to property in an agrarian order previously dominated by dense and embedded social relationships of the

---

[22] Kolff 1990.   [23] Peers 1995.   [24] Habib 1998. See also Stokes 1978.

Mughal world. In a general sense, first material considerations and then fear of rural rebellion motivated colonial enterprise.

3.3 FEAR, THEN GREED: WESTERN, CENTRAL, AND SOUTHERN INDIA

For decades after the conquest of Mughal provinces of the north and east, the Company footprint in southern and western India remained slight, comprising small enclaves and coastal districts around the ports of Madras and Bombay; its presence in central India was nonexistent. By the middle of the 1800s, however, this limited presence had been transformed into instances of the most significant state penetration into agrarian society in India. In other places across southern, western, and central India, however, colonial authorities affirmed princely rule, leading to chieftaincies and feudal princely states, such as those in Rajputana, or modernizing state projects under suzerain arrangements, such as Travancore and Cochin. This trifurcation highlights the governance complexity of colonial India.

The expansion of British rule in southern, western, and central India, despite the best intentions of the Company to limit costs involved in intervention and conquest, arose from the threats to expanding British influence. Powerful indigenous polities challenged the colonial enterprise and threatened its core mercantile pursuits, resulting in a series of wars in which colonial armies subdued rivals and established territorial control or influence across the rest of the subcontinent. These dynamics built into the normally frugal colonial enterprise a dynamic cycle of territorial conquest.[25]

Specific threats to Company power to the west and south arose from the period of Mughal decline over the eighteenth century. Regional kingdoms and successor states had expanded their independent authority as the influence of the Mughal Empire waned, and increasingly clashed with the Company's mercantile and strategic interests. First, the Nizam of Hyderabad and his French allies challenged the Company control over the Madras hinterland and the Carnatic Coast, as discussed earlier. The Company deployed a combination of coercive diplomacy and armed force to neutralize Hyderabad's independent power, establishing it as a grudging ally of the colonial project.

Two powerful indigenous state projects remained significant threats to British power, however: Mysore and the Maratha confederacy. Haider Ali and then his son, Tipu Sultan, became de facto rulers of the massive southern kingdom of Mysore from the 1760s; they were significant state-builders who consciously sought to establish a powerful post-Mughal kingdom in southern India.[26] Mysore was engaged in both military conflict and diplomatic maneuvers with Hyderabad and the Maratha confederacy over the control of

[25] Galbraith 1960. [26] See Ehrlich 2020b.

the South, involving both British and French companies.[27] In the late eighteenth century, the Company was drawn into costly wars against Mysore's armies, which had been threatening British presence in Madras.[28] Mysore was defeated in 1799, but conflict with disparate armed local rulers in the region – known as the Polygar Wars – continued until around 1805.

The second main antagonist was the Maratha confederacy.[29] The legendary leader Shivaji united Marathi-speaking warriors in the western Deccan in the middle of the seventeenth century, subsequently conquering vast Mughal territories in western, central, and southern India and by the early eighteenth century, Maratha armies had captured Delhi and invaded Bengal. By the mid-1700s, however, Shivaji's empire had fractured into several confederated states led by different Maratha nobles. Nevertheless, these kingdoms together represented a powerful challenge to the Company. A first war with the Marathas between 1775 and 1782 involved rival British- and French-allied claimants to Maratha central authority in Pune, in which the Company's army suffered heavy losses. The Second and Third Anglo-Maratha Wars, in 1803–1805 and 1817–1818, were fought over the very existence of independent Maratha power in the Deccan plateau. British conflict against the Marathas thus represented a struggle over the final control of the balance of coercive resources of South Asia, in which armed conflict was embedded in broader arenas of political contention and diplomacy.[30]

The Company's wars against Mysore and the Maratha confederacy represented struggles against powerful indigenous states seeking to expand and consolidate territorial authority, in ways that seriously threatened the Company's material interests as well as its survival. The British eventually prevailed in these conflicts in part because of the material basis of the colonial project. As a fundamentally commercial enterprise, it could borrow funds more easily and cheaply from both indigenous and overseas sources than its competitors to mobilize and equip mercenary armies, even though such debt burdens led to repeated fiscal-military crises.

Mysore and the Maratha states, by contrast, were more constrained in their capacities to borrow or extract resources.[31] As indigenous state-builders, they needed to mobilize funds, raise and maintain armies, and construct administrative capacities while maintaining legitimacy with key internal allies. The Company needed only to frustrate their state-building projects to accomplish its own more concrete (and venal) material interests. Alternative state formation projects were unlikely to prevail when faced with an adversary so fundamentally ambivalent about state-building, thus maintaining greater flexibility and fiscal space.[32] But these conflicts and their consequences emphasized the central nature of the colonial enterprise in "the military-fiscal state," that is, as much a martial organization as an extractive one.[33]

[27] Subrahmanyam 1989.   [28] Wilson 2016, 159.   [29] See Gordon 1993.
[30] Kolff 1990; Cooper 2003.   [31] Wink 1983.   [32] Roy 2013.   [33] Bayly 1994.

At the end of the Third Anglo-Maratha War in 1818, the Company had achieved paramountcy over most of the territory of the Indian subcontinent through direct rule or indirect influence. Yet conquered or otherwise subjugated territories were governed in distinctly different ways according to the nature of the threat in different territories, as well as the costs associated with its governance and the wealth to be gained from that governance. The establishment of governance institutions across provinces and districts, princely states and agencies were thus deeply implicated in territorial politics during this period.

3.3.1 Settled Districts and Cultivator-based Tenure

Central, southern, and western India represented fissured regions where Mughal authority and administrative structures were weak or absent, due to more recent Mughal conquest and the fragmentation of authority associated with sustained armed conflict. Instability in southern India had roots in the disintegration of the Vijayanagar Empire and the subsequent efforts of Aurangzeb to expand the Mughal Empire southward, yielding a fractured territorial space where Mughal soldier-administrators clashed with armed Nayar aristocrats. This intense regional competition allowed for the consolidation of Mysore under Haider Ali, but following his defeat, *palliayakkar* or "polygar" rulers continued to resist colonial rule, necessitating repeated campaigns of pacification.

Similarly, after the end of Maratha rule in central and western India, former soldiers entrenched control over territories and challenged the expansion of the Company. Company armies engaged in military campaigns to disperse *Pindaris*, Muslim irregular troops who had previously fought for Maratha states. Like the Polygar campaigns in the south, the Pindari campaigns represented the final steps to the establishment of stability in the Maratha territories in the Deccan plateau, agrarian arrangements of which had been disrupted by decades of armed conflict. Thus in both the South and the West, a significant amount of coercion was necessary to reestablish social order. Cultivator-based arrangements were an important byproduct of that reestablishment.

The fragmentary nature of governance and the legacies of war in the countryside yielded a fundamentally different set of agrarian relationships than the ones in Bengal. At the root of Thomas Munro's *ryotwari* innovation – land revenues collected directly from cultivators – in Madras Presidency, and its subsequent extension to Bombay Presidency, was the perceived need to eliminate the intermediary armed chieftains previously in control of Mysore and Maratha territories.[34] The Company's direct engagement with cultivators was thus a consequence of the destruction of

---

[34] Washbrook 2004, 491.

intermediaries that, unlike zamindars in the North, were seen as enemies rather than allies.

Once Company officials achieved direct rule over these particular territories, they established ryotwari arrangements. These were not the implementation of a conscious policy framework from above, but rather the pragmatic and expedient application by district collectors of demands for both revenue collection and political stability. District officials recruited members of hereditary village-level record-keeping and accounting communities – *patels*, *desais*, *chaudhrys* – as well as other upper-caste groups directly into the colonial administrative apparatus in these areas. These new "native" officials managed the direct taxation of *ryots*, or peasant-cultivators, once aristocratic intermediaries were eliminated through armed conflict.[35] These positions then became entrenched in agrarian society and supported by a coercive interventionist state, yielding more quotidian administrative presence than landlord-based arrangements in the north.

Thus in regions with ryotwari arrangements, there were traditions of greater penetration between the colonial state and indigenous society, while maintaining and reinforcing social hierarchies. At the same time, interventionist state institutions had real limits; in the early nineteenth century, local elite resistance in Madras Presidency kept the implementation of liberal reforms at bay.[36] Ryotwari arrangements were often, in practice, mechanisms for the concentration of wealth within upper caste communities, collaborating with colonial officials.[37] Further, the intrusion and uneven integration of India within the imperial economy led to a decades-long economic depression in the region, the wholesale destruction of a prosperous craft economy and the reinforcement of deeply hierarchical relations in agricultural production.[38] Critically, arrangements of cultivation in southern India involved the extensive exploitation of *Dalits* ("Pariahs"). These communities comprised lower-caste "untouchable" landless laborers working under ryots and the upper-caste village aristocracy in conditions of agrestic slavery.[39] The salience of caste hierarchies in southern India, relative to the North, is thus an unintended consequence of the processes of stabilizing and administering the region.

3.3.2   Variations in Southern, Central, and Western India

Any straightforward relationship between the elimination of the warrior-aristocracy and ryotwari arrangements can also be complicated by the persistence of some aristocratic arrangements. Price analyzed two zamindaris in South India – formerly princely states that had sided against the British in the Poligar Wars and were annexed into Madras Presidency, while maintaining

---

[35] Rabitoy 1975.   [36] Washbrook 2004, 507.   [37] Washbrook 2004, 506–509.
[38] Chaudhuri 1974; Washbrook 2004.   [39] Viswanath 2014.

their status as feudal estates – and highlighted some continuities in political practice from the precolonial period. In these cases, colonial rule tempered rather than simply eliminated aristocratic authority. Former princely zamindaris controlled structures of honor, fealty, and protection in the local polity through patronage, even while British institutions constrained the exercise of their actual power.[40] Thus, landlord-based arrangements were not completely alien to South India.

The complex politics of incorporation into colonial rule also played out in different ways in central India. The Maratha- and Hyderabad-ceded territories of what would become the "Central Provinces and Berar" represented two distinct regions that had differentiated politics. Berar constituted districts ceded from Hyderabad as repayment of debt; they were administered, much like Madras and Mysore, on the cultivator-based ryotwari system. As territories of annexed states at the peripheries of the Maratha Empire, by contrast, the districts of the Central Provinces constituted a mixture of zamindari estates and village-based arrangements of tenure. This suggests the ways in which British power was overlaid on differential patterns of precolonial governance in a region that at least initially had little economic promise.

3.3.3   Variations in Princely Rule

Even more variation was evident in the princely states in western, central, and southern India, a region which contained most of the significant "native" states in the Indian subcontinent, which persisted until independence. How they were confirmed through treaties and how they ruled themselves had much to do with their relationships with the British during the wars with Mysore and the Marathas, and crucially on whether they were allies, adversaries, or simply tools of colonial power.

Certain princely rulers represented close collaborators of the Company against both enemies and insurrectionary forces. Some of the most powerful princely states in the South, including Travancore and Hyderabad (present-day Kerala, Telengana, and parts of Karnataka and Maharashtra), were Mysore and Maratha antagonists in early eighteenth-century state-building conflicts and subsequently became allies of the Company. Their long-standing alliances limited colonial penetration. As a result, they could pursue internal state formation projects, becoming increasingly integrated into regional and overseas commerce and making use of the governance technologies of British colonial agents, in order to maintain relative independence and foreclose the possibility of colonial interference or annexation.[41] Similarly, the kingdom of Mysore after the defeat of Tipu Sultan in 1799 became a powerful and modernizing princely state under the Wodeyar Dynasty and a close British ally. Distinctively, it was

---

[40] Price 1996.   [41] Das Gupta 1967; Desai 2005.

administered directly as a British province between 1831 and 1881, during which time the British commissioner established ryotwari arrangements, but then returned to its previous status as a princely state from 1881 to 1947.

Often seen as prototypical examples of princely rule, the Rajputana kingdoms in western India – now the state of Rajasthan – had been under the paramountcy of the Mughals and then the Marathas. In the course of conflicts between the Company and Marathas, they sought and achieved early subsidiary alliances with the British as a way of preserving, sustaining, and consolidating princely authority. However, their internal governance focused on feudal, martial cultures that reflected British "ornamentalism" and, unlike states like Travancore, largely abjured investments in modernization.[42]

By contrast, adversaries like the Maratha states needed to be kept under control, but the mandate of frugality precluded their complete annexation. The princely states of major Maratha clans like the Scindias and Holkars, in present-day Karnataka and Madhya Pradesh, represented the vestigial remains of vast Maratha territories, but the British maintained and preserved them in order to minimize the threat of renewed warfare.[43] The Maratha clan of Gaekwads made a separate, proactive peace with the British after the Second Anglo-Maratha War, leading to the preservation of Baroda state, in present-day Gujarat, one of the largest and wealthiest princely states in India. Thus, previous adversaries of the Company in the Mysore and Maratha wars saw their territories severely contracted and isolated from one another, but princely rule itself persisted.

Lastly, a large number of "princely states" were in fact small fiefdoms under the vassalage of greater powers. They were relative bystanders rather than active participants in the dramatic conflicts at the turn of the century. The Company co-opted their rulers and thus affirmed scores of petty princely states and chiefships. For example, Oriya states or "tributary mahals," largely in present-day Jharkhand and Chhattisgarh on the frontiers of the Maratha confederacy in the east, were placed under British suzerainty in 1804. They constituted small chieftaincies with tribal majorities subject to significant restraint by colonial authorities, given their tribal social structures and positions on the periphery of colonial economy and society. These princely states, many of them the size of a contemporary district and others significantly smaller than that, were thus insignificant holdovers from previous empires, which British authorities formally recognized as vassalages within conquered or ceded territories but in which otherwise they had limited strategic or material interest.

To balance the pursuit of colonial interests with the demands of frugality, residents sought political means, including intervening in the internal politics of princely states and even replacing an disruptive ruler, to guarantee their

---

[42] Rudolph 1963; Rudolph and Rudolph 1967. See also Cannadine 2001.
[43] See, for example, Farooqui 2011.

quiescence. This also meant that even large and formerly powerful princely states had limited means to engage in the defensive state-building available to early allies of the Company. The importance of the military to the colonial enterprise implicated princely states, which were increasingly integrated into the colonial military complex through the provision of allied forces and bases. Three of the biggest military cantonments in central and southern India – Mhow, Bangalore, and Secunderabad – were located in the princely states of Indore, Mysore, and Hyderabad; they remain significant bases of the Indian army today. Further, state militaries were often called upon as auxiliary units to support the Indian army.

The creation – or more properly, the variable preservation and augmentation – of much of the princely rule in early colonial India was a function of the violent and contentious politics of the British campaigns to frustrate and eliminate alternative state formation projects in western and southern India. These politics, along with colonial imperatives of security and frugality, yielded locally quite disparate outcomes in the size and "statedness" of princely states, in addition to their preservation or elimination.

Further, some "progressive" princely states developed governance arrangements in parallel with and increasingly isomorphic to colonial rule, increasingly integrated into domestic and international economies. The lived experience in Mysore or Travancore state would have been similar to adjoining districts in Madras Presidency.[44] These states developed a sophisticated government, active civil society, and even investments in industrialization.

In others, British residents and princely rulers colluded in the preservation of both *de jure* and de facto distinctions that kept princely rule apart from the various forms of colonial governance in colonial India. Princely states like Jaipur and Jodhpur empowered notables from Rajput clans to collect taxes and administer justice on behalf of the Maharaja, yielding relatively febrile central administration. As a result, variation within the category of princely rule can be as significant as variation among agrarian arrangements in administered districts, as a result of territorial politics.

3.4 THE PERVASIVENESS OF GREED: METROPOLISES

The cities of colonial India, principally Madras, Bombay, and Calcutta, represented the very first instantiations of the British presence, as early as the seventeenth century, when it was focused entirely on overseas commerce. These centers of economic and political power remained distinct even as territorial authority expanded, developing modes of governance deeply implicated in commercial activities. The transformation of resources into commodities and capital required a particularly dense form of institutional capacity.

---

[44] Boehme 2015.

Institutional economists have long emphasized the need for strong states to enforce contracts and protect property rights, in order to enable capitalist production and exchange.[45] Particular pan-imperial judicial and financial institutions facilitated the integration of colonial metropolises into the international economy. Colonial administrators made tangible investments in housing, health, education, employment, legal institutions, though also imposing increasingly racialized social norms.[46] Municipal corporations formed early, durable patterns of self-governance that provided key services and managed relations among the various colonial officials, expatriate traders, service professionals, and indigenous elites. Crucially, the apparatus of colonial government in cities had more interest in engaging (some of) its "citizens" directly, albeit in racially distinct fashions, rather than relying on mediating institutions. The state deployed greater capacity to manage some of the core activities of exchange at the intersection of overseas and internal commerce.

Beyond concrete institutions, philosophies of liberal reform were critically important for the development of urban governance. Liberal reformers were dedicated to colonialism as a form of modernization. Nineteenth-century liberals viewed India as a deficient or primitive case within a broad, universalistic narrative of progress and development. They felt that India could be paternalistically "treated" with the application of rationality, abstract principles, and fixed rules and thus abandon constraints of tradition and particularism.[47] The application of liberal thought in colonial India was closely associated with capitalist transformations in the economy and the establishment of universal social principles and legal norms. While proposed liberal reforms in governance faced significant challenges throughout much of the hinterland that precluded their actual implementation, they had much greater purchase in the administrative practices and social mores of metropolitan India.[48]

The hegemony of liberal paternalism inspired conscious reactions and responses among indigenous elites who formed an active and contentious civil society in the metropolises.[49] That reaction was most developed in Calcutta, the city at the heart of the imperial project but also the birthplace of the Bengali Renaissance. Important figures engaged with and critiqued empire based on the shared understandings of political and social life in the colonial city. Writers and thinkers such as Raja Ram Mohan Roy and Bankim Chandra Chattopadhyay critically engaged colonial liberalism by fashioning alternative, radical discourses and intellectual and cultural movements.[50]

Similar intellectual exercises arose in other colonial metropoles. The headquarters of the Theosophical Society, an international religious, mystical, and intellectual movement that had a powerful influence on Indian nationalism,

---

[45] North 1991.   [46] Arnold 2006.   [47] Mehta 1991.   [48] See Ehrlich 2018.
[49] On civil versus political society, see Chatterjee 1993.
[50] See Chatterjee 2010. See also Sartori 2014 for more "vernacular liberalism."

were established in Madras in 1882.[51] The wealth, industry, and urbane multiculturalism of Bombay attracted lawyers, bankers, and traders and represented the very heart of the Indian economy.[52] Cities like Pune too presented the development of civil society, but they were largely islands in seas of agrarian relations, more connected to other metropolises than to the hinterland. Critically, the intense and sustained encounter with colonial liberalism, in the governing structures that gave rise to movements of nationalist resistance, was only possible in fully articulated fashion in cities where the state was omni present. Metropolitan governance, which was heavily influenced by liberalizing reforms both in terms of colonial action and proto-nationalist reaction, thus constituted a territorially particular politics.

3.5 THE PERVASIVENESS OF FEAR: FRONTIERS

As the Company's authority expanded to the limits of its territorial influence in the mid-1800s, new existential threats emerged, particularly from other empires engaged in their own colonial expansion. The Russian Empire, expanding southward through Central Asia, constituted a particular source of alarm, because it was Britain's major strategic competitor across Asia and beyond. For the next century, Britain and Imperial Russia, and then the Soviet Union, conducted, in effect, a cold war – called the Great Game – in which spies, diplomats, soldiers, and indigenous allies vied with one another for advantage, especially in the client state of Afghanistan and across the northwestern frontier. The British in India and the Qing Empire also contested authority over the uplands along the northeastern frontier in what is now Arunachal Pradesh.

Critically, neither frontier was easy to govern. They encompassed ill-defined boundaries along the high valleys and mountain passes of the Hindu Kush and the Himalayas, populated by tribal societies that had never been meaningfully integrated into precolonial empires. Neither frontier was endowed with commodifiable resources or an agricultural surplus, which might make administrative investments cost-effective. Rather, insecurity and frugality were dominant, but opposing, forces. Some coercive state presence was, however, necessary to interdict foreign agents and forestall raids on settled areas by tribal groups. Political agents deployed different forms of exceptional governance arrangements, while explicitly refraining from the costly deployment of regular laws and administrative practices. They formed tenuous relationships, tinged with coercion and bribery, with tribal groups in the regions that served as strategic buffers against external, imperial threats.

The combination of unsettled borders, light state presence, and exceptional governance arrangements would have serious consequences after independence and partition. Pakistan's long and contested border with Afghanistan became the site of the last major Cold War confrontation between the United States and

---

[51] Bevir 2003.   [52] Chandavarkar 1993, 1998.

the Soviet Union, and subsequently the major battleground for the War on Terror, as well as a brutal, only recently ended, insurgency in Pakistan's northwest. India's Northeast – now, the states of Assam, Arunachal Pradesh, Meghalaya, Mizoram, Nagaland, Tripura, and Manipur – has been the site of multiple, overlapping insurgencies since India's independence, as well as ongoing strategic confrontations between India and the People's Republic of China across the contested international border, including a war in 1962. The exceptional nature of political order along colonial India's borders has had concrete and lasting effects on exceptional state–society relations in both countries to this day.

3.5.1   Assam and the Northeast Frontier

The last major expansions of the borders of colonial India eastward and westward occurred in the mid-nineteenth century, through expansionary armed conflicts against the Burmese Kingdom and against the Sikh Empire in Punjab and the remnants of the Durrani Empire in Afghanistan. The conquest of politically important agrarian societies in northeastern and northwestern India brought the Company into contact with unstable and threat-saturated borderlands. This led to conflicts over the defense of new territories at their jagged and uneven edges, eventually coupled with the threat of encroachment by other empires in Asia and thus geostrategic competition. This sense of insecurity, unlike the threat of Mysore and the Maratha states in the early nineteenth century, was existential and ongoing. Moreover, the agents of empire had fewer instruments for managing these threats, because cost-ineffectiveness precluded the overwhelming military campaigns against indigenous state-builders of earlier decades.

Expansion eastward from Bengal occurred first. The Company annexed parts of Assam and present-day Myanmar in 1826 after the First Anglo-Burmese War against the Alaungpaya Dynasty, following the latter's annexation of the Ahom kingdom in present-day Assam in the early 1820s. The Company also established suzerainty over the princely state of Manipur.[53] Subsequent wars and annexations brought all of Assam (and eventually all of Burma) under British control, initially administered as part of Bengal Presidency but ultimately under its own provincial government.

Colonial agents developed land tenure arrangements in the lowland areas of the Brahmaputra Valley in two stages. First, district officials confirmed an intermediary class of estate-owning landowners (*chamuadars*) alongside peasant-cultivators and village officers. Second, governance largely shifted to the ryotwari cultivator-based system of land tenure after the collapse of the chamuadari system.[54]

---

[53] A second princely state, Tripura – or "Hill Tippera" – was under Mughal suzerainty and had been included in Bengal Presidency.

[54] Prajapati 1982.

Tea cultivation and plantation agriculture complicated agrarian relations. In the 1830s, the "discovery" of tea plants in upland Assam led Company officials, keen on decreasing the reliance on Chinese imports, to undertake the immigration (under duress) of bonded labor from outside Assam for tea plantations and the clearance of forested hills for cultivation. Plantation agriculture created radically different agrarian arrangements and created a substantial expatriate labor force, both of which became implicated in Assam's contentious and violent politics after independence.[55]

Finally, the tribal-dominated, highland regions of Assam, particularly along the undefined borders with Tibet under Qing suzerainty, were unsettled and unregulated. Taxation, if and when it occurred, was assessed by polls or housing rather than agricultural surplus. The infrastructure of the colonial state was massively underdeveloped beyond areas of lowland cultivation and sites of plantation agriculture.

Threats against British India from the northeast arose at the turn of the twentieth century. Qing dynasty officials from Sichuan asserted more direct rule over Tibet and started conquering the territory on Tibet's southern borderlands in the eastern Himalayas, territory that was thought to be under the jurisdiction of the Assamese provincial authorities. Qing expansionism inspired a series of expeditions of British political agents into the hills and valleys to the north, engaging with tribal societies with little engagement with either Tibet or Assam in what might be thought of as far-western Zomia.[56] Brief episodes of geostrategic competition against the Chinese in the eastern Himalayas thus established the pattern of colonial interventions designed to accomplish cost-effective interdiction against expansionism, first under the Qing and then under Chinese Republican governments, with colonial Indian and Chinese states shadowing one another's governance activities in a pattern that would continue after independence and the establishment of the People's Republic.[57]

3.5.2 Punjab and the Northwest Frontier

In the Northwest, the Company's last major colonial conquests brought with them hazardous frontiers that became a singular focus of threat for colonial India. Punjab, arguably the most valuable Mughal province, had been captured by the Afghan Durrani Empire in the mid-1700s. Ranjit Singh expelled the Durranis and established the Sikh Empire in Punjab in 1801. The Sikh state was deeply embedded in the martial and agricultural society of the Punjabi plains and thus developed strained relationships with Pashtun communities west of the Indus River but east of an undefined border with still Durrani-controlled Afghanistan.

---

[55] Dasgupta 1983; Varma 2017.
[56] Karlsson 2013; Misra 2013. On Zomia, see Van Schendel 2002; Scott 2009.
[57] Guyot-Rechard 2016.

The Sikh empire came into contact with the territory of the Company south of the Sutlej River, when the latter captured Maratha territory in the hinterland of Delhi in the early 1800s, leading to relationships of mutual suspicion. After Ranjit Singh's death in 1839, the Company exerted indirect influence over the Sikh royal court until finally, through wars in 1845 and 1848, it annexed Punjab, including the northwestern frontier. At the same time, the Company gave the old Mughal province of Kashmir to the Maharaja of Jammu, a former vassal of Ranjit Singh, for the support he provided to the Company in the Anglo-Sikh Wars, creating a massive princely state in the extreme northwest of India.

Colonial authorities governed Punjab and the northwest quite differently from Bengal. As with Jat and Rajput society in western and central United Provinces discussed earlier, the Persianate aristocracy had been largely displaced due to both Durrani and Sikh conquest, yielding agrarian organization among the largely Muslim peasantry that emphasized joint-ownership among clans and joint families, in other words, *mahalwari* or intermediate village-based arrangements. British systems of land revenue accorded new proprietary rights to headmen who collected revenue from clan elders, thus concentrating rural power, but from a base of relative dispersion.[58] Directly to the south, the Company annexed Sindh from the Talpur nawabs in 1843 and included it in Bombay Presidency. In this province, there was a much greater concentration of wealth and power in the hands of hereditary religious elites, *pirs* and *makhdooms*. What is now southern Punjab, largely under the princely state of Bahawalpur, had similar arrangements.

Punjab was at the very core of the British military complex after 1857–8, building what Yong terms a Garrison State by heavily recruiting "martial races" – Sikhs, Punjabi Muslims, and Pashtuns from lowland areas – and providing veterans with land in "canal colonies," as well as preventing land transfers and incorporating notables into the administrative structures of the province.[59] The philosophies and praxis of governance in Punjab self-consciously departed from liberal anglicizing reforms; Henry Lawrence, agent to the Governor-General and resident in the 1840s, and his brother John Lawrence, first Chief Commissioner in Lahore and later Viceroy in the 1860s, cultivated a group of soldier-administrators with military experience on the frontier who could preserve extant traditions and social order in Punjab, at a time when liberal universalism held sway in Calcutta.[60]

The annexation of Punjab was deeply implicated in the making of British India's fraught western and northwestern frontiers along its borders with Afghanistan, the site of significant insecurity and the focus of military deployment from the mid-nineteenth century until Partition. The roots of this insecurity were located in the internal politics of the Kingdom of Afghanistan,

---

[58] Nazir 1981. There are significant diversities among different villages even within the mahalwari system in western Punjab, with long-term political consequences. See Mohmand 2019, 49–84.
[59] Yong 2005.   [60] Lee 2002. See Condos 2017 for a general overview.

emerging out of the remnants of the Durrani Empire. In 1839, a Company army intervened to return the exiled Shah Shuja to the throne in Kabul and create a stable buffer state against threatened Russian encroachment. The First Anglo-Afghan War was a strategic disaster, during which thousands of soldiers and camp followers were killed. After Punjab was conquered, the British sought to create stable relationships with Pashtun tribes within the Sikh Empire's jurisdiction. Lawrence's agents established tribal political agencies, while the settled agrarian lands west of the Indus became regular administrative districts, which were eventually incorporated into the North West Frontier Province (NWFP).

A similar set of institutions were established in the western frontier. In Balochistan, British intervention in the Khanate of Kalat, a former vassal to both Mughals and Durranis, yielded districts under exceptional British administration, with the remainder as a princely state under subsidiary alliance. From the 1870s, Robert Sandeman initiated a series of campaigns of tribal pacification, exploiting divisions between the Khan of Kalat and tribal chiefs in order to expand influence and project authority in the region.

3.5.3 Governance Exceptionalism in the Northwestern and Northeastern Frontiers

In western, northwestern, and northeastern frontiers, agents of the colonial state faced contradictory mandates; they needed to secure the subcontinent from fears of foreign intrusion – from the Russians in central Asia from the mid-1800s, and from the briefly assertive Qing Empire in China in the early 1900s – without deploying costly military and administrative resources in regions with little economic benefit. As Punjab, the NWFP, and Assam were integrated into the regular governance practices of colonial India, colonial agents had the additional responsibility of managing the relationships between frontier tribal groups, pastoral in nature, and settled agrarian societies. What resulted was a particular form of indirect rule, where the quotidian institutions of colonial governance, in the form of laws and administrative procedures, were held in abeyance.

In these regions, governance was bifurcated between district administration in the NWFP and Assam proper, and a series of political agencies further west and east between internal administrative boundaries – the Inner Line in the Northeast, the administrative border through Pashtun territory separating lowland districts and highland agencies in the Northwest. International boundaries were (weakly) specified only in the twentieth century: the disputed Durand Line between northwestern India and Afghanistan to the west and the disputed (and secret) MacMahon Line between northeastern India and Tibet to the east.

Beyond these administrative boundaries, political agencies were established, in which agents, operating largely beyond regular administrative hierarchies, would operate as part-soldiers, part-diplomats, and part-spies to establish and maintain relations with tribal leadership and interdict foreign influence. Political agents had two sets of tools to accomplish their objectives: carrots, in the form of "allowances" or bribes to tribal leaders, or sticks in the form of coercion. The quotidian coercive apparatus took the form of frontier constabularies and militias, recruited from tribal populations or adjacent lowland groups, but under the command of British soldiers or policemen. Moreover, there was also implicitly the threat of more severe military intervention, in the form of "punitive expeditions" of regular military forces from permanent encampments in centers of colonial authority, such as Wana and Miranshah in the northwest and Sadiya in the northeast.

There was much debate throughout the late nineteenth and twentieth century about the nature of frontier governance, particularly between greater intervention and greater restraint. In relation to the northwestern frontier, White associates the difference between the Forward Policy and the "Close Border" policy to differences in the philosophies of colonial rule, in effect between liberal interventionism and conservative protection of tradition.[61] Essentially, the dual mandates and exigencies of agents on the frontier led to an intermediate ground that established and institutionalized an exceptional form of "indirect" governance, in which the colonial state explicitly shared coercive authority with tribal groups, rather than either monopolizing it or subcontracting it.[62] This was the outcome of a mandate for flexible security, based on fears of external intervention, coupled with frugality in regions where costs were high and benefits, in terms of taxation or protection, were not forthcoming.

3.6 CONCLUSION

The complex patchwork of governance institutions across the political geography of the Indian subcontinent during the period of colonial rule had specific roots in the politics surrounding the nature of colonial conquest and initial, uneven state-building efforts in India, from the late eighteenth to the mid-nineteenth centuries. Colonial administrators and their interlocutors faced incentives, interests, threats, and constraints that varied from one place to another. The specific politics behind conquest, annexation, the affirmation of princely rule, or the fashioning of exceptional institutions of governance, as well as even more specific practices of colonial administration, are well-understood by historians. In this chapter, I have sought to integrate their insights through a narrative of the ways in which the colonial administration sought to maximize greed and manage fear in different places in various ways, while operating within a cost-benefit framework driven by the frugality of the colonial enterprise.

[61] White 2008.   [62] Naseemullah 2014.

4

The Patchwork Nature of Colonial Governance

The politics of colonial India need to be examined on its own terms in order to understand the legacies of colonial rule. These politics were territorially differentiated in nature because of the nature of colonial conquest, as we saw in Chapter 3, constituting a patchwork of different forms of authority. Across the subcontinent, different governance institutions managed relationships between colonial authorities and indigenous populations. As a result, the political experiences of both rulers and subjects across India varied significantly from one place to another. But what did these various institutions actually look like, and how did they manifest in the ways that colonial India was governed?

This chapter demonstrates the ways in which different territorial governance arrangements formed in the late eighteenth and early nineteenth centuries persisted and shaped colonial rule after 1858. For all the greater institutionalization of colonial rule in the late nineteenth century, variations in governance arrangements continued to exert their influence, not just in the durability of princely states and political agencies but also in the distinctions in the ways that power was exercised within districts under the juridical authority of the colonial Indian Government. Indeed, one might even go so far as to consider the "state" in colonial India as Potemkin, gauzing over a geographically diverse pattern of governance institutions that were quite different in character from one another.

In order to provide some evidence for the presence and persistence of governance variation, I present data on differences in key political and social processes and outcomes across districts, agencies, and princely states during what is often considered the apotheosis of colonial rule of India, in the decade before World War I. These include the extent of quotidian coercive capacity, the nature and extent of agricultural surplus extraction, the deployment of military resources, and the nature of integration into the formal economy and international markets. In so doing, the chapter aims to provide some initial insights into the production of the legacies of colonial rule in the nature and purpose of local state institutions, which then persisted after the end of colonialism.

Finally, this chapter foregrounds some of the changes in the politics of the Indian subcontinent in the final decades of colonial rule, including the rise of the nationalist movement and the responses of colonial authorities to the Great Depression and wartime mobilization. The violent ruptures of partition and the independence of Pakistan and India have their roots during this period of significant flux, but the varieties of governance arrangements that persisted even throughout this period of transformation critically fashioned the nature of statehood and its consequences, as I will discuss further in Chapter 5.

4.1 COLONIAL RULE AT THE APEX OF EMPIRE, 1858–1918

The six decades between the 1858 Rebellion and the end of World War I represented the height of the British Empire globally, as well as that of colonial rule in the subcontinent. The full development of colonialism as a self-understood (though of course, odious) system of governance was deeply situated within Victorian and Edwardian self-satisfaction of British hegemony. It is the stability of this period, along with the application of the technological innovations like the railways to colonial rule in the later nineteenth century, which has led some to fashion positive assessments of the imperial enterprise.[1] Yet the self-satisfaction and stability of colonialism in the late nineteenth and early twentieth centuries masked the patchwork nature of governance that was formed during India's initial conquests and persisted until independence.

4.1.1 The 1858 Rebellion and the Governance Transformations?

The Rebellion of 1857–1858 constituted an existential crisis and a critical juncture for British rule in India. In the spring of 1857, more than 100,000 *sepoys* or native soldiers of the Bengal Army rebelled against their officers, capturing Delhi and much of the United Provinces and reinstating the aging Mughal emperor as paramount ruler. The revolt was joined by peasant rebels as well as disaffected aristocrats and landowners in Awadh, though it was largely confined to north-central India, from modern-day Haryana to Bihar.[2] Indigenous elites and populations in Bombay and Madras Presidencies, the powerful princely states in the south, and the recently conquered province of Punjab supported the Company. The roots of the rebellion itself were complicated, ranging from the class dynamics and patterns of peasant unrest to the grievances of the soldiers of the Bengal Army and their wider

---

[1] See especially Ferguson 2012.   [2] Mukherjee 2002.

communities in northern India.³ It was ruthlessly crushed by military expeditions, including forces from Punjab, in the autumn of 1858, leading to the deaths of more than 150,000 people, most of them civilians, in campaigns of vengeance by British and allied forces.

Following the brutal suppression of the Rebellion, the British transformed the structures of colonial rule. The East India Company was dissolved as a governance organization and the Government of India Act 1858 transferred its sovereign powers to the British Crown. Queen Victoria was crowned Empress of India, replacing the ailing Mughal Emperor, the restoration of whom had served as a key symbol for the rebels. The new Indian government was distinct from but formally responsible to the India Office in Whitehall, even though many of the structures of the subordinate bureaucracy under the East India Company largely persisted. The Indian military was also reorganized. The Bengal Army was greatly reduced in size and the three Presidency armies were integrated into one force. The focus of recruitment and deployment shifted to the northwest, establishing a garrison state capable of interdicting Russian threats from Afghanistan and Central Asia, on which more will be discussed later. The decade following the 1858 Rebellion thus constituted an important critical juncture, during which British colonial authorities self-consciously established and operated modern state structures.⁴

The new British *raj* in India also sought to reverse the liberalizing, universalist, and expansionist impulses of the early nineteenth century, particularly under Governors-General Bentinck, Hardinge, and Dalhousie. The actual import of these impulses can certainly be overstated. There were always contrary traditions among colonial officials; Henry and John Lawrence in Punjab were prime examples. Moreover, actual dynamics on the ground rather than abstract philosophies in Calcutta drove the actual governance practices of officials.

However, Victoria's 1858 Proclamation did formally reject earlier policies of liberal universalism as well as specific objectionable practices like Christian proselytization.⁵ This resistance to universalism had firm intellectual roots. Henry Maine, Law Member of the Governor-General's Council and a key theorist of colonial rule, characterized India as a traditional society subject to ageless customs, rather than formal laws and rationality. For him and his colleagues, the objective of colonialism was to protect this society from the disruptions of modernity by empowering traditional actors like landlords, chieftains, and religious authorities, in effect implementing and sustaining indirect rule by creating and sustaining "native" authority.⁶ Thus, rather than bringing civilization by transforming Indians into educated, liberal subjects, the colonial government would seek only to preserve authority, adjudicate disputes, and keep the peace among India's communities, principalities, and religious

---

³ Stokes 1978; Habib 1998.   ⁴ Kohli 2004, 228–240.   ⁵ Mehta 1991; Sartori 2014.
⁶ Mantena 2010; Mamdani 2012.

traditions in the subcontinent, ruling through them to protect the sanctity of the empire, as well as their own venal objectives.

4.1.2 Governance Practices and Differentiation

Regardless of the reorientation of the stated rationale of colonial rule, actual governance practices continued to vary significantly across the subcontinent. Although key mandates of greed, fear, and frugality changed in character, they did not diminish as standing principles of colonial governance at the local level. In the major cities that represented one extreme of state presence, liberal universalism, and associated institutions from high courts to municipal corporations, continued to operate based on the mutual engagement between the government and an active, if not inclusive, civil society engaged in commerce and finance. At the frontier, the informal practices of political agents emphasized light footprints for fear of incurring costly and ongoing military intervention. A generation of political officers with frontier experience consolidated such practices, backed up by a special, delimiting legal and administrative apparatus.[7]

In the agrarian hinterland, the differences in land tenure arrangements among districts empowered different constellations of elites and established durable, if flexible, relationships with agents of the state. The zamindari system continued to privilege the interaction between colonial officials and proprietary elites, who dominated district boards and maintained order in the countryside. The ryotwari system had incorporated a larger number of individuals from elite communities directly into state employment, and the administrative machinery heightened demands on poorer ryots and landless laborers.[8] These different mutual expectations between the state and social elites did not exactly guarantee stability, but they did continue to structure patterns of governance.

Princely states too were set on different trajectories because of the period of greater intervention in the early nineteenth century. Some rulers turned toward mimetic modernization to maintain internal legitimacy, preventing intervention by British Residents, even as threats to outright annexation had receded.[9] For others, however, imperial recognition of the traditional foundations of their rule froze distant state–society relationships and weak state apparatuses in place. Princely states in Rajputana and chiefships in eastern India continued to empower intermediaries rather than investing in internal state apparatuses.[10]

There were certainly some signs of greater institutionalization after 1858. The Indian government started establishing legislative councils in 1860 that included Indians, with councils and assemblies increasing in participation and

---

[7] White 2008; Naseemullah 2014.   [8] Viswanath 2014.   [9] Desai 2005.
[10] Rudolph 1963; Cannadine 2001.

prominence in the following decades. In addition, the impact of technological innovations on government were significant; the railroad, the telegraph, and the steamship brought Britain much closer to India, and parts of India closer to each other, allowing with more immediate coordination within administrative structures. Yet the patchwork of governance institutions formed by the conquest of India persisted and the resulting variation state-society relations did not disappear. They continued along separate trajectories, and in fact were even more rigidly defined and developed without a guiding narrative of convergence driven by liberal universalism.

These distinctions continued until the eve of Partition, although the last three decades of British rule saw the colonial state responding to dramatic shocks and challenges to its authority that will be discussed later. The Victorian and Edwardian eras, roughly from the 1857 Rebellion until World War I, represented colonial India at its most constant, and thus the turn of the century represents a valuable perspective into the operations of the various governance institutions over Indian territory.

4.2 THE PRACTICES OF PATCHWORK GOVERNANCE

In this section, I explore the impacts of these institutions in relation to how governance was actually practiced, and to what effects. In what follows, I explore the impact of governance categories on key political and social indicators in the first decade of the twentieth century, in the districts, princely states, and political agencies in what is now India, Pakistan, and Bangladesh. The data come from either the Imperial Gazetteer or from provincial or princely state administration reports, unless otherwise indicated, and represent a snapshot of governance in the first decade of the twentieth century.[11]

4.2.1 Revenue Extraction

The most basic form of the extraction of resources was in the form of taxation, principally of agricultural surplus in the form of land revenue but also on other forms of wealth and economic activity. There was not necessarily any straightforward correspondence between the nature and extent of colonial governance and the gains to be made from extraction. Rather, it is important to see the institutional forms of taxation as representing the product of historical processes that can have lasting consequences in colonial governance, state capacity, and state–society relations. Taxation is thus an

---

[11] Provincial and princely state administration reports can be found in volumes V/10 and V/22 of the India Office Records (IOR), in the Asia and Africa Collection of the British Library, as well as National Archives in Delhi, Dhaka, and Islamabad. A note of caution must be struck on exceptional governance; precisely because it was set apart from quotidian governance arrangements, agents produced regular political reports rather than yearly administrative ones.

important indicator of the power of the state and the nature of state–society relations at the local level.

The Imperial Gazetteer has data on land revenue and total revenue for districts and princely states, which I report here on a per capita basis (Figure 4.1).

The different systems of land tenure embedded in governance arrangements yield different levels of revenue: modernizing and intermediate cases yield more by way of agricultural surplus extraction than conservative cases, because of both the limited investment in state extractive apparatus and the compact inherent in the Permanent Settlement that fixed revenue demands. This is despite the greater agricultural productivity of regions, like Bengal and Bihar, governed under conservative arrangements.[12] Chieftaincy governance institutions mobilize significant land revenue despite the limited nature of the state. This may be due to the fact that proprietary landlords in princely states were often of the same clan or community as the ruling family, thus part of the governing apparatus, and as a result, have less compunction in maximizing extraction.

Of course, the colonial state had other sources of taxation apart from land revenue. The government received income from excise on liquor and opium,

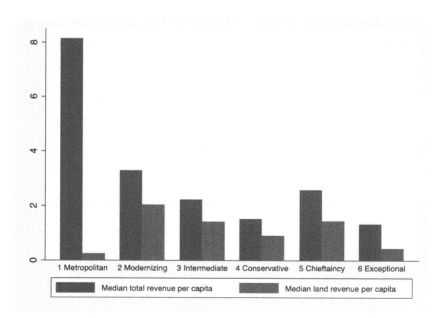

FIGURE 4.1 Land revenue and total revenue per capita

[12] Banerjee and Iyer 2005.

from instruments of registration, from forest products, and increasingly from income and corporate taxes. In terms of total revenue, it is not at all surprising that metropolitan districts have twice as much revenue as the next highest category, despite negligible land revenue; the wealth and the density of economic transactions of urban areas, not to mention the customs duties gathered at ports, represented a much wider and deeper base from which revenues could be generated.

4.2.2 Legal and Economic Institutions

The expansion of judicial institutions was significant, though uneven. Statutes, courts, and the common law became primary arenas for managing the institutions of a growing and deepening colonial economy; they constituted the primary means of monopolizing adjudication of disputes over property and the protection of transactions. The expansion of legal institutions and the incorporation of economic transactions into structured legal frameworks signaled Tilly's "protection" and Olson's "stationary bandits," as introduced in the first chapter: the enabling of economic activity benefitted colonial power, by sustaining trade balances, providing a market for industrialized goods, and generating customs revenue for the metropole.[13] Theories that associate these rational-legal institutions and economic growth hold that the quantum and density of transactions necessary for growth must be enabled by institutions with the power and authority to protect property rights, enforce contracts and restrain the arbitrary exercise of coercive power.[14] This required greater institutional investments. Historians have highlighted the many different ways in which the colonial state shaped the ways that Indian communities engaged with the economy.[15]

Further, by the turn of the twentieth century, indigenous capitalism emerged and consolidated, albeit at the margins of European commercial activity, concentrated in managing agencies exporting commodities like tea and indigo.[16] Despite marginal positions and active discrimination, however, indigenous banking and trading communities were able to deploy their capital for mercantile and eventually industrial investments.[17] These communities would become important in the rise of nationalist mobilization.

Law and the judiciary played a paramount role with regard to the enabling of transactions, the defense of property rights and the enforcement of contracts inherent in this deepening of a colonial economy in which both Europeans and Indians participated. Yet the presence and strength of these institutions were geographically uneven, concentrated in metropolitan cities and dissipating in the deeper hinterland.

---

[13] Tilly 1985; Olson 1993. [14] North 1990. [15] Bayly 1983; Birla 2009. [16] Bagchi 2002.
[17] Chandavarkar 1993; Leadbeater 1993.

The effectiveness of these institutions is certainly endogenous to economic activity. The nature of colonial conquest in the late eighteenth and early nineteenth centuries prefigured certain sites in which the density of transactions, among Indians and Europeans alike, necessitated strong formal institutions that managed relationships among individual actors rather than groups. In many other places, colonial governance involved the maintenance of social order and the de facto subcontracting of coercive authority to local elites to manage the population. As a result, we would expect geographic variation in both the level of economic activity and the capaciousness of institutions designed to enable and discipline this activity, based on the nature and purposes of the different governance arrangements.

Assessing the strength and capaciousness of legal and judicial institutions is difficult, however, because data in the colonial archives on both judicial activity, such as the number of civil suits, and capacity, such as the number of judicial officers, are not comprehensive across the various provinces and are especially absent in the administrative reports of many princely states. Moreover, other important institutional features like the drawing of contracts took place outside court. Such activities do not appear in records of the civil judiciary until they are contested and need to be adjudicated. To deal with this patchiness, I present data on an indirect but powerful measure: that of the incidence of stamp tax.

The Indian Stamp Act of 1899 required the payment of duty for the legal recognition of documents. There were two kinds of stamps: judicial and nonjudicial. Judicial stamps were required for documents involving any judicial procedure, as civil court fees. The payment of stamp duty was (and continues to be, to the present day) necessary for the official recognition of documents to be used in legal proceedings, from affidavits to initial complaints. Nonjudicial stamps were (and continue to be, to the present day) necessary for registering documents with legal standing outside the context of courts: wills, contracts, the transfer of property, mortgages, and during the colonial period, *hundis* and bills of foreign exchange.

As a result, judicial and nonjudicial stamp tax represent indicators for the density of formal economic transactions and judicial proceedings channeled through the formal-legal institutions of the colonial state. These institutions have the advantage of being applied to all princely states (with the exception of Kashmir) as well as British-administered provinces. The meticulous records of the collections of tax, both by provincial officials and by princely governments, provides a more comprehensive picture than the somewhat more partial records of judicial administration.

Stamp tax administration reports from Indian provinces and state administration reports provide district-/princely state-level of the incidence of judicial and nonjudicial stamp tax per capita (Figure 4.2).

It is not at all surprising that the incidence of stamp tax is qualitatively different in cases of metropolitan governance, the key metropoles with active

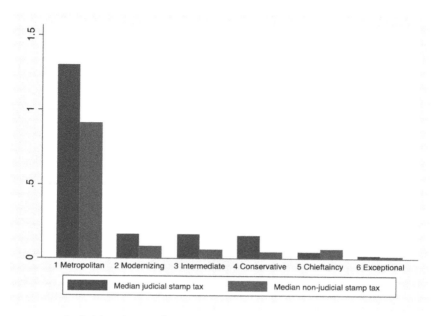

FIGURE 4.2 Judicial and nonjudicial stamp tax per capita

civil societies, complex economies, and deep integration into international markets. The fact that modernizing, intermediate, and conservative categories have essentially the same incidence of judicial stamp tax, though slightly decreasing incidences of nonjudicial tax, is interesting. Magistrates' and superior courts were most present and effective in British districts or the more institutionally developed princely states, and the need for adjudication among zamindars could be every bit as onerous, even though the specific issues would have varied. The significantly lower incidents of judicial stamp tax for chieftaincy and exceptional governance is not surprising; these cases are explicitly and deliberately less integrated into the formal-legal institutions of the Indian economy.

A second window into the operation of formal-legal institutions is that of income tax, which was introduced in 1869. There is a longstanding argument in the political economy of development that the ability to tax the income of specific individuals, rather than land, requires a significant amount of capacity, because of the density of information necessary for assessment and the infrastructure for collection. Yet at the turn of the twentieth century, only a tiny fraction of the population paid income tax. These included salaried government employees, professionals, wealthy traders, and absentee landlords whose regularized contacts with the colonial state afforded them particular status as notable subjects.

Although the revenue garnered from income tax paled in comparison to excise, customs and indeed land revenue, income tax assessment provides a useful indirect indicator of the proportion of the population that is recognized by the colonial state as individuals endowed with specific characteristics, rather than as undifferentiated parts of indigenous communities. This suggests civil society rather than political society in Chatterjee's terminology, or "citizen" rather than "subject" in Mamdani's.[18] We would expect that the number of people to be so identified is very small, but geographically uneven, depending on the requirements of the colonial state to identify and tax individuals across categories of governance.

Figure 4.3 reports total income tax assessments and the number of government servants paying income tax, as a proportion of the population, including and excluding metropolitan governance categories.

Even though the proportion of the population assessed for income tax is tiny – less than two per hundred people in the metropoles, less than one per thousand elsewhere – there is significant variation, signifying differences by which governance institutions engage with individual agents or manage groups through social elites. The relatively higher number of bureaucratic officials in chieftaincy and exceptional categories may be due to uncertain data, but could also result from relatively low populations and the greater requirements among princely states to be seen to govern their territories. Yet the very low proportion of "gazetted" government servants to the population reflects a mandate to frugality, in terms of restraining the numbers of officers who must be paid, housed, and protected.

The tiny number of employees officially recognized by the state suggests, rather, that a variety of actors operated to create and maintain social order in the fuzzy boundaries between the state and society, including proprietary landlords and village leaders, as well as local councils, caste panchayats, and a variety of brokers and intermediaries with important – but difficult to quantify – institutional relationships to the state. As independence neared, many of these were more officially incorporated in an expanding state apparatus, bringing dense social relationships into the operations of the state.[19] As a result, any measurable variable of state capacity, such as the number of government servants, may be less important than categorical distinctions among different forms of state–society relationships that persisted and fashioned durable legacies.

4.2.3   Police and Political Order

Insecurity also drove the nature of colonial governance, and it was only heightened after the 1857 Rebellion.[20] This pervasive existential anxiety took two broad forms. The first was a set of external threats, chiefly the Russian Empire but also the Qing Dynasty and the German Empire around World War

---

[18] Chatterjee 1993; Mamdani 1996.   [19] Gould 2010.
[20] For an excellent overview, see Condos 2017.

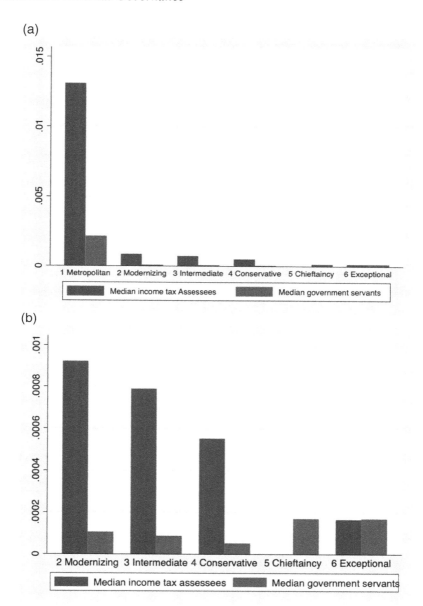

FIGURE 4.3 Proportion of the population assessed for income tax

I and the Soviet Union and the Axis powers in the 1930s and 1940s, all of which challenged British India through subversion along its fuzzy and ill-integrated frontiers. Yet frugality as a standing order of empire meant that these frontiers would never be fully integrated into India proper, yielding governance exceptionalism in the context of "the Great Game."

A potentially far greater, though more inchoate, sense of insecurity arose from within Indian society. Movements of religious reform of the late nineteenth century took on a more explicitly political and contentious character. The turn of the century heralded the first stirrings of assertive nationalism and thus the specter of the violent overthrow of British rule from within, echoing the Rebellion of 1857. The Indian National Congress, a liberal, elite body of both Indians and Europeans founded in 1885 to advocate for greater representation of "natives" in the colonial government had, by the early twentieth century, started calling for total freedom (*"purna swaraj"*) from British rule. Lord Curzon's 1905 partition of the province of Bengal led to mass civil unrest; the policy was reversed just six years later. British attempts to allow select Indians greater participation in colonial governance – the Indian Councils Act of 1909, known as the Morley-Minto Reforms – sought to undercut nationalist mobilization and draw on support from moderate elites against radical nationalists, while establishing the policy of separate electorates for Muslims and other corporate groups to forestall a united Indian opposition.[21] Yet, despite British efforts of accommodation and divide and rule, the palpable anxiety of political and social disorder persisted and increased after World War I.

There were various understandings of and responses to the nature of domestic disorder. Valentine Chirol, a liberal imperialist commentator, provided a wide-ranging account of the sources of contemporary Indian unrest in the early twentieth century – from Swami Dayanand Saraswati's Arya Samaj to the radical politics of Ranade and Tilak to the Swadeshi movement of Congress – as an elite Hindu revolt amid ancient sectional rivalries in the context of modernization.[22] The report of the 1917 Rowlatt Committee on sedition associated the rise of the increasingly radical nationalist movement and rising labor militancy with efforts of Bolshevik and German agents to destabilize British rule in India. The subsequent Rowlatt Act, a peacetime extension of the Defence of India Act 1915, authorized widespread censorship, preventive detention, and warrantless arrest of those suspected of conspiracy, treason, and sedition; these are exceptions to due process that continue in different forms in South Asian states today.

To manage threats of political disorder, the British developed a wide-ranging internal security apparatus. This followed an all-India set of legislative instruments but was operated by differentiated colonial governance institutions, from the local *chaukidars* charged with village watch and ward

[21] Territorial representation in these new expanded legislative bodies, particularly at the provincial level, further instantiated distinctions between governance institutions, as those elite Indians who had been familiar with particular forms of state–society relationships would legislate on the basis of furthering their interests.

[22] Chirol 1910.

to the district police to the Special Branch and the Intelligence Bureau to courts and prisons, and as importantly, a dense network of informers and elite allies that worked with colonial officials. The colonial state deployed variegated "coercive networks," that included colonial officials, the army, and different forms of intermediaries, both in directly ruled provinces and princely states such as Hyderabad.[23] The composition of these networks would vary, however, by the nature of coercive and disciplinary capacity arrayed among state and non-state actors, including landlords and tribal chieftains. As a result, the different forms of colonial governance managed internal security – and especially the fear of internal revolt – in different ways.

We can see this variation in looking at the ways that the most basic version of coercive capacity – the police – is deployed across the governance units of colonial India. Figure 4.4 represents median police per capita and police per square mile, by governance categories.

The variation exhibited here represents differences not in the level of internal security but rather how internal security was practiced, and by whom. Focusing on police per capita and excepting the expected higher incidence in metropolises, we see a significant difference between modernizing and intermediate cases and conservative ones, suggesting that in conservative districts, internal security was managed by intermediates. The higher incidence of police per capita in chieftaincy and exceptional cases represents an anomaly, but this is because "police" in certain princely states included palace guards and even the state militia responsible for internal security rather than a distinct police force. Similarly, in exceptional cases in the northwestern and northeastern frontiers, "police" could include special paramilitaries and constabularies, such as the Tochi Scouts, the Khyber Rifles and the Assam Rifles, and tribal levies; these cases also have very low populations and large territories. Many of these forces, in frontier and hinterland political agencies, represent the roots of many central paramilitary forces today, including those that operate in Indian-administered Kashmir and the erstwhile Federally Administered Tribal Areas and Balochistan in Pakistan.

4.2.4   Military Organization and Capacity

Military forces in India represented a key instrument against threats to British India and the wider British Empire from external forces as well as the last resort in cases of internal disorder. From 1857, they consisted of the Indian Army and units of the British Army in regular rotation, and constituted one of the largest (highly trained, volunteer) armies outside Europe, representing a territorial complement to the dominance of the Royal Navy in maintaining British global hegemony throughout this period.[24] Indian army units were active in most of the conflicts of the height of the British Empire, from Egypt in the 1880s

---

[23] Sherman 2010.   [24] Darwin 2009.

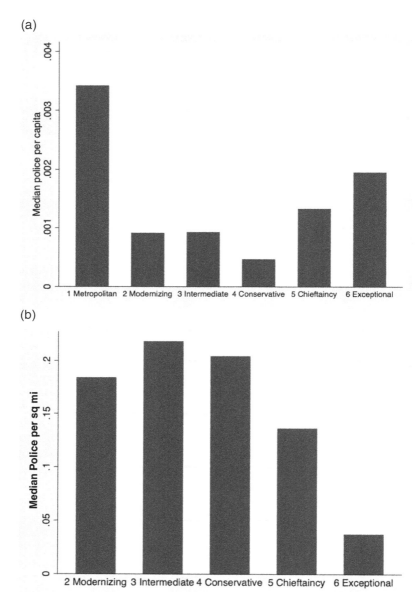

FIGURE 4.4 Police deployment per capita and per square mile

to the Boxer Rebellion and the Boer War in the early 1900s. The Indian Army supplied over a million soldiers for overseas deployment in World War I, particularly in the Mesopotamian campaign against Ottoman forces but also on the Western Front, and two and a half million in World War II, mostly on the Burma front against the Japanese but also in North Africa and other theaters.[25] Within the subcontinent, the Indian Army interdicted the most serious internal rebellions and proximate conflicts, including the Second and Third Anglo-Afghan Wars, the long counterinsurgency campaign against Mirzali Khan, "the Faqir of Ipi," and conducted numerous punitive expeditions in the northwestern and northeastern frontiers.

However, the 1857 Rebellion proved that such a large and concentrated army on Indian territory could be a source of insecurity as well as an important coercive asset. The discipline and deadly expertise of Indian army troops could, if they mutinied, bloodily displace British rule across the Indian subcontinent. Yet when not deployed on overseas campaigns, there was nowhere for the Army to be stationed but in India. The solution to managing this potential threat while maintaining it as an important asset is to set the military apart from society, in base-enclaves known as cantonments. Units of the British Army deployed to India, as well as the Indian army itself, would regularly rotate among these enclaves. This rotation could maintain unit cohesion and corporate identity, often among soldiers recruited from the same communities, without maintaining any close or permanent ties between the army and the populations surrounding them. The segregation between military and society was an institutional legacy of the innate hybridism of the earlier East India Company, between a corporation and a military-expansionist enterprise. Segregation between civil society and "khaki society" would have profound consequences during and after Partition and are still felt today, particularly in Pakistan's fraught civil–military relations.[26]

There was also significant geographical variation in military recruitment among communities and their deployment, with both concentrated toward the northwest. The spatial dynamics of recruitment arose from the legacies of the 1857 Rebellion, where rebelling soldiers were concentrated among Muslim and Rajput Hindu communities in the United Provinces, whereas Sikh and Muslim forces from Punjab did not revolt and they, along with soldiers deputed from princely states, assisted the British in quelling the rebellion. These distinctions were codified, through Victorian-era race theory, into the classification of so-called "martial races."[27] The British recruited heavily from particular communities in these areas of the country. Sikhs, Punjabi Muslims, Pashtuns, Rajputs from western princely states and Jats from India's northwest, as well as Gurkhas from Nepal, constituted the bulk of the army by the early twentieth century. Others, such as Tamils, Bengalis, and Gujaratis, were massively underrepresented.

Data on the composition of the Indian army from Army Lists bears this out.[28] The Indian Army after 1858, integrating the erstwhile Bengal, Madras, and Bombay Armies, was made up of regiments, organized for symbolic and

---

[25] Karnad 2015; Raghavan 2017.   [26] Peers 2007.   [27] Barua 1995.
[28] I use the January 1911 Army List, Asia and Africa Collection, British Library.

administrative purposes but also as tactical units as components of brigades. Infantry regiments were made up of eight companies of between 100 and 120 soldiers each. Companies were ethnically homogenous and ethnically defined, while regiments could either be homogenous or heterogenous. For instance, the 6th Jat Light Infantry, raised at Fatehgarh in 1803, was made up of eight companies of Jats, while the 61st Pioneers, originally raised at Fort St. George in Madras in 1758, comprised four companies of Tamils, two companies of "Madrasi Muslims," and two companies of "Christians and Pariahs."[29] For this reason, examining the ethnic composition of the army by infantry company provides a sense of where military recruitment was concentrated. Out of 912 companies, 518 companies or 56.7 percent of the infantry were comprised of members from five ethnoreligious communities, all concentrated in the northwest: Sikhs and Muslims from Punjab, Pashtuns from the North West Frontier Province, Dogras from the State of Jammu and Kashmir, and Jats from the Doab region in the western United Provinces. In addition to the recruitment of some regiments directly recruited in Rajputana – 78 companies or 8.5 percent of the total from this sparsely populated region – the extant state armies from the Rajput kingdoms such as Jaipur, Jodhpur, and Bharatpur represented supplemental armed forces that were often deployed with the Indian Army.

A more fine-grained look at soldiers' geographic origins across the districts and princely states of British India is to look at the fatalities of Indians serving in World War I, based on a dataset kept by the Commonwealth War Graves Commission.[30] Of the more than 70,000 records of those serving with the Indian Army who died in service, around 40,000 have identifiable family homes; an additional 10,000 were Gurkha soldiers from Nepal. Many of those who died in the war were not soldiers, but rather served in a variety of auxiliary positions, from locomotive engineers to laborers to mule-drivers; I treat those with military ranks or designations as distinct. Figure 4.5 reports total deaths per capita and deaths of soldiers per capita, by the different governance categories.

The concentration of fatalities among those from intermediate districts is striking; it is higher than all other categories combined. Districts under intermediate governance are concentrated in colonial India's northwest: the ten districts or princely states with the highest concentrations of fatalities among soldiers serving in World War I – Kohat, Rawalpindi, Gujrat, Jhelum, Rohtak, Kangra, Ludhiana, Attock, Hoshiarpur, and Jind State – are all in either Punjab or in the North West Frontier. Intermediate governance institutions have higher concentrations of social power, based on clans, than ryotwari systems, but where power is nonetheless more dispersed than in places

---

[29] For an excellent account of the nature and consequences of the ethnic composition of the Indian Army, see Wilkinson 2015.

[30] Data available at www.cwgc.org/find/find-war-dead. See Jha and Wilkinson 2012 for an excellent application of this dataset to explaining the dispersion of partition violence.

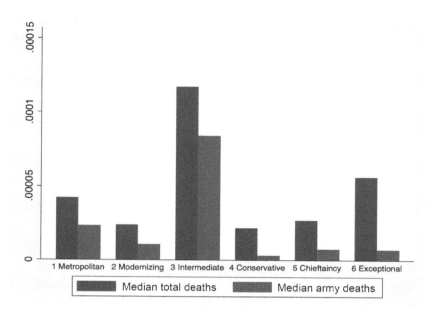

FIGURE 4.5 Casualties and deaths of soldiers per capita in World War I

with the domination of proprietary landlords, became increasingly endogenous to military societies in the northwest. The elective affinity between populations in those areas and military employment would have serious political consequences, which I will briefly discuss later and detail in subsequent chapters.

The military's patterns of regular deployment also concentrated forces in India's northwest. As a result of Russian expansionism and the "the Great Game," the strategic orientation of coercive power was focused toward Afghanistan. In 1903, Kitchener implemented a reorganization and redeployment of the military that focused on the North West Frontier. Kitchener's plan was to create a series of cantonments and secondary bases on two east–west axes to the north and the south – in effect, two spears, the heads of which would lie in the northwest and the points of which would face the tribal frontiers along the Durand Line. What resulted in 1905 were three regional commands. Northern Command – focusing on the northwest frontier – had divisions at Peshawar, Rawalpindi, and Lahore and Kohat, Bannu, and Derajat Brigades. Western Command – focusing on Balochistan and the Arabian Peninsula – had divisions at Quetta, Poona, and Mhow in Indore state, and the Aden Brigade. The Eastern Command – retained largely for internal security – maintained divisions at Meerut and Lucknow. When not deployed overseas, the balance of responsibilities of the Indian Army between frontier defence and internal security decidedly shifted in favor of the former.

Division and brigade deployments across the various cantonments and operating bases were static while regiments were dynamic, regularly rotating among these postings. As a result, we have a fairly accurate picture of how the Indian army was systematically deployed across the various districts, provinces, and princely states. Figure 4.6 reports the total proportion of the Indian Army in addition to supporting state forces stationed across the different governance categories, based on data from the Imperial Gazetteer and Army Lists.

The proportion of the military in territories of intermediate governance parallels the concentration of recruitment. The reasons are more straightforwardly geographical: the mass of forces were concentrated at the base of the spearhead rather than its point, in the garrison towns of Peshawar and Rawalpindi as well as other deployments throughout Punjab, NWFP, and the western United Provinces.

The comparatively low proportion of the military stationed in areas of exceptional governance is deliberate; apart from two permanent encampments at Wana and Miranshah in Waziristan, colonial authorities sought to deploy military force in the northwestern frontier only as a last resort, instead utilizing the diplomatic and espionage capacities of political agencies, the coercive capacity of constabularies and relations with tribal elders to maintain peace. The relatively high proportion of the military in areas under chieftaincy governance reflects the importance of maintaining

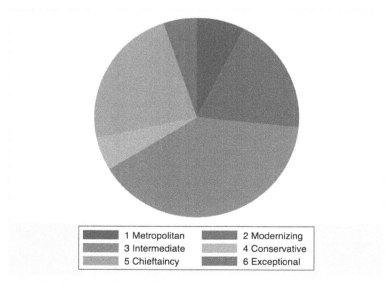

1 Metropolitan	2 Modernizing
3 Intermediate	4 Conservative
5 Chieftaincy	6 Exceptional

FIGURE 4.6 Deployment of the Indian Army in 1911

princely state armies both as a tool for internal security and martial honor. It also reflects a compact embedded in the subsidiary system that princely states would quarter and provision units of the Indian army in permanent cantonments; three of the largest bases for the Indian Army, then as now, were Mhow, Secunderabad, and Bangalore, in the states of Indore, Hyderabad, and Mysore, respectively.

Patterns of recruitment and deployment had profound implications on Indian politics both during and after colonial rule. This was less because of what the army actually did in India. Beyond the horrific (but exceptional) use of force by soldiers in instances like the Jallianwala Bagh massacre, the application of force to exert control in the hinterland was conducted by police, paramilitaries, the intelligence apparatus, as well as the coercion of social elites. Rather, the deliberate separation of the military from society, along with other ways that the military apparatus penetrated society in specific regions in specific ways, created dynamics that have had long-term consequences in both India and Pakistan, if not also in Bangladesh.

In particular, the elective affinities with and concentrations of military recruitment and deployment in territories under intermediate governance, particularly in Punjab, had enormous consequences. Punjab constituted a "garrison state," in which the importance of the army was undergirded by a number of institutions: legislation against land alienation, investments in canal irrigation that provided agricultural grants to veteran soldiers, and the emergence of structures of administration and intercommunal agrarian representation.[31] One might think of Punjab as a subnational, colonial example of what Slater has termed a "protection pact," in which state and society develop cooperative political structures in defense of their interests against external and internal enemies.[32] The particular nature of governance in Punjab would have enormous implications in terms of the influence of the military in the Muslim-majority areas of northwest India that would become (West) Pakistan after Partition.

4.3 CHANGES AND DISRUPTIONS IN COLONIAL GOVERNANCE: 1918–1947

From the point of view of the colonial state, the relatively placid and self-satisfied years of British rule in India, within the broader hegemony of the British Empire, came crashing to an end with World War I and the subsequent political revolutions and social disruptions. When the guns of August finally fell silent, the world had changed. The multinational empires in Europe collapsed and new national states arose, establishing powerful precedents for the right to self-determination exemplified by Wilson's

---

[31] Yong 2005. [32] Slater 2010.

Fourteen Points. The success of the Bolshevik revolution yielded a novel and puissant form of state and political organization that represented a mortal threat to the interests of western capitalist states and their overseas empires. Colonial India was far from immune from these influences.

4.3.1 Pressures on the Colonial State

British rule in India faced two particular challenges in the interwar years. First, the collapse of the nineteenth-century world order and the emergence of radical new alternatives like communism, together with the participation of subject peoples in the European war, placed significant normative pressures on colonial powers to address new nationalist demands for increased self-governance. The Indian National Congress (INC, or Congress) transformed from an elite club of liberal professionals into a mass membership organization, social movement, and political party in the 1920s. Under the leadership of Gandhi, it launched a series of civil disobedience campaigns that fundamentally challenged the basis for British colonial rule. The guiding philosophy of Congress challenged the colonial precept that India was not one nation but many communities in perpetual conflict with one another. As such, it represented a political organization that self-consciously sought to flatten out the diversities of governance by rejecting British governance practices, while crafting a cohesive Indian nationhood deserving of state power.

Second, the global economic crisis of the 1930s and then wartime mobilizations of the 1940s transformed the colonial economy, society, and the state apparatus. Together, these shocks forced colonial officials to formulate new forms of intervention that addressed economic disruptions and later, enabled wartime production targets. The Great Depression led to the collapse of agricultural prices that precluded balanced-budget and free trade policies, leading to the introduction of tariffs. Such revenue requirements impeded India's capacity to serve as a market for British-manufactured goods.[33] In order to address economic crises, the nature of economic governance swung radically from the free market orthodoxy of the nineteenth century to early attempts at activist economic policy. The ultimate failure of reformers within the British Indian government to resolve economic challenges, in the face of opposition by traditional colonial authorities, provided additional strength to nationalist assertions for self-rule.

Wartime mobilization also transformed India's economy and polity. When Britain declared war on Germany in 1939, so did the viceregal government, on behalf of 400 million Indians. Congress actively opposed Indian participation without a solid guarantee of independence after the war. It launched the contentious Quit India Movement and as a result, much of the nationalist leadership spent the war under detention, while the Muslim League and, later,

---

[33] Tomlinson 1982, 135.

the Communist Party of India (CPI) enthusiastically supported British war aims. Indian participation in the war was monumental. Two and a half million Indian soldiers were mobilized to fight the Axis, distinguishing themselves in the many theaters of the conflict, from North Africa and Burma to Italy.

World War II impacted India more directly as well. Eastern India became the base of operations for American efforts to support the Chinese nationalist army. The Northeast briefly served as the front against Japanese advances in the Burma Campaign. The Indian economy was more generally reoriented to support the war effort, and Britain borrowed billions of pounds from India in order to fund its own wartime efforts. This military and economic mobilization caused significant suffering for the civilian population through domestic inflation, as well as causing a deadly famine in eastern India in 1943, in which up to three million lost their lives and for which colonial policies were directly culpable.[34] Yet it also greatly expanded the capacities of the state, which implemented rationing systems, industrial production policies, infrastructure, and social welfare policies in order to meet the demands of wartime mobilization.[35]

One might expect, then, that the ways that the Indian polity and economy responded to the nationalist movement, the impact of the Depression and related policy response and wartime mobilization might diminish the scope of governance variation. Certainly, the capacities of the Indian government expanded dramatically, and increased the capacities of Indian politicians, particularly from the Congress, to formulate legislation. But there are also reasons why these political and economic changes might have simply reinforced geographical distinctions in governance practices.

4.3.2 Nationalism and Self-Government

In response to agitations by the nationalist movement and in order to shore up the flagging legitimacy of British rule in India, colonial authorities implemented a series of political reforms that increased the participation of Indians in self-government and introduced a (strictly limited) franchise for elections to legislators in new councils and assemblies. The Government of India Acts of 1919 and 1935 increased the power of elected Indian representatives to formulate policies in taxation, spending, and investment, though unelected British officials retained authority over finance, security, defense, and foreign affairs.

Increasing Indian participation in colonial governance, adjudicated through elections, represented a massive opening in political opportunity for Congress; few other organizations had the capacity to conduct subcontinent-wide electoral mobilization. In the 1920s and the 1930s, Congress fielded candidates for elections and coordinated electoral strategies, even while conducting agitations

[34] Sen 1981. [35] Rothermund 2002.

and civil disobedience campaigns. Decades before independence, therefore, the electoral and governance practices of Congress – often seen as "a programmatic, multiclass organization"[36] – might present important moves toward the homogenization of governance.

Yet, there are reasons to believe that Congress did not – indeed, could not – fill this role. First, the British designed the institutions of government to disperse, decentralize, and fragment representation and, in so doing, create internal contention within assemblies and councils. Apart from the so-called general constituencies for the Hindu population, there were separate electorates for Muslims and other religious and lower caste minorities and representation for corporate groups such as business, labor, and farmers. Powerful leaders of these communities – like Muhammad Ali Jinnah of the All-India Muslim League (AIML), B. R. Ambedkar, of the Republican Party representing Dalits, and Periyar, of the anti-Brahminical and Tamil nationalist Justice party – clashed in assemblies with Congress politicians representing largely upper caste Hindu constituencies. Second, Congress itself was divided. Jawaharlal Nehru and Subhas Chandra Bose led an assertive socialist contingent within the party. But electoral mobilization in the 1937 elections involved the incorporation of wealthy peasants and small-town merchants with vested interests in reforming but not destroying the status quo.[37] Third and perhaps most crucially, Congress-dominated provincial and central legislative assemblies had limited reach in the actual governing of India at the local level. The strength and autonomy of district governance institutions, long understood as the backbone of the civil service, were preserved even as assemblies debated bills and passed legislation regarding government spending and taxation.

This reflected the challenge of principal–agent coordination deeply embedded in colonial rule. Even as the principals changed, the agents and their practices might persist in their practices. Of course, princely rulers still maintained quasi-absolute authority over their subjects, under British paramountcy, thus limiting representation to only the two-thirds of the territory of the subcontinent under the administration of the British Indian government; only a couple had established assemblies of their own by independence.

Data on the primary membership of Congress at the eve of Independence bears out some of this unevenness. Congress was a self-understood mass membership organization, with low membership fees relative to other political parties and a multitiered structure, with district and provincial Congress committees nominating attendees to the annual meeting and appointing members of the policymaking All-India Congress Committee and Congress Working Committee. Thus, primary membership as a proportion of population is thus a meaningful indicator of the strength of Congress influence on the ground. Figure 4.7 reports Congress primary members per 1,000 people

---

[36] Tudor 2013.   [37] Weiner 1967; Kochanek 1968.

across districts and states, by governance categories, based on the Congress Handbook of 1946.[38]

We can see a number of key features of this mass membership. First, it is highest in metropolitan districts. The high membership of conservative cases relative to modernizing and intermediate ones might represent the fact that the latter two categories contain princely states as well as districts; analyzing only British districts, the modernizing category have an average of twenty-one and intermediate and conservative categories have an average of seventeen members each per 1,000 people.

There was also significant variation by British-administered province: Bombay, Madras, Bihar, and United Provinces had on average over twenty members per 1,000, while Punjab, Bengal, Balochistan, and Orissa had less than ten. While in many ways, this tracked the Hindu population and presaged the dynamics of Partition, it also reflected the uneven penetration of Congress into different parts of India. Of course, Congress membership itself could mean different things: a committed trade unionist in the Bombay cotton mills and a *thakur* in an agrarian district in the United Provinces reflected different aspects of the same Congress organization, engaging in very different politics, even as they are both party members.

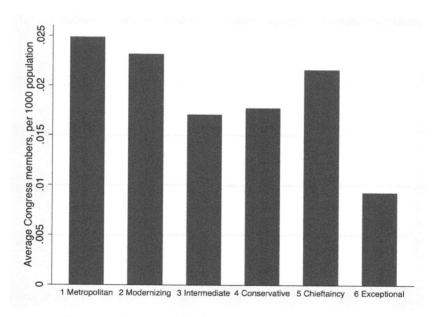

FIGURE 4.7 Congress primary membership, 1946

[38] Available online at https://searchworks.stanford.edu/view/3504852.

4.3.3   Disruptions and Transformations of Governance?

Beyond changes in political participation, there are other ways in which colonial political economy changed, impacting local governance. Due to military procurement and wartime inflation in World War I, India saw massive growth in indigenous manufacturing, transforming cities and their wealthy peripheries and forcing modernization of governance structures.[39] World War II's mobilization led to inflationary financing, which, coupled with the increase of industrial production focused on strategic goods, meant increased purchasing power and a shortage of consumer goods. The government's response during and after the war was to institute a bureaucratic system of rationing and price controls that vastly increased the state's capacity to manage the economy and intervene in society.[40]

These changes in the political economy of late colonial India represented shifts from the perceived timelessness of colonial rule during the Victorian and Edwardian eras. Yet the impact of these disruptions was, in turn, spatially specific. In cities and wealthy rural areas, the disruptions of the crisis years and the opportunities of the boom years in industry led to significant urban migration, particularly among Dalits, and thus spurring movements for political and social reform and subsequent Dalit mobilization in the Bombay and Madras Presidencies.[41] At the same time, elite revolts against taxation and redistribution, particularly based on income taxes, occurred in those areas, prefiguring the class politics that came to the fore in post-independence India.[42] However, in other areas of continuing social intermediation and the domination of traditional structures, colonial officials and local elites cooperated to suppress demands for even moderate redistribution and reform, let alone radical transformation.

In princely states under chieftaincy governance arrangements, traditional governance largely persisted, quelling change, even as other princely states, such as Mysore and Travancore, were engaging in some of India's most significant modernization and innovation programs and yet others, like Hyderabad, faced insurgent revolt. Finally, the frontier saw waves of tribal rebellion and the application of modern tools of war, including aerial bombardment, even while the exceptionalism of governance operated by political agents continued. Thus, even as India profoundly changed and both independence and partition neared, it continued to be governed varied in territorially distinct ways.

Reproducing indicators from analysis in the 1910s for the 1940s presents some circumstantial evidence of this endurance; these data are less consistent and comprehensive than those of the 1910s, because we need to rely on provincial

---

[39] Chandavarkar 1993.   [40] Tomlinson 1993, 161–162.   [41] Ahuja 2019.
[42] Suryanarayan 2017.

and princely state administrative reports without the comprehensive and standardizing Imperial Gazetteer, but they are nonetheless suggestive. Figure 4.8 presents land revenue in the early 1940s.

Here we see similar dynamics as thirty years earlier, except that there is increasing convergence between modernizing and intermediate categories and a dramatic increase in the chieftaincy category, though because data from princely state administration reports are quite sketchy, it is worth taking this with some skepticism. Figure 4.9 represents median police per capita in the early 1940s across different governance categories.

Figure 4.10 represents median judicial stamp tax across different governance categories.

The data presented here more or less recapitulates the analyses of the 1910s, and as such, demonstrates some broad continuities, despite dramatic changes in the Indian economy, society, and polity. This reflects our commonsense understanding of institutional "stickiness" and path dependence: that even the most dramatic shocks are likely to impact different institutions in different ways, based on antecedent conditions. Even at the very threshold of independence and partition, the governance of India was institutionally differentiated, which would have significant impact on the ways that postcolonial countries are subsequently ruled.

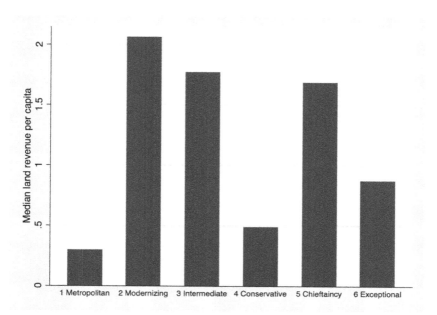

FIGURE 4.8 Land revenue per capita, early 1940s

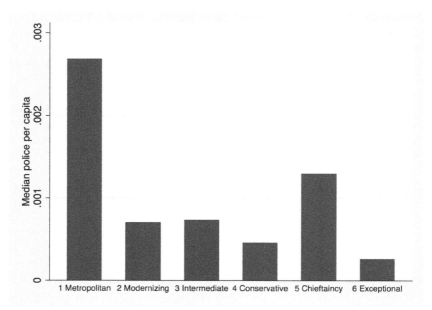

FIGURE 4.9 Police per capita, early 1940s

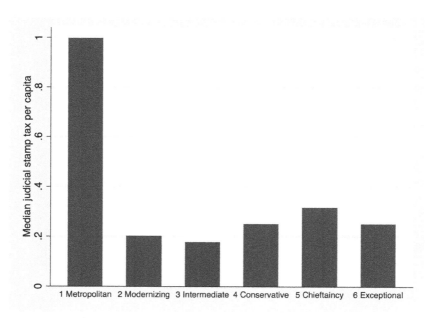

FIGURE 4.10 Judicial stamp tax per capita, early 1940s

4.4 CONCLUSION

This chapter surveyed the nature and impact of governance variation through important political, social, and economic indicators in the Victorian and Edwardian periods, as a proof of concept that these categories constitute meaningful distinctions in how colonial India is governed. It also explored the ways in which India was changed by the political and economic dynamics of the interwar period, in the subcontinent and beyond. These changes did not erase the governance variations that were established in the nineteenth century; rather, they represented structures through which political and economic change was mediated, amplified, or suppressed. As I will argue in Chapter 5, a similar dynamic was similarly evident in the ways that postcolonial states sought to revise governance variation to accommodate the demands of independent statehood.

5

Postcolonial Patchwork States

This book argues that understanding the spatially differentiated politics of conflict and competition in contemporary South Asian states requires examining the origins of state institutions, initially developed in the subcontinent under colonial rule. We must also pay attention to the ways that governance changed with decolonization, however, through the efforts of nationalist leaders to alter the destinies set by colonialism through their own efforts at postcolonial state-building. These leaders had shaken off the yoke of imperial domination and thus could operate differently from the mandates of colonial rule.

The independence of India and Pakistan from Britain in 1947 created two sovereign states in the place of a territory that was in no way sovereign – it was under colonial control for almost 200 years, and moreover fragmented into provinces, princely states, and political agencies that did not constitute a coherent, unitary, modern state. The spatially differentiated structures of the state were very much in the evidence at the eve of decolonization. New governments thus faced a daunting challenge of transforming these structures to suit new national purposes. Postcolonial governments attempted, each in their own way, to form new national solidarities and political practices and establish the structures of the modern state. In so doing, they attempted to counteract the patchwork nature of colonial governance.

This project was not wholly successful, however. The governance variation we see today is the concrete product of the persistence of colonial patchwork governance that could only be partly unraveled by the efforts of postcolonial state-builders. Some institutions of colonial governance were clearly incompatible with modern statehood, such as that of princely states, and these were eliminated, though in India more quickly and energetically than in Pakistan. Other forms of de facto variation, however, represented less of a fundamental challenge to the state's authority, and thus have persisted and become embedded in contemporary variations in state capacity and state–society relations.

The limitations of postcolonial state-building had three sources. First, political leaders had serious disagreements over the meaning and purpose of independent nationhood. These internal conflicts meant that postcolonial states could not follow a straightforward monopolization of authority, as with revolutionary states like China. Second, the ideological or strategic orientations of policymakers in governments in India and Pakistan, even when there was broad agreement, were not strong enough to overpower other considerations, such as the high costs, in blood and treasure, of revising governance arrangements among resisting populations. Third and relatedly, Indian and Pakistani governments absorbed and extended the administrative structures initially established by colonial rule. Collectors, district magistrates, and superintendents of police continued to represent the state at the local level and operate under many of the same formal laws and informal practices as their colonial predecessors. As a consequence, the bureaucratic tools available for reform of the state were themselves unevenly effective.

This book recognizes the ways in which postcolonial governments revised governance by narrowing the sixfold colonial governance typology to four postcolonial governance categories: metropolitan, modernizing, conservative, and exceptional. This narrowing reflects the integration of princely states, albeit with varying thoroughness both within and between India and Pakistan, and the postindependence political contention against landlords that attended modernization, which again varied in its intensity. Crucially, exceptional governance has persisted and even expanded, though it operates in different and arguably more conflictual ways today than it did previously, as recent impulses toward monopolization, following capitalist and geostrategic motivations, have replaced governance restraint.

As a result, India and Pakistan continue to constitute patchwork states, with varying governance arrangements as concrete legacies of colonial rule and postcolonial revision. This governance variation explains the spatial variation in the nature of political conflict and competition that I will outline in Chapters 6–8. Bangladesh represents an exception to the patchwork state left over from colonial rule, because it was cut from whole cloth rather than assembled from disparate elements as Pakistan and India were. As a result, political violence and competition in Bangladesh are national in scope and centripetal in character.

5.1 THE ORIGINS OF THE MODERN STATE AND THE STATE SYSTEM IN SOUTH ASIA

It is among the most stale truisms in the study of South Asia that partition transformed the subcontinent. It becomes more meaningful, however, when one considers the paths not taken and indulges in a little counterfactual conjecture. Partition itself represented the failure of serious negotiations on a constitutional settlement, one that might have prevented the complete rending apart of Hindu- and Muslim-majority provinces into two separate sovereign states. This failure foreclosed the possibility of an altogether different way of governing South Asia after British rule, which might have preserved in more pristine form the patchwork of colonial governance and decreased the distance between the goals and the capacities of postcolonial states.

5.1.1   Paths Not Taken

Partition meant the independence of India and Pakistan as sovereign (and immediately rival) states juridically recognized by the state system, though with significant variation of "empirical" state capacity within their borders.[1] There was a radically different, but ultimately foreclosed, possibility for how postcolonial India might have been governed: a federation of India under a common umbrella of postimperial jurisdiction, containing within it a heterogeneous grouping of polities. This would have included (Hindu- and Muslim-majority) provinces but also kingdoms and even tribal agencies – thus strong, if heterogeneous regional governments and a weak central one – under an overall framework of "national" rights and responsibilities.

If the possibility of this Indian federation – essentially a regional state system rather than two states – seems exotic to the point of absurdity now, and normatively dubious to boot, it was in fact a viable option for postcolonial India as late as the 1940s. Further, it represented a more straightforward continuity of extant constitutional arrangements and structures of representation of the time, as well as following a real-world model for political order after decolonization: that of "dominion status" that had been granted to white-settler colonies like the Canadian and Australian federations in the previous century.[2]

The British Indian government had introduced constitutional reform measures in the early twentieth century, in order to incorporate more Indians into governance structures and thereby bolster the legitimacy of colonial rule against nationalist challenges. However, they were established in such a manner as to reinforce distinctions and divisions within Indian society. Muslims, Sikhs, Christians, and Dalits were elected – on the basis of separate electorates – and representatives of corporate groupings, from labor unions to landlords, were selected to populate legislative assemblies. There was even a Council of Princes representing the differentiated interests of "native states" to the Indian government. Further, elections to "unreserved" seats in legislative assemblies were conducted on the basis of plurality rules in territorially delimited constituencies, just as elections to Pakistani, Indian, and Bangladeshi parliaments

---

[1] See Jackson and Rosberg 1982.   [2] Nathan 1922; Gey van Pittius 1931.

and assemblies are conducted in this manner today. This form of representation meant that aspirant politicians had to mobilize voters in constituencies with specific concerns. The representation of interests would look different in the city of Madras from rural districts in the province, let alone Bihar or the NWFP; Congress party candidates representing these diverse locations would differ as much as they would agree.

The first institutions of participatory governance thus reflected the profound (and self-fulfilling) belief among colonial rulers that India was diverse and internally divided: not one nation, but many. It also represented strategies of divide and rule that pitted communal groups against one another and forestalled the emergence of a coherent nationalist challenge to colonial rule.[3] From the 1920s, the Indian National Congress (INC, or Congress) sought to overcome these divisions through mass popular mobilization. Its politics attempted to create alternative cleavages along nationalist lines, between those who supported British rule and those who opposed it.

The INC included both Europeans and Indians from many different communities when it was founded in 1885, and advocated the greater participation of Indians in the administration of their own country. The nineteenth-century Congress promoted liberal values of individual dignity, rights and the rule of law, calling colonial authorities to account for not living up to those professed ideals and decrying the racism that enforced distinctions between European and Indian peoples. Early nationalist leaders – Mahadev Govind Ranade, Ferozeshah Mehta, Dadabhai Naoroji, Gopal Krishna Gokhale – were university-educated lawyers, scholars, and social reformers who sought to expand institutions to serve the diverse Indian population. Many of its early leaders were from the minority Parsi community, and were thus not naturally moved by majoritarian impulses. They represented a powerful moderate faction against radical activists like Bal Gangadhar Tilak and Lala Lajpat Rai. Muhammad Ali Jinnah, a successful Muslim barrister, was an acolyte of Mehta and Naoroji; he joined Congress in 1906, led its delegations to London in the 1910s and brokered the Lucknow Pact on Hindu and Muslim representation in 1916.

Jinnah, like many Congress moderates, was an enthusiastic proponent of "home rule," demanding that Britain allow India full self-determination as a Dominion within the overall protection of the British Empire, providing all Indians with full rights and protections as citizen-subjects. Home rule represented a fulfillment of promises extended to other colonies like Australia and Canada. It would have replaced British officials with Indians in the crafting of national policies, but it would not fundamentally challenge the structures of power and inequality inherent in colonialism. Indeed, the rights to property enjoyed by landlords and the suzerain authority of princely states would be guaranteed as central components of the rule of law. Jinnah, as the probate

---

[3] Chiriyankandath 1992.

attorney for several princely rulers, had an affinity with this cosmology of constitutional and legal governance over more radical and disruptive nationalist mobilization. As such, home rule represented a managed continuity of governance heterogeneity consistent with self-determination, rather than more assertive decolonization.

The movement for home rule failed, for two reasons. The first is the infamous perfidy of Albion. Nationalist leaders in both Ireland and India were extended promises of Home Rule in exchange for support behind British war aims in the 1910s. As Irish and Indian soldiers fought and died for the British Empire in World War I, successive British governments broke these promises, due in large part to party competition in Westminster.

Beyond British perfidy, however, the moderate home rule position failed against the more radical nationalist tendencies of the Congress, which became a mass movement under Gandhi's leadership from the 1920s. Gandhi advocated a radical break from not just formal British rule but also British institutions, norms, values, and ways of organizing society and the economy.[4] This provided a platform that could unify, if temporarily, the feuding sets of Congress activists and politicians. Socialists saw a radical break from Britain as a necessary step to economic and social transformation brought about by a strong modernizing state, following the economic planning of the Soviet Union.[5] Conservatives, by contrast, saw in the ejection of British norms and institutions the possibilities of a return to the hierarchies of the agrarian order as well as a challenge to the authority of British-allied princely rulers.[6] Neither faction was enamored by the continuities promised by a constitutional settlement with home rule at its center.

Both socialist and conservative nationalisms from the early 1920s to the mid-1930s alarmed moderates, who believed in liberal rights and principles, especially the defense of property rights under legal and constitutional frameworks and the protection of minority communities, as a necessary basis for self-rule. Congress itself was an organization dominated by upper-caste Hindus, who were not naturally attracted to minority protection or the rights of feudal landowners. Its mass mobilization deployed Hindu idioms as repertoires of anti-colonial contention; Gandhi explicitly used the term *Ram rajya*, or the rule of the Hindu deity, to characterize an ideal India after independence. Gandhi also allied with populist religious movements, such as *khilafat*, as a way of mobilizing minority communities against the British. This communal populism alarmed liberals like Jinnah, who saw religion as largely a matter for the private sphere, and intercommunal harmony as only possible through the recognition of rights and the balancing of interests among different religious communities.

By the mid-1930s, Jinnah had left Congress and assumed the leadership of the AIML, a political party advocating for the interests of the Muslim

---

[4] Gandhi 1909; see Brown 1991; Devji 2012.   [5] Zachariah 2005.   [6] Erdman 1967.

community. It had adopted Iqbal's "Two-Nation" theory, that Muslims and Hindus constituted distinct nations with distinct homelands within India. As a result, Jinnah began to focus on highlighting territorial nationalism in regions where Muslims constituted a majority. For him, establishing and protecting the autonomy of a national homeland constituting the Muslim-majority provinces in the northwest of India would geographically concentrate Muslim interests within a broader federation of India after the end of colonial rule, and thus ensure Muslim influence in Hindu-majority India.[7] Other significant differences existed between the constituencies and programs of the Congress and the League. Most obviously, the AIML was essentially a one-issue political party, with a largely elite following, whereas Congress represented a broader arena of interests.[8]

Jinnah, as "sole spokesman" of the cause of the Muslim minority, sought a constitutional settlement with the British authorities and Congress that would allow the Muslim provinces of the northwest to remain as a distinct component in an Indian union under a loose federal structure that reserved substantial power to the provinces.[9] In effect, the League was arguing for a consociational framework for Indian constitutionalism after Independence, whereas Congress remained committed to majoritarian structures.[10] Such consociationalism was more consistent with the actually existing governance heterogeneity at the end of colonial rule than Congress' vision of nationalist majoritarianism. In pursuit of this settlement, the AIML gathered significant political capital with British authorities by cooperating with war aims during World War II, at a time in which Congress launched the Quit India campaign of civil disobedience. Additionally, the League's success in Muslim-reserved seats in the 1946 elections bolstering the sense that Muslims constituted a distinct community and that the AIML spoke for this community.

That year, the Attlee government sent a cabinet mission, under Stafford Cripps, which sought to establish a final constitutional settlement plan for an independent India. The plan suggested groupings of autonomous provinces formed on the basis of religion and a weak central government that would have jurisdiction over defense, foreign affairs, and communications. But the Cabinet Mission Plan was rejected by Congress leaders of the left and the right, the former because it would foreclose plans for state-led industrialization and the latter because it might present a fillip for recognition of demands of other social groups.

5.1.2 The Violent Emergence of the Modern State and Governance Challenges in South Asia

As a result, India was divided into two separate, sovereign states – India and Pakistan – based on Hindu-majority and Muslim-majority provinces, with the

[7] Fatefully, Iqbal's notion of a Muslim state within India did not include the Muslim-majority Bengal.
[8] Tudor 2013. [9] Jalal 1994. [10] Adeney 2002.

provinces of Punjab and Bengal themselves partitioned based on Muslim- and Hindu- (or Sikh-) majority districts.[11] Widespread massacres and forced migration due to communal violence, especially in Punjab, accompanied Partition. Hindus, Sikhs, and Muslims in the police and especially the army, who had been colleagues and comrades, viewed one another with suspicion, and acted with brutal effectiveness upon those suspicions in a classical but tragic case of the security dilemma.[12] The violence surrounding the formation of the Indian and Pakistani states finally destroyed the possibilities of pan-Indian cooperation based on common rights and constitutional frameworks that would have entailed greater continuity between colonial and postcolonial governing structures.

Over just a few months, the common if heterogeneous governance arena that had been colonial India – with provinces and districts, princely states, and political agencies – was abruptly and violently transformed into a state system of two sovereign entities, taking on obligations to monopolize authority internally and compete with one another, but with limited resources.[13] The new structures of the postwar international order, like the United Nations, universalized the norms of "juridical" statehood, and the dynamics of cold-war competition in the 1950s crafted the contours of a bipolar system, about which India was deeply critical and Pakistan more enthusiastic.[14]

Partition, the subsequent conflict over the princely state of Kashmir (on which more later), and the general context of the postwar state system indicated a formally convergent model, in which the Weberian coercive monopoly should be extended to the limits of international borders. But this in turn highlighted the gaps between that model and the realities of continued diversity in territorial governance – in other words, the patchwork nature of the state in empirical terms as opposed to the formal homogeneity of the juridical state built on external recognition.

A necessary mandate in the pursuit of establishing sovereignty was the integration of princely states, as the existence of these ruling entities was inconsistent with the notions of national sovereignty and common citizenship rather than princely subjecthood. Both Pakistan and India integrated princely states within their territory through both negotiation and coercion. Much of this integration passed without incident, but obstreperous rulers such as the Nizam of Hyderabad saw their realms forcibly taken by the Indian government, and Pakistan put down a rebellion of the Khan of Kalat and integrated southern Balochistan in much the same manner.[15]

The princely state of Jammu and Kashmir represented a particular problem, because it lay at the intersection between two orthogonal principles: sovereignty

[11] Adeney 2002, 17.
[12] Posen 1993. For more on partition violence, see Jha and Wilkinson 2012.   [13] Jalal 1990.
[14] On Nehru's policies of "non-alignment" in greater regional context, see Raghavan 2010.
[15] See Benichou 2000; Axman 2008.

and national self-determination.[16] As a Muslim-majority state with a Hindu ruler, the Maharaja and his government had titular authority, based on British interpretations of subsidiary treaties, to decide whether the state would join India, join Pakistan or, if it were a possibility, become an independent kingdom. While the Maharaja vacillated over which direction Kashmir should go, facts on the ground intervened. A local nationalist movement in Kashmir against the Maharaja's government created a situation of increasing instability. Pashtun tribal warriors from the now Pakistani NWFP, under the covert direction of officers of the Pakistani army, then entered Kashmir in support of this movement, in order to overthrow the princely government and integrate the state forcibly into Pakistan. The Maharaja asked for protection from the Indian government, which the latter indicated it would provide only if Kashmir acceded to India. This resulted in the first war between India and Pakistan. The conflict ended with the matter being referred to the United Nations for resolution, which called for the withdrawal of troops and the conduct of a plebiscite. This withdrawal and plebiscite never occurred, however, and both Pakistan and India have been disputing the entire territory of the erstwhile state of Jammu and Kashmir ever since.

The Kashmir conflict brought early and vigorous interstate competition between two sovereign powers, with vastly unequal sizes and resources, into a South Asia that had previously seen threats only from the frontier and from civil unrest. The enduring nature of the conflict – over three wars and numerous smaller engagements – militarized the borders between India and Pakistan and made the borders between India and Bangladesh highly salient. What used to be the fields, canals, and roads that separated districts on an administrative map of the province of Punjab – or the Thar Desert between Sindh and the princely states of Rajputana – became the locus of both countries' military and paramilitary assets. This has meant a continued focus on the military as a key institution for national defense and the maintenance of security, heightening and concretizing previously inchoate security concerns, though of course more in Pakistan than in India.

It also meant that the provision of security – in grand and narrow senses, from internal and external sources – remained an important priority for both governments. The overdeveloped surveillance and internal security state apparatus that had been developed under colonial rule split in half and was redeployed against one other, yielding highly institutionalized suspicion within and outside borders.[17] States also took on threats from insurrection internally, as concrete legacies of colonial rule. Newly independent India, for instance, inherited and continued to prosecute Hyderabad state's conflict against peasant rebels in Telengana, and newly independent Pakistan put down Baloch tribal rebellions. Of course, in India, Pakistan, and Bangladesh, security has meant different things to different people within national populations. Armies and

[16] See Schofield 1996; Ganguly 2003; Bose 2009.   [17] Zamindar 2007.

security forces in all three countries could represent guardians or persecutors, depending on whether populations are behind or facing the sharp edge of the state's coercive force.

At the same time, postindependence governments mobilized their national populations based on promises of the greater distribution of resources, particularly among the vast populations that had been excluded from the largesse of the state. Since colonial rule had axiomatically meant underdevelopment, its end came with it the promise of development unfettered by colonial structures and the mandate to achieve those outcomes through social and economic transformation. This came with early and enduring competition and, indeed, violent conflict among different communities over the distribution of the goods of the state, as well as resistance to measures by state authorities to change or transform this distribution. Thus the politics of postcolonial development, as well as that of postcolonial security, have been contentious and often violent, though in different ways for Pakistan, India, and Bangladesh, both at the national level and in terms of local variation. These differences, I argue, are the consequences of the persistence of patchwork state institutions.

5.1.3   Preserving the Patchwork State

In the face of the immediate, manifold challenges of postcolonial rule, states in South Asia largely retained and built upon the formal administrative structures left by the British, in terms of the elite civil and police services, military and paramilitary forces, systems of taxation and infrastructure, as well as frameworks for the provision of public goods, public health, and instruction. This is in stark contrast to several cases in Southeast Asia, where Japanese conquest dislodged European colonial authorities and subsequent political conflict disrupted extant agrarian arrangements and structures of state authority. In some of these cases, following wartime disruption and the collapse of the colonial *ancien régime*, revolutionary forces supported by the Soviet Union effected a wholesale demolition and rebuilding of the state. In others, counterrevolutionary forces mobilized against challenges from insurrectionary movements.[18]

In India and Pakistan, there was no serious wartime devastation or Japanese occupation. Even though the Japanese threatened the Coromandel Coast in 1942, invaded northeastern India at the latter stages of their Burma campaign and sponsored the anti-colonial Indian National Army, wartime India – though wracked with inflation, famine in Bengal and nationalist agitation – saw the structures of British administration remain intact. Further, though both the British government and the Congress party feared rising Communist influence in agrarian and industrial India in the 1920s and 1930s, the CPI actively

[18] See Slater 2010; Vu 2010.

collaborated with the British colonial authorities after the Soviet Union joined the Allied coalition, and largely pursued electoral politics and labor mobilization in India after independence. As a result, even though colonial administration was on the verge of collapse during the violence preceding Partition, its structures remained intact throughout this period and persisted after independence.

Political elites in both India and Pakistan relied on the maintenance of these structures to accomplish their concrete aims and protect their legitimacy. Congress, though a mass organization, had nothing like the cadre-based structures of the Chinese Communist Party, and so could not substitute for seasoned bureaucrats, even if they were trained in colonial governance practices. The Indian Administrative Service, the successor to the Indian Civil Service, represented continuities between colonial and postcolonial regimes; both were seen as the "steel frame" of the state.[19] Both conservatives and socialists in Congress relied on extant bureaucratic structures. Nehru's plans for state-led industrial transformation were drawn up by a group of elite technocrats in the Planning Commission in New Delhi, including those drawn from the civil service. While he established a novel system for local development, these structures fit within and were overseen by district administration. Patel, Nehru's deputy and Home Minister, went to great lengths to preserve and maintain the authority of the central superior services, in order to maintain the discipline and public security that he saw as necessary for independent India.

In Pakistan, the de facto collapse of the Muslim League after the death of Jinnah and the assassination of Liaqat Ali Khan, and the subsequent fractiousness of Pakistani provincial politics, led to alliances between the elite bureaucracy and the military to maintain order and preserve central authority. This implicitly authoritarian governance system was bolstered by the executive arrangements of the Government of India Act 1935, which remained in place after the failure of the Constituent Assembly to frame and ratify a new constitution for independent Pakistan. This de facto "white- and khaki-collared" governing alliance subverted the redistributive demands of provincial political forces, to reserve resources for national defense, and developed eventually into Ayub Khan's military bureaucratic-authoritarian regime in 1958.[20] While this was formally a military regime, the elite bureaucracy, as a concrete legacy of colonial governance, played a leading role in governing the country.

Thus, despite the epochal political changes in politics after Independence, the bureaucracy at the district level maintained its formal structures and much of its power; it changed its practices, but haltingly and gradually relative to other postcolonial regimes in Asia. This meant that, despite the efforts of postcolonial governments to revise colonial governance arrangements, the main vehicles for

---

[19] Gupta 1996.   [20] Jalal 1990.

achieving such revision were the very structures governments sought to revise. Both the durability and the unevenness of district-level governance meant that such revision could only be partially successful, and the persistence of variation among territorial governance arrangements continues to have profound consequences in national and subnational politics today. In the next sections, I will outline the particular trajectories of the three countries, before turning to the analytical application of postcolonial patchwork governance to contemporary conflict and competition.

5.2 THE LIMITED REVISION OF PATCHWORK STATE IN INDIA

5.2.1 The Politics of India under Congress Hegemony

As India became independent, two very different visions of postcolonial state – the Nehruvian focus on economic and social transformation through state-driven socialist planning and the conservative preservation of traditional social structures – framed the contentious politics of postcolonial India. These debates involved fundamental conflicts among different visions of development and patterns of distribution in postcolonial India, over issues like the implementation of policies of land reform and the pace of industrialization.[21] These significant and sustained conflicts reflected the fundamentally ambivalent nature of Congress, which functioned as both a hegemonic political organization and as a de facto party system with significant contention among constituent elements.[22]

In practice, however, these conflicts were also situated in distinct territorial politics. Modernizing, transformational perspectives of governance dominated in and around the growing metropolises and statist enclaves surrounding key resources, which drew populations toward industrial employment at some remove from agrarian structures of social domination. Competition among these groups over these jobs and other public resources has repeatedly led to social violence. Deep in the agrarian heartland, by contrast, traditional hierarchies and social structures remained largely uncontested, with the capture of state power and resources by dominant proprietary elites and hard political limits on the implementation of land reform, and the exercise of violence to maintain hierarchy.

Democratic competition and the activities of politicians and activists led to different outcomes in different places. In the erstwhile Bombay and Madras presidencies, the political mobilization of Dalits, led by figures such as B. R. Ambedkar and Periyar E. V. Ramaswamy, forced dominant political parties – both Congress and its opponents – to incorporate their concerns in politics and policy.[23] This mobilization, in turn, arose from the ways that the brutality of the pre-Independence ryotwari system inspired migration to cities,

---

[21] Frankel 1971, 2005; Herring 1983.   [22] Kothari 1964.   [23] Ahuja 2019.

incorporation into public institutions including the Army, as well as emerging political resistance to the domination of upper-caste elites.

Modernizing disruption of traditional norms was also evident in particular princely states. Malayali nationalist mobilization in the princely states of Travancore and Cochin that would, along with the district of Malabar, form the state of Kerala prefigured the transformation of politics under political competition between Congress and the Communists after Independence.[24] In others, however, princes and their subordinate elites influenced the local state and dominated society, either directly or through political proxies. Rudolph and Rudolph, in a classic study, argued that "traditional" structures like caste associations can mobilize collective purposive action and thus enable Indian democracy. Apart from forming a basis for collective action, the Rajput Sabha at the heart of their analysis represented systems of social domination in the former princely states of Rajputana or contemporary Rajasthan.[25]

The subnationalist successes of social development in Kerala and Tamil Nadu are predicated on the continued impacts of modernizing governance in both former princely states and British-ruled provinces. In areas of northern and eastern India formerly under zamindari arrangements, however, the unity and strength of elites – either with landlords reinventing themselves as rich and powerful cultivators or intermediaries taking over and consolidating lands left by absentee landowners – led to the capture of the state at the local level and the successful resistance of liberalizing reforms. The Congress leadership in states such as West Bengal, Uttar Pradesh, Orissa, Bihar, and Madhya Pradesh in the two decades after independence reflected the consolidation of proprietary elites and the exercise of violence to maintain hierarchies.[26]

5.2.2 India's Politics of Conflict and Competition

More political mobilization and bifurcation between modernizing and conservative governance arrangements occurred in the 1970s and beyond. This represented the era of Congress decline, a long and contentious process during which the grand coalition of different interests that had been part of the party's internal coalition structures fractured. Former Congress leaders with particular constituencies thus began articulating their politics independent of the Congress organization.[27] In northwestern India, Chaudhry Charan Singh's mobilization of rich peasants from the Jat community reflected a aspirant peasant politics that abjured the elite structures associated with Congress. Charan Singh served as the first non-Congress chief minister of Uttar Pradesh and briefly, prime minister under the Janata coalition. He represented a new form of modernization in which vigorous party competition accompanied

---

[24] Desai 2007; Singh 2016. [25] Rudolph and Rudolph 1967.
[26] Weiner 1967; Kochanek 1968; Jaffrelot 2017. [27] Rudolph and Rudolph 1987; Kohli 1990.

competition over the direction of state investment and the distribution of state resources.[28]

The Green Revolution aided the mobilization by wealthy peasants and exacerbated their power in relation to smallholders, tenants, and agricultural laborers. The expensive but lucrative inputs allowed those landowners and cultivators with capital to invest to become even more wealthy and politically powerful.[29] The political assertion of rich peasants in the 1970s led to the recognition and incorporation of these affluent rural interests into national politics.[30] These mobilizations in turn invited government intervention into the rural economy, such as the *mandi* system and minimum support prices, proposed reforms of which have led to mass farmers' contention in 2020 and 2021.

Transformations in productivity also generated significant violence, however, as wealthy cultivators suppressed the demands of landless lower-caste communities for redistribution. The Keezhvenmani Massacre in Thanjavur District, Tamil Nadu in 1968 occurred when Dalit laborers demanded higher wages, leading to an attack of a lynch-mob of local landowners, in which around forty-four Dalits, mainly women and children, were burned alive.[31] Similar dynamics of violence against Dalits were evident in Punjab in 1970; both states were ruled under non-Congress governments in which patterns of modernizing governance had made explicit contention and conflict over distribution.

In other areas such as eastern Uttar Pradesh and Bihar, however, it would take another two or three decades for subaltern communities to challenge entrenched social structures, through the idiom of caste. Political mobilization against social dominance in these regions came much later and was much harder to achieve in concrete terms, due to the relative strength of dominant actors, their capture of the state at the local level and the absence of preceding forms of social mobilization during and just after colonial rule.[32] Political challenges have resulted in the collapse of governance, chaos, violence, and criminality.[33]

Perhaps the most remarkable transformation in governance in post-Independence India was the electoral success of the Communist Party of India-Marxist (CPI-M) and formation of a coalition government under its leadership in West Bengal in 1977. The CPI-M engaged in comprehensive agrarian reforms, thereby challenging the hierarchical social domination that had arisen from the zamindari order and the Permanent Settlement. Prior events certainly had disrupted colonial continuity in the state, not least partition, which wrenched absentee upper-caste Hindu landowners from their estates in eastern Bengal, as well as the Maoist uprising in Naxalbari in 1971 and ensuing insurrectionary violence in the countryside and urban areas. However, the success of the CPI-M in capturing and retaining power has had a transformative impact and represented a dramatic reversal – from conservative to modernizing governance.[34] Social mobilization of

---

[28] Brass 2011.   [29] Frankel 1971.   [30] Varshney 1998.   [31] Frankel 1971, 113–118, 45.
[32] Jaffrelot 2003; Ahuja 2019.   [33] Witsoe 2013.   [34] Kohli 1983; Harriss 1993.

this kind, against entrenched structures of domination, has been seen as necessary for Indian democracy to move from being purely formal to substantive in nature.[35]

5.2.3 The Indian State's Approaches to Security

In more existential threats to the sovereign sanctity and security of India, the government's approach of aggressively asserting sovereignty over territory has persisted throughout the postindependence period and been deeply incorporated into foreign and security policy. This has involved taking a rigid approach to defending borders that were incompletely and badly drawn by British colonizers. Such assertiveness has repeatedly led to armed confrontations with India's neighbors over disputed international borders, with Pakistan over Kashmir almost immediately and with China over regions in both the western and eastern Himalayas from the late 1950s. In areas in which India was engaged in territorial disputes and conflict with regional competitors – principally Kashmir and the Northeast – the blunt coercive presence of the military and paramilitary forces has replaced previous traditions of standoffishness that had been followed by colonial agents along frontiers, but without the resources and incentives necessary for building more sustainable state–society relationships.[36]

The deployment of coercive force by New Delhi formally homogenized chieftaincy and exceptional governance arrangements from colonial rule, even while elements of exceptionalism continued in practice in former chieftaincies and political agencies. Article 370 recognized limitations on the applicability of India's laws in Kashmir as a condition of accession, which were hollowed out by 1964 but only revoked in 2019. In the Northeast, the Sixth Schedule of the Indian Constitution gave formal autonomous status for tribal-notified areas, which again has been disrupted and changed over time as the interests of the security state has clashed with the assertions of tribal groups seeking greater autonomy.[37] India–China confrontation in the eastern Himalayas, and tensions between India and Bangladesh over immigration, have made the Northeast a perennial site of contention and conflict, because central state mandates are not easily reconciled with cascading complexities of conflict associated with tribal groups that were never particularly well integrated into the Indian state.

The postcolonial Indian state also inherited the colonial fixation with internal security, which informed the approach of the security apparatus to rebellions against its authority. The nascent government crushed a peasant insurgency in Telangana that had begun under the last years of the Nizam's rule in Hyderabad.[38] This pattern continued in the interdiction of uprisings in

[35] Heller 1999.   [36] Kanjwal 2017.
[37] Hazarika 1995; Baruah 2005; Lacina 2009; Saikia 2017.
[38] Kennedy and Purushotham 2012.

Kashmir and Punjab, as well as during episodes of left wing insurgency in central and eastern India. The former arose from particular dynamics in political competition, which married changing practices of state–society distance with an absolute intolerance to questioning state sovereignty.

In the princely states in the interior of India with large tribal populations, however, local agents of the Indian state tended to maintain the traditions of standoffishness and protection of tribal ways of life; these were discussed in the Constituent Assembly debates on the Fifth Schedule on Scheduled Areas and Scheduled Tribes.[39] In the 1990s, however, policies of economic liberalization replaced statist traditions of Indian economic governance. Due to liberalizing reforms and the empowerment of pro-extraction state governments, remote tribal areas have been increasingly penetrated by capitalist enterprises in pursuit of the accumulation of natural and mineral resources, which has in turn led to insurgent conflict.

Thus, the internal and the external security concerns of the Indian state have meant deploying its coercive capacity in areas where the colonial state had previously maintained a negligible footprint, and the postcolonial state practiced heterodox governance traditions. The result has been the durable, often violent and largely undemocratic legacies of state-making in the assertion of territorial sovereignty in these regions, where autonomy had been granted in theory and denied in practice.[40] This disconnect represents a new postcolonial form of exceptional governance that arises from legacies of exceptionalism crashing into the security imperatives of the modern state.

5.3   THE (MORE) LIMITED REVISION OF THE (MORE) PATCHWORK STATE IN PAKISTAN

In Pakistan for the first three decades after independence, it was not the nationalist party but a bureaucratic-authoritarian state apparatus that inherited and revised colonial state structures. Postindependence Pakistan's emphasis was squarely on security, closely following the logic of "systemic vulnerability" and postcolonial "protection pacts" in Southeast Asia.[41] Yet the politics of competition and conflict over the distribution of resources, patronage, and authority arose from the institutional arrangements of the postcolonial state, leading eventually to the destruction of the Ayub Khan regime in the late 1960s.

After partition, the Pakistan Muslim League, the successor to the AIML, struggled to maintain legitimacy after the loss of its two most prominent leaders to tuberculosis and assassination; much of its grassroots organization was now

---

[39] Constituent Assembly Debates Vol IX, 7–9 September 1949. For more on the specifics of this political geography, see Mukherji 2021.
[40] Shah 2010; Sundar 2016.
[41] Doner, Ritchie and Slater 2005; Slater 2010. See also Naseemullah and Arnold 2015.

in western and northern India. Politicians in the provinces that became West Pakistan had joined the Muslim League in the 1946 elections for relatively cynical purposes. They were mostly drawn from previous "parties of notables" such as the Punjab Unionist and the Sindh United Parties. Moreover, political actors beyond Punjab and Sindh had interests and perspectives that clashed with the Muslim League. Khan Abdul Ghaffar Khan, the leader of the Pashtun nationalist Khudai Khidmutgar movement, was an ally of Gandhi and the Congress.[42] The Muslim League in Bengal had a more radical set of politics than those in West Pakistan, focused initially on challenging the Hindu *bhadralok* elite and its structures of agrarian power. Together, these fissiparous political actors engaged in political contestation largely in order to extract resources from the central state in order to satisfy provincial clients and constituencies, without any uniting force among the civilian political leadership. Pakistan went through seven prime ministers between the assassination of Liaqat Ali Khan in 1951 and the establishment of martial law in 1958.

Elite bureaucrats and the military were alarmed at this squandering of public resources, which they considered necessary for defense against India, just to satisfy the parochial demands of provincial politicians. Due to the failure of the Constituent Assembly, Pakistan remained under the Government of India Act 1935, which retained significant power for non-elected members of the government, particularly in terms of defense, foreign affairs, and law and order. During the chaos of the mid-1950s, alliances formed among civil servants and army officers to frustrate the exercise of popular will by political leaders. The eventual establishment of authoritarian rule arose out of these strategies to centralize and depoliticize the country, in order to meet defense requirements with meager domestic resources, while suppressing the inconvenient political demands of the provinces, particularly Bengal.[43]

The military itself has played a central role in Pakistan's politics throughout its postindependence life, for overdetermined reasons. The regions of northwestern India that became (West) Pakistan constituted a de facto regional security complex in the colonial period – a "garrison state" – in order to interdict Russian designs on the subcontinent.[44] Unlike East Bengal, Sindh, and Balochistan, state and society in northern and central Punjab and the plains of the NWFP was implicated directly or indirectly in this security complex before partition, which became the core of the state after independence.

5.3.1   The Pakistani State's Approaches to Security

The overdeveloped influence of the military and its internal structures are seen as having a significant impact on regime outcomes.[45] The Pakistani military is

---

[42] Banerjee 2000.   [43] Jalal 1990.   [44] Yong 2005.   [45] See Shah 2014; Wilkinson 2015.

coherent and cohesive as an organization,[46] and indeed tightly integrated into agrarian society in northern Punjab. In the fractious nature of Pakistani politics after independence, the military constituted a powerful institution with a clear sense of its own purpose and the resources and ultimately the authority to carry out its interests and objectives. During the height of the military-bureaucratic regime, the focus of the Pakistani state on both internal and external security placed serious limits on the extent to which colonial governance were revised by postcolonial politics, particularly relative to India. In the first three decades after Pakistan's independence, the focus of governance was not transformation but stability.

The persistence of colonial traditions was especially evident in Pakistan's governance in its long northwestern and western frontiers. Pakistan maintained and consolidated frontier governance arrangements that colonial political agents had established a century earlier. In FATA, between the North West Frontier and the border with Afghanistan, political agents, tribal militias, and paramilitary constabularies maintained political order under exceptional legal and administrative practices until the systemic disruptions from regional conflict emerged in the 1980s and then the 2000s.[47] The seven tribal agencies were finally integrated into Khyber Pakhtunkhwa province in 2018, seventy years after independence. Similarly, the princely states of the Northwest – Dir, Swat, and Chitral – were not integrated as other princely states in Punjab and Sindh, but rather ruled as Provincially Administered Tribal Areas, with significant governance restraint, until 1969.[48]

Balochistan represents another form of the persistence of governance exceptionalism. In 1947, the province was formed out of the districts of British Baluchistan, with significant frontier governance characteristics such as political order managed by tribal levies, and the princely states of Kalat, Kharan, and Las Bela. In the mid-1940s, the Khan of Kalat wished to remain independent of Pakistan, but the military coercively integrated the massive princely state into Pakistan, and governed through the empowerment of tribal *sardars*, thus subcontracting coercive power to traditional authorities in order to diminish the residual influence of the Khanate.[49] Not unlike tribal-majority areas in central and eastern India with traditions of governance restraint, the resource wealth of Balochistan has meant increasing state intervention and mineral exploitation, with few of the benefits going to Balochis, leading to deep grievances that have inspired insurgent violence.[50] The more recent incorporation of Balochistan into plans for the China-Pakistan Economic

---

[46] Staniland, Naseemullah and Butt 2020.   [47] Naseemullah 2014.
[48] Parts of the original state of Jammu and Kashmir that were occupied by Pakistan at the end of the war in 1948 – Azad (free) Jammu and Kashmir and the region of Gilgit-Baltistan – are *de jure* independent, with a separate government, though the Pakistani state has overwhelming de facto influence.
[49] Titus and Swidler 2000.   [50] Grare 2013.

Corridor, and the building of the port at Gwadar, has brought a national security dimension to these resource conflicts.

5.3.2 Pakistan's Politics of Conflict and Competition

Even though security was centrally important for the Ayub Khan regime, development and the distribution of resources was also considered a crucial component of national strategy, in keeping with the patterns of bureaucratic authoritarianism elsewhere.[51] The Pakistani state embarked on a rapid and successful program of import-substitution industrialization in the 1960s, for two reasons. First and most obviously, as in India, its leaders understood the production and distribution of resources to be a key tool for legitimation among the population. Second, industrialization and thus self-sufficiency in manufactured goods would mean that foreign currency reserves could be spent on defense acquisitions rather than consumer goods.

The distribution of resources and investment was also highly unequal, however, based on the requirements of state planners and the relative importance of different populations to the Pakistani state. Much of the industrial investment was concentrated in and around Karachi, the nation's first capital. Pakistani state elites formed alliances with mercantile and banking families that had migrated from what is now western India, who were encouraged to invest in industrial development.[52] The result was remarkable growth in Pakistan's "development decade," but also resentment among those who were excluded from the goods of development, including but not limited to the citizens of East Pakistan, which would lead to regime implosion from a rising wave of contention.

This was because development in agrarian Pakistan was limited relative to India, as the Ayub Khan regime sought to maintain stability by empowering proprietary elites and traditional authorities in West Pakistan, while actively suppressing the demands of East Pakistani cultivators for greater investment and spending. Economic downturns of the late 1960s led to a mass uprising of workers, students, and peasants in both East and West Pakistan, led by Mujib ur-Rahman's Bengali nationalist Awami League and Bhutto's Pakistan People's Party (PPP), respectively. Following the 1971 war and the independence of Bangladesh, Bhutto achieved power and (selectively) implemented policies that challenged the dominance of the industrial elite of the Ayub regime, including land reform and greater spending for farmers.[53] The brutal military regime that overthrew Bhutto's government also suppressed the PPP's populism, but also engaged in the politics of competition over resources, with the sponsorship of Nawaz Sharif's electoral coalition of wealthy peasants and petty industrialists in Punjab.

[51] O'Donnell 1988.   [52] Khan 1999.   [53] Herring 1979.

The opening of Pakistan's polity to electoral competition after the death of General Zia ul Haq in 1988 was situated in a much more fragmented interest group environment, in which different groups competed politically and pressed the state for resources, investment, and discretionary goods.[54] Two additional factors enabled these transformations from political management to competition, contention, and routinized conflict. First, the Green Revolution had empowered wealthy peasant-cultivators and diminished the power of old proprietary elites, particularly in northern and central Punjab. Second, violent political movements have confronted structures of traditional authority in some locations; peasant movements in northwestern Pakistan in the 1970s that occupied land and challenged the proprietary elite had tenures regulated by state intervention, once the interests of the government shifted from a focus on overall stability to balancing the interests of constituencies.[55]

Yet there were hard limits to modernizing governance in particular political geographies within Pakistan, particularly toward the south. Before independence, conservative governance based on the domination of landlords was prevalent in the province of Sindh, and southern Punjab was under the rule of the princely state of Bahawalpur. Here, the strength and cohesion of a traditional elite, bolstered by claims to religious authority as hereditary saints and the guardians of Sufi shrines, maintained state capture. This deeply conservative form of governance has kept modernizing influences at bay in postcolonial politics. Many of Pakistan's most powerful political families, including the Bhutto-Zardari dynasty, are part of this largely Shi'a elite in the South. Opposition to it, when it occurs, has been violent and clandestine rather than openly contentious, thus yielding significant sectarian violence. Thus, in Pakistan as in India, while some parts of the countryside have been profoundly affected by the forces of modernization and thus fragmented into interest groups, there are significant conservative holdouts that represent a qualitatively different form of political violence.

Pakistan's cities have followed a different trajectory than those of India. As the focus of political power and the distribution of resources shifted toward more politically assertive actors in Punjab, the interaction between contentious urban politics and the decayed metropolitan governance in Karachi has yielded a cauldron of conflict. Karachi's politics are distinctive due to the large proportion of the population that migrated from India at partition, the *mohajir* community, who were permanently alienated from agrarian relationships.[56] From the 1990s, discrimination against these migrants and violent contention among the different ethnic and concessional groups in the city have led to significant conflict amid significant wealth and quotidian political mobilization.[57]

In addition, the emergence of the Tehreek-e-Taliban Pakistan and territorial insurgency in the Northwest has meant that Pakistan's cities have experienced significant violence, particularly relative to India in the 2010s.[58] With the

[54] Naseemullah 2017a; Mohmand 2019.   [55] Ali 2020.   [56] Zamindar 2007.
[57] Gayer 2014.   [58] Naseemullah 2019.

possible exception of Karachi's much more established violence, however, these serious and sustained incidents of terrorism represent spillovers from dynamics situated in the frontier, much as Naxalite violence in the 1970s spilled over to urban insurgency in Kolkata. Even though levels of disorder of the metropolitan spaces in India and Pakistan have been different, both share key governance institutions and thus parallel politics of (often-violent) competition as a consequence of the density of institutions and state–society interpenetration.

5.4 BANGLADESH: AN EXCEPTION TO THE PATCHWORK?

Bangladesh represents a foil to the patchwork state of both Pakistan and India. It is one-sixth the land area of today's Pakistan, even though its population is 83 percent that of Pakistan; it is far more dense than India, let alone Pakistan, with significant linguistic homogeneity and a broadly uniform agrarian society, though with two populous metropolitan cities and three tribal-majority districts. This compactness influences its governance homogeneity, which has deep convergent historical roots. Indeed, it represented a handful of agrarian districts in the eastern half of Bengal Presidency in British India. After British conquest, the control of land in Bengal shifted from the Mughal aristocracy to upper caste Hindu bureaucrats and professionals with close connections to the colonial state. Many of these *bhadralok* elites lived as absentee landlords in Calcutta while receiving rents from Muslim tenants in estates in the east of the province, overseen by agents but incorporated into a complex agrarian landscape in which *jotedars*, intermediaries between proprietors and tenants, played a large role.[59] From the early twentieth century, Muslim nationalist agitation in Bengal resisted the economic and social dominance of the Bengali Hindu elite; vernacular Muslim Bengali culture was violently excluded from representation. Muslim nationalist agitation explicitly countered that exclusion and highlighted the economic and political disparities between communities in the province.[60]

Partition itself abruptly and violently modernized territorial governance in both East and West Bengal, because new international borders severed many of the most destructive linkages of debt and obligation between peasant and absentee landowner. As a result, in East Pakistan, there was a significant if accidental agrarian reform that gave tenancy rights to the tiller, in a deeper and more straightforward manner than elsewhere in India and (West) Pakistan.

Yet, East Pakistanis experienced a new form of repression under the new government. The bureaucratic-authoritarian apparatus found the political

---

[59] Ray 1979.
[60] Bose 2014. Bengali Muslim leaders even opposed the Partition of Bengal, because they wanted to be the democratic leaders of the whole province, while Bhadralok elites supported it as a means to prevent Muslim majoritarianism that might lead to radical redistribution. See Chatterji 2002, 2007.

assertion of Pakistani Bengalis, with a long tradition of left-wing activism, threatening. The demographic weight of East Pakistan, if it could find full democratic expression, would overpower West Pakistan and undermine the strategic objectives of the state elite. In addition, the rights of Bengalis to self-expression, including official recognition of the Bengali language along with Urdu, were severely curtailed.

The province faced economic discrimination as well. The production of jute for international markets provided the central government with much of its foreign exchange, but public investment in East Pakistan lagged significantly behind that of West Pakistan.[61] These grievances led to Bengali nationalist agitations under Mujib ur – Rahman that demanding greater resources and autonomy for East Pakistan, agitations which would eventually lead to the downfall of the Ayub Khan regime. The Awami League triumphed in the 1970 elections on a manifesto of greater autonomy, leading to repression by the Pakistani military and its collaborators and several months of mass civilian violence against Awami league activists and key figures in civil society that is has been characterized as genocidal in nature. The liberation struggle, joined by Indian intervention, led to independence.[62] As a concrete result of this historical trajectory, Bangladesh emerged not as a patchwork state but rather one cut from whole cloth and undergoing political transformations together.

***

At its founding, Bangladesh was a deeply wounded nation. Mujib ur-Rahman, the founder of Bangladesh, proceeded to construct the new nation on the basis of secularism, socialism, and Bengali nationalism. Initial democratic mobilization gave way to one party rule, however. Following a deadly drought and famine, Mujib was assassinated in 1975 by a group of junior army officers, inaugurating a series of coups and countercoups that ended with the military dictatorship of Zia ur-Rahman, and his establishment as Bangladesh's president at the head of the new Bangladesh National Party (BNP). After Zia's assassination in a coup d'état, General Hussein Muammmed Ershad ruled until pressures for a return to democratic rule in 1990. Since then, the Awami League and the BNP have been in intense political competition, with the League emerging victorious and increasingly hegemonic.

Throughout the turbulent half century since Bangladesh's independence, the political faultlines of competition and conflict have not been particularly territorial in nature, quite unlike the patchwork states of both Pakistan and India. Rather, ideology and the cleavage arising from the traumatic circumstances of the country's founding have driven national politics. They involve the meaning of the state over the whole of its territory, and the primacy of identity within that meaning: whether Bangladesh as a Bengali Muslim state is primarily Bengali or primarily Muslim in nature. The two main political

---

[61] Khan 1999.   [62] For an overview of these events, see Raghavan 2013.

parties represent two different sides of this cleavage, and politics operates around the moral wound at the nation's core, based on retributive justice or forgiveness for Bangladeshis who collaborated with the Pakistani military during the 1971 liberation war. Because the practices of governance are convergent and centripetal, dominant actors on both sides of the national cleavage broadly agree to a central settlement on the conduct of politics in cities and the countryside, although they compete over the fruits of that settlement.[63] As a result, beyond the usual inequalities associated with urban bias, it serves as a case of a more unitary nation-state in South Asia, and thus an explicable negative case for the patchwork states framework.

5.5 POSTCOLONIAL GOVERNANCE CATEGORIES

5.5.1 Recategorization

In practical terms, how can we modify the typology of colonial governance introduced in Chapter 2 to reflect the very real but limited and uneven state-building by postcolonial governance? This process should begin with colonial governance categories, which would have looked much the same the day after partition as the day before; this reflects persistence in its most concrete sense. Yet we must reflect the serious if partial efforts of postcolonial state-builders in incorporating princely states and undermining traditional agrarian arrangements, as well as attendant processes of industrialization and urbanization and particular transformative politics.

In practical terms, this recategorization means narrowing the possible range of governance, from six categories to four, to reflect this convergence. Two categories disappear entirely: chieftaincy and intermediate arrangements. Princely states with chieftaincy governance, as with other princely states, were incorporated into India and Pakistan. In instances where there was an extension of regular governance practices, these are classified as conservative, to reflect the relative weakness and capture of state authority that persisted from colonial rule, as opposed to princely states with modernizing arrangements. But in districts where traditions of standoffishness and significant distance came to characterize governance for the first decades after Independence, such as former princely states with large tribal populations, these new districts are classified as exceptional.

Most intermediate colonial governance converged into modernizing governance arrangements after independence. This was a concrete consequence of the ways that public investment, commercialization, and political competition empowered contending groups of cultivators and destabilized village hierarchies and dominant landowners in otherwise *mahalwari* or mixed forms of land tenure. Some districts in northwestern Pakistan with intermediate arrangements

---

[63] On Bangladesh's convergent political settlement, see Khan 2011; Hassan 2013.

during colonial rule represent a partial exception to this, due to the emphasis on stability in Pakistan's authoritarian regime, in which dominant elite could entrench power even in territories of *mahalwari* tenure; these are classified as conservative.

Beyond these necessary reclassifications, some districts and princely states have changed categories in subtle and more obvious ways. The category of metropolitan governance expanded significantly due to urbanization after independence. And discrete events – such as the impact of partition on East and West Bengal, as well as the advent of CPI-M rule in the latter – led to dramatic shifts in categories from colonial governance traditions to modernizing governance arrangements.

The unit of analysis for these new categories is the administrative district, still the basic unit of administration throughout South Asia. District governance spread across former princely states and political agencies, thus yielding administrative maps that were more homogenous than during the colonial period, with few exceptions.[64] I code formerly princely states based on the district or districts that comprise these territories in the 1970s; princely states substantially smaller than a contemporary district are dropped from the analysis. While districts have proliferated in all three countries, the vast majority of new districts represent subdivisions (*tehsils* or *talukas*) of previously united districts, thus enabling classification to carry over from the 1910s to the 1970s.

Appendix A details the nature of postcolonial governance classification, using colonial governance classification and urban and tribal population data from the population censuses of India (1971), Pakistan (1972), and Bangladesh (1974) in addition to discrete events in the 1950s and 1960s, such as Communist rule.[65] Table 5.1 presents the two typologies.

5.5.2 Applying Postcolonial Governance Categories to Contemporary Outcomes

In applying postcolonial governance categories to contemporary outcomes, in the next three chapters, we must be attuned to the dangers of circularity and endogeneity. To be sure, the formation of colonial governance variation, and its revision by postcolonial state-building, are deeply endogenous processes, informed by a wide variety of factors from physical geography – districts and political agencies with exceptional governance are mountainous or forested,

---

[64] Political agencies in northwestern Pakistan were under explicitly exceptional governance until 2018, and the princely states of Dir, Swat, and Chitral were formally integrated only in the 1960s; India's Northeast Frontier Area was integrated as Arunachal Pradesh, first as a union territory in 1972 and then as a state in 1987.

[65] For providing access to the 1971 Indian census data in electronic form, I thank Francesca Jensenius. For applications, see Bhavnani and Jensenius 2015.

TABLE 5.1 *The postcolonial revision of governance*

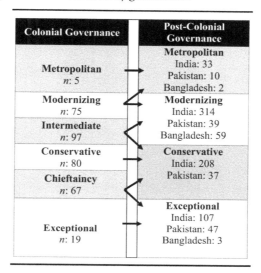

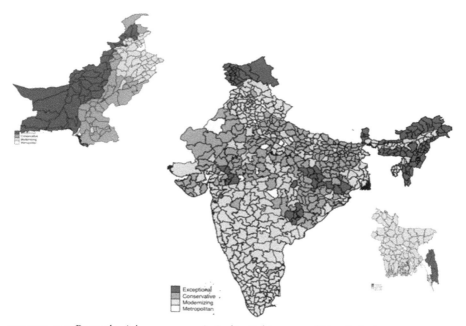

FIGURE 5.1 Postcolonial governance in India, Pakistan, and Bangladesh

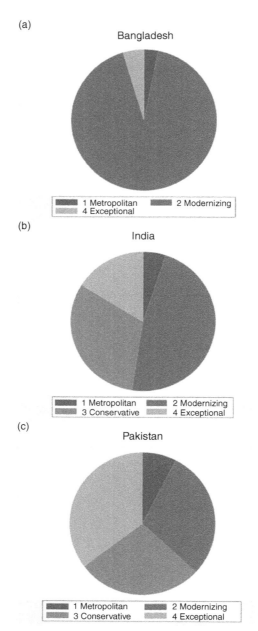

FIGURE 5.2 Distribution of districts by postcolonial governance in South Asia

reflecting the high costs and low benefits of full incorporation – to events like the wars of the early nineteenth century that exhibit significant path dependence. To require plausibly random or exogenous assignment in the complex but legible array of how South Asia was governed across its territory would be asking too much from historical processes that have powerful internal logics and structural features and thus do not yield causal cleanliness.[66]

However, there is another way in which the specter of endogeneity poses a threat to our analysis, by muddying distinctions between explanatory causes – postcolonial categories – and contemporary outcomes like patterns of violence, as well as electoral competition and development. This book guards against this threat in two ways. First, the postcolonial categories, and districts assigned to these categories, represent a snapshot of how South Asian countries were governed at the district level in the early 1970s, almost half a century ago. The several decades-long gap between this categorization and present day outcomes reflects the long-term legacies of postcolonial state-building – itself a revision of colonial governance diversity, in the first two decades after decolonization – rather than simply a characterization of contemporary governance.

Second, intermediary mechanisms of variation in state capacity and state–society relations, as discussed in Chapters 1 and 2, drive outcomes in the contemporary politics of competition and conflict in South Asian countries, rather than reflecting the persistence of institutions themselves. In other words, colonial and postcolonial governance arrangements have influential legacies, but it is obviously the case that governance arrangements do not operate in exactly the same way today, given dramatic changes in technology, political dynamics, and social expectations of the state. This approach takes account of the fact that governance is not the application of a discrete instrument but rather a set of continuing relationships. This in turn helps us see explanatory frameworks in the past and outcomes in the present as plausibly distinct from one another.

I also acknowledge that other important explanations beyond the governance categories of the patchwork states framework inform the outcomes of interest in the politics of conflict and competition in South Asian countries. This is not a determinative argument with full sufficiency, but rather one that suggests a coherent set of causal influences from history that, together with other factors, give us a better understanding of contemporary variations in violence as well as elections and development. In the next three chapters, we will explore the ways in which patchwork governance, its internal explicable variation, and its legacies, shapes the contemporary politics of South Asia.

5.6 CONCLUSION

This chapter has described the processes by which different patchwork postcolonial states in South Asia revised the disparate governance arrangements

---

[66] I return to these themes in Chapter 9.

that originated in colonial rule. Postindependence governments in India and Pakistan faced both internal contention and constrained capacities. The resulting postcolonial state-building constrained the extent of governance differentiation, but did not eliminate it. This is fairly typical of developing countries; few experience revolutionary transformation. The patchwork nature of the postcolonial state is thus a common characteristic. The continuing impact of patchwork governance, rooted in colonial domination, though modified by postcolonial governments, helps us understand the spatial politics of conflict and competition today, in South Asia and beyond.

PART III

CONTEMPORARY CONSEQUENCES

6

Patchwork States and Sovereignty

Explaining Political Violence

The Indian subcontinent is rife with internal violence. South Asian countries have not been strangers to systemic – and deeply political – conflict both against the state and under its auspices in their modern history. Partition itself and the making of its contemporary states was a bloody process that has cast long shadows. Since then, multiple territorial insurgencies in India, Pakistan, and even Bangladesh have raged along frontiers and in deep hinterlands, with government forces fighting rebels seeking to overthrow the state in some or all of its sovereign territory. But these rebellions have coexisted with systemic, violent contention in quotidian politics and society, among ethnic, linguistic, and religious groups and partisan factions. Hindu-Muslim violence in India represents only the most salient example within this wider array of violence within society. These two forms of violence, rebellions and riots, are present in different proportions in different parts of these three countries, giving rise to cross-national and subnational patterns of political violence. They represent qualitatively different relationships between violence and state sovereignty, relationships we will explore in this chapter.

While the study of conflict and political violence in South Asia is quite developed, its patterns across territory are understudied, for two reasons. First, assessing violence across states in South Asia is rarely, if ever, done. Research on conflict in India and in Pakistan are entirely distinct enterprises, even though both countries have the same (variation in) patterns and varieties of political violence.[1] This separateness of national research programs is understandable. Research on political violence and insurgent actors in Pakistan has been thoroughly implicated in the formulation of security policy by western countries, given the country's proximity to and ambivalent

---

[1] Political violence in Bangladesh, though significant, is not particularly salient for analysts of conflict in the region or cross-nationally.

involvement in the American state-building project in Afghanistan. Insurgencies in India are understood largely on their own terms, either as *sui generis* cases or as theoretical anomalies of long-term systemic conflict in a vibrant democracy. Yet the specificity of these disparate research agendas impedes comparative inquiry.

Second, even within countries, different forms of political violence in the region are rarely integrated into one framework. Different arenas of insurgent conflict are rarely studied comparatively, even though they occur within the same national boundaries and engage the same armies, police, and paramilitary forces.[2] Further, research on insurgent conflict is disassociated from enquiries into other forms of political violence, from ethnic riots to electoral clashes.[3] Much of this is the result of research falling between sub-disciplinary stools, with distinct theoretical preoccupations and methodological approaches making it difficult to study both riots and rebellions, as well as terrorism and other forms of social violence, in South Asian countries and beyond.

A focus on the historical roots of these forms of conflict, arising from territorial variations in the nature of state authority, might help to bridge these fissures. To be sure, some forms of political violence in South Asia have always been recognized as colonial legacies and the consequences of decolonization. The origins of the Kashmir conflict, both in terms of interstate competition between Pakistan and India and insurgency within India, can be traced back to the contentious integration of a princely state in the context of partition. Multiple insurgencies in Northeast India are likewise products of abrupt and uneven inclusion into the modern nation-state, among communities that had experienced traditions of colonial governance restraint. The dynamics of Pakistan's recent internal war with the Taliban in the Northwest arises in part from the disruption of "hybrid" governance arrangements fashioned under colonial rule and barely revised after decolonization.[4] Yet these are specific instances within a much broader array of insurgencies and social violence that, individually and together, may be explicable through the historically rooted variations in state power and relationships with society.

In this chapter, I demonstrate how the patchwork state framework can be deployed to explain patterns of violence embedded within the territorial politics of South Asian states. I do this by incorporating different forms of political violence, from riots to terrorism to armed rebellion, into a common conceptual lexicon. I then link local differences in state capacity and state–society relations arising from different governance arrangements with the prevalence of different forms of political violence in different places within national boundaries. The result applies patchwork states as a framework to help us explain the complex but explicable array of political conflict in South Asia today.

---

[2] Staniland (2012, 2021) is an exception to the rule.   [3] Naseemullah 2018.
[4] Baruah 2005; Naseemullah 2014; Guyot-Rechard 2016.

6.1 SOVEREIGNTY, THE STATE AND FORMS OF POLITICAL VIOLENCE

From Max Weber onward, violence and the state are inextricably tied to one another.[5] Charles Tilly's famous dictum – that "the state makes war, and war makes the state" – suggests the bellicose origins of the most powerful states of the world.[6] In addition to interstate conflict, the state's deployment of systematic and brutal *internal* violence to liquidate its rivals and challengers, through civil wars and campaigns against peasant resistance, was vitally important for European state formation. The totalizing ways in which the state used structural violence to flatten governance heterodoxy eventually led to the relative convergence in prosperity and political order among wealthy countries today.

Violence has not yielded the same outcomes in the developing world, however.[7] Borders between countries were drawn by colonial powers and fixed by international norms, and as a consequence, conflict has rarely led to expansion of territory or the establishment of new sovereign states.[8] As a result, we see many more bloody coups, rebellions, and intrastate conflict over the control of sovereign territory than wars of expansion and occupation. Unlike in the West, conflict has tended to weaken rather than strengthen state authority.

South Asian state structures, both before independence and after, were never coherent and powerful enough to unleash the level and form of violence that could bulldoze governance unevenness and liquidate rivals in the service of political order, and state-builders were chary about the benefits of such activities. To quote Lord Curzon in reference to disorder on the northwestern frontier: "No patchwork scheme – and all our present recent schemes ... are mere patchwork – will settle the Waziristan problem. Not until the military steamroller has passed over the country from end to end, will there be peace. But I do not want to be the person to start that machine."[9] In other words, the colonial state's structures were not built and deployed in a manner that would make it a coherent and effective instrument that monopolized the legitimate use of violence. Rather, its constrained capacities could only manage conflict, against rebels and among factions, throughout the period of colonial rule. Postcolonial states continue to have significant unevenness in the state's authority and an immense variety of different forms of violence across their territories.

The absence of any teleology by which, paraphrasing Tilly, the state deploys violence, and violence creates the state, leaves us with questions about the nature of the relationship between the two. There are several aspects to this ambiguity.

---

[5] Weber 1991[1919]. [6] Tilly 1975.
[7] See Cohen, Brown and Organski 1981; Jackson and Rosberg 1982.
[8] Herbst 2000; Philpott 2001; Centeno 2002. [9] Cited in Packer, 2008.

First, non-state actors perpetrate much of the violence in contemporary South Asia, with the state seemingly unable to uphold a monopoly of coercion. At the same time, civil war or state failure are simply not useful characterizations for insurgent violence in either Pakistan, India, or Bangladesh; violent challenges against the state in peripheries and hinterlands coexist with the presence of stable and durable state structures over most of the country.

Second, the government's coercive apparatus perpetrates violence itself, from brutal counterinsurgent operations to extrajudicial killings ("encounters") and the everyday subjugation of minority and subaltern communities. These brutal acts of violence do not conform to constitutional and democratic guidelines of the restrained use of force, in order to protect the rights of citizens. This in turn suggests that state actors are not exactly committed to upholding a legitimate political order over its sovereign territory, but can represent agents of violence with little legitimacy for many citizens.

Third, while patterns may exist among different forms of violence, as this chapter will explore in some detail, there is no overall trend toward either civic peace or state collapse in either India, Bangladesh, or Pakistan. All three countries exhibit a steady state of complex landscapes of violence. The sources of these landscapes reach back decades, but without a trajectory that might suggest the emergence of a straightforward causal relationship between violence and state power or capacity.

The lack of an easy tractability does not mean that we cannot usefully interrogate the relationship between state authority and forms of violence at the subnational level, however. We can usefully begin such an interrogation by focusing on the *purposes* of violent action, either by the state or (perhaps especially) by non-state actors. What are violent actors aiming to achieve by engaging in violence? What is the place of the special authority of the state in relation to the execution of this violence? By answering these questions with regard to different forms of violence, and their relative incidence in different places, we might understand more about their meaning and import for national and subnational politics. We can then locate their sources in the ways that the state was built and has persisted. In other words, the patchwork state concept can usefully explain different kinds, patterns, and incidences of violence.

A key first step in this exercise is to typologize violence in terms of its relationship to state authority. Building on previous work on this subject, I conceptually differentiate *sovereignty-contesting violence* (SCV) and *sovereignty-neutral violence* (SNV). Sovereignty-contesting violence is violence perpetrated by those who fundamentally challenge the legitimacy, authority and ultimately, the sovereignty or monopoly of the legitimate use of force of the state over some or all national territory; the violence perpetrated by state actors to interdict their rivals and thereby reclaim authority also falls within this category, as it represents the other side of the struggle over this authority. At its limit, this type represents the deep and endemic violence associated with civil wars. However, the more limited territorial insurgencies and rebellions, inspiring counterinsurgent activities, and terrorist campaigns that we regularly see in South Asia are instances of SCV, where the authority of the state is under serious contention only in particular areas.[10]

Sovereignty-neutral violence, by contrast, involves the violent activities of actors who take the state's authority as given, operate under its jurisdiction and even endeavor to maximize their influence over its rules and practices. They might even use violence strategically to gain or retain government power through elections, thereby controlling policy and public resources. In other words, this is violent contestation within society over controlling aspects of public authority, rather than contesting that authority. SNV includes ethnic riots, electoral clashes, violent protests, and might even involve assassinations of political opponents, or the coercive suppression of demonstrations by the police. Some significant violence in India is sovereignty-neutral because it represents the coercive actions of the upper-caste elites in demonstrating their domination against subaltern groups that might seek to challenge it, such as Muslims or Dalits, within established structures of state sovereignty. This violence implicates the local state – as with police brutality on behalf of dominant proprietary classes – but this does not contest the state's authority as much as remind us of its partiality. There are versions of this in Pakistan and Bangladesh. Violence by subaltern social actors – villagers *gherao*-ing or beating up a local official for malfeasance, protests that turn violent with police suppression – represents calling the state to account for its promises, rather than fundamentally challenging its authority.

Sovereignty-neutral violence is not normatively better nor necessarily any less serious or deadly than SCV to its victims. Rather, the distinction lies in the place and role of the state in this violence. For SCV, the state is a discrete actor, interlocutor, and antagonist. For SNV, the state is an arena of power and interests within which different actors – police, politicians, civil society activists – try to maximize their advantage through violent action.

To be sure, there are some instances of overlap and some gray areas. Take, for instance, the response of minority communities against pogroms and ethnic riots. Dawood Ibrahim's organized criminal network orchestrated a number of high-profile terrorist attacks in Mumbai in March 1993 in retaliation to the attacks on Muslims by Hindu mobs in the city following the destruction of the Babri Masjid. The responses of minority ethnic communities to attacks by majoritarian groups are rarely symmetric. Further, the contexts of insurgent violence mask local rivalries, criminal activities, and petty contentions

---

[10] Terrorism constitutes a special case. Dramatic terrorist attacks are clearly sovereignty-contesting. Yet terrorists seek locations of maximum salience to the state to perpetrate their most spectacular attacks, often from the locations in which violent geographies might have inspired those attacks. Thus members of the Provisional IRA traveled to London from Belfast to plant bombs in 1973. Radicalized residents of Kashmir, Punjab, and Khyber-Pakhtunkwa have likewise traveled to and perpetrated bombings and suicide attacks in Mumbai, Delhi, Islamabad, and Lahore.

over resources.[11] Moreover, riots or violent demonstrations in the context of regime collapse and violent state response can indeed end up fundamentally contesting sovereignty, as with protests against Bashar al-Assad's government in Syria in 2011 or the movement for Bengali nationalism in Pakistan before Bangladesh's independence in 1971, though these are rare events. While any one typology is not perfect, the difference between SCV and SNV – rebellions and riots, in other words – reflects real and important differences in forms of violence that are at once both prevalent in all three countries and rarely considered together.

6.2   VARIETIES OF POLITICAL VIOLENCE IN SOUTH ASIAN COUNTRIES

Since independence, South Asian countries have experienced various, multiple, complex, and sustained episodes of internal violence. Some of these cases were direct holdovers from the final years of colonial or princely rule, such as peasant insurgency in Telangana.[12] Others arose alongside decolonization as a consequence of the contentious and conflict-ridden nature of decolonization and partition – such as ethnic rebellion in Nagaland, revolts in Balochistan ethnic violence in Punjab and, of course, interstate conflict over Kashmir. Yet as India, Pakistan, and later Bangladesh established trajectories of postcolonial statehood, nationally distinct if internally complex patterns of violence have emerged that are rarely considered comparatively. In what follows, I will survey the landscape of violence in these countries, and how different scholars and analysts have characterized to different purposes, with particular attention to the prevalence of sovereignty-neutral and sovereignty-contesting forms of violence in all three countries.

6.2.1   India

Rebellions and forms of social violence separately arose through the processes of postcolonial politics in India. Much of the early scholarship on political order took the view that such violence was an inevitable consequence of the contentious process of development. Subsequently, the decay of key disciplinary institutions that could manage rising popular demands was seen as the main cause for rising disorder.[13] Thus the ample capacities of the Congress organization to manage language riots in the late 1950s and early 1960s were not present in the government's middling reactions to rising violent contention and insurgent violence in the 1980s.[14]

Over the past two decades, however, there have been few attempts to analyze various conflicts and broader forms of violence in India under a single political

---

[11] Kalyvas 2006.   [12] Kennedy and Purushotham 2012
[13] Huntington 1968; Gurr 1970; Kohli 1990; Brass 1997; Ganguly 1997.   [14] Kohli 1997.

framework, especially given the breadth and complexity of the country.[15] There is one persistent overarching puzzle, however: that of the presence of such sustained and systematic violence in a vibrant democracy. The very fact of democratic governance in India immediately bifurcates theoretical discussions of political violence, into rebellions and riots, however.[16]

Scholars drawn to domestic armed struggle investigate profound challenges to the democratic Indian state and its most basic constitutional settlements. Such work has followed four broad avenues of inquiry. The first follows ethnic grievances and horizontal inequalities within these frameworks that may inspire marginalized populations into rebel.[17] Applications to the Indian case include separatist rebellions in Punjab, Kashmir, and Assam and elsewhere in the Northeast that arose out of a latent sense of group-based inequity, combined with ethnic outbidding by political entrepreneurs and the failure or willful disruption of mechanisms of ethnic management in India's constitutional structure and democratic politics.[18] The second concerns feasibility, where a combination of geographical barriers, resources, and weak state presence might allow for the effective operation of insurgent actors.[19] Such subnational features explain the geographical variation in the intensity and durability of violence within insurgency-impacted regions, such as the Maoist "red belt."[20] The third explores the character and organizational make-up of insurgent groups themselves and how they engage with state actors.[21] Its focus on internal organization and external relationships highlights questions like the cohesiveness of a rebellion, its duration and its resolution, usefully contrasting the trajectories of the Khalistan insurgency to that of the Nagas for instance. Finally, the fourth line of inquiry has assessed the extent to which Indian democratic politics have impacted insurgent conflict and vice-versa.[22] This places the puzzle of rebellion in a consolidated federal democracy in the greatest relief. Yet all these engage with sovereignty-contesting violence, representing profound ruptures with the democratic state, and indeed, "states of exceptionalism" in which regular politics are thought to be suspended.[23]

There are many other scholars who are drawn to explaining riot-based violence which is implicated in an intimate, constant and dark relationship with aspects of India's vibrant traditions of democratic competition.[24]

---

[15] Exceptions include Naseemullah 2018; Staniland 2021.
[16] The most successful attempt to integrate these two forms thus far was by Varshney and his collaborators in the study of group violence in post-New Order Indonesia. See Varshney 2008
[17] Horowitz 1985; Stewart 2008; Cederman, Gleditsch and Buhaug 2013.
[18] Kohli 1997; Baruah 2005; Lacina 2009.
[19] Fearon and Laitin 2003; Collier, Hoeffler, and Rohner 2009.
[20] Gawande, Kapur and Satyanath 2017. See also Mukherjee 2021.
[21] See Staniland 2014a, 2021. See also Baruah 2005; Butt 2017.
[22] Ganguly 1999; Matanock and Staniland 2018; Chandra and Garcia-Ponce 2019.
[23] Agamben 2003.   [24] For a key definition of the term, see Horowitz 2001, 1.

Although there are many forms of riot-based social violence, academics have focused on Hindu-Muslim riots, many of which take the form of anti-Muslim pogroms. Such ethnic riots involve a complex, latent arrangement of violent actors and institutions, which can be activated by political entrepreneurs when required to achieve particular objectives.[25] Besides rioters themselves, the police are key actors. Police forces generally have ample capability to forestall or end riots with even modest application of coercive force. In other words, the persistence and lethality of riots occurs only with the government's tacit permission, suggesting the importance of the motivations of elected officials in enabling or suppressing riots.[26]

Social scientists have offered different explanations for the incidence of Hindu-Muslim riots in Indian cities, which are in turn implicated in different aspects of democratic practice: the presence (or absence) of interethnic civic associations that might prevent (or enable) the distrust at the heart of riot-based mobilization, or the electoral incentives of local politicians to polarize communities and those of state governments to allow riots to occur without impediment.[27] Recent scholarship has explored the roots of violence in material competition and incorporated riots into larger forms of social mediation.[28] In different ways, this form of sovereignty-neutral violence is deeply implicated in democratic competition.

Yet Hindu–Muslim riots have overshadowed other forms of social violence, even those that are ethnic in character, such as the anti-Sikh pogrom in Delhi in 1982, in which 2,500 were killed over four days.[29] The targeting of Christians by Hindu extremists in Orissa, or Muslims by Buddhist gangs in Ladakh, is rarely reported, let alone studied. Systemic violence against subaltern groups like Dalits is likewise deeply understudied.[30] These too have roots in the darker side of political competition.

Similarly, the focus on intergroup violence elides the fact that many riots target quotidian state actors, who often respond disproportionately. Much of the social violence in Kashmir occurs between "stone-pelters" and the police and paramilitaries; teenage rioters have no connection to insurgents, and yet the insurgency has yielded draconian security arrangements that have inspired violent demonstrations. In a radically different context, Patidars in Gujarat and Jats in Haryana have clashed violently with the police over their classification of "backwardness" in relation to India's policies of affirmative action.[31] Further, many incidences of riot-based social violence are explicitly electoral, with the supporters of rival political parties and associated organizations clashing with one another and with the police ahead of national and regional elections.[32]

[25] Brass 1997, 2003.   [26] Wilkinson 2009, 336.   [27] Varshney 2003; Wilkinson 2004.
[28] Berenschot 2009; Bohlken and Sargenti 2010; Mitra and Ray 2014.   [29] Das 1995.
[30] Narula 1999.   [31] Jaffrelot 2016.
[32] For overviews, see Staniland 2014b; Birch, Daxecker and Höglund 2020. I will discuss electoral violence in greater detail in the next chapter.

All of these forms of social violence occur without fundamentally questioning the authority of the state.[33] Indeed, many actors use violence instrumentally to capture state power or influence its policies, thereby implicitly affirming its importance and the use of democratic competition along with violent action to secure it. It may be that riots and forms of social violence represent a perverse but essential aspect of Indian democracy itself. This is quite distinct from armed rebellions, which seek to overthrow the democratic state as a whole.

This distinction complicates the search for integrated, historical causes of the landscape of violence in India. Institutional explanations, detailed in Chapter 2, suggest that both are rooted in the decline of political institutions like the Congress party, yet there is no evidence that either rebellions or social violence were absent even at the height of Congress' power. Indeed, the Naga insurgency began soon after independence, and Hindu-Muslim riots have occurred periodically since independence. Further, scholars have usefully traced the roots of particular forms of violence, from Hindu-Muslim violence in western India to Maoist rebellion in the East, back further, to particular institutions in the colonial period.[34] These enquiries have not been integrated into a single framework, which could explain why different kinds of colonial legacies might inspire some to take arms against the state while incentivizing others to compete (violently) for state power.

The object of this analysis is to bring the two forms of violence together into a such a framework. Both insurgent and social violence are implicated in the nature and characteristics of the Indian state and its relationship to society, as they vary across national territory, inviting us to investigate an uneven geography of violence with historical roots. Such a framework might usefully include Pakistan and Bangladesh as well, as the three countries common historical roots, though the focus of questions of violence in India's democracy and the hybrid regimes of the other countries have not encouraged such inclusion.

6.2.2 Pakistan

Pakistan, like India, is home to a broad array of different forms of violence, from armed rebellion to ethnic riots to violent protest. Due to Pakistan's status

---

[33] A deep, and deeply understudied, arena of social violence concerns sexual abuse and gendered violence. Spatial variation in gendered violence in India is extremely difficult to study, because much of it occurs out of view. When entire communities are involved, such as with extralegal clan gatherings called *khap panchayats* that deploy mobs to execute honor killings, or in dramatic incidents that spark demonstrations, like the 2012 sexual assault and killing of a woman in Munirka, South Delhi, these can shade into other forms of social violence. For more on the nature of gendered violence in India, see Sirnate 2013.

[34] Verghese 2016; Verghese and Teitelbaum 2019; Mukherjee 2021.

as an ambivalent frontline state in the US War on Terror, however, global and regional security policy has dominated research, due to the fears of instability in a nuclear-armed country, and the role of Pakistani state and non-state actors in spreading violence in neighboring countries.[35] Further, the Pakistani state itself is often shorthanded as the military, which is widely framed as the modal actor in the initiation and perpetuation of violence to support ideologies of revisionism.[36] The legacies of authoritarian rule, including the military's reserve domains in policy, tend to obscure the very real political competition within Pakistani society, which like in India, is quite violent in nature.

Events of the last two decades have focused attention on "Af-Pak," or battlefields and arenas of conflict contiguous with America's efforts in counterinsurgency in Afghanistan.[37] This emphasis on this region's systemic insurgent conflict is not misplaced. The Tehreek-e-Taliban Pakistan (TTP)'s rebellion in Pakistan's Northwest from the mid-2000s until the mid-2010s was deeply salient and very violent; even more than insurgent control of territory, it affected the lives of many ordinary Pakistanis through terrorist attacks in major cities. However, the TTP's rebellion has been militarily defeated, although aftershocks periodically occur.[38] Insurgent conflict has continued to rage in other parts of the country, however, including a separatist rebellion in Balochistan associated with maldistribution of mineral resources and increased Chinese investment in the region.[39] Sustained, systemic conflict in the city of Karachi from the 1990s, involving armed clashes between the Mohajir community of Urdu-speaking migrants from India at Partition and the Pakistani security state, has been characterized as insurgent by some analysts.[40]

Moreover, throughout the country, there is a wide array of forms of social violence where the aims of violence are less against the state itself, but rather target particular groups within the Pakistani population. Sectarian violence between Sunni and Shi'a groups has become distressingly commonplace throughout Pakistan, especially in southern Punjab, Sindh, and Balochistan; in Karachi, sectarian rivalries account for most targeted killings.[41] Terrorist attacks against the gatherings and places of worship of religious minorities have also been depressingly frequent. Other instances in the much broader category of social violence involve, in Pakistan just as much as in India, clashes between rival political parties ahead of elections, police violence against protestors, and the violent activities of contentious groups in civil society.

Increasingly, riots, targeted attacks, and other forms of social violence are becoming the dominant form of violence in contemporary Pakistan, as systemic insurgent violence has receded in most of the country beyond Baluchistan.

---

[35] Fair et al. 2010; Cohen 2011 are characteristic.
[36] Fair 2014; Paul 2014. For a review, see Tudor 2015.
[37] Johnson and Mason 2008; Fair and Jones 2009; Hussein 2010; Mir 2018.   [38] Nawaz 2019.
[39] Grare 2013.   [40] See Staniland 2010.   [41] Gayer 2014.

Yet these are imperfectly incorporated into extant explanatory approaches, given the ongoing legacies of policy preoccupation with Afghanistan, even after the establishment of the Taliban regime in 2021. Another source for the obscuring of social violence is that many analysts underestimate the intensity of democratic competition in the Pakistani polity, viewing it as a regime in which the military determines political outcomes. Sectarian violence, for instance, is often coded as the straightforward operation of religious extremism, but it is equally a struggle between different communities over resources, political power, and key policies.[42] Further, electoral violence is quite prevalent; if elections were entirely without meaning, why would political parties engage in conflict with one another?

Both the focus on security policy and the emphasis on the authoritarian legacies of Pakistan, as opposed to democratic India, have emphasized rebellion to the exclusion of violent forms of political competition. Further, due to recent (and quite ahistorical) characterizations of Pakistani political dynamics, there have been few attempts to situate forms of violence in legacies of colonial rule. This parallels India's concentration on postindependence institutions; neither of these traditions of national research study in an integrated fashion the origins of the state in the colonial period, however revised by postcolonial state-building.

6.2.3   Bangladesh

Even more than India and Pakistan, Bangladesh's varied political violence is not a central object of scholarly inquiry. More than either country, however, violence in Bangladesh has meaningful and legibly historical roots, wrapped up in the traumatic events of its birth. The liberation struggle against the Pakistani state in 1971 – with the Pakistani military conducting widespread civilian massacres and insurgents responding with guerrilla warfare – still influences the country's politics half a century later, and has drawn a deep cleavage in Bangladeshi society. This might suggest that to understand the nature and meaning of conflict in Bangladesh, we can look no farther back than this struggle. Yet the patterns of violence in Bangladesh echo some of those in India and Pakistan, suggesting that preexisting patterns of state authority, though much less uneven than either India or Pakistan, can be brought to bear on understanding the relationship between sovereignty, violence, and the state.

Bangladesh has experienced both insurgent and social violence. One territorial insurgency has occurred: a separatist conflict waged by tribal minorities in the erstwhile Chittagong Hill Tracts between 1977 and 1997 over land appropriation and the extension of state authority into these tribal-majority areas.[43] This conflict parallels the multiple, complex conflicts in India's northeast, in turn representing general dynamics of the intrusion of state power

---

[42] See Nasr 2000; White 2012.   [43] See Ahsan and Chakma 1989; Panday and Jamil 2008.

into highland communities with limited previous experience of incorporation.[44] Terrorism has also been prevalent. As in Pakistan, Islamist militant groups with roots in the Afghan mujahidin conflict of the 1980s, as well as more recent ISIS-inspired actors, have targeted foreigners, religious minorities, and self-professed atheist writers and activists in terrorist attacks.[45] These have occurred largely in Dhaka, as militant groups seek to strike the state and associated secular civil society in locations that are the most salient.

However, conflict among groups in Bangladeshi politics and society is widespread and common. Much significant violence has been waged between rival factions over capturing political power at the center and dominating civil society. Political violence has variously taken the form of waves of assassinations, coups, and countercoups in the 1970s and 1980s and the violent contention among parties and associated civil society organizations when Bangladesh's politics became more institutionalized from the 1990s. Intense electoral violence between the two major political parties has been a characteristic feature of Bangladeshi politics over the past decade, with ideological roots over the meaning of the independence struggle but also more quotidian dynamics.[46] Common patterns of different forms of violence in South Asia, despite Bangladesh's distinctiveness in relation to both India and Pakistan, suggest that we need common frameworks of explanation.

***

A key benefit of examining an array of different forms of violence through patchwork governance arrangements during colonial rule, and their subsequent revision by postcolonial governments, is the ability to transcend specific research agendas that have limited that might hinder comparative inquiry. Extant research into the colonial legacies associated with particular forms of violence in India, such as Maoist rebellion or Hindu-Muslim riots, cited earlier represents a promising start, but from the point of view of this book, these separate investigations represent putatively unconnected research islands in what I argue is a causal framework connected by historically situated variations in the state in different locations. Further, studies that focus on colonial legacies are dependent on logics of path dependence that occlude the very real, if partial, state-building projects of postcolonial governments and envelope complex dynamics of state–society engagement into a more unidimensional understanding of state capacity. If we can see South Asia, as a whole, as a historically informed, uneven landscape both in patterns of violence and forms of state authority, then investigations of the relationship between the two may represent a worthwhile endeavor. In the following sections, I deploy the analysis of data on violent events and postcolonial governance categories to undertake such an investigation.

---

[44] Scott 2009.   [45] See Ganguly 2006; Datta 2007; Khan 2017.
[46] For a recent exploration, see Akbar 2016.

6.3 EXPLAINING PATTERNS OF VIOLENCE

Sovereignty-contesting and sovereignty-neutral violence have specific repertoires of conflict that are helpful in coding instances of violence as belonging to one category or another. Guerrilla warfare and terrorism characterizes SCV: armed battles between rebels and security forces, targeted assassinations of government officials, remote bombings against government targets. SNV, by contrast, is largely characterized by riot-like engagements: mass encounters among social groups or with police forces, including protests, rallies, and marches that turn violent based on the government's response and brawling between political party cadres, as well as the more archetypical ethnic riots and pogroms. This could also include targeted violence against civilians, assassinations of the leaders of rival groups, or even acts of terrorism aimed at targets other than the state.

While there are certain violent incidents that require particular judgment as to the aims and objectives of violence, most incidents can be straightforwardly categorized because there is a strong elective affinity between the aims of violence and its methods. Those who attempt to fundamentally challenge the state would be identified and arrested quickly if they chose open rioting over guerrilla warfare. Those who aim to polarize voters through violence to capture state power in elections would be less successful in remote areas. Such a typology can encapsulate the *relative incidence* of different forms of violence across territory, and thus the patterns of violence in a given location. In this way, we may be able to investigate the patterns of violence in relation to state sovereignty, and thus the relationship between violence and the patchwork state.

As described in greater detail in Chapter 5, I have categorized districts in India, Pakistan, and Bangladesh as *metropolitan, modernizing, conservative,* and *exceptional* on the basis of the postcolonial revision of colonial governance arrangements. Different forms of state capacity and state–society relations, associated with these postcolonial governance categories, can shape variations in the prevalence of these two different forms of violence, and subsequent patterns, in contemporary South Asian states. Where the state's presence has been traditionally circumscribed, and where there is little interpenetration between state and society, we would expect violence to be more sovereignty-contesting in nature. This is especially the case when the state more recently has attempted to intervene in these territories, for extractive or strategic reasons, sparking resistance against the contravention of earlier governance restraint. Sovereignty-neutral violence may co-occur with SCV in these contexts as populations reject the ensuing subjugation by police and paramilitaries in the context of counterinsurgent operations.

Where there are higher levels of state presence and state–society interpenetration, we would expect violence to be more sovereignty-neutral. In these contexts, party activists and supporters clash ahead of elections, or ethnic entrepreneurs instigate riots or pogroms to polarize communities, or groups agitate violently for their rights or for changes in policy. Of course, SCV may also be present in these locations, in the form of terrorist attacks, because groups where possible strategically choose targets of greatest salience to the state.

These two types of political violence, and the associated differences in governance that explain their relative prevalence, are rarely considered together. This is due to the study of the politics of individual South Asian countries – Pakistan has long been associated with terrorism and insurgent violence, whereas Hindu-Muslim riots, anti-Muslim pogroms, and now lynchings are more salient in India[47] – as well as differing disciplinary agendas. In what follows, I seek to highlight the importance of both types in all three countries, and argue for the utility of the patchwork state framework in explaining their relative prevalence and resulting patterns across their political geographies. In so doing, this analysis aims to integrate into a common conceptual lexicon the insights of particular case research linking the legacies of colonial rule to communal riots on one hand and insurgencies on the other.[48]

6.3.1 Sources of Data

Sources for empirical data on political violence, which I will use to pursue this analysis, are inherently disputed and controversial. It must be emphasized that there is no clear, tractable, objective universe of political violence with which we might get accurate and unbiased sample; collections of data on political violence, whether reported by government officials, humanitarian actors, NGOs, or journalists, are as socially constructed as the phenomena of political violence itself. Yet my investigation here is principally focused on *patterns* of political violence at the district level, rather than seeking the most objective measures of the incidence of violence.

For analysis of this chapter, I principally use two conflict events databases: the Armed Conflict Location and Event Database (ACLED) and the Upsala Conflict Data Program's Georeferenced Events Database (Upsala).[49] Both databases aggregate publicly available information on conflict events, which are then georeferenced. Importantly, both ACLED and Upsala are cross-regional databases and thus have developed categories and processes that are not South Asia-specific. In addition, I make use of the Pakistan-specific Bueno de Mequita, Fair, Rais and Shapiro (BFRS) database on political violence from 1990 until 2013, based on articles from the *Dawn* newspaper.[50]

---

[47] Varshney 2017.

[48] Naseemullah 2014; Verghese 2016; Verghese and Teitelbaum 2019; Mukherjee 2021.

[49] On ACLED, see Raleigh et al. 2010. On Upsala, see Sundberg and Melander 2013.

[50] Bueno de Mesquita et al. 2015.

The two main datasets complement one another. The Upsala data span a wider timeframe. Its database reaches back to 1989, although I use data for South Asian countries starting in 2000 through 2019, because this subset incorporates information from the South Asia Terrorism Portal. ACLED's data, by contrast, reach back to 2010 for Pakistan and Bangladesh, and 2016 for India and continue in this sample to June 12, 2021, but based on a wider variety of national and regional newspapers and other sources, including NGO reports. The Upsala data are more focused on terrorism and insurgent violence; while there are data on Hindu-Muslim riots in India, for instance, they represent only a small fraction of the total. ACLED has data on many more incidents. For India, the ACLED dataset includes around 25,000 conflict events over five and a half years, whereas the Upsala data include less than 11,000 events over nineteen years. ACLED is also more agnostic with regard to types of conflict events and also includes dense qualitative descriptions associated with every conflict event, which assists with qualitative observations as well as aggregate patterns. I describe the classification of conflict events into SNV and SCV categories for these databases in Appendix B.

6.4 THE PATCHWORK STATE AND PATTERNS OF CONFLICT IN INDIA

There are serious challenges in analyzing patterns of violence in a continent-sized country with significant internal variation, from teeming metropolises to sparsely populated deserts, jungles, and mountains. Nevertheless, the characteristics of districts – their historical governance traditions and contemporary characteristics of violence – represent significant analytical leverage in how the state and its citizens engage with one another in different places, including through violence.

6.4.1 Aggregate Patterns

In order to analyze the relative patterns of insurgent-based and social violence across India's political geography, I begin with a district-level ratio of SCV to total violence in terms of both incidents and fatalities across India's districts, classified by governance category and based on the ACLED data (Figure 6.1).

Districts in the metropolitan category have the lowest proportion of sovereignty-challenging violence to total violence; exceptional districts have the highest proportion, with modernizing and conservative districts in the middle. This is largely in accordance with our theoretical expectations; districts with greater state presence and state–society interpenetration would see a greater proportion of violence that is neutral with regard to the state's sovereign authority, with groups acting to maximize material or political advantage rather than contesting state sovereignty.

Turning to the data on average district-level incidents and fatalities in the data, I measure both sovereignty-neutral and sovereignty-challenging violence,

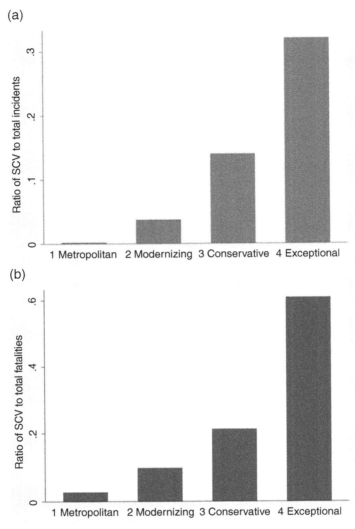

FIGURE 6.1 Sovereignty-challenging to total incidents and fatalities, Indian districts

as a proportion of log population by district, sorted by governance category, for the two datasets. Figure 6.2 presents the ACLED data.

With mean incidents of SCV, we observe a straightforward increase from a negligible level in the metropolitan category, slightly higher for modernizing and then for conservative categories, and then a sharp increase for exceptional districts. Mean incidents of SNV follow a skewed V-shaped pattern: we see SNV

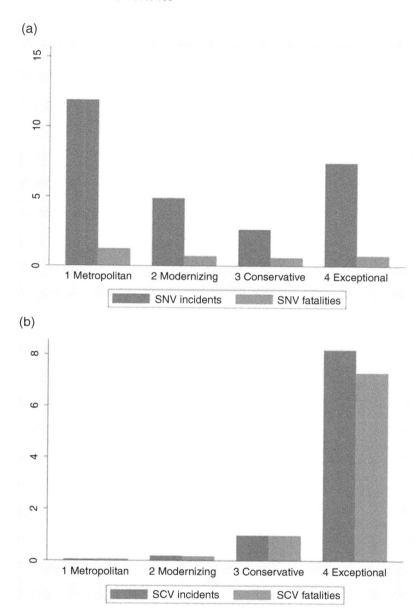

FIGURE 6.2 Mean ACLED incidents and fatalities per Indian district by log population

incidents at its highest point in the metropolitan category, falling with modernizing and then conservative districts, but then rising again for exceptional districts on average. The coercive presence of the state to enforce its writ and interdict rebels tends to lead to grievances among local populations, who might then engage in contentious and even violent social action in response. Kashmiri youth or tribal communities in Maoist-affected areas rioting against the police and paramilitaries are engaging in SNV, even while insurgent violence inspires paramilitary deployment in the first place. In other words, there is a feedback loop between insurgencies and social violence in response to the presence of counterinsurgents that are both endogenous to particular forms and legacies of exceptional governance.

Figures on mean fatalities must be treated with a certain degree of care. Certain forms of violent events, such as bombing a train station or a battle between soldiers and insurgents, are more deadly than others, like riots. The fatalities involved with any one type of event are subject to significant stochastic factors, however, such as timing – how quickly those injured can receive medical attention or how shielded paramilitaries were from an improvised explosive device. Nevertheless, patterns of fatalities generally follow those of incidence. It is worth noting that the vast majority of violence-related fatalities in the ACLED database are associated with SCV in areas under exceptional governance. This is both because much SNV is not as lethal, and because the types of clashes associated with significant fatalities, like armed battles or terrorist attacks on government facilities, tend to occur in districts in the exceptional category.

The Upsala data generally reflects the same patterns of that of ACLED, though because the dataset includes only 209 incidents of plausibly SNV, or about two percent of the total; it is mostly relevant for understanding the distribution of SCV across the different categories of governance (Figure 6.3).

Here we see a similar pattern of increases in the mean incidence of SCV from metropolitan to modernizing and conservative categories, and then a severalfold jump upward with the exceptional category. With fatalities, the relatively high score for the metropolitan category suggests the ways that SCV in urban areas, while rare, can be more deadly, taking the form of mass-casualty terrorist attacks.

The data on India presented here starkly reflect the ways in which different governance categories are associated with different patterns of violence. Violence in relation to sovereignty represents a meaningful typology here. The ways in which governance, state presence, and state–society relations vary through colonial state formation and postcolonial state-building can have a significant impact on the geographic dispersion on different forms of conflict. This suggests that the patchwork state is a useful way of integrating riots and rebellion into a single geography of violence.

6.4.2   Illustrating Sovereignty-Contesting and -Neutral Violence in India

Aggregate patterns tell us relatively little about the specific dynamics of different forms of violence and the different politics within which they are embedded.

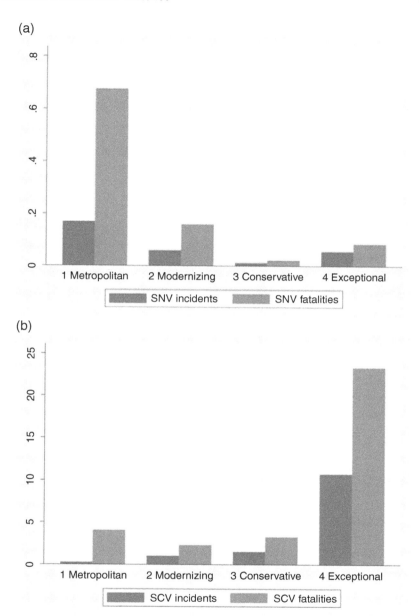

FIGURE 6.3 Mean Upsala incidents and fatalities per Indian district by log population

In order to shed some light on the politics behind violence, I will focus on some of the most deadly recent incidents in India, in both sovereignty-contesting and -neutral forms. As mentioned earlier, there is certainly a stochastic variability to how many fatalities are associated with any particular incident, but high-fatality incidents represent political violence at its most visceral and extreme, and thus can provide a useful entry point into the politics associated with violence.[51]

Turning first to SNV: a single clash between Swadheen Bharat Subhash Sena (SBSS) activists, who had been illegally occupying land, and the police in Mathura, far western Uttar Pradesh, in June 2016 led to the deaths of twenty-nine people, including a police superintendent. The SBSS and the broader Swadhin Bharat Vidhik Satyagrah, a movement with links to the religious leader Jai Gurudev, proclaimed revolutionary aims, such as abolishing British-inspired positions such as prime minister. But these groups were engaged in more everyday contention than insurrectionary violence. Indeed, they were marching on New Delhi to air various – quite strange – demands on the government, like abolition and replacement of the currency, when they stopped and set up a squatter settlement on government land in Mathura's Jawahar Bagh. This settlement persisted, remarkably, for two years with the full knowledge of the local government, until a court ordered its demolition, sparking the violence. While some elements of the Mathura encampment putatively contested state authority – the camp fashioned elements of self-government – commentators framed it as a cult and suggested that its charismatic leader, Ram Vrikesh Yadav, had family connections with powerful leaders of the then-ruling Samajwadi Party; this could explain the government's restraint while implicating the ensuing violence in the state's violent partisan politics.[52]

Other mass casualty events have more explicitly ethno-religious foundations. In August 2017, riots erupted throughout Haryana and Punjab following the conviction of the religious leader Gurmeet Ram Rahim Singh on charges of rape; police killed twenty-nine rioting members of his Dera Sacha Sauda (DSS) sect and injured over 200 in Panchkula, Chandigarh's sister city in Haryana. The DSS is a prominent religious organization in the complex and contentious politics of Sikh Punjab; it operates as a social welfare agency, but also wields enormous political influence, supporting first Congress and then the BJP, and has engaged in conflict with Sikh and Hindu militant groups. In February 2020, fifty-three people were killed in Hindu-Muslim clashes in Northeast Delhi, in response to protests against the CAA promulgated by the Modi government. Together, these incidents are among the most deadly in recent years in India; they all involve communal and sectarian violence, though two involve police attacks on armed activists. Delhi is of course a metropolitan district; Panchkula

---

[51] For these illustrations, I turn to ACLED, which maintains narrative accounts of violent incidents taken from media reports.

[52] A. Singh 2016.

and Mathura are in the modernizing category. In all three, there is serious and violent contention over the control of politics and policy in both explicit and subterranean ways, in regions where state and society exhibit significant interpenetration.

The most deadly incidents of SCV, by contrast, occur hundreds of miles and conceptual worlds away from the wealthy, populous though socially violent parts of northwestern India. In a well-known incident in February 2019, which sparked a tense confrontation between India and Pakistan, including aerial battles, a young militant from the Jaish-e-Muhammed insurgent group rammed a car filled with explosives into a Central Reserve Police Force (CRPF) convoy, killing forty paramilitary personnel in addition to the perpetrator. Pulwama district in Kashmir is the very embodiment of an exceptional district, in which the face of the state is as much that of the army and paramilitaries as the everyday bureaucracy.

Other deadly attacks are perhaps less salient, involving left-wing insurgency in the forested regions in central and eastern India. In April 2018, in the eastern Maharashtrian district of Gadchiroli – categorized as conservative – C-60 Commandos of the Maharashtra State Police and CRPF *jawans* engaged a Maoist force in battle, killing thirty-one rebels. A similar operation with the "Greyhounds" of the Andhra and Telangana State Police and the Odisha police "encountered" Maoists in Malkangiri district, also classified as conservative, leading to thirty-one casualties. In March 2020, Maoist armed cadres ambushed CRPF forces, killing seventeen and injuring fifteen, while twenty-three guerrillas also died in the battle; this occurred in the forests of Sukma District, which was newly formed from the Dakshin Bastar Dantewada district, classified as exceptional, at the epicenter of the insurgency in Chhattisgarh; a similar battle in the same district in April 2021 led to thirty-one deaths. All of these high fatality incidents involve the purposive or inadvertent engagement between government forces and militants or rebels in contexts where the everyday state is largely absent but the security state is present, actively seeking the destruction of insurgents, while rebels seek to attack and retreat in the face of this threat. This is possible only where state and society have significant distance, and where recent disruptions to governance restraint in the form of mineral reaction sparked the most recent era in the Maoist rebellion, from the mid-2000s.[53]

Thousands more incidents of both SCV and SNV are associated with deaths of rebels, security forces, rioters, police, and government officials. The vignettes of violence present here serve only to highlight how different the politics behind these forms of violence are. Further, different types are native to different political geographies, from towns, cities, and a prosperous countryside replete with contentious ethno-religious groups to the forested hinterland where insurgents and counterinsurgent forces clash.

---

[53] Shah 2010; Pandita 2011; Sundar 2016; Mukherjee 2021.

6.5 THE PATCHWORK STATE AND PATTERNS OF VIOLENCE IN PAKISTAN

Studying the geography of violence in Pakistan in comparison to India requires us to shift our conceptual frames. In part, this is because the two countries vary in both size and internal diversity. And of course, the two countries have quite different histories, regime dynamics, and state traditions that all impact the ways in which political violence can occur. As a result, we would naturally expect differences in the composition and aims of violent groups and the repertoires of violence in relation to India.

Yet these differences can be easily exaggerated. The structural composition of the coercive state in both Pakistan and India is very similar, as a result of barely revised common colonial structures in policing and paramilitary formations. As a result, non-state violent actors face similar state interlocutors. Violent repertoires like riots display common characteristics, while others are isomorphic as a result of necessity: insurgent guerrilla warfare anywhere has certain invariant features and tends to be conducted in forbidding physical geographies.

The big difference between Pakistan and India during the period of investigation is the decade-long TTP insurgency from the mid-2000s. Violent actors established territorial control of significant areas in the northwest of the country and executed terrorist attacks much further afield. Karachi also became the site of overlapping ethnic and sectarian conflicts as well as terrorist attacks, merging with the activities of the Taliban in an urban cauldron of violence. This urban conflict has twenty-year roots, making violence in the city qualitatively different from other cities in Pakistan, let alone India.[54] Yet by 2016, concerted action of the military and security services in denying territory to insurgent actors broke the rebellion, leaving Pakistan with more varied patterns of violence. These include the violent rioting of the Pakistan Tehreek-e-Lubbiak over blasphemy legislation, the ongoing ethnonationalist insurgency in Balochstan, and violent clashes among groups within Pakistani society.

6.5.1 Aggregate Patterns

As with India, I begin with the ratio of sovereignty-challenging to total violence using the ACLED data (Figure 6.4).

We see some differences with India, but a substantive similarity: exceptional districts reflect a much higher proportion of SCV in terms of incidents and fatalities. The higher proportion of SCV among districts in the modernizing category for incidents and modernizing and metropolitan districts relative to the conservative category for fatalities reflect dynamics of the insurgency; outside of the exceptional governance contexts of FATA, Balochistan, and

---

[54] Staniland 2012; Gayer 2014.

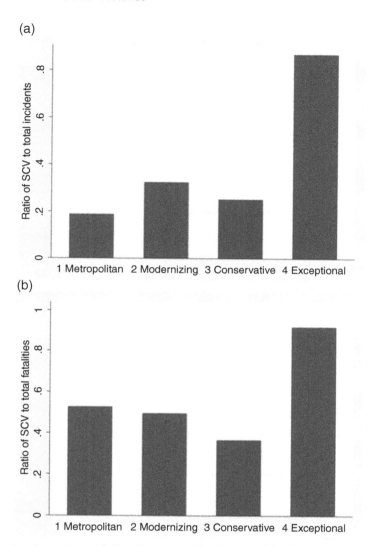

FIGURE 6.4 Sovereignty-challenging to total incidents and fatalities, Pakistani districts

Malakand division, insurgents and terrorists were likely to target relatively wealthier modernizing districts with deadly force.

To begin with a wider spectrum of violence in Pakistan, I start with the Upsala data, which measures average incidents and fatalities per district and covers the period from 2000 (Figure 6.5).

Sovereignty-contesting violence, which is the primary focus of the Upsala dataset, represents a bimodal distribution, with high incidence and fatalities in metropolitan and exceptional districts. The former is driven by Karachi, which

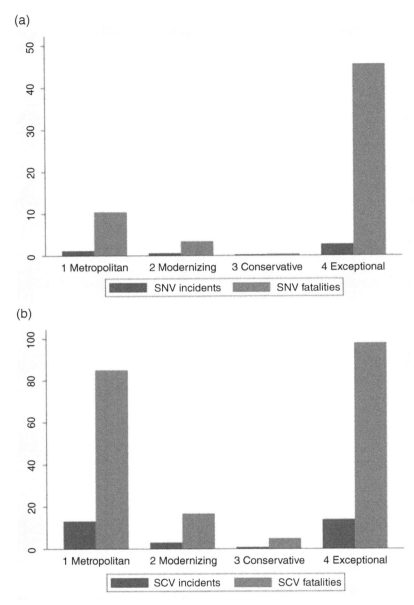

FIGURE 6.5 Mean Upsala incidents and fatalities per Pakistani district by log population

has since the 1990s been home to terrorism and attacks against the state, as well as sectarian violence. Sovereignty-neutral violence follows a V-shaped pattern, but with more incidents and fatalities in exceptional districts relative to metropolitan districts. Sectarian violence against religious minorities, such as the Shi'a community, has been commingled with insurgent violence in the 2000s, especially in Balochistan. Sectarian violence is, while certainly horrific, sovereignty-neutral because the Pakistani state is fundamentally unthreatened by violence between its various communities.

These patterns are largely echoed by the BFRS dataset, which follows the same pattern over an immediately previous time-period, between 1988 and 2001 (Figure 6.6). It represents violent incidents and fatalities as concentrated in metropolitan districts, which is not surprising as it includes the ethnic violence in Karachi in the 1990s as well as more recent insurgent and sectarian violence in the city.

Finally, the ACLED data on Pakistan covers much of the most intense periods of the insurgency in the 2010s, as well as counterinsurgent operations, in fine-grained detail. As such, it represents the ways in which the insurgency affected patterns of violence in the country. Figure 6.7 represents the ACLED dataset from 2010 until mid-2021.

ACLED's data show patterns that we can see elsewhere, but in even more extreme form, with SNV heavily concentrated in metropolitan districts – particularly Karachi – and a bimodal distribution in SCV between metropolitan and exceptional districts.

The most meaningful distinction between India and Pakistan, at least in the twenty-first century, is that violence that contests state power has penetrated urban areas in Pakistan. Terrorism and urban insurgent violence were a feature in India in the 1970s and 1980s, including in major cities like Kolkata and Delhi. Yet recent dynamics in India has meant that anti-state violence has occurred only in areas far from concentrations of state power. In Pakistan, by contrast, anti-state violence became entrenched in Karachi from the 1990s, while sectarian conflict between groups in society also emerged. In the 2000s with the rise of the Taliban insurgency, such violence impacted other areas of the country. This has led to a more existential reckoning of the state's capacity to uphold coercive monopolies at the heart of the country, with serious and self-enforcing consequences for perceptions of stability and investment.[55]

However, apart from relative concentrations of violence in metropolitan districts, other patterns are similar. As Figures 6.1 and 6.4 both show, exceptional districts in both countries are on average associated with a much higher proportion of sovereignty-challenging violence as a proportion of total violence. While it may be tempting to dismiss the exceptional governance category as straightforwardly endogenous to violence that contests the authority of the state, it is worth remembering that these categories were

---

[55] Naseemullah 2019.

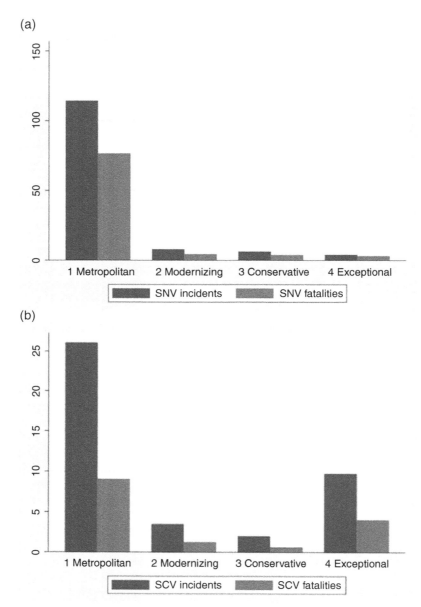

FIGURE 6.6 Mean BFRS incidents and fatalities per Pakistani district by log population

originally formed during colonial rule and revised based on data in the early
1970s in both countries, substantially before the eruption of contemporary
dynamics of insurgent violence. Most districts in the exceptional category,

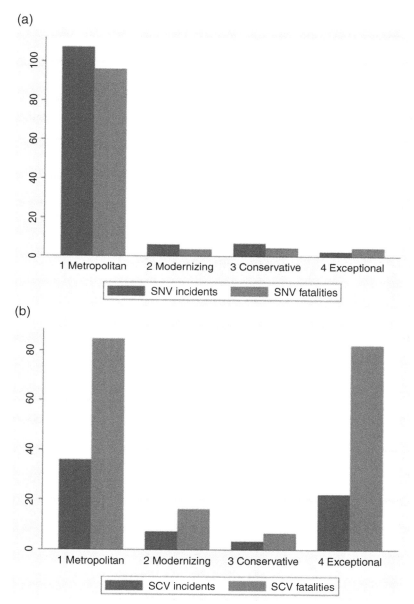

FIGURE 6.7 Mean ACLED incidents and fatalities per Pakistani district by log population

though governed in a heterodox fashion, were peaceful at the time of coding in the 1970s; it is not the case that conflict has continued monotonically from colonial rule to the present day. Subsequent state intervention has done much to disrupt state-society compacts based on governance restraint. Thus while the governance arrangements have roots in exceptional governance under colonial rule, these arrangements themselves are distinct causes rather than simply features of SCV.

6.5.2   Illustrating Sovereignty-Contesting and -Neutral Violence in Pakistan

In order to provide some analytical distance from the insurgency, I will explore high-fatality incidents from 2016, well after the apogee of the TTP's rebellion, beginning with SCV. Between July and August 2017, in the course of operations to destroy the remnants of the TTP in FATA, the army engaged militants in battle in the valleys of Khyber Agency, killing fifty-two militants while two soldiers died. But the decline of the TTP in the face of sustained military operations allowed other militant organizations to establish themselves. In July 2018, in the run-up to national and provincial elections, a suicide bomber from the Islamic State (IS) killed 150 attendees of a rally for a Balochistan Awami Party (BAP) candidate for the provincial assembly in Mastung District, Balochistan. IS has had a relatively marginal presence in South Asia, and dramatic attacks represented opportunities to establish a deadly reputation; along with other groups like Jamaat ul Ahrar, it has perpetrated attacks on other "soft" targets rather than engaging with the security state itself. In February 2017, in Jamshoro District in Sindh, a conservative district, seventy-two were killed and 270 injured in the Lal Shahbaz Qalandar shrine, a noted Sufi place of worship, by an Islamic State suicide bomber. Attacks such as these represent the dark ambiguity between SCV and SNV; the Islamic State clearly aims to contest the state through terror attacks, but its targets reflect the difficulty of striking at a resurgent security apparatus.

More recently, Balochistan – characterized by exceptional arrangements arising from both the Sandeman system of tribal governance and Kalat state before Partition – continues to be the site of significant SCV, even as conflict in the erstwhile-FATA has decreased. Baloch militants follow an ethnic separatist agenda and use guerrilla rather than terrorist tactics. In Dera Bugti District in February 2020, members of the Baloch Liberation Tigers attacked Army personnel, leaving fifteen dead. In May 2021, Baloch Liberation Army cadres opened fire on a Frontier Constabulary post in Bolan District, killing eleven *jawans* and injuring seven. And in October 2020, militants from a third group, Baloch Raaji Aajoi Sanghar, attacked a security convoy accompanying Oil and Gas Development Corporation personnel, killing fifteen. In many ways, the violence in Balochistan in Pakistan and in Chhattisgarh in India echo one another in their common relation to rebellion against the inequities of mineral extraction; I will explore this further in chapter 8. Even after the end of the territorial insurgency in the northwest, sovereign-challenging violence has continued to occur in districts in the exceptional category.

Sovereignty-neutral violence is less salient in Pakistan, yet it is quite prevalent. In July 2017, sixteen people died in a violent clash between rival factions in the Jatoi ethnic community in District Shikarpur, Sindh. Similarly, in June 2019, armed members of two communities clashed over a land dispute in Multan District, leaving ten. In May 2021 in Kashmore District, Sindh, members of the Sabzoi and Jagirani tribal communities, backed by a member of the Sindh Provincial Assembly, attacked the Chachar community and allied activists from the Jamaat Ulema-e-Islam (JUI) party with automatic weapons over a livestock dispute, leaving ten dead; members of political parties are not alien to such disputes. These types of clashes are between organized groups over resources and are more likely to occur in conservative districts like Shikarpur or Kashmore and even modernizing ones, like Multan, than in exceptional districts. Moreover, it is possible that mass-fatality incidents are more likely in conservative districts, or remote locations in modernizing districts, because the police are unlikely to be present to limit the violence, turning disagreements into battles.

The state can be a protagonist in SNV as well, and in unlikely locations. In May 2019, fourteen died in a riot; this clash between security forces and members of the ethnonationalist and human rights-oriented Pashtun Tahafuz Movement (PTM) occurred when a procession in Miranshah, North Waziristan, led by two members of parliament and calling for the advancement of human rights, was stopped by the Army at a checkpoint. The PTM, founded only in 2014, engages in contention and protest but not armed conflict; it is committed not to overthrowing the state, but rather to reforming it, calling for among other things a truth and reconciliation commission on extrajudicial killings by the security forces.

Concentrating on high-fatality incidents overshadows the perhaps less fatal but much more common and dispersed violence among sectarian groups with targeted killings, clashes between partisan cadres, and manifold other sources of violence within Pakistani society. A couple of these events illustrate these dynamics. In June 2016, two years before national elections, four were killed and seven injured in armed clashes between PTI and ANP partisan activists in Mardan, a modernizing district in Kyber Pakhtunkhwa (KP), suggesting that partisan violence can occur even outside the context of an election campaign. In April 2021, the agitations of the Tehreek-e-Labbaik Pakistan (TLP), a far-right Barelvi political organization, turned violent, with a police officer beaten to death by a mob and eleven taken hostage in Lahore; the TLP claimed that twelve of their activists were "martyred" at the hands of police and paramilitaries. The TLP represents the face of social violence in Pakistan; while it targets the police and politicians in its violent agitations, its aims are not challenging the state but forcing (often unpalatable) changes in government policy, such as the expulsion of the French ambassador over blasphemous cartoons or forcing the government to rescind the appointment of an eminently qualified economic advisor from the Ahmedi community. There is thus an important distinction, along with differences in the geography of conflict, between violence that systematically targets the state and violence that occurs between groups or arises from protest and repression. In this way, even though the specific dynamics of India and Pakistan are quite different, they fit within the same conceptual framework.

6.6 VIOLENCE IN BANGLADESH

Bangladesh has a distinctly different profile of violence from both India and Pakistan. There is much less geographic variation than in either country, which largely precludes the kind of "insurgent feasibility" afforded to rebels elsewhere. As a result, patterns of violence tend to be more national rather than regionally specific in character. The substance of violent conflict has also been waged along a single set of national cleavages, along a dimension of secular Bengali nationalism versus Islamism.

This violence has two forms. First, terrorist groups in Bangladesh, including returning mujahidin in the late 1980s and more recently Islamic State affiliates, challenge the secularism of Bangladeshi politics and society and target the government and minority populations with horrific violence. Second, the increasingly violent political competition between the Awami League and the Bangladesh Nationalist Party (BNP) represent two poles of representation on either side of this cleavage. These are implicated in conflicts among broader coalitions involving elite business and civil society. This is quite unlike the fragmented regional political competition that characterizes quotidian violence in both India and Pakistan.

Moreover, the politics of trauma associated with the 1971 Liberation War underline these cleavages, defining electoral and contentious politics as well as political violence. The mass Shahbag protests in central Dhaka in 2013 represented a defining point in recent Bangladeshi politics. This movement called for the execution of Abdul Qadeer Mollah, a member of the Jamaat-e-Islami (JI) convicted in 2013 of atrocities against civilians during 1971, as well as for the banning of the Jamaat from national politics.[56] The protests pushed the ruling Awami League to further prosecute war crimes and were met with counter-demonstrations by the JI and its alliance party, the BNP, leading to clashes with police in which thirty-five were killed and hundreds wounded.

Thus the nationalist-Islamist divide represents a durable cleavage along which Bangladeshi politics and political violence are organized. It suggests

---

[56] Roy 2018; Zaman 2018.

a much more spatially even array of violence, concentrating on Dhaka as the seat of power in a unitary polity, and otherwise unexceptional geographies of violence in the countryside. The one exception to this is the legacies of separatism and continuing suspicion of the state in the tribal-majority Chittagong Hill Tracts. These represent only a small fraction of territory and population and lack the salience of ongoing conflict since peace accords were signed in 1997.

6.6.1 Aggregate Patterns

As with India and Pakistan, I examine forms of violence in districts classified under different governance arrangements. These are a less enlightening than in Pakistan and India, because the vast majority of districts (sixty out of sixty-five) are "modernizing," due to the circumstances of partition and independence that were discussed in the last two chapters. The conservative category is not a feature of Bangladesh, as two partitions and subsequent decades of contentious and competitive politics swept away colonial-era conservative governance arrangements. Only three districts in the Chittagong Hill Tracts – Banderban, Khagrachhari, and Rangamati – are classified as exceptional, and Chittagong and Dhaka are classified as metropolitan. Nonetheless, there are interesting distinctions to be made between urban areas and the hinterland, and between hinterland and peripheries, in a context of an aggressively centripetal polity.

First, I examine the proportion of SCV to total violence, by incidents and fatalities, in different categories (Figure 6.8).

There are some differences among the categories. Metropolitan districts see a lower proportion of incidents, but a higher proportion of fatalities; this makes sense because this form of violence, in the form of terrorist attacks in major cities, is more likely to be deadly. We would also expect exceptional districts to exhibit a higher proportion of this form of violence, but the few remaining insurgent actors are also less likely to be effective in the perpetration of violence against the state, leading to lower casualties. The modernizing agrarian hinterland, constituting most of the country, lies between metropolitan and exceptional districts.

Turning to the actual patterns of violence across territories, Figure 6.9 presents average, district-level incidents and fatalities per log population for the ACLED data from 2010 to mid-2021.[57]

Here we see that metropolitan districts represent much higher SNV and SCV. This is unsurprising, given the centralizing nature of the conflict.

---

[57] The Upsala dataset, while covering a wider time span, is especially shallow for Bangladesh, representing only 382 incidents over more than nineteen years, as opposed to more than 13,500 incidents between 2010 and mid-2021 for ACLED.

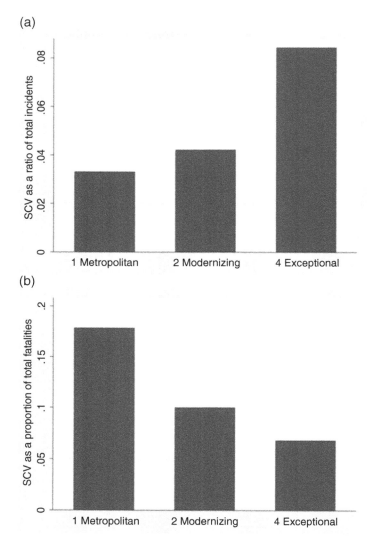

FIGURE 6.8 Sovereignty-challenging to total incidents and fatalities, Bangladeshi districts

Violent partisan competition, targeted killings of political opponents, and ethnic and sectarian violence are all likely to occur close to concentrations of elite political, economic, and social power. Terrorists also target such concentrations in order to maximize their impact.

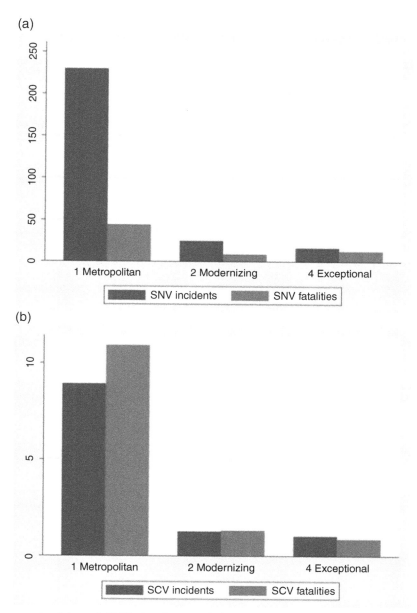

FIGURE 6.9 Mean ACLED incidents and fatalities per Bangladeshi district by log population

6.6.2 Illustrating Sovereignty-Challenging and Sovereignty-Neutral Violence in Bangladesh

To see what these forms of violence mean in practice, it is worth examining some of the high-casualty incidents of each type, as I have done for India and Pakistan. Turning to sovereignty-challenging violence first, Bangladesh's most horrific terrorist attack occurred in the last five years. Five militants with guns, knives, and machetes entered an artisanal bakery in the upscale Gulshan neighborhood of Dhaka in June 2016, taking several dozen hostages – many of them foreign citizens – captive. Twenty-nine people died in the initial attack and counterassault by police and then paramilitary forces; IS claimed responsibility for the attack, but Bangladesh's Home Minister stated that Jamaat ul-Mujahiddin Bangladesh (JMB), a domestic extremist organization, was responsible. Regardless, it reflected a radical assault on the Bangladeshi state and its ability to maintain a monopoly of violence, including the protection of foreign nationals.

The state is sometimes the perpetrator of violence against these groups in order to reclaim authority; in October 2016, members of the Rapid Action Battalion (RAB), a key paramilitary force, killed nine members of the JMB in shootouts in Gazipur, an industrial city 25 kilometers north of Dhaka. Sovereignty-challenging violence also occurs away from Dhaka, in ways that are reminiscent of dynamics in India; in October 2020, the military killed two cadres of the United People's Democratic Front, a political organization demanding greater autonomy for the Chittagong Hill Tracts, in the exceptional Rangamati district. This suggests ongoing violence over the role of the state in this exceptional geography, in which the military rather than the police were involved.

Turning to SNV, electoral clashes are an indelible feature of Bangladesh's politics. Among many other instances, in November 2017, five people were killed in a clash between Awami League and BNP activists over disputed land in Kishoreganj District; partisan clashes can arise from material grievances in addition to electoral mobilization. Social violence involving the police can occur as well; in Chittagong in April 2021, police fired upon power-plant workers demanding a reduction of hours and the payment of wages during Ramadan, killing seven. In the modernizing (and urbanizing) Brahmanbaria District in March 2021, madrassa students and Hefazat-e-Islam activists demonstrated violently against the visit of the Indian prime minister, blockading roads and vandalizing a Hindu temple; in response, the police killed ten over the course of two days of rioting. In many ways, this reflects the Islamist activism of the TLP in Pakistan, but with the police less willing to show restraint. Thus, while some of the broader dynamics of violence in Bangladesh reflect those in India and Pakistan, the particular political context differs significantly.

***

More generally, Bangladesh represents a qualitatively different geography of violence than either India or Pakistan. This has meant that Bangladeshi politics are largely national in character, and so are not subject to varying spatial patterns arising from the patchwork state. It also means that much of the violence in Bangladesh occurs over the nature of the state in ideological terms, in ways that are not as evident in either Pakistan or India.[58] Bangladesh's political and social cleavages and the violence that emanates from them are convergent. Further, they are incorporated into a relatively homogenous, if winner takes all, elite politics and political economy of rent distribution, as well as existential contestation over the meaning of the nation and the state.

This in turn suggests that the distinction between sovereignty-challenging and SNV may not be as useful a typology in Bangladesh as other countries in South Asia. In both Pakistan and India, the state itself can be relatively callous regarding who gets included and excluded from the body politic, as Shi'a and Ahmedi citizens in Pakistan and, increasingly, Muslim citizens in India can readily testify. As a result, violent contestation among groups or pogroms against minorities can coexist with the persistence of the state as a legitimate governance organization. In this context, Sunni extremist attacks on Shi'a communities or anti-Muslim pogroms by Hindu extremists can coexist with the presence the state as a central, if problemmatic, fact of political life. This ambivalence allows for horrific acts of violence to occur without fundamentally challenging political order; such SCV occurs in the exceptional circumstances of organized rebellion or systematic terrorist campaigns, where groups fundamentally want to transform or replace the state in some or all of the territory.

In Bangladesh, by contrast, the meaning and purpose of the state is inextricably bound up with dueling ideas of the nation. It was founded, after a bloody liberation war and mass civilian violence by the Pakistani army and collaborators, on the proposition that Bengali language and culture was the unifying, driving idea of Bangladesh. After the assassination of Sheikh Mujib ur-Rahman and the rise of Zia ur-Rahman, that vision was challenged by an alternative of Islam as a unifying force. Depending on how one understands the substantive meaning of the Bangladeshi state – a meaning that is essentially contested – particular kinds of violence, like the assassinations of atheist bloggers in Dhaka in the years after the Shahbag protests, might contest the state's essential elements in Bangladesh, at least for many, in ways that it might not in India or Pakistan. However, this difference itself is the product of differences between patchwork states in India and especially Pakistan, and a state with a much more even political geography, as in Bangladesh.

---

[58] For more of the ideology of the state, see Staniland 2021.

6.7   THE LIMITATIONS OF THE PATCHWORK STATE
      AS AN EXPLANATION FOR VIOLENCE

While I would argue that the patchwork state framework represents an worthwhile contribution to understanding the patterns and forms of violence in South Asia, it cannot be seen as a totalizing, necessary or sufficient one. For a start, the patterns in the data represent snapshots, with varying exposures, of the landscapes of violence in the twenty-first century. This was a time in which Pakistan was engaged in the rise and fall of a territorial insurgency, closely associated with conflict in Afghanistan, and the rise of the new conservative populist politics of Imran Khan's PTI, which inspired new forms of contention. India, meanwhile, saw the broad resolution of the Naga rebellion, even though Maoist insurgency and violence in Kashmir has continued, as well as civic contention, social violence and ethnic conflict surrounding the policies of Narendra Modi's BJP. Bangladesh has seen various forms of contention alongside the consolidation of de facto one-party rule under the Awami League, on which more in Chapter 7. The patchwork states framework and associated governance categories thus can elucidate key aspects of the geographical patterns of contemporary violence, but it is not clear whether the framework would be as useful if one reaches farther back in time.

If we took a snapshot of South Asia at various points in the 1980s and 1990s, for instance, we would see aspects of political violence, especially in India, that would seem to contradict the theoretical framework. Two of the bloodiest rebellions in recent memory, the Khalistan insurgency and that of ULFA, were raging in the wealthy modernizing districts of Punjab and Assam, respectively; Kashmir, though exceptional, was largely peaceful before 1987. Further, between the destruction of the Babri Masjid in 1992 and the Gujarat pogrom of 2002, waves of Hindu-Muslim violence occurred in cities and towns all over India, without much regard to historical patterns of state capacity and state–society relations. For much of the 1980s, Pakistan was peaceful, if repressively ruled under martial law, and Bangladesh was characterized by the spasmodic violence of coups and assassinations among military and civilian elites over the control of the state. How might we account for this?

For a start, Occam's razor explanations for rebellions – ethnic groups in contention over inequities and grievances, and the manipulation of these grievances by governments to gain, retain, and consolidate power – are powerful and evident in the politics of Congress decline and the fragmentation of the party system.[59] These dynamics go a long way to explaining national or regional eruptions, both in terms of Khalistan or ethnic violence inspired by assertive Hindu nationalism. Such movement-based violence does not have nuanced spatial specificity, certainly at the level of the district. Yet underneath titanic waves of violence associated with the

---

[59] For a classic treatment, see Horowitz 1985. See also Kohli 1990.

fragmentation of national politics and regional mobilization during this period were more quotidian characteristics of how citizens relate to the state, and vice versa; these more specific political geographies shape landscapes of everyday conflict and competition in ways that that are complementary to but distinct from the major waves of political violence. To put it another way, while massive eruptions of violence are associated with particular national and regional politics, attention to the nature, purposes, and relationships surrounding state authority represents an important background dimension of the politics of competition and conflict.

There is another serious limitation to the framework: its fidelity to historical legacies rooted in postcolonial revisions to colonial state-building, measured by data from the early 1970s, ignores subsequent transformations in state–society relations. Karachi is a case in point. It is classified as metropolitan based on its status as Pakistan's capital for more than a decade after independence, the migration of Indian Muslims after Partition and its rapid urbanization. In the 1970s, even with Bhutto's disruptive populism, it was a prosperous if increasingly contentious metropolis. Mass violent conflict with insurgent characteristics between Muhajir activists and the security state in the 1990s, nearly forty years after Partition, has given the city exceptional features, in the presence and pervasive influence of paramilitaries and the security state. This de facto metropolitan-exceptional hybridity may explain some of the differences in the patterns between India and Pakistan, but cannot be easily incorporated into the patchwork state framework while maintaining fidelity to systems of classification.

This, in turn, reminds us to be quite cautious about path dependence in assessing the historical roots of contemporary conflict. Even while exceptional governance arrangements in eastern and central India or western and northwestern Pakistan were present during the colonial period in the light footprint of the state and the subcontracting of governance relationships, the concrete causes of conflict now are due to an entirely different form of exceptionalism: that of the penetration of the security state and the abrogation of governance restraint. Thus, while unevenness of governance in the colonial period might mean different forms of violence today, these are only explicable by actually tracing the historical processes that link institutional origins to outcomes.

6.8 CONCLUSION

A definitional feature of *political* violence is that it is a contest over the distribution of material and symbolic resources, either over the very authority of the state or within its jurisdiction. Such contestation allows for broad comparability, yet researchers are naturally drawn toward inductive explanations of the particular forms of violence they study. Those researching Hindu-Muslim riots in India have limited engagement with those seeking explanations for the spatial distribution of insurgent conflict in the Northeast or Kashmir, let alone that of the Taliban insurgency in neighboring Pakistan or partisan clashes in Bangladesh. In many ways, this is as it should be; in the study of violence more than many other subjects, we are drawn to our objects of study because of their specific theoretical and empirical meaning and import, rather than as the epidemiological distribution within a population, as if violence were a type of virus. But not considering different forms of violence within the same national territories means that we might miss more systematic patterns of conflict across these territories, and thus the historical causes behind these patterns associated with state capacity and state-society relations.

Patchwork states in India and Pakistan, and a state with more even political geography like Bangladesh, are products of the formation of colonial state institutions and subsequent revision by postcolonial governments, determining distinct sets of state–society relations and state capacities across their national territories. These sets of relationships, in turn, have an impact in shaping what people fight over in different places, within national states. This can provide some insights on how the different faces of the state in different places can impact patterns of violent conflict, in ways that attention to particular kinds of conflict or national-level characterizations of state weakness or failure might not.

7

Patchwork States and Patronage

Explaining Electoral Competition

Chapter 6 introduced the idea of social violence over the control of the state as an important aspect of political competition in contexts where the state is capacious and its relationships with society are interpenetrative. Political competition also crucially involves more peaceful and quotidian actions like casting ballots for favored candidates in elections, not just in India but also Pakistan and Bangladesh. If we see these acts, along with violence, as parts of a broader politics of conflict and competition, then we might want to see how institutional unevenness across national territory impacts the meaning of the vote and its consequences of electoral competition in addition to patterns of violence. Such an inquiry, in combination with the analysis in Chapter 6, can also add another dimension to an emergent research program on the interaction between elections and different forms of political violence, from riots to insurgencies.

The patchwork state provides a new perspective on the defining explanatory framework for how Indians vote and why: clientelism. This holds that citizens vote for candidates and parties to maximize the receipt of key discretionary goods, and that parties mobilize constituencies through promising the provision of these goods. While some recent studies have questioned or qualified the ways in which the provision of goods and services impact electoral outcomes, it still represents the most popular explanation for outcomes in a polity with weak parties, endemic poverty and inequality, neo-patrimonial structures and intense electoral competition. Further, there is little reason to think clientelist theories would not be applicable to Pakistan and Bangladesh, despite differences in regime type.

This framework relies on a crucial assumption, however: that quotidian bureaucrats have the resources and capabilities to deliver goods and services on behalf of politicians. This in turn suggests significant levels of state capacity and close, interpenetrative relationships between state and social actors within a context of intense political competition. There are indeed locations across

India, and South Asia more broadly, where this approximates reality on the ground, especially in major cities and their wealthy hinterlands. These are places where parties compete intensely over control of a local state with ample capacities and resources, where active populations expect to receive welfare and other goods, and where brokers, capitalist clients, and social entrepreneurs engage with one another and with politicians to maximize their material advantages.

However, as we have seen, there are many other locations across the territories of South Asian countries in which state capacity is weak and state and society maintains a suspicious distance from one another. Traditional authorities may de facto or *de jure* take the place of the administrative state in providing political order and distributing patronage. In other contexts, the capture of the local state by a coherent dominant elite means that this elite controls the flow of resources, and may even dominate elections. In some other locations, the true avatars of the state might not be local bureaucrats but rather paramilitaries deployed by the security state. The various instances of circumscribed capacity and strained state–society relations complicate settled theoretical relationships among voting in elections and the distribution of patronage resources.

We can see these differences in the differing nature of political competition. There is significant, if largely unexplored, variation in the geographic patterns of electoral competition across both India and Pakistan, within an overall context of fragmentation and intense contests among parties seeking power at national and regional levels. This variation is evident at the constituency level. In some constituencies in both countries, two or three candidates compete credibly for the vote, following expectations from developed democracies. In others, one candidate garners most of the votes, and in yet others, several contenders split the vote, with an overall victor elected with a small plurality. Such variation challenges one of the most cherished regularities in political science, Duverger's Law, which holds that two parties should be in contention at the constituency level due to single-member simple plurality electoral rules.[1]

The patchwork state framework can play a role in explaining these dynamics in India and Pakistan, while also engaging Bangladesh's more recent and dramatic convergence toward one party rule. I argue that spatial differences in state capacity and state–society relations can determine the provision of patronage – by whom, in what ways and to what ends – in a manner that might shape how constituents might see their vote and act upon it. In dense, interpenetrative contexts in which the patronage state is capacious, we would expect a significant proportion of voters acting on the credible expectation of receipt of goods, and thus acting strategically to maximize their chances by voting for the parties most likely to win, consolidating competition toward two or three parties.

---

[1] Duverger 1954.

In contexts where elected officials do not or cannot determine the flow of resources or the direction of government policy through the normal bureaucratic apparatus, a range of other outcomes are possible. Where patronage is channeled through *de jure* or de facto traditional authorities, we might see a fragmentation of the vote, as convergent mechanisms are weak, contenders can win through the support of a small plurality and politicians might seek the perks of elected office itself and could reward their constituents sufficiently through these local funds. In cases of state capture by a coherent set of dominant elites or a party machine, we might see one-party rule. In instances where the coercive state occupies society, various dynamics of polarization or cooptation might be evident.

In some of these contexts, particular forms of authoritarianism characterize the relationship between state and society, but of different kinds with different consequences. Bangladesh has a national party system that represents an extreme instance of this, with vigorous and indeed deadly political competition over patronage resources between two polarized parties giving way to single-party hegemony, and the strategic use of violence to defend that hegemony and the associated rents and patronage resources. In India and Pakistan, however, the unevenness of state authority across national territories has yielded a variety of different electoral expressions of relationships with the state, both across states and provinces and within them. This in turn has significant consequences for the emerging intellectual agenda of electoral violence.

7.1 REGIMES, CLIENTELISM, AND PARTY COMPETITION IN SOUTH ASIA

Quotidian political competition among South Asian countries is a fraught and unsettled enterprise, one that is not as distant from political violence as one might wish. In addition, regime type has been a highly salient concern; democracy itself has certainly been uneven across the region. Some scholars have sought to explain the divergent trajectories of India's consolidated democracy on one hand and Pakistan's (and Bangladesh's) hybrid regimes, with significant authoritarian legacies, on the other.[2] Others have remarked on the puzzle of the stability and vibrancy of Indian democracy, given the absence of features normally associated with the rise of democratic institutions, such as cleavages arising from industrialization and supportive associational structures.[3] The emphasis on Indian democratic exceptionalism, going back to partition-era origins and subsequent path dependence, has elided a more recent convergence in the politics of the three countries, which includes both the institutionalization of party competition in Pakistan and the erosion of

[2] Jalal 1995; Oldenburg 2010; Tudor 2013; Wilkinson 2015.
[3] Varshney 1998b; Chhibber 1999.

democratic governance under Narendra Modi, suggesting that South Asian countries together represent increasingly comparable cases for the study of electoral politics.

Among analysts of Indian politics, however, the balance of inquiry has shifted from explaining the remarkable fact of India's democracy to exploring how it has functioned in practice. Some of the earliest investigations by scholars of Indian democracy highlighted features that were unique to the Indian polity and society, which enabled democratic rule. These included the incorporative, hegemonic Congress party of the 1950s and early 1960s as an organization that served as a key intermediary role between state and society, and the existence of traditional associations that could serve as an alternative to the more formal civil society in the West.[4] More generally, the Congress party was seen as a political institution providing stability and political order; its electoral popularity thus reflected its success in structuring the polity.

By the late 1960s and early 1970s, however, intraparty conflict and the scale of demands from disparate, articulated groups led to the decline of Congress as a hegemonic political organization.[5] This involved a long process of fragmentation of the party system, such that by the 1990s, party competition was most clearly articulated at the level of the states, aggregating up to unwieldy national coalitions, until the return of majoritarian governments under Modi in 2014.[6] As the party system fragmented, moreover, there was a significant increase in the democratic participation of those previously most excluded from politics, including peasant-cultivators and lower-caste communities.[7] The disciplining party-organization of Congress no longer held the key to understanding how Indian democracy functioned.

A search for alternative models led researchers to examine the material micro-foundations of democratic competition, framing the meaning and impact of the fragmented vote through the idiom of patronage, thus reflecting less than sanguine assessments about the quality of democratic competition and associated governance. There is a wide acceptance that competition over resources – who gets what, when, and how – rather than differing ideological and policy programs drives democratic competition in developing countries.[8] Democracy in India has been associated with the pervasiveness of clientelism, or the use of discretionary power to control the distribution of publicly provided goods, services, and privilege for the purposes of electoral mobilization. Rents, a closely associated concept referring to the politically determined assets that yield better-than-average returns, are also prevalent in developing countries and

---

[4] Rudolph and Rudolph 1967; Weiner 1967. By contrast, Kothari (1964) saw Congress as an arena of conflicting and contending perspectives that represented a party system rather than a unified programmatic party.

[5] Rudolph and Rudolph 1987; Kohli 1990.

[6] Yadav and Palshikar 2003; Chhibber and Kollman 2004.   [7] Varshney 1998; Jaffrelot 2003.

[8] See Kitschelt and Wilkinson 2007. For a differing perspective on ideology, see Chhibber and Verma 2018.

are subject to intense competition among partisan actors seeking to attain power to enjoy rentier access.

In attempting to explain important dynamics behind India's fragmented party system, Kanchan Chandra powerfully framed India as a "patronage democracy," in which "the state has a relative monopoly on jobs and services, and in which elected officials enjoy significant discretion in the implementation of laws allocating the jobs and services at the disposal of the state."[9] This axiomatic characterization has structured debates in Indian politics over the past two decades. Chandra built on this characterization to explain the rise of the Bahujan Samaj Party (BSP) through new avenues of clientelism, with Dalit citizens casting votes for the party on the basis of ethnic head counts of the leadership in order to maximize their receipt of patronage, thus tying patronage politics to ethnic voting in elections. Researchers have subsequently extended this model to formulate explanations of the BJP-dominated NDA government between 1999 and 2004, whose successes among subaltern voters were attributed to the provision of patronage by Hindu nationalist civic organizations, as well as the rise of regional parties in the 1990s.[10] New insights have pointed to the crucial role of brokers that serve as intermediaries in the exchange of public resources and electoral mobilization between parties and client populations, and explored the role of elected officials in the dispersal of discretionary goods for elections.[11]

This framework has three advantages. First, it provides an individual logic of voting and electoral mobilization that is consistent with strategic action to maximize utility, in line with dominant intellectual trends and replacing more mechanical, essentialist understandings of voting blocs and caste-based voting. Second, it contrasts clientelism with universal provision of welfare, thus providing a ready explanation of why democratic competition has not yielded positive socioeconomic outcomes. Third and relatedly, it suggests policies of administrative reform that might enable democracy and development to buttress one another. Mobilization against the corruption, by the BJP under Narendra Modi, has become a popular mantra among upper- and intermediate caste voters and has propelled dramatic electoral successes. Yet structures of the state at the local level have not transformed and, as we shall see later, constituency-level variation has persisted despite these convergent outcomes.

Patronage is, if anything, a more universally accepted explanation of politics in Pakistan and Bangladesh, because of the organizational weakness of political parties. Dynastic and personalistic politics have a long tradition in the two countries; with few exceptions, politicians come from long-standing political families. Further, neither Pakistan nor Bangladesh has experienced the rise of lower status groups in the same way as the political assertion of lower caste

---

[9] Chandra 2004, 6.   [10] Thachil 2014; Ziegfeld 2016.
[11] Bussell 2019; Stokes et al. 2013; Auerbach 2020. For a critical commentary, see Naseemullah 2021.

groups in India. It is thus quite easy to view electoral competition, to the extent that it determines the distribution of power, as a competition between different cliques, using patronage to capture power and enjoying its fruits. In Pakistan between the fall of Zia ul Haq in 1988 and the election of Imran Khan in 2018, power alternated between the PPP, headed by the Bhutto family, and Nawaz Sharif's Pakistan Muslim League-Nawaz (PML-N).[12] Politically powerful families have dominated provincial politics in different regions as well.

There are, however, some reasons to be skeptical of characterizing Pakistani electoral politics as simply a competition among cliques based on patronage. Constituency-based analyses have shown more fluidity and dynamism on the part of the voters in choosing between candidates, even as the choice itself is limited by the supply of dynastic parties as the main actors in competition.[13] Of course, in Pakistan, the military still has significant influence in politics and governance. This may well dilute the translation between the preference of voters and the formation and execution of national policy, though in ways that complicate rather than simply subvert political competition.

In Bangladesh, the dynastic and clique-based nature of electoral politics has become more stark over time. After the fall of General Hussein Muhammad Ershad's military regime in 1990, national politics have taken the form of electoral competition between the Awami League, headed by Sheikh Hasina, the daughter of the founder of the country, and the BNP, headed by Khalida Zia, the spouse of a former military ruler, Zia ur Rahman, and its Islamist conservative partisan allies. Hassan has characterized this regime as a "duopolistic partyarchy," with business and civil society associations divided on partisan lines to take advantage of rents from patrons in national and municipal governments.[14] Over the past decade, the Awami League has assumed more hegemonic control of the Bangladeshi state and has monopolized distribution of political patronage without much effective competition.

***

Powerful as they are, frameworks of clientelism suffer from two significant, in the context of this book, related weaknesses: they are ahistorical and aterritorial. Patronage has been a much more venerable feature of political life in the Indian subcontinent than postcolonial democratic competition.[15] Indeed, it represented a key strategy of colonial governments to establish and maintain quiescence and collaboration among elite sections of Indian society. India's "patronage democracy" thus represents only the most recent instantiation of

---

[12] The nine-year interregnum of Pervaiz Musharraf's military regime represented an exception, but Musharraf himself relied on a powerful faction of PML-N rebels, dominated by the Warriach-Chaudhry clan in Gujrat.

[13] Wilder 1999; Mohmand 2019.   [14] Hassan 2013. See also Khan 2011.

[15] For an overview, see Piliavski 2014.

a set of patronage structures that predate by centuries the establishment of democracy and were certainly present and powerful during the assemblies of late colonial India.

The patchwork nature of authority also yielded structures of patronage that have differed significantly across South Asia's political geography, according to the specific interests and strategies of the colonial state in distributing patronage in response to differing opportunities and challenges. Many of those varying patronage structures and practices have persisted, even as the South Asian state itself expanded and deepened after independence. They have become embedded in governance structures and state–society relationships at the local level throughout the three countries. We can see the varying legacies of colonial rule and postcolonial state-building through the persistence of different kinds of patron–client relationships and the nature of rents and resources under public control across national territory. This in turn has consequences for the shape of electoral competition at the constituency level. It suggests that, without attention to differences in political geography and their historical roots – thus the patchwork state framework – we might not understand exactly how patronage and electoral competition interact across the political geography of India, Pakistan, and Bangladesh.

7.2 PATRONAGE AND PATCHWORK AUTHORITY

The patchwork state in South Asia is deeply implicated in the operation of patronage. The Mughal Empire, much like any premodern or early modern polity, operated on patrimonial guidelines, formulating and maintaining complex networks of feudal obligations between patrons and clients.[16] Colonization formally continued this system of patrimonial relations, but broadened and deepened its scope as a key instrument of domination and cooptation.

The investments of colonial governments and their cultivation of local elites meant dramatic increases in patronage resources, adding to both the complexity and the permanence of patronage relationships. Myriad groups and individuals benefited from the state's largesse, as well as rents generated by the colonial mercantile project. Law and administration formalized these patronage arrangements, placing them at the very center of colonial governance, both under the East India Company and afterward. The decentralized ("centrifugist") nature of colonial governance in India enabled the competition over state resources by social elites and thus the establishment of patronage politics, which has persisted after decolonization.[17]

---

[16] Weber 1991 [1919]. For more on Mughal governance and patronage, see Alam and Subrahmanyam 1998.
[17] Kenny 2015.

The specific characteristics of patronage networks under colonial rule varied substantially from place to place, however. Some princely states, receiving substantial largesse from colonial authorities or generating their own resources through taxation, developed sophisticated forms of social penetration and dense, novel patron–client relations. Others, like Rajput kingdoms, relied on much narrower linkages with co-ethnic social elites to enforce social order. Some district officials contended with a competitive and assertive civil society that demanded greater discretionary spending from the state, while others concentrated patronage distribution toward a narrow band of elites that would themselves distribute patronage selectively to the population well beyond the state's ambit. In the political agencies and nonregulated districts that represented exceptional governance during the colonial period, agents disbursed patronage through tribal allowances, along with threats of the use of force, to maintain quiescence without the expenses associated with integration into normal politics and administration.

In the twentieth century, networks of patronage and their relationship to politics deepened even further, as (elite) Indians increasingly participated in elections and enjoyed greater influence in government. Further, increases in state capacity associated with responses to global shocks in the final two decades of colonial rule absorbed heretofore private patronage networks directly into the state apparatus; this absorption established the forms of neo-patrimonialism that have continued to characterize public services throughout South Asia today, in which putatively public officials are nevertheless embedded in patron–client relationships within society.[18] This has intersected with electoral participation in ways that have only reinforced patronage structures.

Patronage politics have certainly persisted after independence but they have also been transformed by democratic structures.[19] To win power in democratic India, one needed to show the ability to disburse patronage for constituents. For the first two decades after independence, that simply meant membership of the Congress party and thus participation in a multilayered system of patronage that flowed from New Delhi and state capitals to core constituencies in districts, tehsils, and villages throughout India, through competition and contestation among rival factions and capture by party notables. As a contemporary commentator colorfully put it, "like a shopkeeper in an Indian bazaar, [Congress] squats with its large flabby shape in the middle of its wares, the heart of a political marketplace in which bargaining and dissent are the language of discourse."[20] This exchange was part and parcel of the Congress system, which involved significantly more contestation, internal disputation, and the need for negotiation than a simple characterization of a programmatic party providing incorporative political order.[21]

---

[18] Gould 2010.   [19] Gupta 2012.   [20] Morris-Jones 1966, 455.
[21] For more on these politics during Nehru's premiership, see Sherman 2022.

As Congress declined, the vote fragmented and multiparty competition became the norm, those seeking office or seeking to retain political power were faced with ever-increasing pressures to extract resources from the state, but they could no longer do so only within the structures and hierarchies of Congress. As a result, those needing to construct minimum winning coalitions at the center of the state would need to negotiate with different partisan actors with capacities to mobilize patronage and rentier networks, including local notables in the hinterlands or bosses of municipal machines, in addition to direct appeals of parties to citizens on the basis of welfare and development programs. Yet other patronage networks were de facto beyond the reach of incumbents or aspirants, due to governance exceptionalism and state capture. This variation in the nature of patronage, and partisan access to it, reflected the unevenness of public authority at the heart of the patchwork state.

In Pakistan, meanwhile, patronage networks that had been embedded in the authoritarian Ayub Khan regime and the system of Basic Democracies fragmented into competing parties and interest groups, leading to the increasingly competitive politics today. Even more than in India, networks of patronage and their relationships to the state have varied across national territory, both within and outside periods of military rule in the 1980s and 2000s. This is due to the legacies and actual persistence of exceptional governance mechanisms in the western and northwestern frontiers, as well as the common practices of managing populations and organizing patronage through influential but footloose "electable" notables; these notables form (often temporary) political alliances and join with different political parties in order to form national and provincial governments in exchange for continued access to patronage and rents. As a result, there is fierce political competition over the ample patronage resources of the state, alongside electoral violence that reflects the darker side of this competition.

In Bangladesh, by contrast, patronage networks have been thoroughly monopolized, initially by two partisan coalitions that alternated in power after 1990, and now increasingly by the de facto one-party rule of the Awami League. These regimes do not reflect Pakistan's complex pattern of different and distinct networks of patronage across its territory, but rather, in effect, nationwide party machines. We would thus expect less spatial differentiation in the party system, as patronage is fully monopolized by the state, which in turn, is fully captured by the dominant party.

For the rest of this chapter, I deploy the patchwork state framework and its application to patronage structures to explain variations in party competition in India and Pakistan and then engage them in discussions of different forms of violence.[22] Based on previous published work with Pradeep Chhibber, I argue that the extent of rents and patronage resources in a given area, and the extent to

---

[22] Bangladesh is an exception to both the state's unevenness and the varying nature of party competition, as I will demonstrate later.

which these are under public, bureaucratic control – rather than that of social notables or private actors – can shape the nature of party competition and electoral coordination at the constituency level, as well as spark violent contention over them. When significant rents and patronage are channeled through governance structures over which elected officials have discretionary control, competition converges around two or three parties. When there are fewer rents and resources, and those present are not under the straightforward control of the administrative state, this limits the capacities for coordination around bi-/triparty competition, yielding to a range of outcomes. The presence of the security, rather than patronage, avatar of the state may also impact the nature of the vote.

7.3   PATCHWORK STATES AND ELECTORAL COMPETITION

In order to engage with these questions, and how they are shaped by the patchwork state, it is important to explore dynamics of electoral competition on their own terms. Variation in the measures of electoral competition at the constituency level represent an important, if underexplored, puzzle in South Asian politics. One of the most cherished empirical regularities in political science is that any electoral system with single-member simple plurality rules – in which the candidate with the most votes relative to her closest competitor in any electoral district wins office for that district – tends to have no more than two candidates in serious competition. Duverger famously argued that the electorate, given these rules, would vote strategically by abjuring their absolute preferences in favor of those closest to policy or ideological preferences but with a realistic chance of winning, thus polarizing the constituency's electorate into two opposing camps, or "local bi-partyism."[23] If there is disagreement as to which parties constitute the more credible challenger to a disfavored party, we might see up to three parties in serious contention consistent with the notion of strategic voting.[24]

In India, Pakistan, and Bangladesh in recent national and provincial elections, held under exactly these electoral rules, the *average* effective number of parties (ENP) at the constituency level stands between two and three, consistent with our theoretical expectations, but this average masks significant variation. Some constituencies represent close to one-party domination and others represent electoral fragmentation, with four or more parties competing for the vote. These outcomes complicate theories of patronage-based voting based on ethnic cues. Voters – if and when casting their votes to maximize their likelihood of receiving patronage goods – would still have to vote strategically at the constituency level. As a result, they would select the party with the most coethnics in leadership positions *that has a credible chance of winning* rather than simply voting based on ethnic head

---

[23] Duverger 1954, 224.   [24] Cox 1997, 31–32.

counts regardless of its consequences. Voting on ethnicity and patronage alone thus suggests a Duvergerian logic, as voting for an ethnic party with no hope of gaining office in the seat would be process-irrational; rather, voters might choose among the two or three parties with the highest co-ethnic head counts in party leadership that also has a credible chance of winning. But what governs the supply, rather than the demand, of such choices?

To answer this question, we must look at parties themselves, and how they compete. There are distinct features of democracies in the developing world, such as weaknesses in party organization, which complicate some of the premises of Duverger's Law. Parties across South Asia are dynastic, leading ambitious politicians without dynastic family connections, and thus little chance of leading the parties in which they have risen to prominence, to form new parties in order to proceed in their careers.[25] This highlights a crucial question of party systems theory as applied to the constituency level: which parties are on the ballot. Electoral coordination around biparty competition is thus the product of not one but two processes: strategic voting by the electorate and the antecedent strategic entry by parties and candidates.[26] In the run-up to elections, parties might selectively decide to (not) compete and campaign in particular constituencies. The importance of party identification for voters in normal circumstances means that serious candidates without tickets from recognizable parties in serious contention are unlikely to succeed, and thus do not enter the race.

Thus, when voters are presented with ballots containing only two or three candidates, strategic entry is sufficient and strategic voting is unnecessary to produce Duvergerian outcomes. However, in instances where there are ten names on the ballot, the ability of the electorate to vote strategically depends on the availability of information as to which candidates are credible and which are not. When parties split or when notables, like former parliamentarians who are no longer party members, stand for office independently or in new parties, it may be quite difficult to separate signal from noise and coordinate around two or three credible competitors.

Of course, the credibility of candidates to win office and thus deliver patronage has been seen as an overriding reason to vote for them. The literature contains few clues as to how patronage is actually distributed, and how this might vary from place to place, however. Most empirical research in South Asia has focused on parliamentarians' discretionary local development funds, because these are the easiest sources of patronage to study and reflect legislators' direct interests and strategies of using funds to mobilize electoral support.[27] Yet these constitute a small fraction of rents and patronage resources in any locality and still require the bureaucratic apparatus to implement distribution.

---

[25] Chhibber, Jensenius and Suryanarayan 2014.   [26] Naseemullah and Chhibber 2018, 83–84.
[27] E.g., Keefer and Khemani 2009.

Politicians' influence over the vast bulk of government spending requires them to maintain vertical linkages with party bosses including those in charge of central or provincial ministries, who might order bureaucrats to target public expenditure, through "legislative cartels."[28] The importance of these vertical linkages require parliamentary aspirants to join major parties and operate within party hierarchies in order to influence spending and thus direct patronage to targeted constituencies, and might in turn lead voters to spurn candidates unaffiliated to parties with credible chances of capturing the ministries that control key government expenditure.

However, this model assumes that patronage and rents from public sources are significant and bureaucrats monopolize their dispersion. Bureaucrats are in turn under the direction of ministers with the power to direct patronage spending to targeted constituencies and populations. Such a monopolization of patronage and rents by the state is a feature of particular political geographies in South Asia, where state capacity is significant and the reach of the state into society is profound, and thus such competition over the state's resources is institutionalized, representing a prized object over which parties would compete. In cities, as well as more developed and commercialized rural areas – such as in central Punjab in Pakistan, in coastal Maharashtra and Tamil Nadu in India, and in most of Bangladesh – this is indeed the case.

What of other contexts? In order to examine these dynamics related to patronage and electoral competition, Chhibber and I examined an extreme form of the opposite, where there was a formal absence of monopolization of patronage by quotidian state structures: that of the erstwhile FATA in northwestern Pakistan. Until the recent integration of FATA into the province of KP, practices of exceptional governance reaching back to the establishment of colonial rule had seen the state formally subcontract governance, and perforce the distribution of rents and patronage, to tribal society. As the (quite limited) largesse of the state was not channeled through the quotidian bureaucracy but rather disbursed to the tribal leadership directly to distribute to their members, elected parliamentarians had little hope of influencing this distribution by virtue of being elected to office. Similar dynamics can occur in cases of less formally exceptional contexts; we found that the absence of local state agencies, like post offices, in northern India is associated with a higher number of parties at the constituency level.[29] In these circumstances, patronage is dispersed through social networks or dominant elites beyond the ambit of the state.

As a result, a key mechanism of electoral coordination is absent because parties in power cannot determine patronage provision, making any candidate – whether affiliated to a major party or not – as credible as any other. Voters, lacking the signals of credibility in patronage or rents delivery, might vote instead for a local leader within their locality in the constituency. If such

---

[28] Naseemullah and Chhibber 2018, 85-86. On legislative cartels, see Cox and McCubbins 1993.
[29] Naseemullah and Chhibber 2018, 96-98.

a candidate is successful, supporters are likely to receive discretionary benefits simply from paltry local development funds associated with parliamentary office or government connections and the candidate's own personal authority or resources. This can lead to fragmentation, given the formidable district magnitudes across rural India and Pakistan, with local champions with various party affiliations as well as independents competing for office.

Moving away from the circumstances of traditional authority, the patchwork state framework suggests that the linkage between patronage and voting can also be diluted in cases where patronage and rents are private or privatized, and thus not subject to competition for control through electoral contests. For example, patrons might seek public office for regulatory favors and thus might be in a position to disburse resources through private *rentier* fortunes. Many members of parliament and state assemblies in India have significant business interests, either as businesspeople who enter politics or as politicians who have significant investments.[30] In other contexts, a party machine might wholly capture the regulatory apparatus and determine such patronage and rents, forcing business and ordinary citizens to support them in return for access to basic goods of the state. Periods of one-party rule of the MQM in Karachi, the Shiv Sena in Mumbai, or the CPI-M in West Bengal were predicated on the implicitly violent efforts of parties to capture and retain rents and patronage, and then operate machines in which dissent means exclusion or coercion, following the logic of protection rackets.

In geographical contexts where the state has significant local authority and state and society interpenetrate, such private rentier-patronage linkage might be drowned out by the sheer weight of public patronage resources, allowing for convergent competition. Politicians might be corrupt, but their private interests do not disrupt mechanisms of public distribution. In conditions of state weakness, absence or capture, however, private patronage and rent-based disbursement might lead to credible competition of independents and electoral fragmentation that is more compatible with narrow targeting than wider distribution. As I have argued throughout this book, the territorial variation of state presence and absence throughout these three countries has historical roots in colonial state formation. All of this suggests that state presence and capacity, and particularly the extent of public resources and the ability of the state to monopolize patronage such that groups would need to influence elected officials, can shape patterns of electoral competition at the constituency level.

7.4 THE EFFECTIVE NUMBER OF PARTIES IN INDIAN ELECTIONS

A key measure of electoral competition at the constituency level is the ENP by votes.[31] We would expect a lower ENP in metropolitan and modernizing districts,

---

[30] Sinha and Wyatt 2019.
[31] I calculate ENP by taking the inverse of the sum of squared proportion of votes for each party, or in other words, the inverse of a Hirschman–Hirfandahl Index. See Laakso and Taagepera 1979.

relative to conservative ones, because the state has more thoroughly penetrated society and thus parties have greater capacity to capture and direct rents and patronage and thus, achieve greater coordinated competition around a smaller number of parties. Districts in the conservative category, by contrast, might exhibit higher fragmentation due to the presence of traditional forms of authority that lead patronage to bypass the state. However, we might also see instances of state capture if elites are sufficiently coordinated to back only one party; as a result, the category should exhibit higher variance around the mean. For districts under exceptional governance, there are fewer stable predictions, because governance exceptionalism can manifest in different ways electorally. In Jammu and Kashmir before 2019, significant intervention by the central government meant that votes for the assembly are less meaningful because critical governance decisions were made in New Delhi, suggesting logics of fragmentation discussed earlier. In former princely states with large tribal populations, we see variable penetration of subaltern-led parties.[32] In the ethnicized politics in the northeast, we see opposing pressures: toward fragmentation based on local assertions of recognition and toward polarization based on support or opposition to the security state.

India's electoral geography constitutes variation at two levels. Vidhan Sabha or assembly constituencies, for state elections, fit within districts. Lok Sabha or parliamentary constituencies are comprised of assembly constituencies, but often from different districts. As a result, I report results for assembly constituencies, on average over the past two or three elections since the last delimitation and the end of 2019. I then report results for parliamentary constituencies at the level of the assembly constituency.[33] Figure 7.1 reports ENP for assembly constituency, based on means and box-and-whisker plots, in terms of distance from the national average, which was 3.03 for assemblies, 2.76 for the parliament.

We see that metropolitan and modernizing constituencies have indeed lower ENP than conservative districts, but also have a smaller variation around the median. Conservative constituencies exhibit a slightly higher than average ENP, but also substantial dispersion of cases; exceptional constituencies exhibit a lower mean but also higher dispersion.

We see similar dynamics when focusing on the differences between constituency-level ENP and statewide averages, holding constant state-specific characteristics and highlighting variation within party systems. Figure 7.2 reports the differences from state averages for assembly constituencies, averaged over the past two to three elections.

Here, we see assembly constituencies in metropolitan and modernizing districts with lower than state averages, conservative districts with slightly higher than state averages, and exceptional districts significantly lower than

---

[32] Chandra and Garcia-Ponce 2019.

[33] All Indian electoral data is provided by the Trivedi Center for Political Data at Ashoka University; I thank its director, Gilles Verniers, for his help. See Boghale et al. 2019.

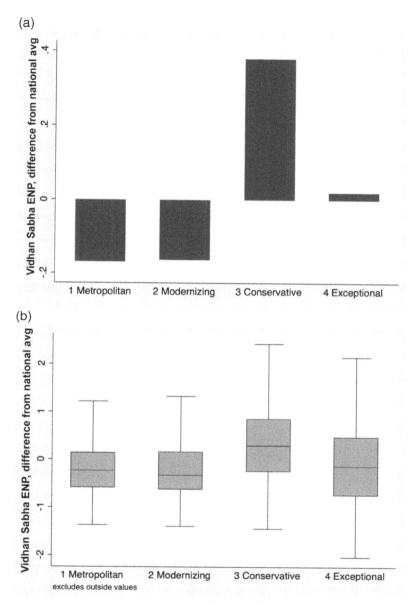

FIGURE 7.1 ENP for assembly constituencies in India

state averages. The outcome in terms of exceptional constituencies should be taken with a grain of salt, given that most exceptional districts exist in states with only exceptional districts, thus limiting the cases in which differences from

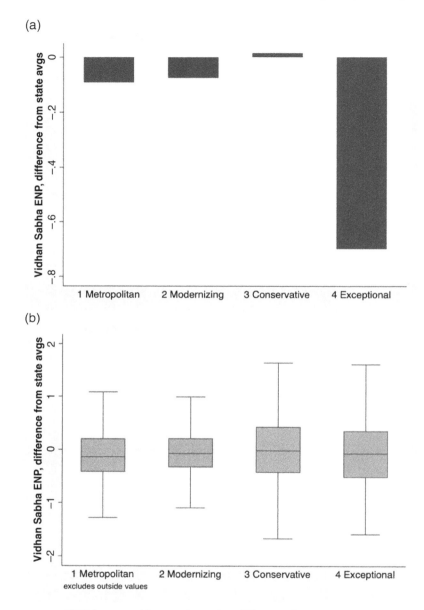

FIGURE 7.2 ENP for assembly constituencies, difference from state average

the state average is a meaningful measure. The box-and-whisker plots present an interesting bifurcation; metropolitan and modernizing districts exhibit significantly less variation than conservative and exceptional districts.

We might expect such an outcome due to networks of patronage that are less regulated by the state can be fully captured by a dominant elite, leading to lower ENP, or else fragmented between different groups within the constituency, leading to higher ENP.

We see similar, if not more dramatic, outcomes in the Lok Sabha. Figure 7.3 presents ENP, in terms of both means and box-and-whisker plots, in relation to the national average over the last three parliamentary elections.

Here we see metropolitan and modernizing districts with ENPs lower than the national average, conservative constituencies higher than the national average, and exceptional districts significantly lower average ENP relative to the national mean. Looking at median and dispersion patterns in the box-and-whisker plots, we see steadily increasing variance from metropolitan, modernizing to conservative districts; exceptional districts have a lower median, but also relatively large variance around the median.

These patterns are similar when looking at the differences from state averages (Figure 7.4).

Here, we see the average constituency ENP for metropolitan and exceptional districts essentially the same as state averages. The non-result of the two categories is not all that surprising. Constituencies in both metropolitan districts and exceptional districts are largely clustered within homogenous states in governance terms (Delhi, Jammu and Kashmir, those in the Northeast).[34] There is however a significant difference between modernizing and conservative constituencies relative to state averages. This is quite revealing. Even controlling for state averages, modernizing districts exhibit greater coordination relative to conservative districts.

Finally, there is a question of the extent to which polarizing elections might transform the party system. The 2019 general election was a watershed in Indian politics; for the first time for decades, an incumbent party was returned with gains in vote-share and in seats, forming a majority government. The transformational mobilization of Narendra Modi and his electoral successes have been seen as signs that India might be transitioning to a new, one party-dominant party system.[35]

This might suggest that the variation in effective parties would be less pronounced given the influence of a thoroughly assertive national politics. To test this, I present ENP in relation to national averages for the 2019 election as well as the 2014 election that initially brought Modi to power and the 2009 election that returned the Congress-led UPA coalition, representing the more fragmented political landscape of the pre-Modi era. Interestingly, average constituency-level ENP was lower in the 2009 election, at 2.45, and in 2014 at

---

[34] My strategy of managing the disconnect between parliamentary constituencies and administrative districts tends to overweight parliamentary constituencies in these states, as they are comprised of a much larger number of assembly constituencies per district.

[35] Chhibber and Verma 2019.

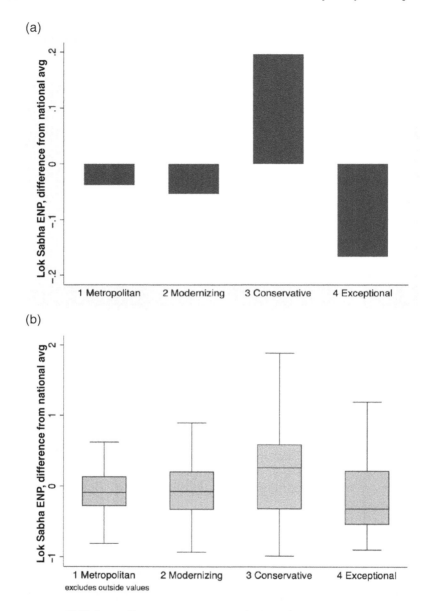

FIGURE 7.3 ENP for parliamentary constituencies in India

2.76, than it was in 2019, at 2.96 which might suggest that Modi's consolidation in terms of seats in parliament was not replicated in terms of votes at the constituency level. Figure 7.5 presents the results of the three elections by governance category.

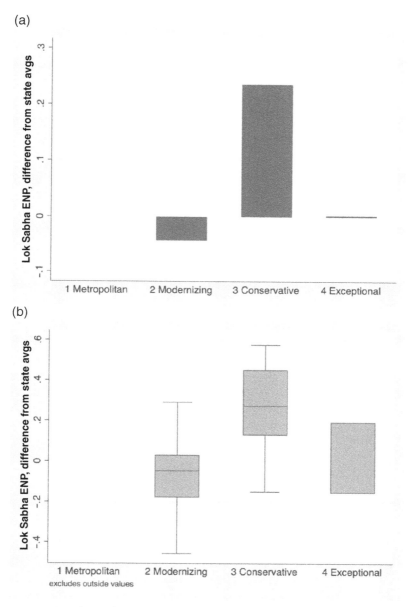

FIGURE 7.4 ENP for parliamentary constituencies, difference from state average

In fact, Modi's re-election in 2019 was consistent with a significantly greater dispersion from the national average based on governance category distinctions than either the 2009 or the 2014 elections. Some of these dynamics may be the

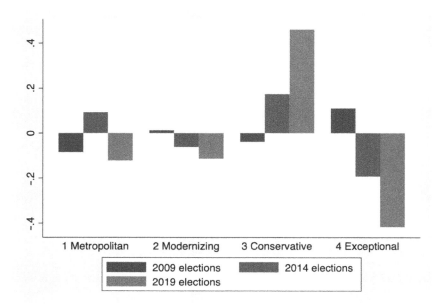

FIGURE 7.5 ENP for 2009, 2014, and 2019 parliamentary elections

natural result of disagreements among opposition parties, but at the very least, a polarizing election by itself cannot even out the variation in the party system.

In assessing electoral competition in India at the constituency level in terms of governance, we see a couple of noteworthy features. First, the data generally followed our theoretical expectations; metropolitan districts have lower ENP than the national average for both parliament and the state assemblies. While this result is not as clear in relation to state averages, given the weight of Delhi as a metropolitan-only state with a large number of elected officials at the state level, it signals that electoral coordination and relatively organized party competition is a feature of governance in cities. Second, in both the national parliament and state assemblies, in relation to the national average and differences from state averages, we see a lower ENP and thus higher average level of coordination for modernizing districts in relation to conservative districts. Constituencies in conservative districts exhibit a wider dispersion than those in modernizing districts, however, suggesting that different dynamics might be present, from fragmentation to capture, that drive electoral outcomes in the context of the lower capacity of the state to penetrate society.

Finally, we see a low average for ENP in constituencies in exceptional districts in India, though with significant variation around that average. We do not have a clear understanding of why that would be the case, and the differing circumstances of exceptional districts in different places – say between Kashmir, tribal-majority former princely states in eastern India and nonregulated districts and frontier agencies in the Northeast – suggest that making generalizations might be hazardous. Nonetheless, several possibilities for electoral convergence as opposed to fragmentation, as suggested by the case of FATA mentioned earlier, present themselves. First, the extraordinary presence of the state in these contexts might polarize communities for or against its coercive intervention. Second, the denseness of tribal societies relative to the state in these contexts might offer a hidden opportunity for coordination outside of electoral campaigns. Of course, these are also areas in which democratic competition does not lead automatically to democratic governance, given the presence and activities of non-state actors and the relatively unaccountable figures of the security state; here, democratic competition might not matter at all for the distribution of state largesse, as we shall see later, yielding subnational authoritarianism.

7.5 THE EFFECTIVE NUMBER OF PARTIES IN PAKISTANI ELECTIONS

Electoral politics and party systems in Pakistan are less salient in the study of South Asian politics than those in India. Unlike India, Pakistan has not enjoyed a long period of consolidated democratic rule; instead, army chiefs have overthrown civilian governments three times and ruled for long periods. Even in periods of relatively democratic rule, the military has still retained command of a number of key areas of policymaking, particularly in relation to foreign, defense, and security.[36] Moreover, the indirectly elected president could dismiss the National Assembly, a power that was exercised regularly in the 1990s, before the Eighteenth Amendment in 2010 rescinded the privilege.

There are also serious allegations that deep state actors have intervened in the conduct of electoral contests. In the run-up to the 2018 elections, the superior judiciary disqualified the head of the incumbent party, based on decades-old corruption charges. Candidates also reported pressure from the security services to break with established parties and run as independents, in order to assist the electoral fortunes of Imran Khan's Pakistan Tehreek-e-Insaaf (PTI).[37] Moreover, party politics itself is based on elite competition. Most parties are dynastic or personalistic in nature, with weak internal organization, inconsistent policies, and without the democratic upsurge among subaltern communities of the Indian party system.

It would, however, be a mistake to dismiss electoral competition in Pakistan. Over the past three elections since the end of the Musharraf regime, electoral turnout averaged around 50 percent, more than ten points lower than India's but still significant relative to other democracies and anocracies. Further, many seats are subject to intense competition. Even as the security state was

---

[36] Adeney 2017.   [37] Abi-Habib and Masood 2018.

attempting to influence outcomes in the 2018 elections toward the PTI and against the incumbent Pakistan Muslim League-Nawaz (PML-N), the PTI was unable to win the majority of seats in Punjab, the biggest province.

This suggests that electoral competition in Pakistan is not simply theater. It reflects a very real and uncertain contestation over political power. Pakistani citizens take the opportunity to express their preferences in the shape of government and perforce the distribution of the state's resources, with vigor and seriousness. The old stereotypes of elections being wholly determined by "feudals," who enforce their will on pliant subject populations, have been challenged by significant evidence of grassroots politics mobilizations that can upend dynasties that were perceived as not delivering for their constituencies.[38]

We have also seen that the Pakistani state is even more of a patchwork than that in India, which can have a significant impact in the ways that electoral competition is structured. Chhibber and I argued that in contexts of the explicit subcontracting of governance to customary authorities, such as in the FATA – a dynamic that is absent in India – we see dramatic electoral fragmentation, because networks of patronage formally bypass the formal bureaucracy and thus elected politicians.[39] Outside these extreme dynamics of subcontracted governance, however, Pakistan is subject to similar dynamics as India. The difference between big cities and the largely agrarian heartland, and between modernizing and conservative districts in the latter, can have serious consequences for the possibilities of electoral competition. The extent of the quotidian state's penetration into society and the subsequent strength and monopolization of patronage and rentier resources by bureaucrats and politicians varies significantly across the political geography, fashioning the possibilities for electoral coordination. Thus, we might expect to see similar, if not even more dramatic, variation in party systems and electoral competition. We might not see precisely the same dynamics, however, as the framework of party politics and the nature of the state are different.

To these ends, I look at ENP at the constituency level for provincial and national assembly elections averaged over 2008, 2013, and 2018 contests. As in India, I report constituency results as difference from national averages; these are 3.24 for provincial assemblies and 3.10 for the National Assembly.[40] First, I present ENPs by governance category for provincial assemblies (Figure 7.6).

In Pakistan just as in India, constituencies in metropolitan districts are associated with lower effective parties. However, all the other categories are reversed. Modernizing and exceptional districts have constituencies that

---

[38] Mohmand 2019.   [39] Naseemullah and Chhibber 2018.

[40] I do not the report the results for variations within provinces, because Pakistan has four provinces and one national territory to India's twenty-nine states and seven union territories. Pakistan has also de facto a less federalized policy than India.

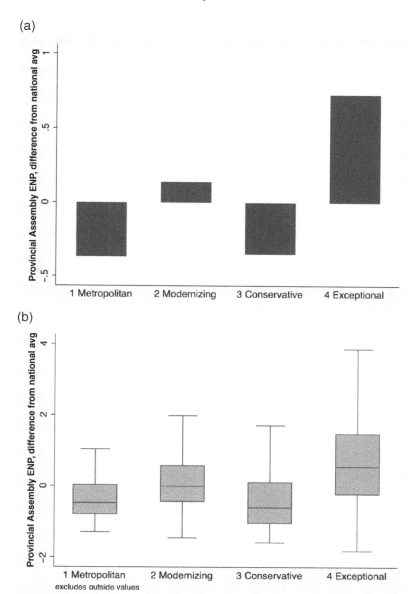

FIGURE 7.6 ENP for provincial assembly constituencies in Pakistan

are higher than average and conservative districts have constituencies that have lower than average ENP.

To make sense of this difference, it is important to recognize that the political dynamics of areas under conservative governance arrangements in

Pakistan can be quite different than those in India. In the former, large landowners and religious notables in constituencies and districts in southern Punjab and interior Sindh operate dominant political machines that produce more concentrated competition, whereas in the latter, the politics of conservative districts in northern and eastern India have are witness to more fragmented competition. Modernizing districts in Pakistan represent the closest to the norm of competition of three parties than other categories.

Constituencies in exceptional districts – those in Balochistan and the former princely states of Dir, Chitral, and Swat, as formerly federal tribal agencies have not yet participated in KP provincial elections – are associated with greater than average fragmentation. Instances of extreme fragmentation in exceptional districts in Pakistan may be the result of patronage and rents formally bypassing the quotidian, bureaucratic state. Yet as in India, we see significant variation around the median, relative to the other categories.

We see similar, if even more dramatic, outcomes in elections to the National Assembly, which are arguably more politically salient given the greater power of the federal government relative to provincial governments in Pakistan (Figure 7.7).

One of the significant reasons why the variation is more dramatic for national assembly constituencies is the inclusion of the erstwhile FATA, which was not part of the provincial-level analysis; these have some of the highest ENP in Pakistan. Since the last election, FATA has been formally incorporated into KP province, which might lead to greater party-based convergence in subsequent elections, as the administrative machinery of the provincial government extends into the former tribal agencies, now districts in KP. Yet some legacies of exceptional rule are likely to persist, as with de facto governance exceptionalism in Balochistan.

Pakistan thus represents different patterns from than those of India in terms of electoral competition measures at the constituency level, because of differences in the specific dynamics of competition, but categories still represent legible differences from one another in both countries. The evidence of variation from national averages by governance categories in Pakistan is, if anything, even more stark. As Pakistan is a less consolidated democracy than India and therefore the norms of electoral competition are less established, this greater variation is unsurprising. However, both Pakistan and India represent patchwork states informed by the historical legacies of colonial rule, and as a result, have long-term differences in the networks and patterns of patronage that shape electoral competition and party systems differently in different places.

7.6   BANGLADESHI EXCEPTIONALISM

Across India and Pakistan, we see significant variation at the constituency level around a mean of between 2 and 3, roughly consistent with our

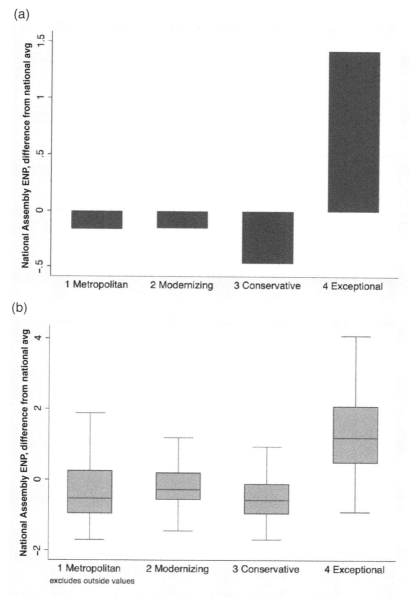

FIGURE 7.7 ENP for parliamentary constituencies in Pakistan

theoretical expectations. Still, the variation is contrary to the norm of strategic voting in democracies with single-member plurality electoral rules and is not straightforwardly explained by extant frameworks of clientelism and ethnic voting. Bangladesh, on the other hand, has dynamics of electoral competition that are quite different from both India and Pakistan. Figure 7.8 presents constituencies in all three countries averaged over the past three national elections.[41]

India and Pakistan are more alike in terms of median ENP, though Pakistan has even greater dispersion, whereas Bangladesh has a much lower median and much tighter variation around the median. How might we make sense of this difference, given that all three countries follow the same electoral rules and share the same general legacies of colonial rule?

I argue that Bangladesh's much more consolidated party system is, at least in part, a consequence of its less uneven political geography, which has meant a much more convergent national politics. Vigorous bipartisan competition between the BNP and the Awami League after the fall of Ershad's military regime in 1990 established itself across the entire country, without the different governance arrangements shaping the basis for different sorts of electoral competition across India and Pakistan. This complete monopolization of patronage networks by party apparatus – in the manner of nationwide political machines – precludes the sort of varied party competition that we see in India and Pakistan.

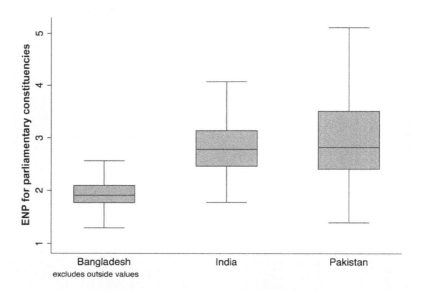

FIGURE 7.8 ENP in Pakistani, Indian, and Bangladeshi parliaments

---

[41] The opposition BNP boycotted the 2014 elections; as a result, I have data for the 2001, 2008, and 2018 elections in Bangladesh.

The difference between the 2000s and the 2010s is that competition between two party machines has consolidated into single-party domination, that of the ruling Awami League. We can see this trend in steadily decreasing average ENP over three elections. In the 2001 elections, the average ENP across constituencies was 2.32, and in 2008 it was 2.1. In the 2018 elections, however, following an election in 2014 that was boycotted by the opposition, the average ENP was 1.44, and the ruling Awami League won 258 seats out of 300 in the Jatiya Sangsad and formed a government coalition with 289 seats.

Some aspects of Bangladesh's regime can be termed electoral authoritarianism, in which the practices of the incumbent government frustrate the free exercise of democratic competition, such as by monopolizing patronage.[42] The subversion of democracy in this context is quite different from the more regionally specific instances of subnational authoritarianism through occupation in India and Pakistan, as in Kashmir and Balochistan, respectively, as well as instances of local state capture or the exercise of traditional authority. This is in large part because of Bangladesh's political geography, which facilitates one-party domination over most of the country through the national capture of the practice of patronage, but is also quite different from military-based authoritarianism that Bangladesh (and Pakistan) experienced in the late 1970s and 1980s.

There are, however, some exceptions to this evenness that have consequences on party competition over time. While most districts and thus constituencies in Bangladesh's agrarian heartland are classified as modernizing, there are two metropolitan districts in Dhaka and Chittagong and three exceptional districts in the Chittagong Hill Tracts. Figure 7.9 represents these discrete variations from the preponderance of Bangladesh's modernizing districts.

We see constituencies in Dhaka and Chittagong have similar medians but much tighter variation around the biparty norm, while the constituencies in Banderban, Khagrachhari, and Rangamati districts (the Chittagong Hill Tracts) see a significantly higher ENP, over three elections. These represent five districts and 39 constituencies, about 13 percent of the total, but suggest that exceptions to Bangladesh's smooth political geography have political and electoral consequences. For the modernizing agrarian hinterland that constitutes much of Bangladesh, however, norms around two-party competition (and later, one-party dominance) predominate.

7.7 ELECTIONS, VIOLENCE, AND THE PATCHWORK STATE

There has been significant recent interest among political scientists in the relationship between elections and political violence. This research includes explicit violence among partisan supporters around electoral contests, but also the conduct of elections in contexts of endemic conflict, and even the capacities of elections to resolve conflicts and marginalize violent actors.

---

[42] Levitsky and Way 2010.

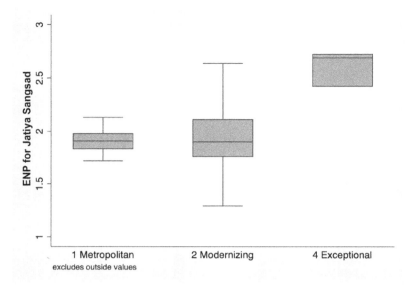

FIGURE 7.9 ENP for parliamentary constituencies in Bangladesh

The patchwork state concept and some associated discussions in Chapter 6 may help us clarify some of the mechanisms and intermediate factors linking elections and violence.

7.7.1 Elections and Sovereignty-Neutral Violence

The literature on elections and violence tends to maintain a distinction between electoral and other forms of purposive political violence, and between armed groups and political parties, even while accepting that some armed groups vary their strategies and could pursue electoral mobilization.[43] In the context of the social violence and competition over patronage and rents in the South Asian context, however, these distinctions may not be helpful. Take, for instance, Bangladesh: ACLED data shows that 369 out of 1,002 violent incidents between November 2019 and mid-June 2021 involved political parties, even though there were only municipal elections during this period. Many of these incidents involved clashes between intra-partisan factions over control of a locality and its associated rents; following 2021 municipal elections in Companiganj upazilla in District Noakhali, members of two factions of the Awami League clashed for supremacy over the Chaprishar Hat locality, killing a journalist and wounding at least fifty other people. Similar deadly fights over control among co-partisans occurred in Kushtia, Bagerhat, Cox's Bazaar, and

[43] Matanock and Staniland 2018; Birch, Daxecker and Höglund 2020.

several other districts occurred. In May 2020, cadres of the Awami League and the BNP clashed in Narsingdi over control over localities, and associated rents. Violence can also occur when opposition party activists rally to mobilize support and end up clashing with police. This suggests that electoral violence can represent mafia-like dynamics, in which electoral mobilization and contentious politics are parts of a broader repertoire aimed at capturing or controlling rents and patronage in localities. Aspects of these dynamics might be specific to Bangladesh's increasingly one-party system, yet the notion of politics intertwined with rent-seeking and contentious or violent mobilization are common to Pakistan and India as well. To understand violence among partisan actors in these contexts of significant state–society penetration, we need to understand local political economy as much as electoral analysis.

The notion of an armed group as a distinct type of actor in electoral politics may also not be that surprising in South Asia where cadres of well-recognized parties are often armed and violent, and may be separated from rebel groups only by the government's recognition or proscription. In Pakistan, while there has been much debate on the mainstreaming of militant groups such as Jamaat ud-Dawa, violent political parties with radical positions engage in contentious and violent action, not least the Tehreek-e-Labbaik Pakistan (TLP), discussed in Chapter 6, which has rioted in the capital and killed police as well as contested in elections.

To take an older example in India, systemic conflict erupted over the establishment of a proposed Special Economic Zone in Nandigram in West Bengal in 2007 and 2008. State police and armed cadres of the ruling CPI-M clashed violently with activists against land evictions, themselves increasingly armed and affiliated with both Maoist rebel organizations and the Trinamool Congress opposition. Trinamool Congress subsequently won the 2011 state elections and dislodged the Communist government for the first time in thirty-four years. Political violence has continued for the next decade, implicating both parties like the CPI-M, Trinamool, and the BJP as well as proscribed groups such as Maoist organizations.

Systematic coordinated violence to capture power and gain control over rents, patronage, and policy is more likely to occur with parties in convergent competition, in which the prize is sufficiently valuable to mobilize activists, electorally and violently, for its achievement. To give a sense of this, I compare aggregate incidents of partisan violence between November 2019 and mid-June 2021 in three large states that had assembly elections during this period – Bihar, Tamil Nadu, and West Bengal – as well as the ENP for constituencies in these elections (Figure 7.10). All three elections were targets of opportunity for BJP mobilization.

Bihar is the most populous of these states, but it has the lowest number of incidents, even though it has long been used as a byword for political disorder.[44]

---

[44] Kohli 1990, 205–237. For an alternative reading, see Witsoe 2013.

(a)

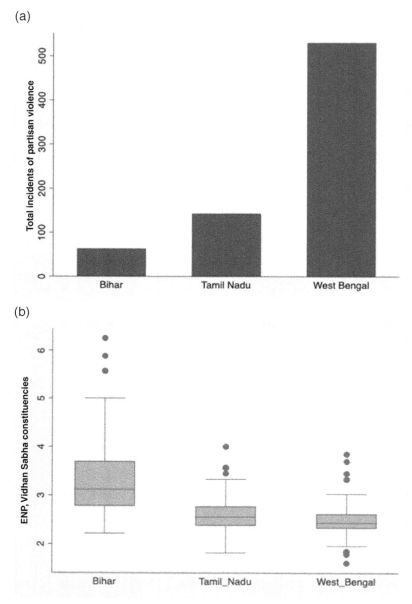

(b)

FIGURE 7.10 Electoral violence and ENP for Bihar, Tamil Nadu, and West Bengal Assemblies

West Bengal, due to dynamics of political contention described earlier, has by far the highest. Bihar also has high median effective parties and a large variance around that mean, whereas there is much more convergent competition at the constituency level in Tamil Nadu and West Bengal. While it is possible that partisan actors were using violence strategically to polarize communities, in the manner of Hindu-Muslim riots in the 1990s,[45] partisan polarization has long been a feature of both Tamil and Bengali politics.

Rather, patchwork state dynamics may be at play. Bihar has only conservative districts as legacies of zamindari arrangements from colonial rule. As a result, constrained bureaucratic capacity and more distant state–society relations would mean significant rents and patronage outside public authority, which in turn would mean both less electoral coordination and less partisan violence over their control. West Bengal and Tamil Nadu, by contrast, have modernizing and metropolitan districts, the former due to ryotwari arrangements during the colonial period, and the latter due to postcolonial revisions after partition as well as subsequent Communist rule. As a result, high state capacity and interpenetrative state–society relations, along with substantial rents and patronage under public control, would mean incentives for both coordinated electoral convergence and violent partisan competition. In other words, both electoral competition and electoral violence are endogenous to variation in patchwork state structures.

7.7.2 Elections and Sovereignty-Contesting Violence

Analysts regularly look to democratic elections as a possible solution to grievances and feelings of exclusion in the context of systemic insurgent violence and suggest that the presence of parties arising in from excluded communities can intervene to deescalate tensions and draw communities away from rebel violence.[46] This possible resolution is complicated by the deployment of a particular kind of subnational authoritarianism in India and Pakistan, however. Most studies of subnational undemocratic regimes focus on patrimonial bosses and party machines, and thus suggest that violence is a minor strategy in comparison to co-optation through patronage.[47] By contrast, in South Asia, electoral competition is subverted in a serious manner by the overwhelming power of the security state, in which decisions over the lives and livelihoods of citizens in insurgency-affected areas are made by policymakers in national capitals, implemented by paramilitaries and other public order officials and governed by exceptional legislation.[48] This is particularly the case when Indian and Pakistani governments feel the threat of separatism, as with Kashmir in the former and Balochistan in the latter.

---

[45] Wilkinson 2004.   [46] Chandra and Garcia-Ponce 2019.
[47] See Gibson 2013; Giraudy 2015; Gervasoni 2018.
[48] For a theoretical framing, see Agamben 2003.

In these contexts, elections themselves do not lead to determination of policy or even the distribution of patronage, as these are determined by the security state according to its own strategies. In the last election to the Jammu and Kashmir State Assembly, before it was disbanded and the state was turned into two union territories in 2019, the average ENP was 3.9 parties, almost a full party more than the national average, along with a 24 percent lower than average turnout for assembly elections. In 2018 provincial assembly elections in Balochistan, the average ENP was 4.1, just less than one party higher than the national average, with lower turnout than that of Punjab and Sindh. This suggests fragmentation consistent with the idea that the object of electoral competition may be for the benefits of office itself, rather than the patronage associated with governments capturing power.

Of course, voters do not only focus on material benefits; Chandra highlighted the importance of "psychic" benefits that parties might provide to voters facing systematic discrimination, in addition to discretionary material goods.[49] Particular types of psychic goods might be important in contexts of insurgent conflict, as citizens resent the repressive measures associated with the government's counterinsurgent practices. Malik, explaining the electoral success of the MQM among the Mohajir community in Karachi despite their dismal record in service provision, suggests that Mohajir voters display "defiant pride" in response to their harassment from paramilitaries and the security services.[50] If political organizations channel these resentments, this might lead to polarization rather than fragmentation.

7.8 CONCLUSION

In India and Pakistan, the nature of electoral competition varies significantly across electoral geography. This is not easily explicable through conventional frameworks, like generative social cleavages, ethnic politics, or electoral rules. Patronage – a virtual leitmotif of Indian democratic politics – may represent a means for understanding the drivers of electoral mobilization. However, the structures of patronage themselves vary significantly, along with differences in state capacity and state–society relations across the territory of South Asian countries. The patchwork nature of the state, as concrete institutional legacies of colonial rule and postcolonial state-building, can help us understand such variation. Capacities for more consolidated electoral competition at the constituency level may be critically conditioned by the ability of politicians and parties to promise and deliver the largesse of the state in power. If rents and patronage are less evident and/or are not under public control, then the incentives for consolidation decrease. The patchwork state has significant consequences for how we understand political competition, with important impacts for both social and insurgent violence.

[49] Chandra 2004.   [50] Malik 2020.

8

The Patchwork State and Development

This book is primarily concerned with understanding the nature of violence across the Indian subcontinent as part of a broader spatial politics of conflict and competition. Development is a key component of these broader politics. The countries of the Indian subcontinent are lower middle-income, with significant poverty and rising inequality. As a result, individuals and communities contend with one another and with the state to receive the key goods for bettering their lives and achieving greater freedom from want: critical infrastructure like roads, bridges, and railways, piped water, sanitation, and electricity, education, health care, jobs with dignity, and welfare for those who need it to lead meaningful lives.[1] While governments are at least rhetorically committed to the provision of these goods as a key source of national legitimacy, demand far exceeds supply, resulting in intense competition for access to goods and services that should be universally provided. As a result, development is an inherently and deeply political enterprise – it is very much a matter of who gets what, when, and how.[2] These intensely competitive politics often bleeds into the incidence of violence, while violence itself shapes patterns of development, on which more later in the chapter.

Spatial variation is a key puzzle in the politics of development in South Asia, particularly India. Scholars have long noticed differences in growth and social development across India's states, despite common membership in a democratic, federal polity.[3] Extant explanations for these variations are usually rooted in postcolonial dynamics of India's states, and particularly on the social coalitions, bureaucratic capacities, and political incentives that drive

---

[1] For a framing of development as freedom, see Sen 2001.
[2] Lasswell 1936. Kruks-Wisner (2018) emphasizes citizen claims-making as a key activity for the receipt of welfare goods in India.
[3] Variations across Pakistani provinces are also very much evident, though less salient in the literature.

subnational politics of welfare and investment. While there has also been some recent research into the historical roots of such variation, stretching back before independence, there has also been insufficient attention to the multiple mechanisms by which historical institutions involved with the governance of the economy shape contemporary outcomes.

This chapter explores how patchwork forms of authority, arising from colonial and postcolonial state formation, might provide additional leverage for the puzzle of subnational variation in development outcomes. It does so by excavating the ways that differences in state capacity and especially state–society relations can shape the nature of material exchange, both across and within India's states. It will focus largely on India, in conversation with a broader literature on subnational development that is hard to translate across borders, but will briefly discuss the variations in subnational development in Pakistan and Bangladesh. Echoing Chapter 7, it will also discuss the ways in which the politics of violence and the politics of development engage with one another across the political geographies of India, Pakistan, and Bangladesh.

8.1   EXPLAINING SUBNATIONAL VARIATION IN INDIAN DEVELOPMENT

Development has been a virtual leitmotif of Indian politics. At independence, many commentators wondered whether its novel political institutions could deliver development. By the 1960s, after India embarked on an ambitious import-substituting industrialization program, scholarly attention shifted to the management of the contention that arises from development.[4] Early, sanguine accounts of India's relative successes in maintaining democracy and initiating industrial development focused on the forms of cultural and social solidarity within the organizing structures of the Congress party, to manage different demands from different populations in different places. In other words, as laid out in Chapter 2, the incorporative dynamics of party-based political order was a core theme of Indian politics and its developmental outcomes.[5]

The decline of the Congress as an overarching, incorporative disciplinary institution gave way to concerns about India's "growing crisis of governability," along with declining investment and stagnation in programs of economic development.[6] The crisis of governance and legitimacy at the center provided opportunities to the development projects of individual states, however. Students of this subnational variation in the politics of development have sought explanations for this variation in accounts of agrarian relations,

---

[4] See Huntington 1968.
[5] Rudolph and Rudolph 1967; Weiner 1967. For a more skeptical perspective, see Frankel 2005.
[6] Kohli 1990.

caste, and class structures.[7] The mobilization of popular energies for public investment and social development, and the political organizations that arose to carry these demands to power, have transformed development outcomes in a number of states.[8] Regionally specific analyses have since been more thoroughly integrated into systematic cross-state comparisons in growth and development, involving factors such as social coalitions, center-state relations, and party systems along with varied mechanisms such as policy consistency and incentives for private investment.[9] Recent scholarship has also examined themes of historically embedded social solidarity, rather than the dynamics of competition and conflict, as key to understanding bureaucratic effectiveness and investment in the provision of social welfare.[10]

The deep and wide-ranging literature on the subnational variations in growth and human development in India represents an uncommon instance of substantive engagement among a community of researchers. This in turn arises from strong normative commitments to understand and address the tragedies of the failure of certain states to provide materially for their populations. Scholars and policymakers also seek out models for successful development that might be replicated elsewhere. This work, with a few exceptions, is deeply grounded in postcolonial democratic politics and India's contemporary states, however. This leaves the possibility that some causal factors may precede postcolonial political structures, the boundaries of which were substantially reorganized in the 1960s.

One such factor is the legacies of colonial rule. Inquiry into the ways that colonial institutions have impacted contemporary development outcomes has become an important object of study, cross-nationally as well as in the subnational Indian context.[11] Banerjee and Iyer, have traced colonial land tenure arrangements, as well as the distinction between administrative districts and princely states, to explain differences in agricultural productivity and the provision of public goods in post-Independence India.[12] Other scholars have explained a range of development indicators through aspects of colonial rule, from early missionary activity impacting human capital endowments to caste mobilization in colonial India shaping developmental politics after independence.[13]

This research constitutes a significant advance in exploring the ways that specific historical institutions might shape contemporary development. As a salutary feature, much of this research focuses on district-level variation rather

---

[7] For an integrated collection of state-level accounts, see Frankel and Rao 1989.

[8] Frankel 1971; Varshney 1998; Heller 1999.

[9] Sinha 2005; Nooruddin 2010; Bussell 2012; Kohli 2012; Murali 2017.

[10] Singh 2016. See also Mangla 2015.

[11] For a popular cross-national explanation, see Acemoglu and Robinson 2012.

[12] Banerjee and Iyer 2005. For critical engagement and elaborations, see Iversen, Palmer-Jones and Sen 2013; Lee 2017

[13] Lankina and Getachew 2012; Lee 2019a.

than that of India's states; districts exhibit greater continuity between the colonial and postcolonial periods than India's states, and thus represent an appropriate level of analysis for examining historical influences. However, there are also some drawbacks in the design of these disparate studies that suggests the need for further elaboration and investigation.

First, the path-dependent characterization of colonial legacies has underspecified the actual causal mechanisms that might transmit the influence of colonial institutions to postcolonial and contemporary outcomes.[14] These mechanisms generally fall under the rubric of state capacity, the relative presence of which drives development. While subnational variations in the capacity of the bureaucracy are both a reality and clearly consequential, this framework by itself is insufficient, for two reasons. First, variations in bureaucratic capacity were substantially (though not wholly) revised by the interventions of the postcolonial state, representing a critical juncture in development trajectories; straightforward path dependence from institutions formulated during colonial rule to more recent outcomes elides this juncture.

More critically, the nature of state–society relations are at least as impactful than the presence (or absence) of administrative personnel and the strength of their capabilities. If we expand our search for mechanisms to include how state and society engage one another over the determinants of material distribution, other possibilities of how institutions in the past might impact contemporary development might present themselves. In what follows, I will explore some of the differentiated ways that colonial authorities governed economic life, which have persisted with some revision after decolonization and have shaped development outcomes. Two sets of these mechanisms – markets and commodification, and rents and investment – are discussed in the next section.

8.2   THE PATCHWORK STATE AND INSTITUTIONAL MECHANISMS

State-level accounts of development variation place much of the explanatory power on the formulation of pro-development policies of subnational governments and on the incentives and capacities of bureaucrats carrying these policies out. While governmental structures, political incentives and bureaucratic capacities are certainly important for explaining growth and development, I introduce a complementary set of institutional mechanisms. These involve the institutionalized relationships between state and society that shape the nature and extent of economic transactions. These institutions, reaching back to colonial rule and revised incompletely by postcolonial politics, reflect the terms by which individuals and communities engage with a material world of relative scarcity and unlimited wants, and as such, manage questions of production, exchange, distribution, and redistribution. They are

---

[14] I elaborate on this in the next chapter.

critically determined by the same patchwork governance institutions that shape other aspects of political conflict and competition.

8.2.1 Markets and Commodification

Markets are institutions that use the price mechanism to adjudicate the exchange of goods, services, and productive assets. For neoliberal thinkers, access to effective market institutions represents a necessary and sufficient condition for development, by providing incentives for long-term investment and unleashing ingenuity and "animal spirits" among the population. Even for contemporary economists of the center-left, markets represent instruments to be used in conjunction with government intervention to achieve sum-positive outcomes.

There has, however. been a fruitful disagreement as to institutional origins: whether markets are naturally occurring phenomena that arise whenever groups of people come together (as long as governments do not intervene to suppress them), or whether they must be built through concerted action by the state. Institutional economics tends to see market-based exchange as universal over time and space, arising automatically as long as transaction costs are sufficiently low.[15] This is a more complicated question when it comes to markets "fictitious" commodities – land, labor, and capital – rather than goods like potatoes or pickaxes. A foundational proposition in Karl Polanyi's *The Great Transformation* is that markets for these fictitious commodities arise only through the concerted action of the modernizing state against the protective carapace of traditional social norms. Polanyi portrayed in vivid terms the construction of these national market-based economies for land and labor as the product of the systematic application of coercion against individuals who resisted the market, yielding a set of discrete, specific, and historically contingent institutions that have roots in violence.[16] The most visceral example of these violent processes, the enclosures in Britain, destroyed agrarian social relations, alienated communities from land, and forced the dispossessed to migrate into cities and into anonymized wage relationships under terrible living conditions. As a result, Polanyi situated the building of markets as a historical process that is intertwined with the building of states, both of which are saturated by violence.

Political economists have thus understood that the violent application of state power was necessary for the integration of market economies. Such violence would eventually lead to prosperity and political order, at least for Western democracies, but only after violent dislocations stimulated subsequent popular demands for compensatory social protection against the power of the market to disrupt lives and livelihoods. The politics of social policy in advanced industrialized countries have at their core the notion of "de-commodification,"

[15] North 1990, 1991.   [16] Polanyi 2001[1948].

or the extent to which governments intervene to protect citizens from the vicissitudes of market forces, once they completely replaced traditional social norms of material exchange.[17]

In colonial India, however, colonial authorities had deeply ambivalent feelings toward the creation of national "self-regulated" markets for land, labor, and capital. The patchwork nature of colonial governance foreclosed national markets in ways that suited the economic purposes of empire and its agents, allowing important economic flows such as the export of key commodities, the import of manufactures, and the drain of capital, but preventing indigenous economic actors from challenging these patterns in any systematic fashion through combining their efforts across regions. Colonial administrators were additionally afraid of the social dislocations and attendant disorder that unrestrained market forces might unleash, and in particular, of peasant rebellion. Fear and frugality thus restrained the spread of market institutions beyond a set of interconnected enclaves – the great metropolises, smaller cities and towns and sites of plantation-based agriculture along networks of road and rail – while maintaining (neo-) traditional practices of landlordism, intermediation, and social hierarchies in the hinterland and peripheries. Thus, under colonial rule, the territory of the subcontinent varied significantly in the extent to which the hierarchical social norms and structures restrained market forces over land and labor. This variation has important consequences today.

In response, the nationalist movement rhetorically framed India as constituting one national society and associated national economy, which was kept divided and empoverished only by the actions of the British. However, it was also bitterly divided over the extent to which the market, even one heavily regulated by the government, could or should replace the structures of moral economy in the countryside.[18] As a consequence, fear of disruption from modernization among conservative nationalists echoed the ambivalence of the colonial government toward the creation of a national market economy.

After independence, the Indian government sought to transform and integrate the previously fragmented economy under colonial rule through state-led industrial development, while guaranteeing some measures of social protection from market forces, such as reserved capacities for craft-based manufacturing.[19] In significant ways, this was a successful enterprise. The integration of princely states, the introduction of a national currency, and common external tariffs meant that Indians no matter their location or station had access to a common medium of exchange. Powerful symbols, spread throughout India, undergirded nationalist policies.[20] But existing, and spatially differentiated, social and economic forces that persisted after independence still shaped the realities on the ground.

---

[17] Esping-Anderson 1990.   [18] Goswami 2004; Naseemullah 2017b.
[19] See Naseemullah 2017a, ch. 3.   [20] Roy 2007.

As a result, market institutions have continued to have a somewhat Potemkin character, with a veneer of "free" market exchange covering powerful mechanisms of traditional socioeconomic regulation, from debt bondage to barter-based economies to explicit coercion to reinforce social hierarchies. In such areas of "pre-commodification," landless laborers face either quiescence or exit through (often-seasonal) migration to cities to work in the informal economy, hundreds of kilometers from their homes and families.[21] In areas that have been more thoroughly penetrated by the market, however, political and economic mobilization yield a more competitive and productive agrarian economy as well as greater violent competition among various politically activated groups.

We can see circumstantial evidence for variable commodification in district-level differences in agricultural productivity, measured by the value of agrarian output divided by the number of agricultural workers. At least for those districts with predominantly agricultural livelihoods, there are ways in which the persistence of traditional social and economic relations can be seen through such productivity measures. Low-productivity agriculture often represents "disguised unemployment," in other words, the presence of more workers than is strictly necessary for production, suggesting that social norms rather than the demand for labor determine who works on the land.[22] The presence and persistence of low-productivity agriculture over time might suggest that social relations are preventing full commodification and the inability of national markets to absorb labor.

High agricultural productivity meanwhile suggests the state-implicated investment of commercializing inputs, which disrupt traditional structures and allow for more highly commodified land ownership and use, in which modernizing and entrepreneurial cultivators can capture gains from productivity for themselves. These inputs were at the very heart of the Green Revolution.[23] Figure 8.1 presents data on agricultural productivity over time, on average for 288 districts divided by governance categories:[24]

We see that agricultural productivity differs among the different categories, following our theoretical expectations, from even before the Green Revolution in the mid-1960s. While productivity continues to increase after the 1960s, differences between categories also increase over time.

Different forms of agrarian labor represent another dimension of commodification. Traditional, hierarchical social obligations and relationships between workers and *saiths* (bosses) in India are not unknown in factories and modern corporations in gleaming office buildings in urban India, but they are most evident in the farms and fields of the deep countryside. Employment figures in the 2011 Indian Census provide us with some evidence for greater or lesser commodification in patterns of agrarian work. In Figure 8.2, we see the

[21] Breman 1996.   [22] Lewis 1954.   [23] Frankel 1971.
[24] Bhallia and Singh 2012. I thank Devesh Kapur for pointing me to these data.

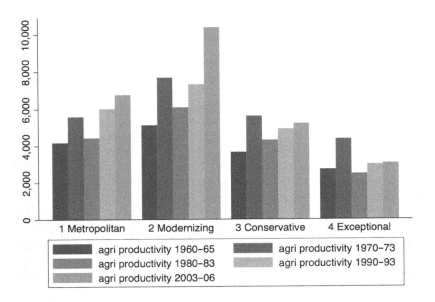

FIGURE 8.1 Agricultural productivity over time

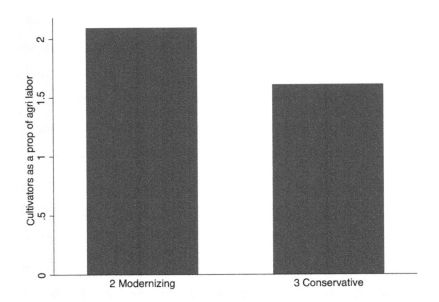

FIGURE 8.2 Ratio of cultivators to agricultural labor

proportion of landed cultivators to landless agricultural workers in modernizing and conservative districts.

Modernizing districts have a higher ratio of cultivators to landless laborers than those in conservative districts. In more modernizing contexts, there were more successful efforts of the government and social movements of empowered peasants to dismantle traditional structures and give land to the tiller.[25] The presence of significant numbers of landless agricultural workers relative to landowning cultivators, by contrast, suggests the persistence of traditional patterns. This distinction can also be seen in the proportions of precarious agricultural workers to the total workforce. In Figure 8.3, we see that marginal agricultural labor[26] as a proportion of the total labor force is roughly twice as high on average in conservative districts as modernizing districts. While these data are only suggestive, they point to differences in the extent of the commodification of labor and land, at least within the Indian countryside.

8.2.2   Rents and Investment

The direct and indirect interventions of the state have also powerfully shaped economic institutions, though in different ways in different places. Many of

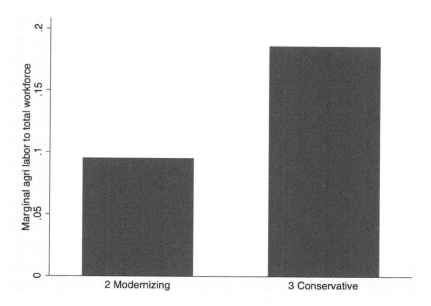

FIGURE 8.3 Marginal agricultural workers as proportion of workforce

---

[25] Herring 1983.
[26] Marginal workers are defined in the Indian census as those who worked less than 180 days a year.

these interventions are implicated in "rents," usually defined as assets that provide returns out of proportion to the resources required for their mobilization. Rents are deeply embedded in politics, in South Asia and far beyond. It is widely accepted that a major objective of everyday politics, particularly but not only in developing countries, is the creation and capture of rents by political actors and distribution of these rents to their clients. These might include lucrative government positions and contracts, licenses for lucrative economic activities, and even the politically determined location of infrastructure investment to favor particular constituencies over others, as well as lucrative contracts for its construction.

The distribution of rents in India has deep roots in colonial rule. Areas with more penetrative governance institutions established patterns of the flow of lucrative rents and other patronage resources to various groups as a means for the government to maintain quiescence from key elites and to "divide and rule" through competition among them. Groups would then become locked in competition with one another to control rentier access; eventually, this competition was adjudicated through elections, as discussed in Chapter 7. This yielded not just expectations of largesse but also mechanisms to absorb it and systematized competition over its capture. However, in other areas where governance was subcontracted – either formally in the maintenance of princely states and political agencies or more informally in steeply hierarchical land tenure arrangements – rents were more parsimoniously deployed to benefit a narrow set of social elites. These geographic contexts have long been associated with public underinvestment and exclusion, and state capture.

Postcolonial states sought to disrupt these mechanisms of colonial governance, but patterns of rentier distribution and more public investment have persisted in many places and were incorporated into postcolonial development. The post-independence investments of the state and allied private sector in industrial production have occurred in locations of significant economic intervention from the colonial period. In other words, the actual mechanisms of state-directed industrial development were themselves predicated on *ex ante* rent-seeking relationships.[27] Postcolonial patterns of rents and investment, when viewed from a perspective of economic geography, mostly reinforced rather than disrupted patterns of rents and investment of the colonial period.

Liberalization in the 1990s significantly restricted the autonomous role of the nationalist state in governing the economy. Yet if anything, the involvement of agents of the state in promoting and intervening in economic activity has grown as regional governments became dominant actors in the political economy of rent creation, distribution, and capture.[28] This has increased the rentier aspects of the economy and heightened their impact, as politically favored corporate

---

[27] Krueger 1974.   [28] Naseemullah 2017a.

groups have sought and received access to expanded arenas of economic activity and access to the capital necessary for these investments. Most of the dollar billionaires in India are concentrated in "rent-thick" sectors, such as mining, telecommunications, and infrastructure, in which they benefit from close ties with government actors.[29]

We can see some indicative evidence of patterns of recent rentier activity in the contemporary Indian economy after liberalization, particularly in local economies dominated by rents. To assess rent-implicated economic activity, I use Gandhi and Walton's definition: "sectors such as real estate, infrastructure, construction, mining, telecom, cement and media are classified as 'rent-thick' because of the pervasive role of the state in giving licenses, reputations of illegality, or information on monopolistic practices."[30] Figure 8.4 represents the proportion of district aggregate income generated by mining, construction, communication, and transportation as these four sectors are the most clearly rent-thick.

There is little discernable difference in the proportion of rents in district income among districts under metropolitan, modernizing and conservative categories, but exceptional districts have a qualitatively higher level of rent-implicated activity. The preponderance of rentier activities, like mining and mineral extraction, in exceptional districts is implicated in relatively recent

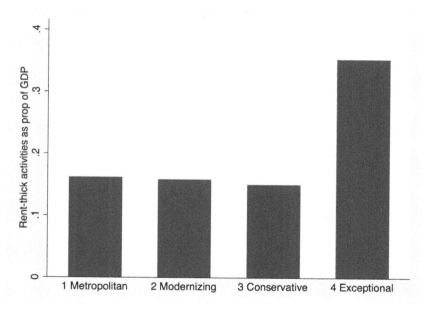

FIGURE 8.4 Rent-implicated activity as a proportion of district income

[29] Gandhi and Walton 2012.   [30] Gandhi and Walton 2012, 12.

extractive intervention in regions previously characterized by "stand-offish" relationships between state and society. This is in turn associated with sovereignty-challenging violence, on which more later.

By contrast, private investment, particularly in the formal corporate sector, has followed the opposite trajectory, as it is concentrated around areas of the greatest state–society interpenetration and the strength and depth of formal institutions supporting economic activity. These have important historical antecedents, with joint-stock companies, managing agencies of expatriate investments, and allied indigenous banking and trading concerns located in the colonial entrepôts of Bombay, Calcutta, and Madras.[31] After independence, nationalist firms like the Tata and Birla Groups, as well as others associated with trading and finance, clustered in many of the same locations, taking advantage of institutional density, despite the stated goals of the government to encourage investment beyond the cities.

Since liberalization, the corporate sector in the economy has grown significantly in wealth, power, and prominence, leading to characterizations of government practices as not pro-market but pro-business, yielding growth but also heightened inequality as gains are captured by oligarchic capital.[32] These remain clustered in locations with the highest institutional density, as well as linkages to the international economy. To assess the concentration and dispersion of corporate investment in India, I use the geographical incidence of the listed companies in the Bombay Stock Exchange (BSE or Sensex), as well as their assets and capital. Publicly listed companies are more legible to the global economy and receive the most institutional investment and regulatory favor. This is especially the case with industries like business processing, financial services, and information technology. Figure 8.5 represents the number of BSE listed firms per district, as well as their assets and capital, during the course of the 2000s, including districts with no BSE listed firms registered.

Districts under metropolitan governance in postcolonial India – and especially the state of Delhi and the six metropolitan districts of Mumbai, Ahmedabad, Chennai, Kolkata, Hyderabad, and Bangalore – account for a lion's share of listed firms. Further, firms in districts under metropolitan governance represent most of the capital and assets, suggesting the extent of concentration of formal private investment in a small minority of districts. These sites of governance are also most closely associated with sovereignty-neutral violence, including Hindu-Muslim violence in Mumbai, Ahmedabad, and increasingly Delhi, and intense electoral violence in Kolkata.

8.3   THE PATCHWORK STATE AND DEVELOPMENT OUTCOMES

In what follows, I will use the governance categories arising from the patchwork state to highlight differences in various outcomes important to development,

[31] Chandavarkar 1993; Birla 2009.   [32] Kohli 2012.

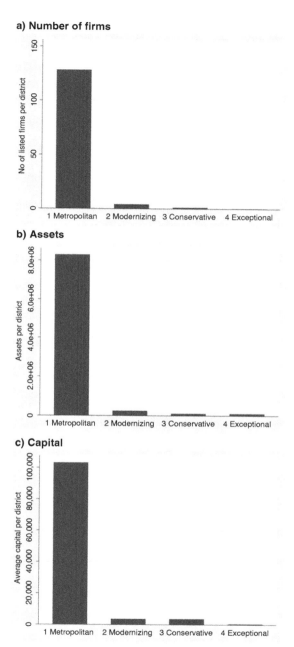

FIGURE 8.5 Firms, and assets and capital of BSE in millions of rupees in 2013

understood quite broadly. In order to highlight dynamics that are not captured by state-level explanations, I report both raw district-level measures and the differences between those measures and state averages. This is intended to capture variation in state capacity and state-society relations that represent legacies of colonial and postcolonial governance arrangements within states, particularly large and heterogeneous ones such as Uttar Pradesh and Maharashtra.

8.3.1 Growth

Studies of the politics of development in India, as elsewhere, are bifurcated between studies of economic growth on the one hand and studies of human development on the other, with only a few scholars attempting to integrate the two.[33] Traditionally, studies of economic growth have not been geographic in nature, focusing on the politics behind growth constraints, including public and private investment and the intersectoral transfer of capital from low- to high-productivity enterprises.[34] Economic liberalization, however, returned the spatial distribution of growth onto the research agenda, as the central state was less committed to managing public investment and redistribution across subnational boundaries, and state strategies and outcomes varied significantly.

To examine the ways in which growth outcomes may be affected by governance institutions and colonial legacies, I analyze per capita income data – which can be thought of as GDP per capita at the district level – through the patchwork state framework. Figure 8.6 presents average district per capita income from the mid-2000s[35] by governance categories.

We can see marked differences among the categories, in expected patterns; we see metropolitan districts much higher in qualitative terms than the others, and we see conservative districts lower than modernizing districts. They are also lower than exceptional districts; this may be a consequence of concentrated government and rentier investment discussed earlier, yet the higher per capita incomes due to these forms of economic activity are unlikely to translate into human development outcomes, on which will be discussed later. We see similar patterns within Indian states. Differences from state averages move in expected directions, with metropolitan districts clearly showing higher incomes and exceptional districts significantly lower than state averages in the 2004 data, with modernizing and conservative districts arrayed in between. These represent variations in outcomes that are unexplained through more popular state-level frameworks.

For an alternate measure of aggregate economic activity, I turn to nighttime luminosity. Brian Min has calculated "nightlights" for villages, districts, and

---

[33] Kohli 2012 is important in this regard.   [34] Pinglé 1999; D'Costa 2000; Frankel 2005.
[35] District GDP measures in the mid-2000s are available from state-level development data in an archived website of the Planning Commission, now under the Niti Udyog website. https://niti.gov.in/planningcommission.gov.in/docs/plans/stateplan/ssphd.php?state=ssphdbody.htm

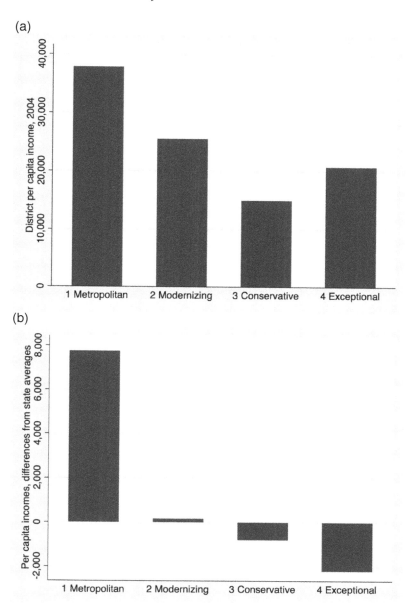

FIGURE 8.6 District per capita income

states over a twenty-year period using satellite data. Nighttime luminosity
can be used as a proxy for both wealth and income, working under the
assumption that greater luminosity at night signals not just electrification

(a)

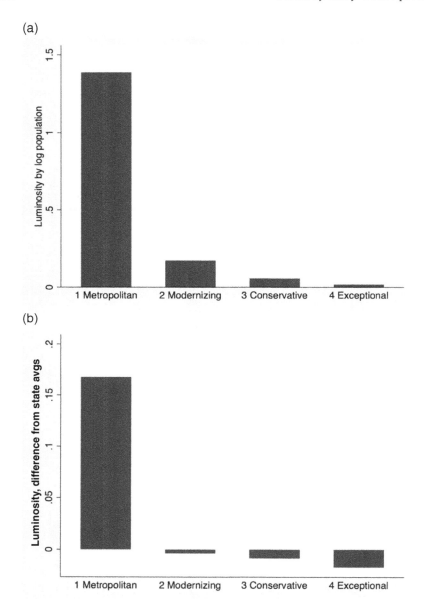

FIGURE 8.7 Nighttime luminosity

but greater use of electricity, which in turn correlates with greater economic
activity.[36] Figure 8.7 represents average luminosity as a proportion of log
population per district for 2013, the last year of the study, itself a measure of

[36] Min 2015; Gaba et al. 2016.

median luminosity over tens of thousands of observations per month, and as difference from state averages.

Here we see a significant decrease in luminosity between metropolitan and modernizing districts, as expected in the distinction between urban and rural, but also more modest decreases over the other three categories. We also see expected differences between state averages and district-level luminosity scores, which is significant because these luminosity data do not include some of the largest metropolitan cases – Mumbai, Chennai, Kolkata, and Bangalore – thus reflects the impact of other urban agglomerations.

8.3.2   Human Development Indicators

Research in India and elsewhere has broadened from focusing narrowly on growth outcomes to a more inclusive understanding of development. Much of the political economy of development today studies the ways in which state interventions, and the capacities and incentives of government agencies to implement them, can expand the essential needs and capabilities of some of the poorest among Indian citizens, including the provision of welfare and essential infrastructure, as well as health care and education.

Research programs in human development have in turn expanded from the technical implementation of human development interventions to examining the politics and social conditions that cause their formulation and condition their implementation. Here, both subnational solidarities and the more cynical incentives of electoral politics can impact variation in development outcomes. More recently, researchers have focused on microlevel political engagements among citizens, brokers, politicians, and bureaucrats that shape when and how poor citizens demand development and make claims on the state.[37] This research investigates the politics of distribution: when and how the poor are successful in forcing the state to provide both statutory and discretionary public and social goods. Yet a focus on these microlevel interactions significantly limits external validity; we know less about the extent to which theories travel across India's varied political and economic geography. An examination of the impact of different forms of governance on human development outcomes may thus be a fruitful addition to debates on both development and distribution. Sorting out the extent to which outcomes are the result of the welfare spending, policy decisions and implementation of state governments, in addition to other factors, is a complicated proposition far beyond the scope of this book. Nonetheless, a focus on the district level and differences from state averages can at least reveal the extent of unexplained variation and suggest the ways in which variations in state capacity and state–society relations might influence these outcomes.

---

[37] Kruks-Wisner 2018; Auerbach 2020.

Here, I present two of the most common measures of human development: literacy and infant mortality.[38] Figure 8.8 represents differences in the literacy rate from the 2011 Census across the different governance categories and the differences between these scores and state averages.

This shows expected outcomes, with metropolitan and modernizing districts with higher literacy than conservative and exceptional districts, both in absolute terms and relative to state averages. The slightly higher literacy of exceptional relative to conservative districts may be due to the more concentrated missionary activity in northeastern states. Figure 8.9 represents infant mortality scores,[39] per district as well as differences from state averages.

With infant mortality we see much the same pattern as with literacy; the variation is, if anything, more dramatic. This may be because illiteracy is more susceptible to the interventions of the state over time than the more complex and tragic problem of infant mortality.

Lastly, employment and the quality of work is a vitally important, though often neglected, aspect of human needs and capabilities. Outside cultivation, workers are employed in various enterprises, and the capacity to earn wages that enable individuals to sustain their livelihood and invest in themselves and their families comes to the very essence of development, as freedom from the obligations of the market. Those who are unable to work fulltime suffer serious challenges, particularly when they are at or below the thresholds for poverty or caloric insufficiency.

In this sense, basic needs like health, education, sanitation, and nutrition are necessary but not sufficient for wageworkers and the self-employed. Being able to work enough to live on one's earnings, self-insure against calamities and save for the future is crucial. In India as in other developing countries, the notion of an "unemployment rate" makes little sense as it relies on regular national surveys of those employed and actively seeking work. Instead, I turn to the concept of "marginal workers" in the 2011 Census, defined as those who worked for less than 180 days during the census year. Employment precarity, signified by this measure, is a deeply detrimental aspect of the contemporary Indian economy, though often overshadowed by health and education indicators that form the basis of most development interventions.[40] Figure 8.10 presents marginal workers as a proportion of the total workforce.

As we can see, employment precarity differs significantly by governance category, from just over ten percent in metropolitan districts to over a third in conservative districts; average difference from state averages also represents

---

[38] Other research has looked at spending on health and education as a key intermediary mechanism, but this is formulated at the state rather than the district level.

[39] Ram et al. 2013.

[40] The Mahatma Gandhi National Rural Employment Guarantee Scheme (MGNREGS) represents an important exception in this regard.

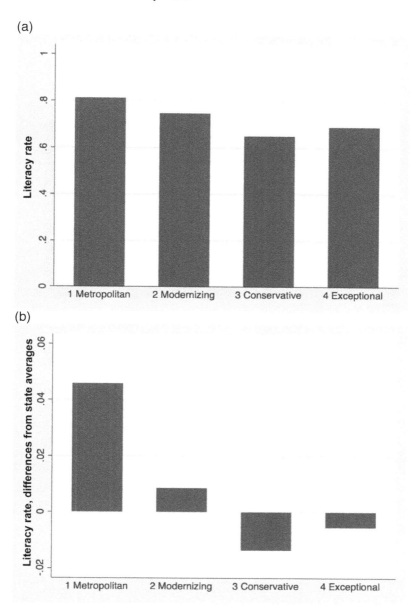

FIGURE 8.8 Literacy rate

differences along expected lines. A significant proportion of this difference might arise from India's slow-moving and complex but serious agrarian crisis, signified by low and unstable prices, higher input costs and a shortage of capital,

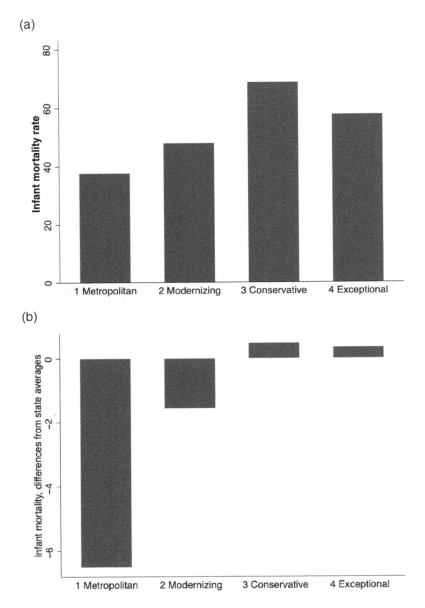

FIGURE 8.9 Infant mortality rate

most tragically illustrated by farmer suicides. However, the impact of that crisis itself differs across political geography, in ways that implicate the patchwork state, and are in turn associated with various patterns of violence.

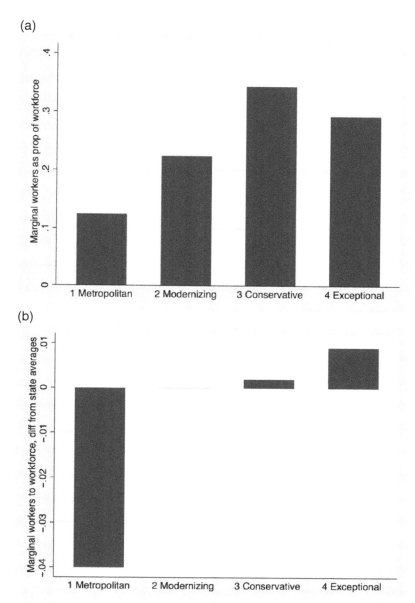

FIGURE 8.10 Marginal workers as a proportion of the workforce

8.4   INDIAN DEVELOPMENT IN COMPARATIVE PERSPECTIVE

Moving from the subnational dynamics of development in India to South Asia in comparative perspective, Bangladesh and Pakistan present stark contrasts in the variations in development outcomes across national territories. Figure 8.11 presents literacy rates for the three countries in the early 2010s, first in terms of raw scores and second in terms of variation from the national average.

While we must be cautious about cross-country comparability of any measure collected by separate national agencies, we clearly see significant variation not just the levels but also variation across these countries; the standard deviation of literacy rates in Pakistan are almost twice as much as Bangladesh, with India in the middle. If anything, this variation is even more stark when it comes to district-level Human Development Index (HDI) scores between Pakistan and Bangladesh (Figure 8.12).

The population of Bangladesh is 83 percent that of Pakistan, both are Muslim-majority countries with legacies of military-authoritarian rule, and both were ruled as part of the same country, and thus subject to not only colonial but also postcolonial administrative structures. How might we account for such a stark difference? I argue that this arises from the starkly different economic and political geographies in contemporary Pakistan and Bangladesh, implicated in the patchwork state framework, which has profound consequences for national development patterns and outcomes.

Perceived existential rather than ideological concerns structured Pakistan's development trajectory from independence. Partition shaped the country, but not with a view to making it economically viable or coherent; the territories that would become present-day Pakistan contained the metropolis of Karachi, the disparate agrarian societies of (West) Punjab, Sindh and what is now KP, along with a long span of frontier territories and tribal-majority princely states that were governed under exceptional arrangements. Due to early, intense regional competition with India, the lack of both administrative and rentier resources and the many demands on the new state by populations seeking development, Pakistan found itself in a state of "systemic vulnerability."[41] The Ayub Khan regime from 1958 responded to this vulnerability by directing resources to where they would be the most productive in generating industrial investment, like Karachi, while extracting resources from the most politically vulnerable, like East Bengal. It otherwise bought off elites and mobilized populations that might pose difficulties for the regime, from Punjabi farmers to Sindhi landlords to Pashtun and Balochi tribal leaders. Different governance arrangements thus conditioned stark differences in the integration of the different parts of Pakistan into the national development project. These differences have persisted despite the fall of the Ayub Khan

---

[41]   Doner, Ritchie and Slater 2005; Naseemullah and Arnold 2015.

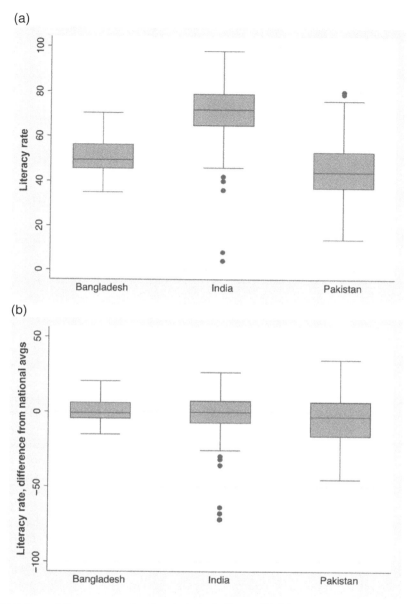

FIGURE 8.11 Literacy rates for Bangladesh, India, and Pakistan

regime and the independence of Bangladesh, Zulfiqar Ali Bhutto's populism and Zia ul Haq's brutal military dictatorship, and the emergence of more systematized electoral competition.

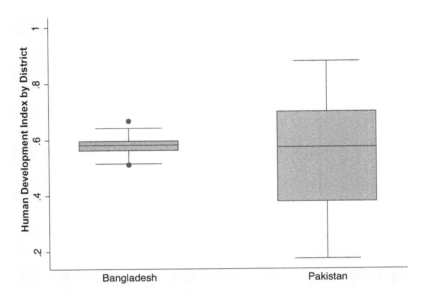

FIGURE 8.12 HDI scores in Bangladesh and Pakistan, 2015

A tension has always existed in the Pakistani polity between centrifugal and centripetal political forces.[42] Centrifugal actors believe that the state's largesse should be directed outward from the center to the periphery. By contrast, centripetal actors – like the military, the bureaucracy, the judiciary – believe that resources should be preserved at the core for the use of the state. Less noted is how this tension operates differently across political geography. In the metropolitan centers like Karachi and Lahore, and the more wealthy and mobilized countryside and smaller cities, centripetal forces can more easily accommodate centrifugal ones, and political and economic competition leads to greater investment and productive state intervention, as well as competition over its resources. In conservative districts in interior Sindh, southern Punjab and parts of KP, however, the emphasis in maintaining social order has meant that dominant elites have colluded with the central elites to restrict competition and monopolize distribution of largesse, leading to more restrained development. In areas under exceptional governance along western and northwestern frontiers, by contrast, the imposition of the security state and the resistance and resentments of local populations that are not well integrated into the Pakistani polity has translated into much worse development outcomes there. The result is massive variation in development driven, at heart, by patchwork state outcomes.

[42] Lieven 2012.

Bangladesh, by contrast, is characterized by remarkable evenness in political geography. With the exception of the Chittagong Hill Tracts and two metropolitan agglomerations, much of contemporary Bangladesh is constituted by the countryside, large towns and small cities with an active and assertive civil society and interpenetration between society and the state. The histories of colonial rule and postcolonial transformations, and the shocks of two partitions, have shaped this exception to the patchwork state, or perhaps more accurately, a state made from a single patch. Contemporary Bangladesh has surprising features in relation to development. From a poverty-stricken country emerging from widespread conflict, in which the bureaucracy and civil society were systematically targeted, Bangladesh has emerged as a relative success story. Further, these salutary human development indicators and successful export-oriented economic growth has coexisted with weak state institutions captured by elites and an economy replete with rent-seeking.

To explain Bangladesh's relative successes from very humble beginnings, scholars have sought to identify the underlying political settlements that enable economic activity in the context of obvious, surface-level dysfunction.[43] Hossain locates Bangladesh's durable socioeconomic consensus in the aftermath of the disastrous and deadly famine of 1974, which coincided with the assassination of Sheikh Mujib ur-Rahman and the end of his short-lived experiment of socialist one-party rule.[44] By this account, Bangladesh's relative development successes are the result of deep and dependent engagement with the international aid community, coming with costs as well as benefits. Such engagement arose out of the consensus among elites that the survival of the ruling class depended on basic welfare, social protection and employment among the poor landed population. In order to do so, ruling elites established a set of credible policy commitments to international donors that they would establish and maintain externally facing pro-market policies. But Bangladesh's relatively even political geography has enabled the construction of social consensus around social protection from the center, but also the penetration of society to a series of development interventions: "A flat, small space with an accessible and homogenous population, the country has many qualities suited to social experimentation."[45] In other words, its development trajectory is endogenous to an even political geography, in stark contrast to that of India and especially Pakistan.

8.5 DEVELOPMENT, VIOLENCE, AND THE PATCHWORK STATE

There is a longstanding debate about the relationship between development and violence. During the heyday of modernization theory, it was understood that the process of economic development – which involved industrialization, urbanization

---

[43] Khan 2011; Hassan 2013. [44] Hossain 2017. [45] Hossain 2017, 14.

and increasing inequality – would be disruptive and could turn violent, particularly when institutions did not have the capacity to accommodate popular demands.[46] Since that time, scholars have studied the ways in which the widespread predation and disinvestment associated with violence undermines development, while solutions to systemic violence in the monopolization of rents also have adverse, long-term consequences.[47] In studying the relationship between development and violence in South Asia, however, it helps to differentiate among different forms of violence, which might have differing impacts, particularly when interacting with patchwork forms of state authority.

8.5.1   Development and Sovereignty-Contesting Violence

Much of the discourse on development policy in South Asian countries focuses on the provision of key public and social goods to individuals and communities in need of them, which is entirely appropriate. Yet this framing of development overshadows another way of understanding development, as transformation through capitalist investment. In cities and the wealthy countryside, this might mean mega-infrastructure projects or investment in new enterprises. However, the extractive dimensions of capitalist transformation have significant implications for violence, particularly in areas of exceptional governance, where the state traditionally had a light footprint ahead of neoliberal reform.

An example of this is the recent investment in mining and mineral extraction in forested areas in eastern and central India that are home to *Adivasi* communities. Domestic oligarchs and multinational corporations have colluded with state governments to gain access to these formerly protected areas, depriving indigenous communities of their traditional livelihoods, displacing villages and causing significant environmental destruction.[48] In this context, Maoist groups claim to fight on behalf of these communities against the state and its capitalist clients, even while both state and insurgent actors operate various forms of protection rackets.[49] Mining operations more directly provide the explosives that Maoists use to perpetrate attacks. Thus the quest for capitalist development, through rentier investments, in these mineral-rich areas of previous government restraint perpetuates violence between those who challenge the state's authority and state actors who violently seek to reclaim that authority.

The link between rentier investment and insurgent violence is at the heart of separatist conflict in Balochistan as well. Mineral engineers discovered Pakistan's biggest gas field at Sui, in the tribal Dera Bugti district, in the early 1950s. Natural gas from Balochistan provides energy primarily for big cities like Karachi; a long-term grievance among Balochis is that the province receives little benefit from the resources of their underdeveloped homeland.[50] In the last

---

[46] See Gurr 1970.   [47] North, Wallis and Weingast 2008; Besley and Persson 2011.
[48] Falkenhagen 2011.   [49] See Shah 2006 for more on these dynamics.   [50] Grare 2013.

decade, however, the insurgency has increased in its scope due to Chinese investment in Pakistan, with Balochistan at the fulcrum of the China-Pakistan Economic Corridor (CPEC). The Pakistani military and paramilitary forces are obligated to protect these investments, bringing Balochi separatists and the security state into regular conflict due to such investments.

Part of the difficulty is that rentier investment, as an avatar of development, and insurgent violence mutually reinforce significant distance between society and the state. Such economic activity may stimulate growth, and thus yield tax revenue (as well as kickbacks). But such growth does not translate into human development, despite efforts by the state to provide discretionary goods to affected populations in order to undermine the insurgency. This is because the state has limited means of engaging society in a manner that could augment the freedom and capacities of citizens under current (and increasingly coercive) forms of exceptional governance.

8.5.2   Development and Sovereignty-Neutral Violence

Other forms of development have much closer relationships to SNV, or the struggle among groups over public resources. This runs the gamut from the violent contention of communities seeking "reserved status," in order to receive the benefits of affirmative action, to the strategic use of Hindu-Muslim violence to capture resources and political power in the context of urban political economy.[51] Beyond state provision of goods and services that has animated much research in the politics of development in India, other aspects of development have significant impacts on the nature and consequences of violence.

In particular, the state-implicated transformation of the agrarian economy toward greater commercialization has been a very bloody process. In 2020–2021, farmers from Punjab and other wealthy areas in northern India marched on Delhi to protest policies that would undermine statist institutions like minimum pricing guarantees and allow the participation of the private sector; the ensuing agitations have resulted in hundreds of deaths. These institutions themselves were the result of earlier struggles between the state and peasant society over agricultural policy, along with significant conflicts over distribution.[52] These politics were implicated in modernizing arrangements of postcolonial governance, in the most prosperous and vibrant areas of the countryside, rather than conservative districts in eastern and central India with significantly lower productivity.

Earlier periods of investment, development, and violence in modernizing districts were associated with the politics of the Green Revolution and clashes between dominant and subaltern communities in the countryside. Some of the most horrific violence that is perpetrated within Indian society has been against Dalits, who are placed by Vedic orthodoxy at the bottom of social hierarchies.

[51] Bohlken and Sergenti 2010; Jaffrelot 2016.   [52] Varshney 1998.

The traditional political, social, and economic weakness of Dalits arose from their lack of access to land, assets and education. They are thus traditionally dependent on landowners, cultivators and dominant elites for agricultural work and often consigned to occupations that violate notions of ritual purity. In the traditional hierarchical society of the Indian village, there was pervasive structural and everyday violence against Dalits but fewer cases of explicit conflict.

The development of the 1960s came with challenges to traditional hierarchies and thus increasing capacities for Dalits to mobilize against their oppression. At the same time, the Green Revolution empowered and enriched middle cultivators, who resisted sharing the spoils of their higher yields. One of the most terrible massacres of Dalits occurred in the village of Keezhvenmani in Nagapattinam District in Tamil Nadu in 1968. When Dalit workers, supported by Communist unionists, agitated for higher wages, forty-four of their family members were murdered.[53] We can see some of the same dynamics of modernizing development and social violence today.[54] Figure 8.13 presents the distribution of violent incidents in which Dalits were victims between 2016 and mid-2021, across different postcolonial governance categories.

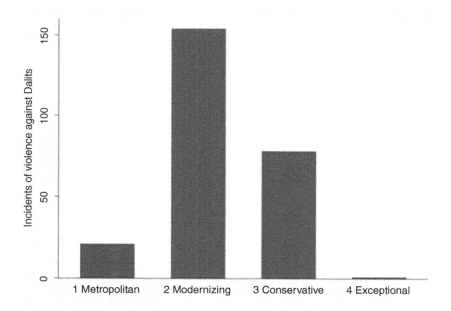

FIGURE 8.13 Violence against Dalits, 2016–2021

[53] Frankel 1971, 113–118.
[54] I am deeply indebted to conversations with Amit Ahuja on these points.

We can see that two-thirds of the incidents of anti-Dalit violence occurred in modernizing districts, reflecting the continuation of a link between development and hierarchy-associated violence in the countryside.[55] Violence against Dalits represents a specific part of a wider category of the darker side of development, in which violence occurs due to challenges to social domination that arise from growth.

***

Violence and development have complex interrelationships in South Asia, particularly beyond the realm of particular development interventions such as the provision of public goods. They suggest the conflict embedded in questions of distribution: who wins and who loses. The unevenness of the state in different parts of South Asia shapes the ways in which different forms of development might spark violence, and how violence might be addressed through development, however. Without attention to the variations in state authority and state–society relations, we might miss intimate connections between these two realms of inquiry that are usually treated separately.

8.6 CONCLUSION

The study of the politics of development in India has generally focused on the politics of its states: their social coalitions, party systems, policy implementation by more or less capable bureaucrats, differences in the strength of civil society. This focus has obscured other causal factors that are rooted in dynamics before the formation of India's contemporary states and operate within them, at the district level. Patchwork states and governance mechanisms highlight district-level variation in growth and development outcomes, while also introducing a complementary set of causal mechanisms that relate how colonial authorities governed economic life differently in different places, with lasting consequences. The differential unevenness of political geography has impacts in terms of national development trajectories, particularly with the polar cases of Pakistan and Bangladesh.

More generally, I argue that the politics of development share a close connection with the politics of competition and conflict discussed in the rest of the book. Forms of violence, electoral competition, and development outcomes, are together products in the spatial variation in state capacity and state–society relations that has its roots in the geographically differentiated nature of colonial rule and attempts by postcolonial states to revise colonial governance.

---

[55] Of course, this could be in part a function of greater reporting in modernizing areas, but this is consistent with hidden, structural violence rather than reported incidents in conservative areas.

PART IV

CONCLUSIONS

9

Researching the Legacies of Colonial Rule

The comparative-historical framework introduced in this book, and its deployment for analyzing the contemporary politics of competition and conflict in South Asian countries, suggests that we might want to revisit the ways we normally approach studying the legacies. There has been a great deal of scholarship in the social sciences on colonial legacies in the past couple of decades, but much of this literature has been preoccupied with cleanly identifying the causal impact of colonial institutions on important social and economic outcomes within and across postcolonial countries, often through the use of through "natural experiments." This dominant approach has certain benefits but also serious drawbacks.

In particular, it has tended to obscure the complex, internally differentiated politics within colonial regimes, which in turn have generated complex, differentiated legacies. Preoccupations with causal inference have led researchers to focus on specific contexts in which a causal instrument – a natural experiment or other form of exogenous or instrumental variable – is available and can be employed to demonstrate with exactitude the import of a particular kind of colonial institution relative to another. These strategies are by their nature selective in their objects of inquiry. They do not – cannot – perceive a complex landscape of spatial variation constituting different kinds of governance arrangements internal to a colonial territory, and the legacies of this variation. In other words, to mix metaphors, they both search for the key where the lamppost is miss the forest for the trees.

Instrumental approaches to colonial legacies have some tricky normative implications as well as analytical drawbacks. Exact specification of the effects of colonial institutions indicates the centrality of questions of whether we can actually measure them. This in turn suggests that there is a serious *analytical* debate on the knowability of the consequences of colonial rule; can we demonstrate that colonial rule has had deleterious effects, in terms of long-term development, despite confounding factors that could muddy such an evaluation?

Is there a serious debate, however? Most historians would agree that colonialism was a social evil, but a rather complicated one, so spend most of their energies understanding the causes, nature, and consequences internal to this complex object of inquiry. Such a debate is, however, a welcome development for those on the right who want to emphasize colonial institutional investments and their legacies that might be associated with positive outcomes.[1] We end up with dueling sets of "good" and "bad" colonial legacies, which talk past one an other and cannot come to a resolution because the nature and consequences of the regime considered as a whole.

Further, the relative "successes" of certain colonialisms associated with long-term positive outcomes, such as settler colonial societies, can only be assessed from the perspective of beneficiaries centuries later.[2] The destruction of alternative sovereignties and the suffering – or wholesale elimination – of indigenous peoples are not often mentioned, let alone analyzed. The exacting specification of the effects of colonial institutions on contemporary outcomes can thus lead to the misspecification of a wider range of impacts and outcomes of colonial regimes, let alone the lived experience of its victims.

We also enter problematic territory in the schematic manner by which researchers tend to understand how colonial institutions transmit their legacies forward, based on a logic of straightforward path dependence. In this framing, once institutions are established, even if centuries before, societies are locked into these trajectories, no matter what they do. The benefits of such an institutional rendering of historical legacies is that it cleanly identifies the sources of transmission, enabling us to see how the past might impact the present. However, it also tends to ignore intervening critical junctures – such as decolonization – through which other institutions are formed; earlier and later institutions interact in a complex fashion to explain present circumstances.[3] The simplicity of initial institutional sorting by causal instrument sets up a temptation to view politics as ending with that sorting.

This denies the agency of anti-colonial activists who forced the end of colonial rule and postcolonial governments who consciously attempted to counteract colonialism's most pernicious legacies; these might not be wholly successful, but they are impactful, complicating any straightforward notion of path dependence in colonial legacies. The political conflict over institutions that occurs both with the resistance to colonial rule and the reckoning with its impacts after decolonization are therefore crucial for understanding the nature and the limits of colonial legacies and yet are generally absent from these discussions. The locked-in framing of institutional legacies, absent the recognition of subsequent critical junctures, represents the spectral hand of the colonial past that forever grips the throat of

---

[1] See Ferguson 2012; Gilley 2017.   [2] Acemoglu and Robinson 2012.
[3] For more on institutional change, see Mahoney and Thelen 2009.

the postcolonial present, rendering the politics of intervening decades and even centuries irrelevant. At the very least, it denies the political dynamism within colonial rule and postcolonial efforts to address its legacies.

This book has suggested a different way of understanding colonialism and its legacies, which frames institutional origins as embedded within and endogenous to complex processes of state formation under colonial rule. It has analyzed how postcolonial governments sought to address the legacies of fragmented governance, which modified but did not eliminate them. In so doing, I abjure concerns about confounders and identification and instead focus on the task of understanding internally complex colonial regimes and their institutions as a whole, and how these might explain the local capacities of the state and its relationships with social actors.

This is not only a better approach for explaining spasmodic and stochastic patterns of violence across territory, but also an important approach for explaining other social outcomes, like subnational variations in development. It does mean accepting, to some extent, the inherent endogeneity of historical processes and not knowing precisely whether this institution led to that outcome. However, with this key disadvantage come other hidden advantages. Certainly, methodological preoccupations are inevitable with any program of research, but recent studies on colonial institutional legacies have ignored the inherent tradeoffs between the problems of confounding on one hand and those related to the specification of the object of inquiry on the other. This chapter explores in further detail what this has meant in the study of colonial legacies, starting with the role of history in comparative analysis.

9.1 WHAT DO WE MEAN BY A HISTORICAL LEGACY?

Most macro-social inquiry, including the study of colonial legacies, is indelibly historical. Absent universal "covering laws," we search for the causes of phenomena in what occurred before: inflation leading to social unrest, the mobilization of the working class leading to the emergence of popular democracy, or colonial rule leading to endemic violence and underdevelopment. Historically minded social scientists must adjudicate the impact of potential past causes that might individually or collectively determine outcomes and identify the most meaningful or powerful among them. Was World War I, for instance, caused by nationalist challenges to continental empires, or by German challenges to British hegemony? While any particular outcome can serve as a cause of some subsequent outcome,[4] a scholar, by making a causal claim, is in effect making an affirmative argument for one important (or neglected) cause or set of causes over others, and then marshaling evidence in support of that claim. This has evolved into a tradition in the social sciences of conducting research based on rival historical arguments, in turn

---

[4] Fearon (1991) called this the "Cleopatra's Nose" problem.

based on different theoretical frameworks, to understand the historical processes that shape consequent politics.[5]

9.1.1   Critical Junctures and Path Dependence

In comparative-historical analysis in political science, a framing of history as that of constant, evolutionary and teleological has given way to a model of punctuated equilibrium, in which social dynamics, strategic decisions, or incidental events during periods of great flux can yield outcomes that persist for a long time along relatively stable trajectories.[6] Ruth Collier and David Collier formalized this approach by specifying "critical junctures" – periods in which structures of normal politics have broken down, opening up multiple possibilities for political trajectories – the outcomes of which are subject to path dependence.[7]

Since this initial formulation, scholars have further specified the framework of critical junctures and path dependence, introducing logics of "increasing returns" and incorporating it more formally into institutionalist analysis.[8] Critical junctures represent a temporal gap between the breakdown of older structures that pattern human behavior and the emergence of new institutions, during which different forms of political organization are possible, and particular variables or influences rise to causal prominence. The contingent outcomes of these dynamics, once institutionalized, have long-term consequences. In more formal institutionalist terms, critical junctures represent the search for new equilibria after a disruptive shock. As a result, the tools of inquiry we use to understand that process are qualitatively different from the forms of analysis appropriate for understanding stable equilibria.[9]

9.1.2   Historical Institutional Legacies

The scholarly work on historical legacies in social science has developed largely apart from the critical junctures-path dependence framework. This is because the objects of historical legacies represent the obverse of the contingency evident in the critical juncture-path dependency model; they represent the *continuation* of the influence of an antecedent cause *despite* the disruption of a critical juncture. Historical legacies "describ[e] the presence of a phenomenon that came into being before and persisted after a critical juncture ruptured the

---

[5] For an overview of this tradition, see Mahoney and Reuschemeyer 2003.

[6] Moore 1966; Skocpol 1979. On punctuated equilibrium, see Baumgartner et al. 2009.

[7] Collier and Collier 1991. For a parallel application, see Luebbert 1991.

[8] Pierson 2004; Capoccia and Kelemen 2007.

[9] Greif and Laitin 2004. Schwartz 2000 by contrast, suggests that an aggressively formal approach to path dependence threatens our abilities to understand the diverse mechanisms of path dependency.

original conditions that gave rise to it."[10] In other words, they represent continuity despite junctures rather than change because of them.

There is an important distinction between two different types of argumentation on historical causes and legacies.[11] The first ("$X_1 \rightarrow X_2$") refers to the same causal factor persisting from one time period to another, such as neo-patrimonial relationships persisting after democratization. The second ("$X_1 \rightarrow Y_2$"), represents a particular cause in the first time period leading systematically to a particular and predictable, but different, outcome in the second period, in the manner of emergent coalitions of industrial workers and middle peasants before World War I leading to social democracy in postwar Scandinavia.[12] The critical issue is whether dynamics in the past fashion later outcomes of a different kind, or whether the past more directly intrudes on the present by means of its influence directly persisting across a critical juncture. The former is most closely associated with work on historical legacies, the latter with critical junctures. For historical legacies, it is vitally important to delineate the nature of past phenomena that could influence present outcomes and how they transmit their influence forward.

While the term "legacies" can be used to refer to the persistence of any causal influence across any change in one state to another – "authoritarian legacies," "Stalinist legacies," "legacies of Thatcherism," "the legacies of the Cold War" – most involve the persistence of institutions, behaviors, and attitudes once a deep, long-standing, and coherent political phenomenon has formally ended. The notion of historical legacies carries the connotation of the long-term impact of grand, coherent, and deeply impactful antecedent conditions. In this, it is quite different from critical junctures, which imply a period of contingency and flux, in which potentially many influences activated within the juncture can have significant long-term consequences.

However, the notion of a new politics that departs from an old order is at odds with the persistence of an old order's impact, despite notional disruption associated with its formal end. The causal grandeur and persistence of historical legacies correspond to single, constant, powerful forces that have common logics, rather than a diverse universe of cases subject to a critical destabilizing shock, like countries in interwar Europe or Latin America in the era of labor mobilization. They focus on the consequences of an intense and often long-term political "treatment," particularly once that treatment has been formally discontinued. The long-run legacies of totalitarian rule represent a modal case in this respect.

The structure of argumentation also differs. The critical junctures-path dependency framework tends to explore the "causes of effects," attempting to

---

[10] LaPorte and Lussier 2011, 645. LaPorte and Lussier proceed to categorize legacy arguments by political, cultural, and economic spheres and then institutional, behavioral and attitudinal levels of analysis.
[11] Wittenberg 2015. [12] Luebbert 1991, 267–271.

excavate the causal factors during a critical juncture that are associated with later outcomes under investigation. Historical legacies, meanwhile, are more often deployed in investigating "effects of causes," where the causes are obvious and well known, and their long-term consequences, even beyond a disruptive critical juncture, are the key object of inquiry.

9.1.3 The Historical Legacies of Colonialism

Most contemporary studies on the institutional legacies of colonial rule focus on the effects of causes. In this, scholars tend to think of colonialism as a cohesive political regime or coherent set of institutions, not unlike communist regimes in Eastern Europe, with a unifying causal and symbolic logic. Common, coherent institutions of that regime then have predictable, coherent effects that persist after the end of the regime. Some scholars emphasize stable institutional differences across colonialisms or within them, but colonial institutions themselves are usually understood to be coherent and stable phenomena, leading to predictable legacies at the national or subnational level.

Certainly, there are reasons why this framing of colonial rule might be apt. After all, colonialism was by its very nature a long-lasting authoritarian regime, with a putatively unifying, if perverse, ideology of racial supremacy. Further, institutionalized practices of profit-making and subordination inherent in colonial rule penetrated and structured different aspects of political, economic, and social life. In this, colonialism might straightforwardly conform to the "$X_1 \rightarrow X_2$" model; indeed, leading institutional scholars of colonial rule argue that the extractive institutions that were established under colonialism persisted after decolonization and have enduring impacts *of the same essential character* today, particularly in the form of neo-patrimonialism and extractive institutions after independence.[13]

There are two reasons to consider this framing to be rather misguided, however. First, colonialism constituted technologies, ideologies, and practices of governance that unfolded and changed significantly over time and across space. Colonial rule in India unfolded over more than 200 years, between the age of sail and the age of aviation, such that its character changed significantly over time. It was also replete with contingency and discontinuous change, as Chapters 3 and 4 have discussed. The manner by which colonizers responded to external events and internal compulsions had lasting effects, but not in ways that would lead to causal homogenization or random assignment. I argue in this book that the disparate and disjointed impacts of colonial rule in South Asia and beyond lasted for centuries and corresponded with the uneven, patchwork building of modern state institutions.

Second and relatedly, the patchwork quality of institutions and outcomes was a feature, if not a guiding principle, of colonial rule, through concrete

---

[13] Acemoglu, Johnson and Robinson 2001.

practices of "divide and rule." Unlike the imposition of state socialism, for instance, it explicitly did not aim to create a homogenous system of governance. Rather, it established an internally differentiated system of institutions that addressed the needs and fears of the colonial power in different locations under its domination, while keeping India fragmented to facilitate this domination.

As a result, the most important legacies of colonial rule were the establishment of differentiated institutions across space, not one institutional treatment or even a coherent set of them. We should not see colonialism, particularly British colonial rule in South Asia, as like a totalitarian regime, with all the ideological coherence and policy consistency that this implies. Rather, it can be more fruitfully understood as an arena of different forms of (authoritarian) politics, developing over time and through contention and cooperation, that yielded a differentiated variety of durable governance institutions across the subcontinent. The geographically differentiated forms of colonial governance that emerged, in different places and times, thus represent the *multiple kinds* of colonial legacies arising from the different governance arrangements in the patchwork state. These yield meaningful outcomes in the politics of conflict and competition in contemporary South Asia.

9.2 COLONIAL LEGACIES AND THE HAZARDS OF CAUSAL INFERENCE

The ways that social scientists have been studying colonial legacies stand in the way of a full appreciation of the differentiated character of colonial rule in South Asia. Particular methodological preoccupations have inhibited the understanding of colonial legacies as internally complex, diverse, differentiated though legible within now-national territories. Much of the extant work on colonial legacies has, by contrast, been concerned with how we might examine the ways that colonial institutions systematically produce outcomes. As a result, researchers are extremely concerned with questions of causal inference, or how one can plausibly conclude that one particular factor, and not other confounding influences, has led to a particular outcome. This, I suggest, has led to researchers ignore other aspects of understanding the impact of colonial rule that are as, if not more, important.

Such methodological preoccupations are relatively recent. Foundational work on the nature and enduring impact of colonialism and imperialism understood them as a set of international economic structures that constrained national economies in the developing world.[14] More recent macro-historical accounts of different forms of colonial rule and their legacies at the national level have highlighted different logics of colonialism, leading to

---

[14] For classic accounts, see Lenin 1911; Gunder Frank 1967; Cardoso and Faletto 1979. For a recent articulation, see Kohli 2020.

underdevelopment in Latin American and Asian cases, and economic success among European settler colonies and East Asia. Differences in the character of British colonial rule among settler and nonsettler colonial possessions have had consequences in democratic and autocratic rule. Structural variation in colonial "style" among European powers is correlated with different incidences of ethnic conflict and related outcomes today.[15] Powerful comparative-historical accounts on colonial rule interrogate how different capitalist processes generate consequences that are not reducible to particular institutions.[16]

9.2.1   Causal Inference and Colonial Legacies

Recent trends in social science have abjured such comparative-historical accounts in favor of analysis driven by causal inference, however. Social scientists have been increasingly preoccupied with the problem of "confounding." When a researcher makes an argument that differences in the nature of colonial rule between two countries leads to differences in their incidence of political violence, for instance, she is faced with the question of whether other factors might actually be driving the outcome: might the two countries' differing size, geography, ethnic makeup, political institutions, or external influences be actually driving differences? Worse still, could some of these factors have caused the nature of colonial rule that in turn drives outcomes? This could potentially confound any causal relationship between an outcome of interest and a proposed cause.

Concerns about confounding have led social scientists to seek incidences of natural experiments and causal instruments, where the universe intervenes to create a random assignment of cases to different causal categories, which then allows investigators to assess causal impact absent confounding factors. Natural experiments of this kind follow the logic of randomized controlled trials, where a researcher in a clinical trial gives participants either a proposed treatment or a placebo ("control") on the basis of random selection. If the treatment group is much less likely to be hospitalized for coronavirus relative to the control group, for instance, we might reasonably conclude that it was the treatment itself, rather than any innate characteristics of the participants in the treatment group, that led to this outcome, because any participant would have been equally likely to be assigned to either group. This approach to investigating causes in social science has gained significant influence, particularly with development interventions, despite some skepticism as to the universal utility of the approach.[17]

Assessing historical causes of contemporary outcomes precludes the direct manipulation of laboratory experiments or clinical trials. Absent time-traveling capabilities and near-omnipotence, it is impossible (and would certainly be

---

[15] North, Summerhill and Weingast 2000; Blanton, Mason and Athow 2001; Tusalem 2016.
[16] Kohli 2004; Mahoney 2010.   [17] Banerjee and Duflo 2012.

unethical) to "assign" treatments and controls to historical cases and then evaluate subsequent outcomes. Instead, methodologists have counseled attention to research design and the deployment of natural experiments to overcome confounding. If, by a particular historical accident, cases under investigation undergo an "as-if" randomization, then the outcomes would theoretically be free of confounding influences. If, say, otherwise similar villages find themselves on different sides of linear boundaries drawn at a conference of European powers thousands of miles away, and thus subject to different species of colonial institutions, then we might plausibly conclude that differences in the prosperity or ethnic tensions on the two sides of the border are due to differences in colonial rule. Natural experiments represent modal instances of a larger category of causal instruments: factors that are exogenous to both independent and dependent variables and that can be said to "assign" cases in an "as-if" random fashion.

The use of such causal instruments have pervaded studies of colonial legacies. Acemoglu, Johnson, and Robinson influentially argued that prior, exogenous disease burdens determined whether Europeans would establish colonial settlements or rule indirectly in conquered territories. Where disease burdens were light, European powers opted for "direct" colonialism, in which European settlers carried with them institutions that included property rights and government restraint. In areas where disease burdens were heavy and thus settlement impractical, European powers established "indirect" colonial rule and extracted resources from the colony with minimal institutional investment.[18] They correlate the contemporary quality of institutions, measured by the risk of government expropriation, as a legacy of this prior institutional assignment. Following in this tradition, political scientists and economists have deployed a variety of natural experiments and causal instruments to explain the impacts of different forms of colonial rule on a variety of different outcomes.[19]

The application of random assignment has been a powerful feature of the analysis of colonial rule and its legacies within India. As mentioned earlier, Banerjee and Iyer, and Iyer powerfully demonstrate the ways that different forms of colonial land tenure institutions in British India and the distinction between directly ruled areas and princely states have long-run developmental consequences, making explicit use of causal instruments central to their analysis.[20] They suggest that the assignment of institutional forms to particular places in the first century of colonial rule was the result of contingency: "We compare the present-day economic performance of different districts of India, which were placed under different land revenue systems by British colonial rulers

---

[18] Acemoglu, Johnson and Robinson 2001.
[19] See, for example, Michalopoulos and Papaioannou 2013, 2014; Mattingly 2017; Faguet, Matajira and Sanchez 2017; Lecher and McNamee 2018; Dupraz 2019.
[20] Banerjee and Iyer 2005; Iyer 2010.

as a result of *certain historical accidents.*[21] They locate the application of the cultivator-based "treatment" – landlord arrangements being taken as the norm or "control" – in the presence of an extant precolonial landlord class, the timing of annexation, reactions to exogenous events like the French Revolution, and the policy proclivities of particular colonial administrators.[22]

Iyer measured the differences in economic performance between districts under direct British rule and princely states.[23] As a causal instrument, she utilizes the "Doctrine of Lapse," an EIC policy of the mid-nineteenth century in which the death of a princely ruler without an heir would result in annexation. Given that the ruler's death (at least by natural causes) can be understood as random and thus exogenous, Iyer was able to compare those districts that were incorporated during this period with those that did not, and found a systematic difference; unannexed districts had greater access to public goods.

This work has represented a significant advance in the study of the legacies of colonial institutions in India, and as such, has highlighted important *subnational* outcomes that are at some remove from debates on cross-national success and failure. By clearly specifying institutional distinctions at the district level and identifying ways in which institutions have impacts separate from confounding factors, they have provided us with extra confidence that those institutions continued to drive subnational impacts after independence. To be sure, historical investigations into variation in different aspects of colonial rule, even absent causal instruments, have been welcome additions to our understanding of subnational variations in the politics of India.[24]

Yet the success of this particular line of research has had the unintended effect of narrowing the field of inquiry. Most obviously, colonial institutions identified by Banerjee and Iyer were as present at the subnational level in Pakistan and Bangladesh as they were in India, and yet there have been no attempts to expand the analysis to include these countries. They also have been used to explore variations in development and local provision of public goods, rather than a wider array of social and political outcomes, not least political violence. Studies of the colonial legacies of political violence have focused on particular sites of variation.[25] More broadly, however, the influence of causal inference and natural experiments has significantly affected the way that historical colonial legacies are analyzed, as the effects of discrete institutional causes. Here, I want to draw back from the specific, and important, research on

---

[21] Banerjee and Iyer 2005, 1190, emphasis added. For a critical discussion, see Banerjee and Iyer 2013; Iversen, Palmer-Jones and Sen 2013.

[22] Banerjee and Iyer 2005, 1196. Lee (2019b) likewise argues that colonial authorities are more likely to disrupt zamindari tenure during exogenous shocks resulting from war in Europe.

[23] Iyer 2010. Chaudhury et al. (2020) by contrast, uses a border design to find that communities with legacies of princely rule demonstrate less cooperation than those under direct rule.

[24] See Lankina and Getachew 2012.

[25] Verghese 2016; Verghese and Teitelbaum 2019; Mukherjee 2021.

colonial institutional legacies in India toward a broader investigation of the assumptions behind causal inference in the application of colonial legacies writ large.

9.3 DRAWBACKS TO CAUSAL INFERENCE IN THE STUDY OF COLONIAL LEGACIES

Any one form of social analysis, from ethnography to cross-national regressions, has benefits and costs, and causal inference is not an exception. Some scholars have highlighted the pitfalls of the emphasis on causal instruments and natural experiments in narrowing the scope of possible research, exaggerating the inferential power of causal instruments and ignoring external validity.[26] In particular, researchers' quest for natural experiments may at its limit be an instance of "looking for the key where the lamppost is," or in other words, abjuring the most important or urgent research questions in favor of those in which a natural experiment or some other form of causal instrument is available. Single-mindedness in the pursuit of clean identification has arisen from the (often mistaken) belief that confounding is the most serious problem facing causal inquiry. This singlemindedness has generated other problems.

In particular, I identify four specific and interrelated drawbacks to a focus on causal inference and the use of natural experiments in the context of colonial legacies, in South Asia and beyond. First and perhaps most seriously, natural experiments frame history and politics, particularly with regard to the "assignment" of institutions, as fundamentally contingent. While this framing of colonialism assists with the claim that a particular form of institution has consequences independent of other confounding factors, it elides the ways that colonial rulers acted to achieve particular mandates and thus quite deliberately instituted particular forms of institutions to accomplish those mandates in different places. The "historical accidents" described in the paper by Banerjee and Iyer would, for historians, constitute deep and meaningful divisions in how India was governed and why, as discussed in Chapter 3.

Broader attention to the actual objectives of colonial rule also suggests other limitations of a focus on causal instruments. Contrary to Acemoglu, Johnson, and Robinson's assertion that disease burdens determined settlement or extraction, it was unequivocally not the case that the British would have ever *intended* settlement or were primarily driven by extraction. The EIC was an enterprise devoted singularly to trade. The tiny population of Europeans resident in the Company's "factories" for the first century and a half of its presence in the subcontinent facilitated that trade, and British conquest of territory in India from the mid-eighteenth century was the concrete

---

[26] Deaton 2010; Heckman and Urzúa 2010.

consequence of threats to that trade and the use of land revenue to pay for its protection. Trade and security, central themes of British colonialism in India and beyond, are thus completely obscured by an emphasis on the dichotomy between settlement and extraction.[27]

Second, natural experiments naturally dichotomize a universe of cases under investigation into "treatment" and "control" groups through randomization or exogenous shocks. This can take different forms: the before-and-after of a particular shock or the spatial discontinuity as a result of administrative borders. In the study of colonial legacies, much of the analysis has focused on the categories of direct and indirect rule (either in *de jure* or de facto terms) as two ideal-type conditions that approximate a treatment or a control, with clever strategies that enable researchers to argue that these colonial institutions were randomly assigned. Yet there is significant, legible complexity and important and explicable variation within these two categories, which tends to be ignored in favor of the cleanliness of the identification.[28] It may be more than two categories are needed to characterize institutional variation, as this book argues, yet more than two categories strain the credulity of random assignment, suggesting that history might contain as much deliberate action as contingency, thus collapsing the logic of a natural experiment.

This complexity is more evident when analyzing the full universe of cases, but natural experiments incentivize analysis of only a small subset that were plausibly subject to as-if randomization. The Doctrine of Lapse is a key case in point. The policy was in place for less than a decade in the late 1840s and 1850s and applied to a small minority of cases of potential annexation, because most annexations of princely territory had in fact occurred decades before that time, in the aftermath of conflict against Mysore and the Maratha states. In addition, the annexations of Punjab and Awadh, during the period under investigation, were outcomes of political machinations that began well before the establishment of the doctrine and had nothing to do with the death of the ruler and the absence of a male heir. This can at its limit lead researchers to miss a complex but legible forest for two species of trees; comparing two categories might be worthwhile, but only while recognizing a broader landscape of variation.

Third, an elective affinity exists between natural experiments in colonial legacies and a particular understanding of institutions, as "the humanly devised constraints that structure political, economic and social interaction."[29] Institutional economists have argued that the presence of institutions reduces transactions costs, protects property rights, guarantees

---

[27] Also, there is even cross-national evidence that nonsettler colonies were not actually associated with greater extractive activity. See Frankema 2010; Mahoney 2010.

[28] Naseemullah and Staniland 2016. Scholars have tended to treat the zamindari–ryotwari distinction as parallel to direct and indirect rule.

[29] North 1991, 99.

contracts, and provides clear sanctions for their contravention, thus enabling economic activity. As importantly, state institutions can credibly guarantee self-restraint and rule-by-law, thereby guaranteeing that citizens do not fear from the predations of the government.[30] In their broader work on explaining national wealth and prosperity, Acemoglu and Robinson have argued that settler colonialism is associated with such "inclusive" institutions more capable of protecting property rights, whereas indirect forms of colonialism are associated with extraction and predation.[31] The supposed inclusiveness of the institutions of settler colonialism ignores darker aspects of these institutions, including eliminationist impulses associated with the genocide of indigenous peoples and the liquidation of indigenous sovereignties.[32]

The transactions cost-reducing, property rights-protecting approach tends to overshadow an alternate framing of institutions as congealed and sedimented power relations.[33] Colonial rule is, by its very nature, the exercise of power, and colonial authorities were effective at "mobilizing the bias" and setting political agendas such that outright resistance was sublimated into a more complicated politics of contestation and collaboration. If one is less focused on the randomized assignment of broad categories of institutions – their presence or absence, their inclusiveness and extractiveness – we might understand how colonial authorities established *particular kinds* of institutions in different places for furthering mandates of fear, greed, and frugality, managing social demands and resistance. In other words, they fashioned particular institutional solutions to specific challenges, resulting in diverse but specific institutional strategies. These institutions were not limitless in terms of variety, but they yielded categories of governance that were more complex than a simple division between direct and indirect rule would suggest, while responding to the actual politics of conquest and domination.

Fourth, analyses of colonial legacies focusing on causal inference tend to elide the mechanisms of institutional perpetuation, particularly across other disruptive shocks, including decolonization. The heavy lifting of random assignment is often seen as obviating these concerns, leading researchers to assume rather than investigate the causal pathways among institutions during colonial rule that would lead to postcolonial outcomes. However, this empties the various territorial politics of colonial rule of their substance. Power might be exercised and state and society might interact in consequentially different ways in different places, and in ways that might change over time in response to subsequent shocks. It is ultimately these continuing politics rather than initial institutional assignment that produce the outcomes we seek to explain.

---

[30] North and Weingast 1989; Olson 1993.   [31] Acemoglu and Robinson 2012.
[32] See Wolfe 2006.
[33] See Bachrach and Baratz 1963; Lukes 1974; Gaventa 1980; MacIntyre 2002.

Further, decolonization is by any reasonable account a significant *endogenous* shock or critical juncture to institutions established during the course of colonial rule. The object of many social scientists is often to demonstrate that outcomes after the shock follow institutional assignment before the shock, following "effects of causes" logics discussed earlier. But early postcolonial politics, just like colonial conquest, constitutes a distinct critical juncture in which there is an arena of conflicting interests that engage with one another to produce outcomes. These may be deeply influenced by pre-juncture institutions, but are unlikely to be completely determined by them.

Any mechanical notion of the path dependence of colonial institutional assignments negates the political agency of postcolonial governments and other actors to revise the legacies of colonial rule. Perhaps the best example of this is Banerjee and Iyer's classification of Bengal Presidency as landlord-based, leading to disappointing developmental outcomes in West Bengal in the 1960s. This is indeed accurate! Yet it is also incomplete, because the contentious politics of West Bengal in the 1970s, from the Naxalbari uprising to the CPI-M's assumption of power, led to a throughgoing land redistribution and transformation of state–society relations that makes the "landlord" assignment inappropriate for assessing more recent development outcomes. In general, the inferential power of random assignment of institutions naturally abstracts away ongoing *politics*: the contention, competition, and conflict surrounding the distribution of resources and political power that is as much a feature of colonial societies as postcolonial ones.

9.4 CONCLUSION

For these reasons, I take the view that the overwhelming attention paid to causal inference in the study of colonial legacies can, on balance, be counterproductive. While natural experiments and causal instruments have yielded some insights regarding the lasting influence of colonial institutions, inference-driven research designs have obscured far too much in the nature and consequences of the complex politics of colonial rule to provide us with a reliable guide as to the ways that colonial (and postcolonial) institutions shaped the diverse politics of competition and conflict in contemporary South Asian countries. It certainly should not be the only such guide.

Instead, I suggest that we might return to the comparative-historical tradition by analyzing institutional origins and political dynamics in contexts of critical juncture, such as with colonial conquest, and examining the durability of different kinds of institutions and their impacts on the state after other critical junctures, such as decolonization. Further, it may not be the best idea to throw data away in the pursuit of causal identification. Rather, characterizing and thus explicating the roots and nature of institutional diversities can represent another way of understanding different historical dimensions of subnational politics. Experimental designs might help us to more exactly specify the impacts of particular institutions, but it is not useful for understanding institutional diversity.

This book has laid out such a framework for understanding patchwork state formation, as a set of processes that shaped spatial variation in colonial and postcolonial governance institutions, which in turn shape a political geography of conflict and competition today. This framework requires different tools and forms of analysis from that of natural experiments and instrumental research designs, and they can be correctly indicted for not solving problems of confounding and endogeneity. Yet equally, they have capacities for understanding the diverse arrangements of colonial rule and postcolonial state-building that inference-based approaches do not, and as such, may represent a more flexible and durable way of understanding the historical roots of subnational politics of conflict and competition.

10

The Patchwork State in Comparative Perspective

This book has been chiefly concerned with two core questions: (1) how complex politics of colonial expansion and domination yielded differentiated governance arrangements, with postcolonial state-building projects (only incompletely) revising these arrangements, led to patchwork states of different kinds and thus distinct national trajectories today, and (2) how the resulting differences in state capacity and state–society relations shape the contemporary subnational politics of conflict and competition. In so doing, it brings together a number of strands of social science inquiry that are usually kept separate: political violence and contention, electoral competition, state-implicated development, colonial legacies, subnational political analysis, and the processes of state formation in postcolonial countries.

The book also provides a distinct subnational perspective on the national politics of South Asia. Both India and Pakistan sought to revise colonial governance practices, though to different extents for different purposes, but the variegated institutional legacies of the patchwork state have persisted in enduring differences in state capacity and state–society relationships among cores, hinterlands, and peripheries, providing a spatial dimension to key aspects of national politics. Bangladesh, meanwhile, emerged as a country with more homogeneity in governance as a result of partitions that cut its sovereign territory from whole cloth, resulting in more convergent national politics. The book highlights how the ongoing patchwork nature of the state can help us understand the complex subnational politics of violence, as well as representation and development, across three states that together constitute a fifth of the world's population, but also how that might frame national political contention in these countries. In this last chapter, I will focus on the meanings of governance differentiation and institutional persistence for the politics of South Asian countries in broader comparative perspective.

In what follows, I extend the implications of this argument in two different directions. First, I further elaborate on what the patchwork state concept might mean for the national political order of India, Pakistan, and Bangladesh, from the perspective of a set of comparable countries in South, East, and Southeast Asia. Second, I place the patchwork state in South Asia in more global and historical context, sketching out the terms for a broader investigation into the comparative politics of imperialism and its consequences, engaging with extant cross-national frameworks. These two related investigations reflect on a venerable discussion of the theoretical relationship among different forms of violence, state and regime consolidation, and the character of national politics.

10.1 PATCHWORK STATES AND NATIONAL TRAJECTORIES: SOUTH ASIA IN COMPARATIVE PERSPECTIVE

A major challenge for conducting analysis of subnational political outcomes is, in the end, facing the political science profession's infamous, favored question: "so what?" Particularly with regard to relatively understudied South Asian countries, it is not immediately clear why many would care about internal spatial variation: why any district in India or Pakistan would see riots, rebellion, or a combination of forms. Identifying and explaining variation might represent a worthy exercise in such large and heterogeneous polities. However, doing so without arguing for the intellectual stakes of explaining that variation would be to embark on a directionless search for meaning in fractal complexity.

Comparative politics has traditionally been concerned with the politics of entire countries and differences among them, rather than that of bits within them, even when they are as populous and internally complex as Pakistan and Bangladesh, let alone continental countries like India. Subnational outcomes, when properly investigated, ideally shine a light on the whole, of which provinces and districts are constituent parts.

To this end, the subnational empirical investigations of this book can bring into sharper focus the *processes* of the expansion and transformation of state authority in the modern era and how that reflects the nature of national politics. Nearly every country has been forced to manage abrupt transitions from more mediated and patrimonial forms of social organization to forms of more direct, sustained, and often violent intervention of rational, bureaucratic state power into the lives of regular citizens. These processes were together once known as modernization. They are spatially uneven in nature, particularly in developing countries. Modernization they proceeded more rapidly and vigorously in some national cases rather than others, but it was also more thoroughgoing in some places than others within national borders, creating different kinds of conflict and competition, political order and disorder over their disruptive dynamics and inequitable consequences.

There is a perhaps inevitable success bias built into the study of the comparative politics of developing countries. Perhaps not deliberately or consciously, we tend to frame the most successful cases of the institutional deepening and geographical spread of state authority – western European and settler-colonial countries, revolutionary and developmental states – as the norm and all others as divergences from, or even failures to live up to, that norm. This has enormous consequences in how we might understand the national trajectories of developing countries. More often than not, such trajectories are measured against the world's wealthiest and most powerful countries, rather than analyzed against more directly comparable cases.

This book represents an investigation among more comparable national cases. India, due to its size and complexity, is the most deeply studied of the three countries in contemporary social science, but it is often analyzed in *sui generis* terms or among the BRICs or the G20 category of powerful, developing countries. But India arises from the same colonial institutions as Pakistan and Bangladesh. All three thus share common features of the politics of conflict and development that can be highlighted when placed in that comparative context.

Comparing India, Pakistan, and Bangladesh, the distinctiveness of national trajectories is at least in part a consequence of what portions of the patchwork of governance from colonial India they inherited, precisely because unlike in much of East and Southeast Asia, colonial patchworks persisted, albeit with some modification, after decolonization. The relative national economic success of India is rooted in the modernizing portions of the west, northwest, and south, balancing the underdevelopment of northern and eastern India; political compacts among groups under modernizing arrangements over the distribution of patronage and largesse has kept systemic, insurgent violence largely to peripheries since the 1990s, while allowing for significant social violence. Pakistan inherited much of the exceptional governance of the western and northwestern frontier from colonial rule, however, along with martial, if also modernizing, state institutions in the hinterland. That has prefigured a conflict between the centripetal and centrifugal aspects of the state, and thus a greater propensity toward systemic, insurgent conflict and highly uneven growth concentrated in central Punjab and Karachi. Bangladesh, by contrast, emerged from independence in 1971 as largely a whole square in the previously fragmented patchwork of governance in the eastern subcontinent, transformed – together – by two partitions. As a result, conflict persists in the meaning and purpose of the state as a whole.

The variable preponderance of different patchwork forms in these three countries at the core of the Indian subcontinent thus provides us a useful starting point for comparative enquiry. The distinctiveness of their national trajectories can be highlighted in even more stark terms by contrast with the smaller countries in South Asia and those in East and Southeast Asia. The two main dimensions that begin this broader inquiry are the relative evenness of governance from colonial rule, and the relative penetration and monopolization of particular forms of coercive, bureaucratic state authority.

10.1.1 Patchwork Authority in Greater South Asia

It is possible to incorporate some of the book's insights into the understanding of some of the other countries in South Asia. Nepal was a client kingdom of the British – a princely state that achieved sovereignty out of its suzerain status – and contains extreme variation in political geography. This shaped the structural inequality and political exclusion that ultimately led to the Maoist-instigated revolt, largely among upland ethnic minorities ruled indirectly or exceptionally by a political elite in the Kathmandu valley. Subsequent struggles to redefine identity and representation after civil war have focused on creating federal structures that allow for such differentiation to receive meaningful political expression.[1]

Sri Lanka under colonial rule, by contrast, was a Crown Colony with significant governance homogeneity and a highly interventionist colonial economy based on migrant plantation labor. After independence, these dynamics encouraged winner-take-all politics and ethnic outbidding among majoritarian groups based on a single, deep cleavage of religion and ethnicity, against minorities privileged under colonial rule. These politics and political economy led to a qualitatively different civil war – based on identity rather than topography – between Tamil separatists and the Sinhala-dominated government, the aftershocks of which are still being felt today. Though both Nepal and Sri Lanka experienced significant civil conflict, they did so for different purposes and to different effects, because Nepal is a highly variegated form of patchwork state, while in Sri Lanka, a deep ethno-religious cleavage dominates national politics in similar, though much more violent, ways as Bangladesh.

Farther afield, on the borderlands of South Asia, Afghanistan and Myanmar were subject to British colonial intervention – as a buffer client state and a directly administered province, respectively – and were shaped by extreme variation in the presence or absence of the state. By the time of recognition as an independent state by the British in 1919, Afghanistan maintained significant state authority only around Kabul, the Panjshir Valley and other cities, with little presence in the vast hinterland. This has resulted in systemic civil conflict and state failure when Afghanistan was violently integrated into geopolitical competition in the Cold War and the War on Terror. Myanmar, by contrast, was unevenly integrated into the plantation agriculture and the extraction of agrarian surpluses of British India, but with zones of governance exceptionalism along long and uncertain frontiers with China. These cleavages became fractures with Japanese invasion and the construction of the postwar revolutionary state,

---

[1] Lawoti 2007; Hangen 2009.

not unlike other countries in Southeast Asia, on which more in the next section. Sixty years later, we see institutional differentiation between the Irrawaddy basin, under homogenized if often authoritarian rule, and exceptional peripheries with active insurgent conflict.

Thus, greater South Asia is characterized by states of different patchworks of authority that were created, directly or indirectly, by the presence of British colonial rule, with subsequent variation in the capacity of the state to implement governance homogenization. This makes this region distinct, at least within Asia, and suggests that in order to understand national trajectories of violence and political order, examination of the historical roots of subnational politics is important. This in turn suggests that national success and failure on a broader cross-national canvas may well be impacted by the ways in which broader imperial projects yielded states of variable governance heterogeneity, and how postcolonial states reacted to this homogeneity. I will lay out these first in broader Asia and then further afield.

10.1.2 Governance Differentiation and Consolidation in Comparative Asian Perspective

The comparative analysis of colonialism and its consequences across Asia is far too grand an enterprise for this book, rooted as it is in the specific experiences of the subcontinent. However, there are general trends of colonial rule and the nature of decolonization and postcolonial politics that have an important bearing on national trajectories across most of the continent. These include (1) the internal variations of governance within colonial territories, (2) the impact of prewar Japanese colonization or wartime Japanese conquest and occupation, and (3) the extent to which Communist insurgencies and reactionary governments resulted in cohesive national states through coercive state-building in the context of emergent Cold War competition.[2] As this book has argued India is an extreme case of governance variation in colonial rule. The legacies of that variation were transmitted more powerfully to postcolonial statehood in India and Pakistan (though not Bangladesh) than many countries to its east, because Japanese intervention was limited and the threat of postwar Communist revolution or insurgency was negligible. In what follows, I provide an overview of how these dynamics played out differently in East and Southeast Asia.

Scholars have remarked upon the theory and praxis of colonial rule among the different European powers – that the French were considered to be much more universalizing than the British, for instance, and the Belgians were more extractive, while the Spanish and Portuguese Empires are considered categorically different from later European colonial expansion.[3] Yet in Asia, colonial territories exhibited significant internal variation. French Indochina,

[2] I thank Bill Hurst for these insights.   [3] See J Hart 2003; Mahoney 2010.

for instance, was divided into five territories, four of which were ruled indirectly as princely protectorates while Cochinchina was ruled directly by a French colonial government. British Malaya was similarly bifurcated into the Straits Settlements, ruled directly by the EIC and then as a Crown Colony, and Federated and Unfederated Malay States, which were governed by indigenous rulers under British suzerainty. As a result, while India lay at one extreme in terms of governance variation, internal differences in *de jure* forms of rule and de facto governance were characteristic of all European colonial territories in Asia. Further, the influence of European powers extended to countries which they did not conquer; European powers placed large swaths of late Qing and Republican China under conditions of indirect domination and dependency from the middle of the nineteenth century onward.

The rise of Japan as an economic and military power in the twentieth century transformed the region, first in East and then Southeast Asia. Its imperial expansion included the colonization of Taiwan in 1895 and Korea from 1905, the invasion and rule over Manchuria in the early 1930s and then, from 1938, the invasion and occupation of most of northern and central China, including major coastal cities. By 1942, Japan occupied a quarter of China's territory, with a third of its population.

With World War II and its devastating military campaigns across Southeast Asia, Japanese forces displaced – and often eliminated or imprisoned – colonial authorities, established puppet regimes of varying longevity and supported anti-colonial nationalists, but this also inspired guerrilla resistance against Japanese occupation in what is now the Philippines, Indonesia, Vietnam, Myanmar, and Malaysia. The retreat and then defeat of the Japanese Empire allowed colonial governments to return to power, but they did so without their previous authority. Nationalist governments of varying composition then succeeded in dislodging colonial rule, either through armed conflict (Indonesia, Vietnam) or negotiated changes in constitutional status (Malaysia, the Philippines) between the mid-1940s and mid-1950s.

Of course, the independence and partition of India followed the latter pattern, but largely because of internal dynamics. The Japanese navy threatened an invasion of the Coromandel Coast and the Japanese army briefly invaded northeast India and sponsored the anti-colonial Indian National Army (INA), yet India was largely beyond the limits of Japanese expansion. As a result, unlike much of East and Southeast Asia, Japanese invasion and occupation did not serve as a significant shock to the institutions and structures of colonial rule.

Following the war and decolonization, early Cold War competition and the Soviet Union's sponsorship of Communist insurgents, as well as US support for conservative nationalist governments, led to variably powerful regimes that more or less fundamentally revised state–society relations. The most dramatic transformations occurred in East Asia. The Chinese Communist Party defeated the western-allied Kuomintang (KMT) in 1949, establishing the People's

Republic and beginning a destructive but fundamentally successful project of extending and consolidating territorial authority to the far peripheries at the limits of Qing power, while transforming the economy and remaking the regional security order. Taiwan was, in turn, transformed by the exiled KMT from the mainland, consolidating a developmental nationalist regime under single-party rule with security and economic assistance from the United States. Following the Korean War that disrupted the agrarian order in South Korea, an institutional vacuum allowed the emergence and consolidation of a military-led bureaucratic-authoritarian regime under Park Chung-Hee, also with substantial US support.[4]

In Southeast Asia, meanwhile, postcolonial state-building and the alignment of fragmented societies along cleavages inspired by Communist insurgencies and conservative nationalist reactions, inspired by decolonization and Cold War competition, had varying strengths and took on different national characters.[5] The Viet Minh defeated the French military at Dien Bien Phu in 1954, establishing a Communist regime in the North, while Ngo Dinh Diem consolidated a conservative nationalist regime in the South, with backing from the United States. The creation of both North and South Vietnam involved brutal state-making violence against rival coercive organizations and populations unintegrated by the sovereign authority of either state; the assassination of Diem in 1963 and the collapse of South Vietnamese Republic in 1975 brought all of Vietnam under the control of the Communist regime. Similar but even more destructive regime consolidation under the Pathet Lao and the Khmer Rouge in Cambodia accompanied the withdrawal of US aid and influence. The consolidation of Communist regimes forced the displacement of millions fleeing conflict and Communist consolidation in Indochina.

Archipelago Southeast Asia largely presented conservative state-building in reaction to the threat of Communist influence. In Indonesia, the anticolonial resistance that separately involved the elite Javanese nobility, Islamists, and Communists led to the establishment of a nationalist regime under Sukarno, with support from the Communist PKI; in 1965, Sukarno's government was overthrown by the military, and General Suharto established the New Order regime and conducted a widespread and systematic anti-Communist purge. In the transition between British Malaya and contemporary Malaysia and Singapore, the eventual success of counterinsurgent operations against (largely ethnic Chinese) Malayan Communist guerrillas resulted in the consolidation of a conservative nationalist Malaysian regime, with roots in Malay agrarian aristocracy and – following ejection from the Malaysian federation – an urban, multiethnic but conservative city-state in Singapore. In the Philippines, anti-Japanese Hukbalahap guerrillas persisted in their revolutionary demands after independence, leading to a bloody counterinsurgent campaign. The election and then authoritarian rule of

---

[4] See Cumings 1984.   [5] See Vu 2010; Slater 2010 for comparative analysis.

Ferdinand Marcos was associated with the US-supported project to extirpate Communists from Filipino politics and society.

***

Comparing South with East and Southeast Asia highlights the ways that comparability in terms of colonial (and broader imperial) governance variation before the 1940s led to significant disjuncture in the nature of political order and postcolonial state-building after World War II. Postcolonial politics in South Asia, including both India and Pakistan, are largely distinct from the political experience further to the east, but for explicable reasons. First, Japanese invasion did not yield such a shock to colonial governance. Second and relatedly, it did not inspire (Soviet-supported) Communist guerrilla resistance against Japanese occupation, which persisted in various forms after Japanese defeat, either eventually creating Communist regimes or inspiring reactionary ones engaged in counterinsurrectionary mobilization. In South Asia, the threat of Communist insurrection in the countryside, which was palpable in the 1920s and seen as a real threat by both the colonial government and Congress, receded during the war as the Communist Party of India collaborated with the British government after the Soviet Union joined the Allies in mid-1941. After independence, Communists in India largely turned toward parliamentarism and union organizing, except in the case of rebellion in exceptional geographies; active as Maoist groups have been in certain locations at certain times, they have not defined national cleavages evident in East and Southeast Asia. Communism in Pakistan, though often dismissed, represented a significant political movement particularly among Karachi's workers, but was destroyed during the course of successive military regimes.[6] The influence of the Cold War on the domestic politics of South Asia more broadly was relatively marginal, with both Pakistan and India using geopolitical competition only in order to further internal and regional goals. The spatial distinctiveness of political conflict and competition rooted in patchwork colonial rule has persisted, without being reoriented by vigorous transformative state-building.

10.2 VIOLENCE, GOVERNANCE UNEVENNESS, AND THE COMPARATIVE POLITICS OF EMPIRE

This brief survey of state-building trajectories across Asia illustrates a well-known maxim in comparing national trajectories of state formation: that the most systemic violence have led to the most successful and powerful states. The brutal violence of the enclosures and the Highland clearances from the sixteenth to the eighteenth century – "a revolution of the rich against the poor" – enabled pastoral-commercial agriculture, while demolishing peasant societies and

---

[6] See Ali 2015.

creating an industrial labor force, that shaped modern Britain.[7] Both the Soviet
Union and the People's Republic of China undertook economic transformation
through the systemic, mass state violence associated with the collectivization of
agriculture and the solution to "the peasant problem," in which tens of millions
died.

How does this relationship between state-building and violence apply to
the study of colonialism and the postcolonial world more broadly? Recent
assessments of colonial legacies have largely elided the role of systemic
violence, in favor of the more antiseptic language of institutions. Popular
cross-national comparisons assess the inclusiveness of institutions between
settler and nonsettler colonial societies – understood as a key to explaining
why some countries are rich and peaceful, while others are poor and
conflict-ridden – and as such, ignore the generative power of violence in
the politics of colonial rule.

The scholarship on colonial legacies has particularly considered why some
former colonial territories, like Canada or Australia, are rich and peaceful,
while most other countries with colonial legacies are poor, underdeveloped,
authoritarian, and rife with political violence? Acemoglu, Johnson, and
Robinson's answer to this puzzle, which has achieved a dominant status in
these debates, involves the quality of institutions.[8] European settlers
incorporated inclusive institutions able to protect property rights, thereby
enabling innovation and investment. In nonsettler colonial societies, by
contrast, indirect European domination over indigenous populations yielded
widespread extraction, predation, and rent-seeking that has persisted long after
decolonialization. They thus contend that settler societies thus represent a key
determinant of institutional quality. Where colonists achieved widespread
settlement, institutions were more efficacious. However, where settlement was
impossible, due to heavy disease burdens facing potential colonists, purely
extractive impulses yielded weak and malignant institutions. Other
researchers have come to slightly different conclusions, while maintaining
a framework of different forms of colonialism and domestic institutional
differentiation at the national level.[9]

The variable quality of national institutions has come to be seen as the modal
legacy of colonial rule, for two reasons. First, it employs the conceptual
framework of institutions to causally link different forms of colonial rule to
postcolonial outcomes across a vast array of different cases. Second, the link
between colonial extraction, weak institutions, and postcolonial predation is
evident in the most extreme and salient cases of colonial rule. The neo-
patrimonial kleptocracy of Zaire under Mobutu arises from the horrific
extractive systems of the Congo under Belgian rule, because the Belgians did
not invest in inclusive institutions.[10] The extractive dynamics of colonial rule in

---

[7] Moore 1966; Polanyi 2001 [1945].   [8] Acemoglu, Johnson and Robinson 2001.
[9] Lange 2009; Mahoney 2010.   [10] Kabwit 1979; Evans 1989; Hochschild 1998.

India, though less stark, nevertheless certainly yielded weak national institutions.

Frameworks that link different "treatments" of colonial rule to the quality of national institutions after decolonization leave a lot to be explained, however. First, the size and homogeneity of these two categories are quite uneven. Outside the intermediate cases of creole societies in Latin America, the majority of settler colonial societies are Anglophone, and with the exception of the United States, represent vast territories with relatively small populations in the British Commonwealth. As a result, they represent convergent institutions as a result of direct transfer and subsequent modification of institutions from Britain.

Nonsettler colonial societies under the domination of European countries, by contrast, run a gamut of different forms: a mixture of settlement, plantation, and much more prevalent indirect rule over much of Africa, the mandate system in the Middle East, and various combinations of direct and indirect rule in the Asia-Pacific, Russian domination over Central Asia to the cooperative European hegemony over an ailing Qing dynasty leading to Japanese colonial domination over much of China and its proximate tributary states. The categories of settler and nonsettler colonialism are thus vastly different in size and level of heterogeneity. This makes direct comparison rather challenging.

Second, the assignment of different forms of colonial rule to different territories, and subsequent effects in domestic institutions, assumes no endogenous relationship between these different forms of rule. The assumption that cases of settler and nonsettler colonial rule are causally independent of one another is worth interrogating, however. After all, the overall rubric of British imperialism was responsible for both the white settler dominions and the colonies that would become the United States of America, as well as "indirect" rule over much of Africa and Asia. The specific agents of this imperial project certainly transcended these boundaries: to take an obvious example, Charles Cornwallis, the general commanding British forces in the American revolutionary war, went on to become Governor-General and commander-in-chief in India, and then Lord Lieutenant in Ireland. Such distinctions thus leave out linkages in the *motives* of imperial powers.

Third, as I have argued throughout this book, assessing institutional outcomes at the cross-national level represents a challenge. Certainly, the countries that arise out of settler colonial experience have relatively inclusive and capacious institutions, but they are also surprisingly homogenous across (vast) territories. For all its differences in the politics of federal units and the character of "frontier societies,"[11] the formal practice of the rule of law and the protection of property rights in the United States operates in much the same fashion in Wyoming or Hawai'i as it does in Massachusetts. By contrast, many developing countries represent incoherent national institutional frameworks,

[11] Foa and Nemirovskaya 2016.

but looking below the national level, we see patchworks of different institutions that operate consistently, but differently in different places.

Ultimately, I argue that greed and fear animated settler colonies just as much as in India, but the relative absence of frugality is a defining difference that led initially to horrific, structural violence and subsequent peace and prosperity in settler colonial societies relative to those of postcolonial Asia and Africa. Frugality thus serves as a generator and consolidator of differentiation during colonial rule, and subsequent weaknesses of state capacity – absent subsequent revolutionary or reactionary transformations, as discussed earlier – preserves such differentiation after decolonization, thus leading to patchwork states with diverse spatial politics, endemic violence, and underdevelopment today. Frugality's absence as a governance mandate led to national cohesion and consolidation in successful settler colonial societies, but only after genocidal violence against opponents.

For these reasons, I believe that an application of the framework of the book can be helpful in filling in the gaps behind explanations linking different categories of colonial rule to national wealth and poverty, order and disorder. In doing so, I focus on the discrete interests of various colonial projects in establishing governance arrangements. Some were deliberately constructed to be institutionally differentiated, thus patchwork states. Others were made convergent and homogenous by the application of systemic violence. States with enduring patterns of patchwork authority, in and beyond South Asia, face greater difficulties in the national consolidation and transformation of polity, economy, and society, and thus greater poverty and disorder. Settler colonial societies, by contrast, violently pulverized governance differences – including pockets of indirectly ruled indigenous sovereignties – yielding a much less uneven institutional landscape, and thus greater economic success and political order following long periods of annihilationist violence.

10.2.1 Direct and Indirect Colonial Rule

Taking the British empire as a whole, there was a significant difference as the means and ends of the colonial enterprise: as to whether financiers (or religious communities) sent entire populations to found isomorphic societies or enterprises in new lands, or whether mercantile companies sent representative agents to establish trading relationships with faraway empires.[12] For the latter, as we see in colonial India, frugality ruled the EIC even as its agents managed organizational imperatives of greed and fear, and the resulting governance institutions were established in various ways in different places, with lasting consequences. While the details of British colonial rule across Africa, in Malaya, and even in Middle Eastern mandates were quite different from the longevity and complexity of British India, they all followed strict cost-benefit calculations

---

[12] These distinctions follow Mahoney's logic of "liberal" colonialism. See Mahoney 2010.

focused on commerce and strategic mastery in the nineteenth and early twentieth centuries.

Settler or "direct" colonial rule, by contrast, represented an antecedent phenomenon of the direct extension of power and population beyond the British Isles. The first, and the most fraught, was the invasion and domination of Ireland, first by medieval Norman nobles and then by English (and Scottish) Protestant settlers in successive violent conquests. Policies of plantation alienated land for settlement and interdicted counter-reformationist forces, thereby subjugating the Catholic majority under British settler rule through the destruction of indigenous sovereignties.

The policies and practices of systematic discrimination of the vice-regal government and those of their clients in the Protestant Ascendancy against Irish Catholics accompanied the annihilation of traditional Gaelic civilization. Until the early nineteenth century, Irish was the dominant language, but now a small minority are native Irish speakers. Centuries of subjugation eventually led to nationalist uprising and, following civil war in the 1920s, independence for the Irish republic. However, concentration of colonial settlement and expulsion of Catholics from the north, known as the Ulster Plantation, resulted in the partition of the island of Ireland and long-term conflict among Catholic Republicans, Protestant Unionists, and the state in the North. Both fear and greed ruled British colonialism in Ireland, but without restraint.

Similar motivations drove settler colonialism in the American colonies, Canada, Australia, and New Zealand. Unlike Ireland, North America by the seventeenth century had already been substantially depopulated by pandemic disease brought by European colonizers a century before. Britain's North American colonies had diverse commercial and extractive motivations – particularly following the introduction of slavery in 1619 – as well as religious and ideological ones. All these colonies represented an overseas extension of British agrarian and commercial society, along with its political institutions, which expanded over territories as indigenous societies were forcibly removed and destroyed. Moreover, the existential insecurity of competition with France and Spain over the North American continent drove expansion, anxiety and conflict.

Similarly, colonies of settlement in the South Pacific expanded in the eighteenth century as the aboriginal population decreased dramatically through disease and were forcibly dispossessed of lands to allow for commercial agriculture and mining. In both instances, the shock of dramatic disease burden *on the original inhabitants* – not to mention more deliberate genocidal displacement and elimination – enabled widespread settlement and the establishment of "yeoman" institutions that could emphasize liberty and self-restraint, though by and for European settlers. As Wolfe writes, "settler colonialism destroys to replace," dissolving and erasing indigenous societies and erecting a new society on expropriated territories, while forcing the integration of indigenous peoples based on rigid and alien racial, religious, and cultural codes.[13] Thus within imperialist projects, settler colonialism responds to greed and fear with aggressive and totalizing logic of elimination, quite unlike the logic of preservation and differentiation in contexts where frugality was a guiding mandate.

10.2.2 Settler Colonialism and Hegemony in the American Empire

Another important example of the bifurcated nature of imperialism is that of the United States, as it emerged from British rule and consolidated national authority in the 1780s. If we take the first thirteen states as the original polity, we might understand its expansion across the continent to the Pacific Ocean as a dramatic instance of settler colonialism. The interweaving of fear and greed drove forces in this expansion, but frugality was completely absent. Rather, the expansionist universalism embedded in "manifest destiny" animated settler colonialism from independence to the incorporation of the last continental territory of Arizona as the forty-eighth state in 1912.

Significant ideological forces drove this expansion and homogenization, allowing no space for frugality. The United States was founded in part on a Jeffersonian ideal of a yeoman republic of independent farms and small, self-governing communities. The highly commercialized and financialized slavery-based plantations, like Monticello, were a gross hypocrisy in this respect, yet the ideal drove the universalizing alienation of land and resources for (white) Americans. As Susanne Rudolph has argued, America's Lockean universalist tradition brooks no preservation of tradition or fundamental difference of worldview, as propounded by Edmund Burke and practiced (though selectively) by the British in India; the American liberal tradition "elicits an impulse to impose Locke everywhere."[14] Nowhere was this impulse more evident than the American Conquest of the West. Turner's 1893 essay portrayed the teleological expansion of the frontier as the keystone of American "composite nationalism," transcending sectionalism, realizing rugged individualism wedded to technological and "civilizational" progress.[15]

Such ideologically and materially motivated expansion crushed competing sovereignties, including Native American tribes that had originally been considered sovereign nations. The destruction of indigenous sovereignties began in earnest under the Andrew Jackson administration; subsequent war, deportation, reservation land-grabbing, and paternalistic projects of individuation led the final end to tribal sovereignty and treaty obligations in 1871.[16] This aspect of America's frontier history stands in marked contrast with the restraint of governance exceptionalism at the northwestern frontier of British India, which was marked by an awareness of the costs of governance.

---

[13] Wolfe 2006, 388.   [14] Hartz cited in Rudolph 2005.
[15] Turner 1920, 22–28. See also Heitala 1985, Kens 2005.
[16] White 1991, 87–109. See also Otis and Prucha 1973.

Material opportunities, and threats to those seeking to take advantage of them, shaped the incentives of settlers, but it was ultimately the federal government that would intervene to preserve and protect the greed and fear of its (white) citizens. In the face of uncontrolled settlement and land grabs, the federal government reneged on treaties, then formed new ones with dubious authority, and waged bloody annihilationist wars with the tribes capable of resisting settler expansion. The military might of the federal army annihilated Indian nations *qua* nations, relegating them to reservations under US control and establishing absolute sovereignty for resource extraction efforts of the United States in the West. It thus privileged the interests of the settlers, miners, ranchers, other fortune-seekers, and ultimately eastern capital and midwestern industry over sovereign treaty commitments. Thus insecurity and economic opportunity, intertwined with one another and unrestrained by frugality, yielded a settler colonial state across the North American continent over the nineteenth century.

This stands in stark contrast to America's overseas imperial possessions and broader hegemonies in the twentieth century, which similarly operated according to capitalist opportunities and geostrategic threats, but in which frugality was very much in evidence. Following the Spanish-American War in 1898, America gained control of the remaining Spanish overseas possessions, such as Guam, Puerto Rico, and the Philippines, but these were not incorporated directly into the territory of the United States and subject to settlement. Rather, America's overseas empire was kept at arm's length and subject to an autonomous bureaucratic apparatus, implicated in Progressive-era administrative reforms, which in turn would shape the capacities of the American state itself.[17]

However, overseas possessions constituted a small fraction of what we might consider the American empire, particularly after World War II.[18] It included treaties and treaty systems in East Asia and Western Europe, which represented important bulwarks against the Soviet Union throughout the Cold War. These arrangements represented fear rather than greed, although European countries did provide key markets for America's manufacturing goods. The United States' naval and broader military presence is global and has at times been compared to Britain's hegemonic position in the nineteenth century. It has resulted in both deployment for specific objectives – such as ensuring the flow of energy resources to the Gulf – and also overreach, resulting in costly wars with limited strategic benefits in Southeast Asia and more recently, "the forever wars" in the Middle East.

The American empire is the most fully articulated in its *hegemony* over Latin America, which incorporated greed, fear (of Communist influence), and frugality. The United States never formally colonized any Latin American countries, but it put in place arrangements of domination and quiescence,

---

[17] Moore 2017.   [18] For a brilliant synopsis, see Kurth 2019.

which ensured that economic benefits largely flowed northward, at significant cost to the autonomy and developmental capacity of Latin American countries themselves.[19] These arrangements ensured the persistence of "colonial pacts" of unequal exchange between US industry and these largely agrarian countries. The navy established a dominant presence through Caribbean (later Southern) Command and through the training and equipping of US-allied national militaries. The United States implicitly or covertly supported military dictatorships or de facto oligarchies, with patrimonial and extractive relationships with their own citizens.[20]

American hegemony in the western hemisphere had varying economic and security dimensions – greed in uneven trade and resource flows and fear in the threats from Soviet-backed and broader socialist movements – that led to differing strategies and practices with regard to Central America. Given the proximity to Cuba, American intervention was often more explicit and violent, with the CIA overthrowing a left-wing government in Guatemala in 1954 and supporting insurgent Contras against the Sandinista government in Nicaragua in the 1980s. While some of these dynamics have changed after the Cold War, the hegemonic influence of the United States in the hemisphere is still significant.

It can therefore be useful to compare the settler colonization of the United States across the North American continent (as well as Alaska and the Hawai'ian islands) in the nineteenth century to the establishment and persistence of hegemonic relations in Latin America in the twentieth. Both are driven by often closely linked imperatives of economic opportunity and security, that is, greed and fear. Both correspond in different ways to a world of often-violent and discriminatory hierarchies rather than inclusive liberalism.

What truly distinguishes the two is *frugality*, or the extent to which governments and their clients are restrained in their expenditures for maintaining domination over subject peoples. In twentieth-century Latin America, with a few exceptions, the United States executed its objectives and that of its capitalist clients through maintaining its influence with elite clients, supporting local juntas, threatening of economic sanctions or executing covert action, rather than by direct action. The territorial expansion of the United States westward throughout the nineteenth century, however, was not a restrained enterprise. Settlers and the commercial, financial, and industrial clients of the US government sought to fully alienate the land and resources of the continent, thereby liquidating all alternative sovereignties and governance arrangements, particularly of indigenous peoples; to the extent that this impulse was resisted, such resistance was crushed by the might of the American military.

The relative unevenness of governance in North and South America can account for some of the important differences in development outcomes and mechanisms. In the sovereign territory of the United States, the violet flattening

[19] Kohli 2020, ch. 4–6.   [20] Kurth 2019, 32. See also Grandin 2006.

of governance difference meant that land, resources, and labor were alienated and commodified early, allowing for the unrestrained operation of capitalism. However, the US hegemony over Latin America in effect preserved the unevenness and incoherence of Latin American countries, particularly in the maintenance of patrimonial relationships and resistance to centralizing reforms.[21] "Brown spots" in the capacity of the state have had significant impacts in limiting the spread of democratic competition, particularly in provinces that are located far from metropolitan influence, reflecting a patchwork state logic.[22]

***

Chapter 10 has sought to place the complex nature and far-reaching impacts of colonial rule in India and the subsequent politics of conflict and competition in South Asian states in a wider comparative context, utilizing the logic of the patchwork state. In South Asian cases, we examined the roots of this patchwork authority in the particular politics of colonial rule, not as a unitary treatment but a complex though legible set of processes that established domination in different places for different reasons, yielding different governance arrangements. Postcolonial states in South Asia inherited different patterns of patchwork authority after independence, and sought to homogenize some (though not all) of this governance differentiation, yet postcolonial revision was limited in practice. The patchwork state has thus had a defining impact on patterns of subnational politics as well as the nature of national trajectories in three countries that together represent a fifth of the world's population. But this framework can help us understand the broader global canvas of wealthy, stable and poor, unstable countries by highlighting how histories of colonial rule and imperial domination have yielded both powerful states with violently homogenized governance and weaker states with traditions of differentiated and thus disjointed governance traditions, with consequences for contemporary politics.

[21] Soifer 2015.   [22] O'Donnell 1993.

Classification of Governance Institutions

COLONIAL GOVERNANCE ARRANGEMENTS

Typologizing variations in governance institutions into discrete categories across political geography represents interrelated conceptual and empirical challenges. It is always difficult to reconcile our own intellectual needs for clean classification and the making of distinctions with the lived experiences of those who actually conducted, or were subjected to, colonial governance. Archival sources suggest a diverse world of rulers and agents that is more variegated than social–scientific concepts like direct and indirect rule might suggest, even while sharing many common tropes, languages, and prejudices. Colonial records on how India was governed are also unfortunately, if unavoidably, partial; besides gaps in the records themselves, they represent the (often *ex post*) assessments and self-justifications of the dominators, and their pathological need to classify and judge subject populations, with tragic consequences. The worldviews, perspectives, and interests of indigenous actors often appear only indirectly in systematic colonial governance records and then through the distorting, self-interested lenses of the colonizers. As a result, it is crucial to avoid all but the most tentative and suspicious credulity in relation to the colonial state's assessments of India, particularly but by no means only in relation to caste and religion.

At the same time, if we want a systematic account of governance across the Indian subcontinent, the records of the colonial state are unavoidable. The voice of the colonial government is the loudest and clearest precisely because of its dominance and its interest in gathering information to sustain that dominance. We must proceed, with utmost caution, by focusing on the assets, liabilities, and self-reported activities of the colonial apparatus in different places, in order to build a dataset from which we can undertake classification. In order to be as systematic and comprehensive as possible in classification, I use the 26-volume *Imperial Gazetteer of India*, in an edition published in 1909.[1] It represents a virtual encyclopedia of colonial governance across South Asia that collected, organized, and abstracted reports from agents of empire into standardized entries on provinces, districts, and princely states. Due to their inclusion in the same publication, we can expect a minimum standard of comparability across entries, even though the language of governance can differ markedly from one region to another. The gazetteer has clear operational assumptions that are useful to us for identifying basic distinctions: districts, princely states, and political agencies are labeled as such. However, the aim of this exercise is not to take these categories for granted. Rather, it is to find the distinctions in the ways that different regions are governed *in practice*, which requires us to remain vigilant with regard to differences within and similarities across these categories, based on formal systems of rule and land tenure administration.

Metropolitan: This signifies those very few populous districts where at least half of the population is urban. At the turn of the twentieth century, this comprised of only the Presidency cities – Calcutta, Madras, and Bombay – along with Hyderabad in Hyderabad State, and the hill station district of Simla, which served as the summer capital of the colonial government from 1863 onward. Delhi is only included in assessments of governance in the 1940s, decades after it became the capital of colonial India in 1911.

Modernizing: Cases of modernizing governance constitute both districts and princely states with at least two-thirds of their territory under the ryotwari or cultivator-based land tenure arrangements. I include both districts and princely states in this category because of a deliberate isomorphism as a strategy of governance in "native states."

Intermediate: Cases of intermediate governance are complex and represent several different kinds of governance that characterize a middle ground between high and low levels of intermediation. They involve both administrative districts and princely states, based on the logic outlined earlier. Cases are included in this category based on two conditions: (1) there is a preponderance of mahalwari/ malguzari or village-based land tenure, with landlord-dominated villages, mahals, or territory under landlord-based tenures constituting less than half of the total in the United and Central Provinces, Punjab, and the North West Frontier Province[2] or (2) there are zamindari or jagirdari estates in otherwise cultivator-based districts or states that constitute more than one-third of its territory, or government estates or khalsa, or crown lands in otherwise

---

[1] The Imperial Gazetteer is available at the Asia and Africa Collection in the British Library and online at the University of Chicago's Digital South Asia Library: https://dsal.uchicago.edu/reference/gazetteer/

[2] In the United Provinces, Punjab, and the North West Frontier, tenures are divided by village into bhaicharya, pattidari, and zamindari. In the Central Provinces and Berar, I follow Iversen, Palmer-Jones and Sen (2013) in classifying *malguzari* tenures as village-based, with landlord-based tenures usually recorded as square miles under jagirdari tenure or *inam* grants.

landlord-based districts and princely states that represent more than a third of the territory.

Conservative: Cases of conservative governance constitute those districts where more than two-thirds of the land was subject to the Permanent Settlement or otherwise alienated to proprietary landlords, or more than half of the villages or mahals in otherwise mahalwari regions are under zamindars or jagirdars.

Chieftaincy: Cases of chieftaincy governance constitute those princely states in which the khalsa territory represent less than a third of the total area, and/or where crown lands are administered using zamindari arrangements.

Exceptional: This heterogeneous category of cases include the political agencies of the Northwest, the exceptionally governed districts of British Balochistan, and the "hill" districts of Assam in which less than a quarter of the total area was subject to surveys for the purposes of revenue. They have in common areas in which settled agriculture is limited, and the colonial government has formulated some form of exceptional governance over largely tribal populations.

POSTCOLONIAL GOVERNANCE ARRANGEMENTS

The unit of analysis for postcolonial governance is contemporary administrative districts, still the basic unit of administration throughout South Asia; I classify them into postcolonial governance arrangements using data from population censuses from the 1970s. While districts have proliferated in all three countries, the vast majority of new districts represent subdivisions (tehsils or talukas) of previously united districts, thus enabling classification to carry over from the 1970s until today.

Metropolitan: To acknowledge urbanization as a significant and deliberate consequence of state-building, I classify in the metropolitan governance category all districts with urban populations constituting 40 percent or more of the total population in the 1970s; I use 40 rather than 50 percent to reflect the spread of urban influence over peri-urban and proximate rural areas.

Modernizing: I classify all Indian districts in the 1970s that were previously districts and princely states under modernizing and intermediate governance under colonial rule. In addition, due to the nature of Partition and subsequent disruptions of dominant agrarian relations in both East and West Bengal, districts in West Bengal and Bangladesh not classified as metropolitan are categorized as modernizing. In Pakistan, all modernizing and intermediate districts with greater than 15 percent literacy in 1972 are classified as modernizing.

Conservative: I classify all Indian districts in the 1970s that were previously districts under conservative governance under colonial rule as under the postcolonial conservative governance, with the exception of the aforementioned erstwhile Bengal presidency. In addition, princely states under chieftaincy governance arrangements with tribal populations constituting less than 40 percent of the total population are also classified as under postcolonial conservative governance. In Pakistan, districts formerly under the princely rule of Khairpur and Bahawalpur, conservative districts under colonial rule and intermediate districts with lower than 15 percent literacy are classified as conservative, to reflect Ayub-era Pakistan's more cautious approach to political management, thus increasing the scope for state capture.

Exceptional: Districts and political agencies under exceptional governance in postcolonial states are difficult to classify systematically, because they represent self-conscious departures from governance orthodoxies. This means different things in different countries, as well as different places within the same country. In India, I include districts that were princely states but had tribal populations greater than 40 percent in the 1971 Census, districts under the Fifth and Sixth Schedules that delineated tribal autonomy in the Northeast, and the districts of Jammu and Kashmir, given its (nowrescinded) special constitutional status. In Pakistan, I classify as cases under exceptional governance the erstwhile FATA, the districts of the former Malakand division that constituted the tribal-majority princely states of Dir, Chitral, and Swat, and all districts in Balochistan province.[3] In Bangladesh, I classify as exceptional the three districts in the Chittagong Hill Tracts.

---

[3] This might seem overly broad, given the existence of a Balochistan provincial government, but exceptional features of governance in British Baluchistan, including the reliance on sardars and tribal levies to maintain law and order, were extended across the princely states of Kalat and Las Bela after Independence. The Pakistani state, despite its overweening presence in the province through a huge military cantonment and significant paramilitary forces, has deliberately not integrated Balochistan into the regular political norms and practices of Punjab and Sindh.

APPENDIX B

Classifying Political Violence

For the analysis in Chapter 6, we need to first classify violent incidents as sovereignty-contesting (SCV) or sovereignty-neutral (SNV). With reference to the ACLED data, I do this by means of two features of the data: event types and interaction codes, which signify the actors involved.[1] First, I exclude incidents that are classified as strategic developments or involving outside forces, such as firing between Indian and Pakistani soldiers across the Line of Control. Battles are classified as SCV, unless the battles are between social actors such as communal militias. Riots are always classified as SNV. Together these two categories represent a plurality of the incidents. For other categories such as remote violence or violence against civilians, I make use of interaction codes. Violent altercations between government forces and rebel actors (1-2) or between rebel actors and civilians (2-7), for instance, are classified as SCV. For other interactions, such as between ethnic or political militias and civilians (3-7 or 4-7), I code incidents individually based on the details of the case. Moreover, these cases are nationally specific: sectarian violence in Pakistan, for example, is sovereignty-neutral, because attacks on Shi'a community do not constitute a profound challenge to the authority of the Pakistani state.

In order to provide some alternative measures to the ACLED data, I analyze two other datasets of geolocated violent events. For the Upsala data, which mostly incudes SCV and excludes SNV, I use "type of violence" (state-based, non-state and one sided) and "dyad-name" to classify conflicts. For the BFRS data, I classify incidents based on event type and leave cases with "other" as unclassified.

The most important limitation of these data as a whole is that they represent a (wider or narrower) contemporary snapshot of the patterns of violence in these three countries, rather than tracing the nature of conflict over time. These patterns would look significantly different, for example, in the late 1980s in India, where violence was concentrated in the wealthy cities and countryside of

---

[1] See Naseemullah 2018, Appendix 1. For details, see the ACLED codebook. www.acleddata.com/wp-content/uploads/dlm_uploads/2017/10/ACLED_Codebook_2019FINAL_pbl.pdf

the northwest due to the Khalistan insurgency, or in the early 1970s, when the leftwing insurgency that started in Naxalbari spread to urban violence in Kolkata.[2] In many ways, this cannot be helped; systematic data collection on political violence is too intensive an exercise to go back in time with the level of detail necessary for district-level work. I have endeavored to specify the scope conditions of the argument and indicate how these patterns might look different in the presence of ethno-national separatist conflict, an important causal factor that lies beyond the explanatory framework. Another key factor complicating the analysis is spillover. Specifically, the extent to which regionally specific insurgencies are able to penetrate concentrations of state power and thus affect outcomes elsewhere through terrorist violence can impact district-specific analysis. This is especially important for understanding the differences in the dynamics between India and Bangladesh on one hand and Pakistan on the other. The Taliban insurgency in the early 2010s pervaded much of the country, yielding qualitatively different patterns of national violence at variance from theoretical expectations. I leverage the successful victory over the insurgents in the last three years of the decade to compare the two patterns across time.

[2] I wish to thank both Devesh Kapur and Pradeep Chhibber for this insight.

References

Abi-Habib, Maria and Salman Masood. 2018. "Military's Influence Casts a Shadow Over Pakistan's Election." *New York Times*, July 21. www.nytimes.com/2018/07/21/world/asia/pakistan-election-military.html

Acemoglu, Daron, Simon Johnson, and James Robinson. 2002. "Reversal of Fortune." *The Quarterly Journal of Economics* 117(4): 1231–1294.

2001. "The Colonial Origins of Comparative Development." *American Economic Review* 91(5): 1369–1401.

Acemoglu, Daron and James Robinson. 2012. *Why Nations Fail*. New York: Crown.

Adeney, Katharine. 2017. "How to Understand Pakistan's Hybrid Regime." *Democratization* 24(1): 119–137.

2002. "Constitutional Centring." *Commonwealth & Comparative Politics* 40(3): 8–33.

Agamben, Georgio. 2003. *State of Exception*. Chicago: University of Chicago Press.

Agarwala, Rina. 2013. *Informal Labor, Formal Politics, and Dignified Discontent in India*. Cambridge University Press.

Ahsan, Syed and Bhumitra Chakma. 1989. "Problems of National Integration in Bangladesh." *Asian Survey* 29(10): 959–970.

Ahuja, Amit. 2019. *Mobilizing the Marginalized*. New York: Oxford University Press.

Ahuja, Amit and Pradeep Chhibber. 2012. "Why the Poor Vote in India." *Studies in Comparative International Development* 47(4): 389–410.

Ahuja, Amit and Rajkamal Singh. 2020. "Why Electorally Secure Modi Govt Cracked Down on CAA Protesters so Brutally." *The Print*, January 8. https://theprint.in/opinion/why-electorally-secure-modi-govt-cracked-down-on-caa-protesters-so-brutally/345543/

Akbar, Nafisa. 2016. Outside the Institutional Box. PhD Dissertation, University of California.

Alam, Muzaffar and Sanjay Subrahmanyam. 1998. *The Mughal State, 1526–1750*. Delhi: Oxford University Press.

Ali, Kamran Asdar. 2015. *Communism in Pakistan*. London: IB Tauris.

Ali, Noaman. 2020. "Agrarian Class Struggle and State Formation in Post-Colonial Pakistan, 1959–1974." *Journal of Agrarian Change* 20(2): 270–288.

Amin, Samir. 1977. *Imperialism and Unequal Development*. New York: Monthly Review Press.

Amsden, Alice. 1989. *Asia's Next Giant*. Oxford: Oxford University Press.

Anderson, Benedict. 1983. *Imagined Communities*. London: Verso.
Anderson, Perry. 1974. *Lineages of the Absolutist State*. London: Lew Left Books.
Arias, Enrique and Daniel Goldstein, eds. 2010. *Violent Democracies in Latin America*. Durham: Duke University Press.
Arjona, Ana. 2016. *Rebelocracy*. Cambridge University Press.
Arnold, Caroline. 2006. Claims on the Common. PhD Dissertation, University of California.
Auerbach, Adam. 2020. *Demanding Development*. Cambridge: Cambridge University Press.
Auerbach, Adam and Tariq Thachil. 2018. "How Clients Select Brokers." *American Political Science Review* 112(4): 775–791.
Auyero, Javier. 2007. *Routine Politics and Violence in Argentina*. Cambridge: Cambridge University Press.
Axmann, Martin. 2008. *Back to the Future: The Khanate of Kalat and the Genesis of Baloch Nationalism, 1915–1955*. Oxford: Oxford University Press.
Bachrach, Peter and Morton Baratz. 1963. "Decisions and Nondecisions." *American Political Science Review* 57(3): 632–642.
Bagchi, Amiya Kumar. 2002. *Capital and Labour Redefined*. London: Anthem Press.
Balcells, Laia. 2017. *Rivalry and Revenge*. Cambridge: Cambridge University Press.
Banerjee, Abhijit and Esther Duflo. 2012. *Poor Economics*. London: Penguin.
Banerjee, Abhijit and Lakshmi Iyer. 2013. "Response to 'a Re-examination of Banerjee and Iyer'." *Journal of Development Studies* 49(12): 1647–1650.
    2005. "History, Institutions, and Economic Performance." *The American Economic Review* 95(4): 1190–1213.
Banerjee, Mukulika. 2000. *The Pathan Unarmed*. Woodbridge: James Currey.
Bardhan, Pranab, Sandip Mitra, Dilip Mookherjee, and Abhirup Sarkar. 2009. "Local Democracy and Clientelism." *Economic and Political Weekly* 44(9): 46–58.
Barkey, Karen. 1994. *Bandits and Bureaucrats*. Ithaca: Cornell University Press.
Barnes, Nicholas. 2017. "Criminal Politics." *Perspectives on Politics* 15(4): 967–987.
Barua, Pradeep. 1995. "Inventing Race: The British and India's Martial Races." *The Historian* 58(1): 107–116.
Baruah, Sanjib. 2005. *Durable Disorder*. Delhi: Oxford University Press.
Bashir, Shahzad and Robert Crews, eds. 2012. *Under the Drones*. Cambridge, MA: Harvard University Press.
Bates, Robert. 1981. *Markets and States in Tropical Africa*. Berkeley: University of California Press.
Baumgartner, Frank, Christian Breunig, Christoffer Green-Pedersen, et al. 2009. "Punctuated Equilibrium in Comparative Perspective." *American Journal of Political Science* 53(3): 603–620.
Bayly, Christopher. 1994. "The British Military-Fiscal State and Indigenous Resistance: India 1750–1820." In Lawrence Stone, ed., *An Imperial State at War*. Abingdon: Routledge: 322–354.
    1983. *Rulers, Townsmen and Bazaars*. Cambridge: Cambridge University Press.
Bendix, Reinhard. 1978. *Kings or People*. Berkeley: University of California Press.
Benichou, Lucien. 2000. *From Autocracy to Integration: Political Developments in Hyderabad State, 1938–1948*. Delhi: Orient Blackswan.
Bensel, Richard. 1990. *Yankee Leviathan*. Cambridge: Cambridge University Press.

Benton, Lauren. 1999. "Colonial Law and Cultural Difference." *Comparative Studies in Society and History* 41(3): 563–588.

Beramendi, Pablo. 2012. *The Political Geography of Inequality*. Cambridge: Cambridge University Press.

Berenschot, Ward. 2009. "Rioting as Maintaining Relations." *Civil Wars* 11(4): 414–433.

Berman, Eli, Joseph Felter, Jacob Shapiro, and Vestal McIntyre. 2018. *Small Wars, Big Data*. Princeton: Princeton University Press.

Besley, Timothy and Torsten Persson. 2011. *Pillars of Prosperity*. Princeton: Princeton University Press.

Bevir, Mark. 2003. "Theosophy and the Origins of the Indian National Congress." *International Journal of Hindu Studies* 7(1–3): 99–115.

Bhalla, Gurwinder Singh and Gurmail Singh. 2012. *Economic Liberalisation and Indian Agriculture*. Delhi: Sage.

Bhavnani, Rikhil and Francesca Jensenius. 2015. "Socioeconomic Profile of India's Old Electoral Constituencies, 1971–2001." In Mohammad Sanjeer Alam and K. C. Sivaramakrishnan, eds., *Fixing Electoral Boundaries in India: Laws, Processes, Outcomes and Implication for Political Representation*. Delhi: Oxford University Press.

Birch, Sarah, Ursula Daxecker, and Kristine Höglund. 2020. "Electoral Violence." *Journal of Peace Research* 57(1): 3–14.

Birla, Ritu. 2009. *Stages of Capital*. Durham: Duke University Press.

Bhogale, Saloni, Sudheendra Hangal, Francesca Refsum Jensenius, et al. 2019. "TCPD Indian Elections Data VI," Trivedi Centre for Political Data, Ashoka University.

Blanton, Robert, David Mason, and Brian Athow. 2001. "Colonial Style and Post-Colonial Ethnic Conflict in Africa." *Journal of Peace Research* 38(4): 473–491.

Boehme, Kate. 2015. "Smuggling India: Deconstructing Western India's Illicit Export Trade, 1818– 1870." *Journal of the Royal Asiatic Society* 25(4): 685–704.

Bohlken, Anjali and Ernest John Sergenti. 2010. "Economic Growth and Ethnic Violence." *Journal of Peace research* 47(5): 589–600.

Boone, Catherine. 2014. *Property and Political Order in Africa*. Cambridge: Cambridge University Press.

   2003. *The Political Topographies of the African State*. Cambridge: Cambridge University Press.

Bose, Neilesh. 2014. *Recasting the Region: Language, Culture, and Islam in Colonial Bengal*. Delhi: Oxford University Press.

Bose, Sugata. 1993. *Peasant Labour and Colonial Capital*. Cambridge: Cambridge University Press.

Bose, Sumantra. 2009. *Kashmir: Roots of Conflict, Paths to Peace*. Cambridge, MA: Harvard University Press.

Bowen, Huw. 2005. *The Business of Empire*. Cambridge: Cambridge University Press.

Brass, Jennifer. 2016. *Allies or Adversaries?* Cambridge: Cambridge University Press.

Brass, Paul. 2011. *An Indian Political Life*. Delhi: Sage.

   1997. *Theft of an Idol*. Princeton: Princeton University Press.

Bratton, Michael and Nicolas Van de Walle. 1994. "Neopatrimonial Regimes and Political Transitions in Africa." *World Politics* 46(4): 453–489.

Breman, Jan. 1996. *Footloose Labour*. Cambridge: Cambridge University Press.

Brown, Judith. 1991. *Gandhi: Prisoner of Hope*. New Haven: Yale University Press.
Bryant, Gerald. 2013. *The Emergence of British Power in India, 1600–1784*. Woodbridge: Boydell and Brewer.
Bueno de Mesquita, Ethan, Christine Fair, Jenna Jordan, Rasul Bakhsh Rais, and Jacob Shapiro. 2015. "Measuring Political Violence in Pakistan: Insights from the BFRS Dataset."*Conflict Management and Peace Science* 32(5): 536–558.
Bull, Hedley. 1977. *The Anarchical Society*. London: Red Globe.
Bussell, Jennifer. 2019. *Clients and Constituents*. New York: Oxford University Press.
2012. *Corruption and Reform in India*. Cambridge: Cambridge University Press.
Butt, Ahsan. 2017. *Secession and Security*. Ithaca: Cornell University Press.
Cannadine, David. 2001. *Ornamentalism: How the British Saw their Empire*. New York: Oxford University Press.
Capoccia, Giovanni and Daniel Kelemen. 2007. "The Study of Critical Junctures." *World Politics* 59(3): 341–369.
Cardoso, Fernando and Enzo Faletto. 1979 [1971]. *Dependency and Development in Latin America*. Berkeley: University of California Press.
Cederman, Lars-Erik, Kristian Gleditsch, and Halvard Buhaug. 2013. *Inequality, Grievances, and Civil War*. Cambridge: Cambridge University Press.
Cederman, Lars-Erik, Andreas Wimmer, and Brian Min. 2010. "Why Do Ethnic Groups Rebel?" *World Politics* 62(1): 87–119.
Centeno, Miguel. 2002. *Blood and Debt*. State College: Penn State Press.
Chandavarkar, Rajnarayan. 1998. *Imperial Power and Popular Politics*. Cambridge: Cambridge University Press.
1993. *The Origins of Industrial Capitalism in India*. Cambridge: Cambridge University Press.
Chandra, Bipan. 1968. "Reinterpretation of Nineteenth-Century Indian Economic History." *Indian Economic and Social History Review* 5: 1–15.
Chandra, Kanchan. 2004. *Why Ethnic Parties Succeed*. Cambridge: Cambridge University Press.
Chandra, Kanchan and Omar Garcia-Ponce. 2019. "Why Ethnic Subaltern-led Parties Crowd Out Armed Organizations." *World Politics* 71(2): 367–416.
Chatterjee, Partha. 2010. *Empire and Nation*. New York: Columbia University Press.
2004. *The Politics of the Governed*. New York: Columbia University Press.
1993. *The Nation and its Fragments*. Princeton: Princeton University Press.
Chatterji, Joya. 2007. *The Spoils of Partition: Bengal and India, 1947–1967*. Cambridge: Cambridge University Press.
2002. *Bengal Divided: Hindu Communalism and Partition, 1932–1947*. Cambridge: Cambridge University Press.
Chaudhuri, Kirti. 1974. "The Structure of Indian Textile Industry in the Seventeenth and Eighteenth Centuries." *The Indian Economic & Social History Review* 11(2–3): 127–182.
1978. *The Trading World of Asia and the English East India Company: 1660–1760*. Cambridge: Cambridge University Press.
Chaudhary, Latika, Jared Rubin, Sriya Iyer, and Anand Shrivastava. 2020. "Culture and Colonial Legacy." *Journal of Economic Behavior and Organization* 173: 107–129.
Chaudhry, Kiren. 1993. "The Myths of the Market and the Common History of Late Developers." *Politics & Society* 21(3): 245–274.

Chhibber, Pradeep. 1999. *Democracy without Associations*. Ann Arbor: University of Michigan Press.

Chhibber, Pradeep and Ken Kollman. 2004. *The Formation of National Party Systems*. Princeton: Princeton University Press.

Chhibber, Pradeep, Francesca Jensenius, and Pavithra Suryanarayan. 2014. "Party Organization and Party Proliferation in India." *Party Politics* 20(4): 489–505.

Chhibber, Pradeep and Rahul Verma. 2019. "The Rise of the Second Dominant Party System in India." *Studies in Indian Politics* 7(2): 131–148.

—— 2018. *Ideology and Identity*. Oxford: Oxford University Press.

Chibber, Vivek. 2003. *Locked in Place*. Princeton: Princeton University Press.

Chiriyankandath, James. 1992. "'Democracy' under the Raj." *Commonwealth & Comparative Politics* 30(1): 39–63.

Chirol, Valentine. 1910. *Indian unrest*. London: Good Press.

Chua, Amy. 2002. *World on Fire*. New York: Doubleday.

CMS. 2019. *Poll Expenditure, the 2019 Elections*. Delhi: Centre for Media Studies.

Cohen, Stephen. 2011. *The Future of Pakistan*. Washington, DC: Brookings Institution Press.

Cohen, Youssef, Brian Brown, and Kenneth Organski. 1981. "The Paradoxical Nature of State-Making." *American Political Science Review* 75(4): 901–910.

Collier, David and Ruth Collier. 1991. *Shaping the Political Agenda*. Princeton: Princeton University Press.

Collier, David, Jody LaPorte, and Jason Seawright. 2012. "Putting Typologies to Work." *Political Research Quarterly* 65.1: 217–232.

Collier, Paul, Anke Hoeffler, and Dominic Rohner. 2009. "Beyond Greed and Grievance: Feasibility and Civil War." *Oxford Economic Papers* 61(1): 1–27.

Condos, Mark. 2017. *The Insecurity State*. Cambridge: Cambridge University Press.

Cooper, Randolf. 2003. *The Anglo-Maratha Campaigns and the Contest for India*. Cambridge: Cambridge University Press.

Corbridge, Stuart. 2002. "The Continuing Struggle for India's Jharkhand." *Commonwealth & Comparative Politics* 40(3): 55–71.

Cox, Gary. 1997. *Making Votes Count*. Cambridge: Cambridge University Press.

Cox, Gary and Mathew McCubbins, 1993. *Legislative Leviathan*. Berkeley: University of California Press.

Cumings, Bruce. 1984. "The Origins and Development of the Northeast Asian Political Economy." *International Organization* 38(1): 1-40.

Cunningham, Kathleen. 2011. "Divide and Conquer or Divide and Concede." *American Political Science Review* 105 (2): 275–297.

D'Costa, Anthony. 2000. "Capitalist Maturity and Corporate Responses to Economic Liberalization in India." *Contemporary South Asia* 9(2): 141–163.

Dalrymple, William. 2019. *The Anarchy*. London: Bloomsbury.

Damodaran, Harish. 2008. *India's New Capitalists*. New York: Palgrave Macmillan.

Darwin, John. 2009. *The Empire Project*. Cambridge: Cambridge University Press.

Das Gupta, Achin. 1967. *Malabar in Asian Trade 1740–1800*. Cambridge: Cambridge University Press.

Das, Veena. 1995. "Privileging the Local." *Seminar* 425:97–102.

Dasgupta, Keya. 1983. "Plantation Economy and Land Tenure System in Brahmaputra Valley, 1839–1914." *Economic and Political Weekly* 18(29): 1280–1290.

Datta, Sreeradha. 2007. "Islamic Militancy in Bangladesh." *South Asia* 30(1): 145–170.

Deaton, Angus. 2010. "Instruments, Randomization, and Learning about Development." *Journal of Economic Literature* 48(2): 424–455.

Desai, Manali. 2007. *State Formation and Radical Democracy in India*. Abingdon: Routledge.

2005. "Indirect British Rule, State Formation, and Welfarism in Kerala, India, 1860–1957." *Social Science History* 29(3): 457–488.

Devji, Faisal. 2012. *The Impossible Indian*. Cambridge, MA: Harvard University Press.

Digby, William. 1901. *"Prosperous" British India: a Revelation from Official Records*. London: Unwin.

Dirks, Nicolas. 1987. *The Hollow Crown*. Cambridge: Cambridge University Press.

Doner, Richard, Bryan Ritchie, and Dan Slater. 2005. "Systemic Vulnerability and the Origins of Developmental States." *International Organization* 59(2): 327–361.

Downing, Brian. 1993. *The Military Revolution and Political Change*. Princeton: Princeton University Press.

Dunning, Thad. 2012. *Natural Experiments in the Social Sciences*. Cambridge: Cambridge University Press.

Dupraz, Yannick. 2019. "French and British Colonial Legacies in Education." *The Journal of Economic History* 79(3): 628–668.

Dutt, Romesh Chander. 1902. *The Economic History of India, vol I*. London: Kegan Paul.

Duverger, Maurice. 1954. *Political Parties*. New York: Wiley.

Eck, Kristine. 2009. "From Armed Conflict to War." *International Studies Quarterly* 53(2): 369–388.

Ehrlich, Joshua. 2020a. "Anxiety, Chaos, and the Raj." *The Historical Journal* 63(2): 777–787.

2020b. "Plunder and Prestige." *South Asia* 43(3): 478–492.

2018. "The Crisis of Liberal Reform in India" *Modern Asian Studies* 52(6): 2013–2055.

Erdman, Howard. 1967. *Swatantra Party and Indian Conservatism*. Cambridge: Cambridge University Press.

Erikson, Emily. 2014. *Between Monopoly and Free Trade*. Princeton: Princeton University Press.

Ertman, Thomas. 1997. *Birth of the Leviathan*. Cambridge: Cambridge University Press.

Esping-Andersen, Gosta. 1990. *The Three Worlds of Welfare Capitalism*. Princeton: Princeton University Press.

Evans, Peter. 1995. *Embedded Autonomy*. Princeton: Princeton University Press.

1989. "Predatory, Developmental, and other Apparatuses." *Sociological Forum* 4(4): 561–587.

Faguet, Jean-Paul, Camilo Matajira, and Fabio Sánchez. 2017. "Is Extraction Bad? Encomienda and Development in Colombia since 1560." Unpublished Paper, London School of Economics. https://papers.ssrn.com/sol3/papers.cfm?abstract_id=3007769

Fair, Christine. 2014. *Fighting to the End*. Oxford: Oxford University Press.

Fair, Christine, Keith Crane, Christopher S. Chivvis, Samir Puri, and Michael Spirtas. 2010. *Pakistan: Can the United States Secure an Insecure State?* Santa Monica: Rand Corporation.

Fair, Christine and Seth Jones. 2009. "Pakistan's War Within." *Survival* 51(6): 161–188.

Falkenhagen, Adrea. 2011. "Mining and the Maoists." Occasional Paper, Program on Environmental Security, Stimson Center. www.stimson.org/2011/mining-and-maoists/

Farooqui, Amar. 2011. *Scindias and the Raj*. Delhi: Primus Books.

Fearon, James. 1991. "Counterfactuals and Hypothesis Testing in Political Science." *World Politics* 43(2): 169–195.

Fearon, James and David Laitin. 2003. "Ethnicity, Insurgency, and Civil War." *American Political Science Review* 97(1): 75–90.

Ferguson, Niall. 2012. *Empire: How Britain Made the Modern World*. London: Penguin.

Fisher, Michael. 1991. *Indirect Rule in India, 1764–1858*. New York: Oxford University Press.

1984. "Indirect Rule in the British Empire." *Modern Asian Studies* 18(3): 393–428.

Foa, Roberto and Anna Nemirovskaya. 2016. "How State Capacity Varies within Frontier States." *Governance* 29(3): 411–432.

Frankel, Francine. 2005. *India's Political Economy*. Delhi: Oxford University Press.

1971. *India's Green Revolution*. Princeton: Princeton University Press.

Frankel, Frankel and MSA Rao. 1989, eds. *Dominance and State Power in India*. Delhi: Oxford University Press.

Frankema, Ewout. 2010. "Raising Revenue in the British Empire, 1870–1940." *Journal of Global History* 5(3): 447–477.

Frykenberg, Robert. 1988. "Modern Education in South India, 1754–1854." *American Historical Review* 96(1): 37–65.

1981. "On the Study of Conversion Movements." *Indian Economic and Social Review* 17(2): 121–138.

Fukuyama, Francis. 2015. *Political Order and Political Decay*. Princeton: Princeton University Press.

2011. *The Origins of Political Order*. New York: Farrar, Straus and Giroux.

Furnivall, J. S. 1957. *Colonial Policy and Practice*. Cambridge: Cambridge University Press.

Gaba, Kwawu, Brian Min, Anand Thakker and Chris Elvidge. 2016. nightlights.io: Twenty Years of India Lights.

Galbraith, John. 1960. "The 'Turbulent Frontier' as a Factor in British Expansion." *Comparative Studies in Society and History* 2(2): 150–168.

Galtung, Johan. 1971. "A Structural Theory of Imperialism." *Journal of Peace Research* 8(2): 81–117.

Gandhi, Aditi and Michael Walton. 2012. "Where do India's Billionaires Get their Wealth?" *Economic and Political Weekly* 47(40): 10–14.

Gandhi, Mohandas K. 1909. *Hind Swaraj*. Ahmedabad: Navajivan.

Ganguly, Sumit. 2006. "The Rise of Islamist Militancy in Bangladesh." Special Report 171. United States Institute of Peace. https://www.usip.org/publications/2006/08/rise-islamist-militancy-bangladesh

2003. *The Kashmir Question*. Abingdon: Frank Cass.

1997. *The Crisis in Kashmir*. Cambridge: Cambridge University Press.

Gaventa, John. 1980. *Power and Powerlessness*. Oxford: Oxford University Press.

Gawande, Kishore, Devesh Kapur, and Shanker Satyanath. 2017. "Renewable Natural Resource Shocks and Conflict Intensity." *Journal of Conflict Resolution* 61(1): 140–172.

Gayer, Laurent. 2014. *Karachi: Ordered Disorder and the Struggle for the City*. Oxford: Oxford University Press.

Gerring, John, Daniel Ziblatt, Johan Van Gorp, and Julian Arevalo. 2011. "An Institutional Theory of Direct and Indirect Rule." *World Politics* 63(3): 377–433.

Gervasoni, Carlos. 2018. *Hybrid Regimes within Democracies*. Cambridge: Cambridge University Press.

Gey van Pittius, Ernst. 1931. "'Dominion' Nationality." *'Journal of Comparative Legislation and International Law* 13(4): 199–202.

Gibson, Edward. 2013. *Boundary Control*. Cambridge: Cambridge University Press.

Gilley, Bruce. 2017. The Case for Colonialism. Unpublished Paper. Portland State University. www.web.pdx.edu/~gilleyb/2_The%20case%20for%20colonialism_at2Oct2017.pdf

Gilman, Nils. 2003. *Mandarins of the Future*. Baltimore: JHU Press.

Gilpin, Robert. 1975. *US Power and the Multinational Corporation*. New York: Basic Books.

Giraudy, Agustina. 2015. *Democrats and Autocrats*. New York: Oxford University Press.

Gordon, Stewart. 1993. *The Marathas, 1600-1818*. Cambridge: Cambridge University Press.

Goswami, Manu. 2004. *Producing India*. Chicago: University of Chicago Press.

Gould, William. 2010. *Bureaucracy, Community and Influence in India*. Abingdon: Routledge.

Grandin, Greg. 2006. *Empire's Workshop*. New York: Metropolitan Books.

Grare, Frederic. 2013. *Balochistan: the State vs the Nation*. Carnegie Papers, Carnegie Endowment for International Peace.

Greif, Avner and David Laitin. 2004. "A Theory of Endogenous Institutional Change." *American Political Science Review* 98(4): 633–652.

Guha, Ranajit. 1997. "Not at Home in Empire." *Critical Inquiry* 23(3): 482–493.

 1983. *Elementary Aspects of Peasant Insurgency in Colonial India*. Delhi: Oxford University Press.

 1963. *A Rule of Property for Bengal: An Essay on the Idea of Permanent Settlement*. Paris: Mouton.

Gunder Frank, Andre. 1967. *Capitalism and Underdevelopment in Latin America*. New York: Monthly Review Press.

Gupta, Akhil. 2012. *Red Tape*. Durham: Duke University Press.

Gupta, Shaibal Kumar. 1996. *A Foot in the Door of the Indian Civil Service, 1859–1943*. Kolkata: Papyrus.

Gurr, Ted. 1970. *Why Men Rebel*. Princeton: Princeton University Press.

Guyot-Réchard, Bérénice. 2016. *Shadow States: India, China and the Himalayas, 1910–1962*. Cambridge: Cambridge University Press.

Habib, Irfan. 1998. "The Coming of 1857." *Social Scientist* 26(1): 6–15.

 1985. "Studying a Colonial Economy without Perceiving Colonialism." *Modern Asian Studies* 119(3): 355–81.

Habib, Irfan, ed. 2002. *Confronting Colonialism: Resistance and Modernization under Haidar Ali and Tipu Sultan*. London: Anthem.

Haggard, Stephan. 2018. *The Developmental State*. Cambridge: Cambridge University Press.

Hamilton, Alexander. 1791. "Report on Manufactures." US House of Representatives, December 5. https://founders.archives.gov/documents/Hamilton/01-10-02-0001-0007

Hangen, Susan. 2009. *The Rise of Ethnic Politics in Nepal*. Abingdon: Routledge.

Hanson, Albert. 1966. *The Process of Planning*. Oxford: Oxford University Press.

Hardgrave, Robert. 1964. "The DMK and the politics of Tamil nationalism." *Pacific Affairs* 37(4): 396–411.

Harriss, John. 1993. "What Is Happening in Rural West Bengal? Agrarian Reform, Growth and Distribution." *Economic and Political Weekly* 28(24): 1237–1247.

Hart, Jonathan. 2003. *Comparing Empires*. New York: Palgrave.

Hassan, Mirza. 2013. "Political Settlement Dynamics in a Limited-Access Order: The Case of Bangladesh." ESID Working Paper No 23. https://ssrn.com/abstract=2386698

Hazarika, Sanjoy. 1995. *Strangers of the Mist: Tales of War and Peace from India's Northeast*. Delhi: Penguin.

Heckman, James and Sergio Urzua. 2010. "Comparing IV with Structural Models." *Journal of Econometrics* 156(1): 27–37.

Heitala, Thomas. 1985. *Manifest Design*. Ithaca: Cornell University Press.

Heller, Patrick. 1999. *The Labor of Development*. Ithaca: Cornell University Press.

Herbst, Jeffry. 2000. *States and Power in Africa*. Princeton: Princeton University Press.

Herring, Ronald. 1999. "Embedded Particularism." In Meredith Woo-Cumings, ed. *The Developmental State*. Ithaca: Cornell University Press.

 1983. *Land to the Tiller*. New Haven: Yale University Press.

 1979. "Zulfikar Ali Bhutto and the 'Eradication of Feudalism' in Pakistan." *Comparative Studies in Society and History* 21(4): 519–557.

Hochschild, Adam. 1998. *King Leopold's Ghost*. New York: Mariner.

Holsti, Kalevi. 1996. *The State, War, and the State of War*. Cambridge: Cambridge University Press.

Horowitz, Donald. 2001. *The Deadly Ethnic Riot*. Berkeley: University of California Press.

 1985. *Ethnic Groups in Conflict*. Berkeley: University of California Press.

Hossain, Naomi. 2017. *The Aid Lab*. Oxford: Oxford University Press.

Huntington, Samuel. 1968. *Political Order in Developing Societies*. New Haven: Yale University Press.

Hurrell, Andrew. 2007. *On Global Order*. Oxford: Oxford University Press.

Hussain, Zahid. 2010. *The Scorpion's Tail*. New York: Simon and Schuster.

Islam, Mozahidul. 2015. "Electoral Violence in Bangladesh." *Commonwealth & Comparative Politics* 53(4): 359–380.

Iversen, Vegard, Richard Palmer-Jones, and Kunal Sen. 2013. "On the Colonial Origins of Agricultural Development in India." *Journal of Development Studies* 49(12): 1631–1646.

Iyer, Lakshmi. 2010. "Direct vs Indirect Rule in India." *The Review of Economics and Statistics* 92(4): 693–713.

Jackson, Robert and Carl Rosberg. 1982. "Why Africa's Weak States Persist." *World Politics* 35(1): 1–24.

Jaffrelot, Christophe. 2017. "The Congress in Gujarat (1917–1969)." *Studies in Indian Politics* 5(2): 248–261.

 2016. "Quota for Patels?" *Studies in Indian Politics* 4(2): 218–232.

 2003. *India's Silent Revolution*. London: Hurst.

Jalal, Ayesha. 1995. *Democracy and Authoritarianism in South Asia*. Cambridge: Cambridge University Press.

 1994. *The Sole Spokesman*. Cambridge: Cambridge University Press.

1990. *State of Martial Rule in Pakistan*. Cambridge: Cambridge University Press.

Jamil, Ishtiaq and Pranab Panday. 2008. "The Elusive Peace Accord in the Chittagong Hill Tracts of Bangladesh and the Plight of the Indigenous People." *Commonwealth & Comparative Politics* 46(4): 464–489.

Jha, Saumitra and Steven Wilkinson. 2012. "Does Combat Experience Foster Organizational Skill?" *American Political Science Review* 106(4): 883–907.

Johari, Shuba. 2012. "Implementation of Tenancy Tenures in the Central Provinces in the 1860s." *Proceedings of the Indian History Congress* 73: 853–860.

2007. "Annexation of Nagpur." *Proceedings of the Indian History Congress* 68: 547–552.

Johnson, Chalmers. 1982. *MITI and the Japanese Miracle*. Palo Alto: Stanford University Press.

Johnson, Thomas and Chris Mason. 2008. "No Sign until the Burst of Fire." *International Security* 32(4): 41–77.

Jones, Stephanie. 1992. *Merchants of the Raj*. New York: Springer.

Kabwit, Ghislain. 1979. "Zaire: The roots of the continuing crisis." *The Journal of Modern African Studies* 17(3): 381–407.

Kaldor, Mary. 2012. *New and Old Wars*. Cambridge: Polity.

Kalyvas, Stathis. 2006. *The Logic of Violence in Civil War*. Cambridge: Cambridge University Press.

Kanjwal, Hafsa. 2017. Building a New Kashmir. PhD Dissertation, University of Michigan.

Kapur, Devesh and Milan Vaishnav, eds. 2018. *Costs of Democracy: Political Finance in India*. Oxford: Oxford University Press.

Karlsson, Bengt. 2013. "Evading the State." *Asian Ethnology* 72(2): 321.

Karnad, Raghu. 2015. *Farthest Field*. London: William Collins.

Keefer, Philip and Stuti Khemani. 2009. "When Do Legislators Pass on Pork?" *American Political Science Review* 103(1): 99–112.

Kennedy, Jonathan and Sunil Purushotham. 2012. "Beyond Naxalbari." *Comparative Studies in Society and History* 54(4): 832–862.

Kenny, Paul. 2015. "Colonial Rule, Decolonisation, and Corruption in India." *Commonweath & Comparative Politics* 53(4): 401–427.

Kens, Paul. 2005. "A Promise of Expansionism." In Sanford Levinson and Bartholomew Sparrow. eds., *The Louisiana Purchase and American Expansion*. Lanham, MD: Rowman and Littlefield: 139–164.

Khan, Mushtaq. 2011. "The Political Settlement and its Evolution in Bangladesh." Unpublished Paper, School of Oriental and African Studies. https://eprints.soas.ac.uk/12845/1/The_Political_Settlement_and_its_Evolution_in_Bangladesh.pdf

1999. "The Political Economy of Industrial Policy in Pakistan 1947-1971." Unpublished Paper, School of Oriental and African Studies. www.soas.ac.uk/economics/research/workingpapers/file28876.pdf

Khan, Shahab Enam. 2017. "Bangladesh: The Changing Dynamics of Violent Extremism and the Response of the State." *Small Wars & Insurgencies* 28(1): 191–217.

Khilnani, Sunil. 1997. *The Idea of India*. London: Hamish Hamilton.

Kipling, Rudyard. 1901. *Kim*. London: Macmillan.

Kissane, Bill. 2016. *Nations Torn Asunder*. Oxford: Oxford University Press.

Kissinger, Henry. 2014. *World Order*. New York: Penguin.

Kitschelt, Herbert and Steven Wilkinson, eds. 2007. *Patrons, Clients and Policies.* Cambridge: Cambridge University Press.

Kochanek, Stanley. 1968. *The Congress Party of India.* Princeton: Princeton University Press.

Kohli, Atul. 2020. *Imperialism in the Developing World.* Oxford: Oxford University Press.

2012. *Poverty amid Plenty in the New India.* Cambridge: Cambridge University Press.

2004. *State-Directed Development.* Cambridge: Cambridge University Press.

1997. "Can Democracies Accommodate Ethnic Nationalism?" *The Journal of Asian Studies* 56(2): 325–344.

1990. *Democracy and Discontent.* Cambridge: Cambridge University Press.

1983. "Parliamentary Communism and Agrarian Reform." *Asian Survey* 23(7): 783–809.

Kolff, Dirk. 2010. *Grass in their Mouths.* Leiden: Brill.

1990. *Naukar, Rajput and Sepoy.* Cambridge: Cambridge University Press.

Kothari, Rajni. 1964. "The Congress 'System' in India." *Asian Survey* 4(12): 1161–1173.

Krueger, Anne. 1974 "The Political Economy of the Rent-Seeking Society." *The American Economic Review* 64(3): 291–303.

Kruks-Wisner, Gabrielle. 2018. *Claiming the State.* Cambridge: Cambridge University Press.

Kurth, James. 2019. *The American Way of Empire.* Washington, DC: Washington Books.

Laakso, Markku and Rein Taagepera. 1979. "'Effective' Number of Parties." *Comparative Political Studies* 12(1): 3–27.

Lacina, Bethany. 2009. "The Problem of Political Stability in Northeast India." *Asian Survey* 49(6): 998–1020.

Lake, David and Donald Rothschild. 1997. *The International Spread and Management of Ethnic Conflict.* Princeton: Princeton University Press.

Lange, Matthew. 2009. *Lineages of Despotism and Development.* Chicago: University of Chicago Press.

Lange, Matthew and Andrew Dawson. 2009. "Dividing and Ruling the World? A Statistical Test of the Effects of Colonialism on Postcolonial Civil Violence." *Social Forces* 88(2): 785–817.

Lankina, Tomila and Lullit Getachew. 2012. "Mission or Empire, Word or Sword?" *American Journal of Political Science* 56(2): 465–483.

LaPorte, Jody and Danielle Lussier. 2011. "What is the Leninist Legacy?" *Slavic Review* 70(3): 637–654.

Lasswell, Harold. 1936. *Politics: Who Gets What, When, How.* New York: Whittlesey House.

Lawoti, Mahendra, ed. 2007. *Contentious Politics and Democratization in Nepal.* Delhi: Sage.

Leadbeater, Simon. 1993. *The Politics of Textiles.* Delhi: Sage.

Lechler, Marie and Lachlan McNamee. 2018. "Indirect Colonial Rule Undermines Support for Democracy." *Comparative Political Studies* 51(14): 1858–1898.

Lee, Alexander. 2019a. *Development in Multiple Dimensions.* Ann Arbor: University of Michigan Press.

2019b. "Land, State Capacity, and Colonialism." *Comparative Political Studies* 52(3): 412–444.

2017. "Redistributive Colonialism." *Politics & Society* 45(2): 173–224.

Lee, Harold. 2002. *Brothers in the Raj*. Oxford: Oxford University Press.

Lenin, Vladimir. 1920. *Imperialism: the Last Stage of Capitalism*. London: Lawrence and Wishart.

Lerner, Daniel. 1964. *Passing of Traditional Society*. Glencoe: Free Press.

Lessing, Benjamin. 2017. *Making Peace in Drug Wars*. Cambridge: Cambridge University Press.

Levitsky, Steven and Lucan Way. 2010. *Competitive Authoritarianism*. Cambridge: Cambridge University Press.

Lewis, Arthur. 1954. "Economic Development with Unlimited Supplies of Labour." *The Manchester School* 22(2): 139–191.

Lewis, David. 2013. "The Paradoxes of Bangladesh's Shahbag Protests." LSE South Asia. https://blogs.lse.ac.uk/southasia/2013/03/21/the-paradoxes-of-bangladeshs-shahbag-protests/

2011. *Bangladesh*. Cambridge: Cambridge University Press.

Lieven, Anatol. 2012. *Pakistan: A Hard Country*. New York: Public Affairs.

Lipset, Seymour. 1959. "Some Social Requisites of Democracy." *American Political Science Review* 53(1): 69–105.

List, Friedrich. 1856. *The National System of Political Economy*. Philadelphia: Lippincott.

Luebbert, Gregory. 1991. *Liberalism, Fascism and Social Democracy*. Oxford: Oxford University Press.

Lukes, Steven. 1974. *Power: A Radical View*. London: Red Globe.

MacIntyre, Andrew. 2002. *The Power of Institutions*. Ithaca: Cornell University Press.

Mahoney, James. 2010. *Colonialism and Postcolonial Development*. Cambridge: Cambridge University Press.

Mahoney, James and Kathleen Thelen, eds. 2015. *Advances in Comparative-Historical Analysis*. Cambridge: Cambridge University Press.

2009. *Explaining Institutional Change*. Cambridge: Cambridge University Press.

Mahoney, James and Dietrich Rueschemeyer, eds. 2003. *Comparative Historical Analysis in the Social Sciences*. Cambridge: Cambridge University Press.

Malik, Mashail. 2020. "Defiant Pride." Working Paper, Depart of Government, Harvard University.

Mamdani, Mahmood. 2012. *Define and Rule: Native as Political Identity*. Cambridge: Harvard University Press.

1996. *Citizen and Subject*. Princeton: Princeton University Press.

Mampilly, Zachariah. 2011. *Rebel Rulers*. Ithaca: Cornell University Press.

Mangla, Akshay. 2015. "Bureaucratic Norms and State Capacity in India: Implementing Primary Education in the Himalayan Region." *Asian Survey* 55(5): 882–908.

Mann, Michael. 2008. "Infrastructural Power Revisited." *Studies in Comparative International Development* 43(3–4): 355.

1984. "The Autonomous Power of the State." *European Journal of Sociology* 25(2): 185–213.

Mantena, Karuna. 2010. *Alibis of Empire*. Princeton: Princeton University Press.

Markovits, Claude. 2009. "The Political Economy of Opium Smuggling in Early Nineteenth Century India: Leakage or Resistance?" *Modern Asian Studies* 43(1): 89–111.

Marx, Karl. 1978 [1853]. "The British Rule in India." In Robert Tucker, ed., *Marx-Engels Reader*. New York: WW Norton.

Matanock, Aila and Paul Staniland. 2018. "How and Why Armed Groups Participate in Elections." *Perspectives on Politics* 16(3): 710–727.

Mattingly, Daniel. 2017. "Colonial Legacies and State Institutions in China." *Comparative Political Studies* 50(4): 434–463.

Mehta, Uday. 1991. *Liberalism and Empire*. Chicago: University of Chicago Press.

Metcalf, Thomas. 1994. *Ideologies of the Raj*. Cambridge: Cambridge University Press.

McDonnell, Erin. 2020. *Patchwork Leviathan*. Princeton: Princeton University Press.

McGarry, John and Brendan O'Leary. eds. 2013. *The Politics of Ethnic Conflict Regulation*. Abingdon: Routledge.

Michalopoulos, Stelios and Elias Papaioannou. 2014. "National Institutions and Subnational Development in Africa." *The Quarterly Journal of Economics* 129 (1): 151–213.

2013. "Pre-Colonial Ethnic Institutions and Contemporary African Development." *Econometrica* 81(1): 113–152.

Migdal, Joel. 2001. *State and Society*. Cambridge: Cambridge University Press.

1988. *Strong Societies, Weak States*. Princeton: Princeton University Press.

Migdal, Joel, Atul Kohli, and Vivienne Shue, eds. 1994. *State Power and Social Forces*. Cambridge: Cambridge University Press.

Miliband, Ralph. 1970. "The Capitalist State: Reply to Nicos Poulantzas." *New Left Review* 59(1): 53–60.

Min, Brian. 2015. *Power and the Vote*. Cambridge: Cambridge University Press.

Mir, Asfandyar. 2018. "What Explains Counterterrorism Effectiveness?" *International Security* 43(2): 45–83.

Misra, Sanghamitra. 2013. *Becoming a Borderland*. Abingdon: Routledge.

Mitra, Anirban and Debraj Ray. 2014. "Implications of an Economic Theory of Conflict." *Journal of Political Economy* 122(4): 719–765.

Mohmand, Shandana Khan. 2019. *Crafty Oligarchs, Savvy Voters*. Cambridge: Cambridge University Press.

Mohsin, Amena. 2003. *The Chittagong Hill Tracts, Bangladesh*. Boulder: Lynne Rienner.

Moore, Barrington. 1966. *Social Origins of Dictatorship and Democracy*. Boston: Beacon Press.

Moore, Colin. 2017. *American Imperialism and the State, 1893–1921*. Cambridge: Cambridge University Press.

Morris, Morris. 1983. "The Growth of Large-Scale Industry to 1947." In *The Cambridge Economic History of India, Volume 2*. D. Kumar, ed. Cambridge: Cambridge University Press: 553–667.

Morris-Jones, Wyndraeth. 1966. "Dominance and Dissent: Their Inter-Relations in the Indian Party System." *Government and Opposition* 1(4): 451–466.

Mukherjee, Rudrangshu. 2002. *Awadh in Revolt, 1857–1858: a Study of Popular Resistance*. London: Anthem Press.

Mukherjee, Shivaji. 2021. *Colonial Institutions and Civil War*. Cambridge: Cambridge University Press.

Murali, Kanta. 2017. *Caste, Class and Capital*. Cambridge: Cambridge University Press.

Naipaul, Vidiadhar Surajprasad. 1990. *India: A Million Mutinies Now*. London: Picador.

Naoroji, Dadabhai. 1901. *Poverty and Un-British Rule in India*. London: Sonnenschein.

Narula, Smita. 1999. *Broken People: Caste Violence Against India's "Untouchables."* New York: Human Rights Watch.

Naseemullah, Adnan. 2021. "Patronage vs. Ideology in Indian Politics." *Commonwealth & Comparative Politics* 59(2): 193–214.

2019. "Violence, Rents and Investment." *Comparative Politics* 51(4): 581–601.

2018. "Riots and Rebellion." *Political Geography* 63: 104–115.

2017a. *Development after Statism*. Cambridge: Cambridge University Press.

2017b. "The Political Economy of Economic Conservatism in India." *Studies in Indian Politics* 5(2): 233–247.

2016. "The Contested Capacity of the Indian State." *India Review* 15(4): 407–432.

2014. "Shades of Sovereignty." *Studies in Comparative International Development* 49(4): 501–522.

Naseemullah, Adnan and Caroline Arnold. 2015. "The Politics of Developmental State Persistence." *Studies in Comparative International Development* 50(1): 121–142.

Naseemullah, Adnan and Pradeep Chhibber. 2018. "Patronage, Sub-Contracted Governance, and the Limits of Electoral Coordination." *Comparative Politics* 51 (1): 81–100.

Naseemullah, Adnan and Paul Staniland. 2016. "Indirect Rule and Varieties of Governance." *Governance* 29(1): 13–30.

Nasr, Vali. 2000. "International Politics, Domestic Imperatives, and Identity Mobilization." *Comparative Politics* 32(2): 171–190.

Nathan, Manfred. 1922. "Dominion Status." *Transactions of the Grotius Society* 8: 117–132.

Nawaz, Shuja. 2019. *Battle for Pakistan*. New York: Penguin.

Nazir, Pervaiz. 1981. "Transformation of Property Relations in the Punjab." *Economic & Political Weekly* 16(8): 281–285.

Nooruddin, Irfan. 2010. *Coalition Politics and Economic Development*. Cambridge: Cambridge University Press.

North, Douglass. 1991. "Institutions." *The Journal of Economic Perspectives* 5(1): 97–112.

1990. *Institutions, Institutional Change and Economic Performance*. Cambridge: Cambridge University Press.

North, Douglass, William Summerhill, and Barry Weingast. 2000. "Order, Disorder and Economic Change," in Bruce Bueno de Mesquita and Hilton Root, eds., *Governing for Prosperity*. New Haven: Yale University Press.

North, Douglass, John Wallis and Barry Weingast. 2008. *Violence and Social Orders*. Cambridge: Cambridge University Press.

North, Douglass and Barry Weingast. 1989. "Constitutions and Commitment." *The Journal of Economic History* 49(4): 803–832.

O'Donnell, Guillermo. 1993. "On the State, Democratization and Some Conceptual Problems." *World Development* 21(8): 1355–1369.

1988. *Bureaucratic Authoritarianism*. Berkeley: University of California Press.

Oldenburg, Philip. 2010. *India, Pakistan, and Democracy*. Abingdon: Routledge.

Olson, Mancur. 1993. "Dictatorship, Democracy, and Development." *American Political Science Review* 87(3): 567–576.

Otis, D. S. and Francis Prucha. 1973. *The Dawes Act and the Allotment of Indian Lands*. Norman: University of Oklahoma Press.

Packer, George. "Risk Factors." *The New Yorker*, December 15, 2008. www .newyorker.com/magazine/2008/12/15/risk-factors

Palit, Chittabrata. 1975. *Tensions in Bengal Rural Society.* Kolkata: Progressive Publishers.

Pandita, Rahul. 2011. *Hello Bastar.* Chennai: Westland.

Paul, Thazha Varkey. 2014. *The Warrior State.* Oxford: Oxford University Press.

Peers, Douglas. 2007. "Gunpowder Empires and the Garrison State: Modernity, Hybridity, and the Political Economy of Colonial India, circa 1750-1860." *Comparative Studies of South Asia, Africa and the Middle East* 27(2): 245-258.

    1995. *Between Mars and Mammon: Colonial Armies and the Garrison State in Nineteenth Century India.* London: IB Tauris.

Petras, James and James Kurth. 1993. *Mediterranean Paradoxes: Politics and Social Structure in Southern Europe.* New York: Berg.

Philpott, Daniel. 2001. *Revolutions in Sovereignty.* Princeton: Princeton University Press.

Pierson, Paul. 2004. *Politics in Time.* Princeton: Princeton University Press.

Piliavski, Anastasia, ed. 2014. *Patronage as Politics in South Asia.* Delhi: Cambridge University Press.

Pitts, Jennifer. 2005. *A Turn to Empire: The Rise of Imperial Liberalism in Britain and France.* Princeton: Princeton University Press.

Pinglé, Vibha. 1999. *Rethinking the Developmental State.* New York: St. Martin's Press.

Polanyi, Karl 2001[1948]. *The Great Transformation.* Boston: Beacon Press.

Posen, Barry. 1993. "The Security Dilemma and Ethnic Conflict." *Survival* 35(1): 27–47.

Posner, Daniel. 2004. "The Political Salience of Cultural Difference." *American Political Science Review* 98(4): 529–545.

Poulantzas, Nicos 1969. "The Problem of the Capitalist State." *New Left Review* 58(1): 67–78.

Prajapati, S. L. 1982. "Chamuadari Settlements in Assam, 1826-1874." *Proceedings of the Indian History Congress* 43: 494–8.

Prasad, Nandan. 1964. *Paramountcy Under Dalhousie.* Delhi: Ranjit Publishers.

Price, Pamela. 1996. *Kingship and Political Practice in Colonial India.* Cambridge: Cambridge University Press.

    1996b. "Revolution and Rank in Tamil Nationalism." *The Journal of Asian Studies* 55(2): 359–383.

Przeworski, Adam and Fernando Limongi. 1997. "Modernization." *World Politics* 49 (2): 155–183.

Rabitoy, Neil. 1975. "System v. Expediency: The Reality of Land Revenue Administration in the Bombay Presidency, 1812–1820." *Modern Asian Studies* 9(4): 529–546.

Raghavan, Srinath. 2017. *India's War.* London: Penguin.

    2013. *1971.* Cambridge, MA: Harvard University Press.

    2010. *War and Peace in Modern India.* London: Palgrave.

Raleigh, Clionadh, Andrew Linke, Håvard Hegre, and Joakim Karlsen. 2010. "Introducing ACLED." *Journal of Peace Research* 47(5): 651–660.

Ram, Usha, Prabhat Jha, Faujdar Ram, et al. 2013. "Neonatal, 1–59 Month, and Under-5 mortality in 597 Indian districts, 2001 to 2012" *The Lancet Global Health* 1(4): e219–e226. https://ars.els-cdn.com/content/image/1-s2.0-S2214109X13700731-mmc1.pdf

Ramusack, Barbara. 2004. *The Indian Princes and Their States.* Cambridge: Cambridge University Press.

Ray, Ratnalekha. 1979. *Change in Bengal Agrarian Society, c. 1760–1850*. Delhi: Manohar Publications.

Richards, John. 2011. "The Finances of the East India Company in India, c. 1766–1859." Unpublished Paper, London School of Economics. http://eprints.lse.ac.uk /37829/1/WP153.pdf

2002. "The Opium Industry in British India." *The Indian Economic & Social History Review* 39(2–3): 149–180.

1981. "The Indian Empire and Peasant Production of Opium in the Nineteenth Century." *Modern Asian Studies* 15(1): 59–82.

Rostow, Walt Whitman. 1960. *Stages of Economic Growth*. Cambridge: Cambridge University Press.

Rothermund, Dietmar. 2002. *An Economic History of India*. Abingdon: Routledge.

Rothstein, Bo and Ayesha Warraich. 2017. *Making Sense of Corruption*. Cambridge: Cambridge University Press.

Roy, Anupam. 2018. "Shahbag Stolen? Third Force Dynamics and Electoral Politics in Bangladesh." *South Asia Research* 38(3_suppl): 1S–24S.

Roy, Srirupa. 2007. *Beyond Belief: India and the Politics of Postcolonial Nationalism*. Durham: Duke University Press.

Roy, Tirthankar. 2019. *How British Rule Changed India's Economy*. London: Palgrave.

2013. ""Rethinking the Origins of British India: State Formation and Military-Fiscal Undertakings in an Eighteenth Century World Region," *Modern Asian Studies* 47 (4): 1125–1156.

Rudolph, Lloyd and Susanne Rudolph. 1987. *In Pursuit of Laxmi*. Chicago: University of Chicago Press.

1967. *The Modernity of Tradition*. Chicago: University of Chicago Press.

1966. "Rajputana under British Paramountcy." *The Journal of Modern History* 38 (2): 138–160.

Rudolph, Susanne. 2005. "The Imperialism of Categories." *Perspectives on Politics* 3 (1): 1–8.

1963. "The Princely States of Rajputana." *The Indian Journal of Political Science* 24 (1): 14–32.

Said, Edward. 1978. *Orientalism*. New York: Pantheon.

Saikia, Smitana. 2017. Explaining Divergent Outcomes of the Mizo and Bodo Conflicts in the Ethno-Federal Context of India's Northeast. PhD Dissertation, King's College London.

Sartori, Andrew. 2014. *Liberalism in Empire*. Berkeley: University of California Press.

Sarvarkar, Vinayak. 1909. *The Indian War of Independence*. Bombay: Sethani Kampani.

Schofield, Victoria. 1996. *Kashmir in the Crossfire*. London: IB Tauris.

Schwartz, Herman. 2000. "Down the Wrong Path: Path Dependence, Increasing Returns, and Historical Institutionalism." Unpublished Paper, University of Virginia. www.people.virginia.edu/~hms2f/Path.pdf

Scott, James. 2009. *The Art of Not Being Governed*. New Haven: Yale University Press.

1999. *Seeing Like the State*. New Haven: Yale University Press.

1977. *The Moral Economy of the Peasant*. New Haven: Yale University Press.

Sen, Amartya. 2001. *Development as Freedom*. Oxford: Oxford University Press.

1981. "Ingredients of Famine Analysis: Availability and Entitlements." *The Quarterly Journal of Economics* 96(3): 433–464.

Sen, Sudipta. 1998. *Empire of Free Trade: The East India Company and Making of the Colonial Marketplace*. Philadelphia: University of Pennsylvania Press.

Shah, Alpa. 2010. *In the Shadows of the State*. Durham: Duke University Press.

2006. "Markets of Protection: The 'Terrorist' Maoist Movement and the State in Jharkhand, India." *Critique of Anthropology* 26(3): 297–314.

Shah, Aqil. 2014. *The Army and Democracy*. Cambridge, MA: Harvard University Press.

Sherman, Taylor. 2022. *Nehru's India*. Princeton: Princeton University Press.

2010. *State Violence and Punishment in India*. Abingdon: Routledge.

Siddiqa, Ayesha. 2007. *Military, Inc*. London: Pluto.

Singh, Ajay. 2016. "Mathura Clash: How Cabals in Mulayam Singh Yadav's Clan Bloodied UP Politics." *FirstPost*, June 3. www.firstpost.com/politics/mulayam-singh-yadav-ram-vriksh-yadav-akhilesh-yadav-ram-gopal-yadav-mathura-2815680.html

Singh, Gurharpal. 1996. "Punjab since 1984: Disorder, Order, and Legitimacy." *Asian Survey* 36(4): 410–421.

Singh, Prerna. 2016. *Sub-Nationalism and Social Development*. Cambridge: Cambridge University Press.

Singh, Rajkamal and Rahul Hemrajani. 2018. "Concentric Clientelism." *Studies in Indian Politics* 6(2): 247–266.

Sinha, Aseema. 2005. *The Regional Roots of Development Politics: the Divided Leviathan*. Bloomington: Indiana University Press.

Sinha, Aseema and Andrew Wyatt. 2019. "The Spectral Presence of Business in India's 2019 Election." *Studies in Indian Politics* 7(2): 247–261.

Sirnate, Vasundhara. 2013. "The Gender Terrorists." *Economic and Political Weekly* 48(13). www.epw.in/journal/2013/13/web-exclusives/gender-terrorists.html

Skarbek, David. 2014. *The Social Order of the Underworld*. Oxford: Oxford University Press.

Skocpol, Theda. 1979. *States and Social Revolutions*. Cambridge: Cambridge University Press.

Skowronek, Stephen. 1982. *Building a New American State*. Cambridge: Cambridge University Press.

Slater, Dan. 2010. *Ordering Power*. Cambridge: Cambridge University Press.

Slater, Dan and Diana Kim. 2015. "Standoffish States: Nonliterate Leviathans in Southeast Asia." *TRaNS* 3(1): 25–44.

Slaughter, Anne-Marie. 2004. *A New World Order*. Princeton: Princeton University Press.

Snyder, Richard. 2001. "Scaling Down." *Studies in Comparative International Development* 36(1): 93–110.

Soifer, Hillel. 2015. *State-Building in Latin America*. Cambridge: Cambridge University Press.

Staniland, Paul. 2021. *Ordering Violence*. Ithaca: Cornell University Press.

2014a. *Networks of Rebellion*. Ithaca: Cornell University Press.

2014b. "Violence and Democracy." *Comparative Politics* 47(1): 99–118.

2012. "States, Insurgents, and Wartime Political Orders." *Perspectives on politics* 10(2): 243–264.

2010. "Cities on Fire: Social Mobilization, State Policy, and Urban Insurgency." *Comparative Political Studies* 43(12): 1623–1649.

Staniland, Paul, Adnan Naseemullah, and Ahsan Butt. 2020. "Pakistan's Military Elite." *Journal of Strategic Studies* 43(1): 74–103.

Stern, Philip. 2011. *The Company-State.* Oxford: Oxford University Press.

Stewart, Frances, ed. 2008. *Horizontal Inequalities and Conflict: Understanding Group Violence in Multiethnic Societies.* London: Macmillan.

Stewart, Frances. 1985. *Planning to Meet Basic Needs.* London: Macmillan.

Stokes, Eric. 1978. *Peasant and the Raj.* Cambridge: Cambridge University Press.

 1959. *English Utilitarians and India.* Oxford: Oxford University Press.

Stokes, Susan, Thad Dunning, Marcelo Nazareno, and Valeria Brusco. 2013. *Brokers, Voters, and Clientelism.* Cambridge: Cambridge University Press.

Subrahmanyam, Sanjay. 1989. "Warfare and State Finance in Wodeyar Mysore, 1724–25." *The Indian Economic & Social History Review* 26(2): 203–233.

Subrahmanyam, Sanjay and Christopher Bayly. 1988. "Portfolio Capitalists and the Economy of Early Modern India." *Indian Economic and Social History Review* 24 (4): 401–424.

Sundar, Nadini. 2016. *The Burning Forest.* Delhi: Juggernaut Books.

Sundberg, Ralph and Erik Melander, 2013, "Introducing the UCDP Georeferenced Event Dataset," *Journal of Peace Research* 50(4): 523–532.

Suryanarayan, Pavithra. 2017. "Hollowing Out the State." Unpublished Paper, Johns Hopkins University. https://papers.ssrn.com/sol3/papers.cfm?abstract_id=2951947

Thachil, Tariq. 2014. *Elite Parties, Poor Voters.* Cambridge: Cambridge University Press.

Tharoor, Shashi. 2018. *Inglorious Empire: What the British Did to India.* London: Penguin.

Tillin, Louise. 2007. "United in Diversity? Asymmetry in Indian Federalism." *Publius: The Journal of Federalism* 37(1): 45–67.

Tilly, Charles. 1991. *Coercion, Capital and European States.* New York: Wiley.

 1985. "War-Making and State-Making as Organized Crime." In Peter Evans, Dietrich Rueschemeyer, and Theda Skocpol, eds., *Bringing the State Back In.* Cambridge: Cambridge University Press: 169–191.

 1975. *The Formation of National States in Western Europe.* Princeton: Princeton University Press.

Titus, Paul and Nina Swidler. 2000. "Knights, not Pawns: Ethno-Nationalism and Regional Dynamics in Post-Colonial Balochistan." *International Journal of Middle East Studies* 32(1): 47–69.

Tomlinson, B. R. 1993. *The Economy of Modern India, 1860–1970.* Cambridge: Cambridge University Press.

 1982. "The Political Economy of the Raj: the Decline of Colonialism," *Journal of Economic History* 42(1): 133–137.

 1979. "Britain and the Indian Currency Crisis, 1930-32," *Economic History Review* 32(1): 88–99.

Tudor, Maya. 2015. "Pakistan's Security State of Mind." *Perspectives on Politics* 13(4): 1097–1102.

 2013. *The Promise of Power.* Cambridge: Cambridge University Press.

Turner, Frederick. 1920. *The Frontier in American History.* New York: Henry Holt.

Tusalem, Rollin. 2016. "The Colonial Foundations of State Fragility and Failure." *Polity* 48(4): 445–495.

Vaishnav, Milan. 2017. *When Crime Pays: Money and Muscle in Indian Politics.* New Haven: Yale University Press.

Van Schendel, Willem. 2002. "Geographies of Knowing, Geographies of Ignorance: Jumping Scale in Southeast Asia." *Environment and Planning D* 20(6): 647–668.

Varma, Nitin. 2017. *The Coolies of Capitalism*. Berlin: de Gruyter.

Varshney, Ashutosh. 2017. "Crime and Context." *Indian Express*, July 7, 2017.

  2008. "Analyzing Collective Violence in Indonesia." *Journal of East Asian Studies* 8(3): 341–359.

  2003. *Ethnic Conflict and Civil Life*. New Haven: Yale University Press.

  1998. *Democracy, Development and the Countryside*. Cambridge: Cambridge University Press.

  1998b. "India Defies the Odds: Why Democracy Survives." *Journal of Democracy* 9(3): 36–50.

Venugopal, Rajesh. 2018. *Nationalism, Development and Ethnic Conflict in Sri Lanka*. Cambridge: Cambridge University Press.

Verghese, Ajay. 2016. *The Colonial Origins of Ethnic Violence in India*. Palo Alto: Stanford University Press.

Verghese, Ajay and Emmanuel Teitelbaum. 2019. "Conquest and Conflict: The Colonial Roots of Maoist Violence in India." *Politics & Society* 47(1): 55–86.

Viswanath, Rupa. 2014. *The Pariah Problem*. Princeton: Princeton University Press.

Vogel, Steven. 2018. *Marketcraft*. Oxford: Oxford University Press.

Vu, Tuong. 2010. *Paths to Development in Asia*. Cambridge: Cambridge University Press.

Wade, Robert. 1990. *Governing the Market*. Princeton: Princeton University Press.

Waldner, David. 1999. *State Building and Late Development*. Ithaca: Cornell University Press.

Wallerstein, Immanuel. 1976. *The Modern World-System: Capitalist Agriculture and the Origins of the European World-Economy in the Sixteenth Century*. New York: Academic Press.

Washbrook, David. 2004. "South India 1770–1840: The Colonial Transition." *Modern Asian Studies* 38(3): 479–516.

  1993. "Economic Depression and the Making of Traditional Society in Colonial India 1820–55." *Transactions of the Royal Historical Society* 6(3): 237–263.

Weber, Max. 1991 [1919]. "Politics as a Rocation." In W. W. Gerth and C. Wright Mills, eds., *From Max Weber*. Abingdon: Routledge.

Weiner, Myron. 1967. *Party-Building in a New Nation*. Chicago: Chicago University Press.

Weinstein, Jeremy. 2007. *Inside Rebellion*. Cambridge: Cambridge University Press.

White, Joshua. 2012. "Beyond Moderation: Dynamics of Political Islam in Pakistan." *Contemporary South Asia* 20(2): 179–194.

  2008. "The Shape of Frontier Rule." *Asian Security* 4(3): 219–243.

White, Richard. 1991. *'It's Your Misfortune and None of my Own': A New History of the American West*. Norman: University of Oklahoma Press.

Wilder, Andrew. 1999. *The Pakistani Voter*. Karachi: Oxford University Press.

Wilkinson, Steven. 2015. *Army and Nation*. Cambridge, MA: Harvard University Press.

  2009. "Riots." *Annual Review of Political Science* 12: 329–343.

  2004. *Votes and Violence*. Cambridge: Cambridge University Press.

Wilson, Jon. 2016. *India Conquered: Britain's Raj and the Chaos of Empire*. New York: Simon and Schuster.

  2008. *The Domination of Strangers*. New York: Springer.

Wilson, Nicholas. 2011. "From Reflection to Refraction: State Administration in British India, circa 1770–1855." *American Journal of Sociology* 116(5): 1437–1477.

Wink, Andre. 1983. "Maratha Revenue Farming." *Modern Asian Studies* 17:591–628.

Witsoe, Jeffrey. 2013. *Democracy against Development*. Chicago: University of Chicago Press.

Wittenberg, Jason. 2015. "Conceptualizing Historical Legacies." *East European Politics and Societies* 29(2): 366–378.

Wolfe, Patrick. 2006. "Settler Colonialism and the Elimination of the Native." *Journal of Genocide Research* 8(4): 387–409.

Wong, Joseph. 2006. *Healthy Democracies: Welfare Politics in Taiwan and South Korea*. Ithaca: Cornell University Press.

Woo-Cumings. Meredith. 1991. *Race to the Swift*. New York: Columbia University Press.

Wood, Elisabeth. 2003. *Insurgent Collective Action and Civil War in El Salvador*. New York: Cambridge University Press.

World Bank. 2007. *A Decade of Measuring the Quality of Governance*. Washington, DC: World Bank.

2002. *Building Institutions for Markets*. New York: Oxford University Press.

1997. *The State in a Changing World*. New York: Oxford University Press.

Wucherpfennig, Julian, Philipp Hunziker, and Lars-Erik Cederman. 2016. "Who Inherits the State? Colonial Rule and Postcolonial Conflict." *American Journal of Political Science* 60(4): 882–898.

Yadav, Yogendra and Suhas Palshikar. 2003. "From Hegemony to Convergence: Party System and Electoral Politics in the Indian States, 1952–2002." *Journal of Indian School of Political Economy* 15(1): 5–44.

Yong, Tan Tai. 2005. *The Garrison State*. Delhi: Sage.

Zachariah, Benjamin. 2005. *Developing India: An Intellectual and Social History c. 1930–50*. Delhi: Oxford University Press.

Zaidi, Akbar. 2005. *Issues in Pakistan's Economy*. Karachi: Oxford University Press.

Zaman, Fahmida. 2018. "Agencies of Social Movements: Experiences of Bangladesh's Shahbag Movement and Hefazat-e-Islam." *Journal of Asian and African Studies* 53 (3): 339–349.

Zamindar, Vazira. 2007. *The Long Partition and the Making of Modern South Asia*. New York: Columbia University Press.

Ziegfeld, Adam. 2016. *Why Regional Parties?* Cambridge: Cambridge University Press.

Index

For EU product safety concerns, contact us at Calle de José Abascal, 56–1°, 28003 Madrid, Spain or eugpsr@cambridge.org.

www.ingramcontent.com/pod-product-compliance
Ingram Content Group UK Ltd.
Pitfield, Milton Keynes, MK11 3LW, UK
UKHW010249140625
459647UK00013BA/1752